Contagions of Empire

Contagions of Empire
Scientific Racism, Sexuality, and
Black Military Workers Abroad, 1898–1948

Khary Oronde Polk

The University of North Carolina Press CHAPEL HILL

This book was published with the assistance of the
Lilian R. Furst Fund of the University of North Carolina Press.

© 2020 Khary Oronde Polk
All rights reserved
Set in Merope Basic by Westchester Publishing Services
Manufactured in the United States of America

The University of North Carolina Press has been a member of the
Green Press Initiative since 2003.

Library of Congress Cataloging-in-Publication Data
Names: Polk, Khary Oronde, author.
Title: Contagions of empire : scientific racism, sexuality, and black military
　workers abroad, 1898–1948 / Khary Oronde Polk.
Description: Chapel Hill : The University of North Carolina Press, 2020. |
　Includes bibliographical references and index.
Identifiers: LCCN 2019046672 | ISBN 9781469655499 (cloth) |
　ISBN 9781469655505 (paperback) | ISBN 9781469655512 (ebook)
Subjects: LCSH: African Americans—Government policy—United States. |
　United States—Armed Forces—African Americans—History. |
　United States—Armed Forces—African Americans—Social conditions.
Classification: LCC UB418.A47 P65 2020 | DDC 355.0089/9607309041—dc23
　LC record available at https://lccn.loc.gov/2019046672

Cover illustration: St. Nazaire stevedores poster. National World War I Museum
and Memorial, Kansas City, Missouri, USA (https://theworldwar.org/explore
/online-collections-database).

To my grandmothers,
Ruby Lee Coleman (1925–2012) and
Helen Louise Polk (1919–2019)

And my grandfathers,
Leroy Coleman (1913–2000) and
Harry Daniel Polk Sr. (1922–1996)

No lie is strong enough to kill
The roots that work below;
From your rich dust and slaughtered will
A tree with tongues shall grow.

—COUNTEE CULLEN, "In Memory of Colonel Charles Young" (1925)

So what do we do with our lives?
We leave only a mark.
Will our story shine like a light,
Or end in the dark?
Is it all or nothing?

—TINA TURNER, "We Don't Need Another Hero (Thunderdome)" (1985)

Contents

Acknowledgments xi
Abbreviations in the Text xvii

Introduction 1

CHAPTER ONE
We Don't Need Another Hero 13
Death, Honor, and the Archive of American Militarism

CHAPTER TWO
Negro Heroines 48
Gender, Race, and Immunity in the Spanish-Cuban-American War

CHAPTER THREE
Charles Young in Five Acts 77
Patriots, Traitors, and the Performance of American Militarism

CHAPTER FOUR
Contagious Immunity 124
Race, Sexuality, and the Black Venereal Body Abroad

CHAPTER FIVE
Communicable Subjects 166
African American Soldiers Trip the Global Color Line

Epilogue 213
The Long Arc of Black Military Opportunity

Notes 221
Bibliography 249
Index 263

Figures

0.1 "Places I've Been While in the Service," journal entry of Harry Polk Sr. xii

1.1 Drawing of Lieutenant McCorkle's gravesite in Cuba 36

1.2 Photograph of the graves of men from the Twenty-Fifth Infantry near Caney 36

1.3 Painting of tree tablets commemorating members of the Twenty-Fifth Infantry killed at Caney 37

1.4 Map of the cemetery of the General Hospital at Siboney 39

1.5 Cemetery of the First Division Hospital 40

1.6 Drawing of Richard Jones's cemetery plot 41

1.7 Richard Jones's report of interment card 42

1.8 Richard Jones's gravestone at Arlington National Cemetery 43

2.1 Newspaper clipping of Mrs. A. M. Curtis (Namahyoka Gertrude Curtis) 54

2.2 Namah Curtis's pension file 59

3.1 Portrait of Captain Charles Young (1905) 78

Acknowledgments

Despite the fact that both of my grandfathers fought in racially segregated units in World War II, and that I, myself, am the child of an African American military family, my efforts to write a theoretical history of black soldiers abroad in the early to mid-twentieth century have, at times, seemed anything but inevitable. In truth, it was only after this project was largely complete that I inquired about the military travels of my male forebears. As it turns out, Leroy Coleman, my mother's father, served as a private in the Philippines during the war, while my father's namesake, Harry Polk Sr., experienced the peripatetic movement of station and nation that exemplified the travels of black military workers overseas during the course of the conflict. Harry Sr. served with the 366th Infantry Regiment, whose motto, "Labor Conquers All Things," aptly captures the intersections of race, labor, and masculinity at the heart of my analysis. My Aunt Ina shared with me a leather-bound pictorial history of the regiment that had been passed down in the Polk family, and within which my grandfather had taken copious notes. In addition to tagging his friends in the photographs—writing "swell pal," "ok," and "crazy" under their faces—he kept a detailed list of the nearly eighty places where he had been stationed during the war on the book's final page (figure 0.1). In the United States, Harry Sr. traveled from the top of the eastern seaboard down to Louisiana, making stops in Yarmouth, Spartanburg, and Baton Rouge along the way before shipping off overseas to North Africa and Europe. After spending time in Oran, Algiers, and Casablanca, his regiment joined the Ninety-Second Infantry Division in Italy, where he made more than twenty changes of station in the country. From Augusta and Palermo in Sicily, he journeyed up and down the boot of the peninsula, seeing Naples, Anzio, Rome, Civitavecchia, Pisa, and Genoa during his tour of duty abroad. Harry Sr. was wounded twice in battle, and received a Purple Heart for his service in World War II.

Though my grandfathers passed on before I came of age to ask them questions about their time in the military, the belated revelation they had both served overseas in places I had written so passionately about proved to me, beyond a shadow of a doubt, that this history—even in its most academic registers—was a personal and familial one. In this regard, I dedicate this

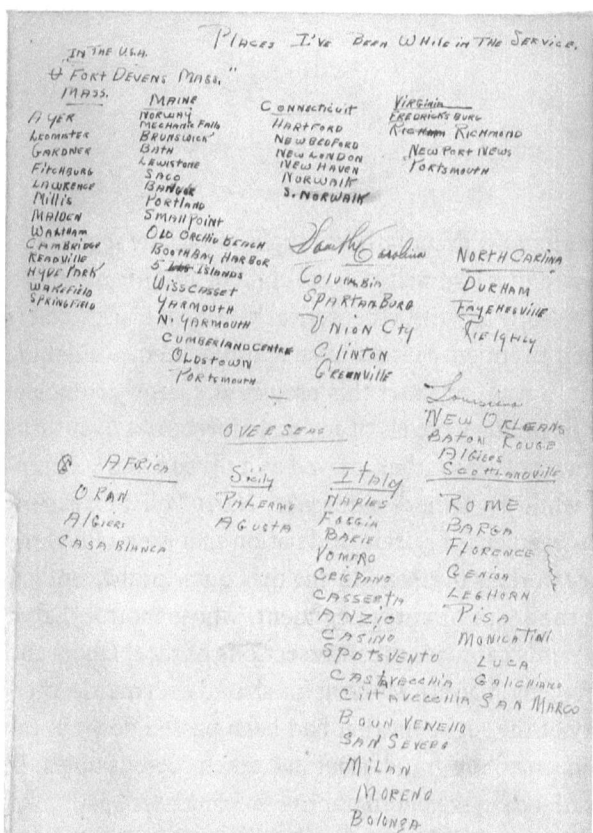

FIGURE 0.1 Harry D. Polk Sr., "Places I've Been While in the Service," journal entry. Courtesy of Ina Jones.

book to the memories of Harry Polk Sr. and Leroy Coleman, as well as the strong-willed women who made them better men and fathers while remaining legendary in their own right, Helen Louise Polk and Ruby Lee Coleman. I thank my grandparents for making a way for their children—and their children's children—to survive and thrive with grace, faith, and persistence. My parents, Bobbie J. Polk and Chief Master Sergeant Harry D. Polk, USAF, Retired, welcomed me into this world as a military brat, and have been my biggest cheerleaders throughout the process of completing this book. Their love and support has meant everything to me, and I hope I make them proud. Likewise, Bill Harper, Tonya Bryant, and Michael Bryant are the best siblings a younger brother could ask for. Through their guidance and good humor, they taught me self-respect, independence, and how to make a home away from home. Last but certainly not least, to all my aunties, uncles, cousins, play-cousins, brother- and sister-friends in the many-headed Polk and Coleman families: this book is but a small reflection of the power, faith, and love you have given to me, and I carry you all with me wherever I go.

This book would not have been possible without the support of countless people and organizations that helped this project come into fruition. I am thankful for the staff at the Ohio History Connection/National Afro-American Museum and Cultural Center, the U.S. Army Heritage & Education Center at Carlisle Barracks, the Allied Museum in Berlin, the Coleman Collection in Akron, Ohio, UMass Amherst Special Collections and University Archives, and Frost Library at Amherst College for providing me access to many of the primary sources I treat in my analysis. In addition to employing traditional historical methods, much of my research was carried out using digital archives. UMass Amherst's Credo Online Repository—which contains the W. E. B. Du Bois Papers—was especially valuable in this respect, as was Readex's "African American Newspapers: Series 1" online archive, which expanded my access to nineteenth-century and turn-of-the-century black periodicals. Many of my genealogical sources in chapter 2 were obtained through Joseph A. Romero's website "The Moors of Delaware: Genealogical Records of the Descendants of a Colonial Delaware Isolate Community," as well as Ancestry.com.

At UNC Press, I'd like to thank my editor, Brandon Proia, for his patience, guidance, and steadfast belief in this project, as well as Steve Barichko and Michael Durnin, who prepared the manuscript for publication. A special note of gratitude goes out to my research assistant, Brian Zayatz, for his meticulous attention to detail and instincts in the archives. His efforts at securing primary source material for the Namahyoka Curtis and Charles Young chapters were especially commendable. Additionally, the manuscript benefitted immensely from the critical feedback it received from Jennifer Terry, Robert Reid-Pharr, Sujani Reddy, andré carrington, Kim M. Everett, Ronaldo V. Wilson, Kristin Moriah, and Sarah Schulman, all of whom were instrumental in helping me refine my argument. I was also quite fortunate to present portions of this work at the Five College Women's Research Center at Mount Holyoke College, the Yale University Working Group on Race and Slavery in the Atlantic World to 1900, the History Department at the University of Hawai'i at Mānoa, the Humanities Institute at UC Santa Cruz, and the African Atlantic Research Group workshops in New York and Berlin. I thank the conveners of these seminars and their participants for their generous insights and pointed critiques. Frank Kelleter's invitation to host me at the John F. Kennedy Institute, Freie Universität Berlin, during my sabbatical was foundational in helping me develop the contours of the book. I remain grateful that he, Martin Lüthe, and David Bosold welcomed me so readily into their intellectual community.

Much of the preparation for writing this book began at New York University, whose departments of Social and Cultural Analysis, Performance Studies, and History shaped the vision and scope of my intellectual potential. It was there that I learned how theory could change the world. I am forever grateful for having worked with Phillip Brian Harper, Jennifer Morgan, Michael Ralph, José Esteban Muñoz, Fred Moten, Daphne Brooks, Michael Dash, Lisa Duggan, Thuy Linh Tu, Awam Amkpa, Andrew Ross, Adam Green, Arlena Davila, and Nikhil Singh. In addition, learning alongside Njoroge Njoroge, Suzanna Reiss, Ted Sammons, Sybil Cooksey, Ifeona Fulani, Christopher Winks, Kobi Abayomi, Steve Fradkin, Adam Waterman, Christina Hanhardt, Peter Hudson, andré carrington, M.J. Grier, Elizabeth Mesok, Seth Markle, Sobukwe Odinga, Natasha Lightfoot, Chinua Thelwell, Carmelo LaRose, Dawn Peterson, Tej Nagaraja, Rich Blint, and Carlos Decena politicized my worldview, sharpened my analytical skills, and expanded my educational horizons.

I completed this book while teaching in two departments well-tailored to my academic training, and whose students, faculty, and staff created a home for me at Amherst College. In Black Studies, John Drabinski, Rhonda Cobham-Sander, Rowland Abiodun, Hilary Moss, Jeffrey Ferguson, Solsiree del Moral, Mary Hicks, Alec Hickmott, Carol Bailey, Dominique Hill, and Olufemi Vaughn brought the best out of me as a teacher and a scholar. With a light touch, they allowed me to grow into my own as an intellectual, and for that, I am forever grateful. In Sexuality, Women's and Gender Studies, Amrita Basu, Michele Barale, Krupa Shandilya, Sahar Sadjadi, Rick Griffiths, Martha Saxton, Manuela Picq, Jessica Vooris, and Aneeka Henderson politicized my understandings of gender, sex, race, and nation, and challenged me to make gender matter in every field of inquiry I approach. I thank them for their support, insight, and critical fierceness. And to a large degree, Stephanie Orion, Robyn Rogers, Karla Keyes, and Dee Brace have made working in multiple departments and committees not only possible, but enjoyable. Their warmth, humor, and wise counsel are greatly appreciated.

My colleagues at Amherst and the broader Five College community have fostered a sense of collegiality and community in the Pioneer Valley. Marisa Parham, Anston Bosman, Judy Frank, Alicia Christoff, Christopher Grobe, Chris Dole, Ted Melillo, Jason Robinson, Adam Sitze, Frank Couvares, Nusrat Chowdhury, Hannah Holleman, Ron Lembo, Nicola Courtwright, Betsey Garand, Niko Vicario, Dwaipayan Sen, Tariq Jaffer, Ashley Carter, Sheila

Jaswal, Christian Rogowski, Anna Schrade, Alex George, Nishi Shah, Joseph Moore, Rafeeq Hasan, Jen Manion, Mark Jacobson, Mike Kelly, Missy Roser, Sara Smith, Dunstan McNutt, Steven Heim, Riley Caldwell-O'Keefe, and Megan Lyster have shown me the best of what the liberal arts can offer. Likewise, Jennifer Guglielmo, Iyko Day, David Hernandez, Kara Lynch, Wesley Chihyung Yu, Whitney Baptiste, Jennifer Hamilton, Stephen Dillon, Elizabeth Pryor, Svati Shah, Laura Briggs, Angie Willey, Banu Subramaniam, Britt Russert, Fumi Okiji, Markeysha Dawn Davis, Daniel Kojo Schrade, Preston Smith, Jina B. Kim, and Ren-Yo Hwang have made the Five College community a site of pathbreaking scholarship, cutting-edge pedagogy, and intellectual generosity.

For close to two decades, my friends and colleagues in New York City have sustained my intellectual and creative lives, and I have been blessed to be in their good company. Robert Reid-Pharr, Chris Fezzuoglio, Emma Taati, Ronaldo V. Wilson, Daniel Silverbusch, Sujani Reddy, Tyler Schmidt, Tavia Nyong'o, Adam Radwan, Scott Cameron Weaver, Ralph Wilde, K. Ryan Yancy, Dagmawi Woubshet, Herman Bennett, Clay Matlin, Sarah McDougald Kohn, Connie McDougald, Christopher Jobes, Robert Escalera, Kristopher Musumano, Shelly Eversley, Mark Grundy, C. Riley Snorton, Cally Waite, Carmen Grau, and YK Hong continue to make a place for me in their hearts and minds, for which I am immensely grateful. Likewise, in Berlin, *mein zweites Zuhause*, Thomas Ebel, Kim M. Everett, Sasha Disko, Cornelia Möser, Rufus Sona, Eric D. Clark, Jared Abbott, Cameron Cook, Ben Miller, Robert James Napier, Giuseppe Piovesan, Sam Wilder, Bill Martin, Satch Hoyt, Troy Lopez, Kirk Henry, Leon Rothenbacher, and Benjamin Hotter have held space for me in their wonderful city, and I thank them for their graciousness and their unmatched hospitality. And for those who have helped me make Western Massachusetts home—Pete Cofoni, Eric Wirth, Paul Specht, Eric LeFlore, Fletcher Clark, Mattea Kramer, and Scott McGinley—thank you for honoring me with the gift of your friendship.

Finally, in memoriam: to my grandmother, Helen Polk, my colleague, Jeffrey Ferguson, and my friends, Christopher Schmidt and Manuel Matos.

Abbreviations in the Text

AEF	American Expeditionary Force
AFRICOM	U.S. Africa Command
AME	African Methodist Episcopal (Church)
ANC	Army Nurses Corps
ASHA	American Social Hygiene Association
CMH	(Army) Center of Military History
DAR	Daughters of the American Revolution
ISIS-GS	Islamic State of the Greater Sahara
JAMA	*Journal of the American Medical Association*
MID	Military Intelligence Division
NAACP	National Association for the Advancement of Colored People
NACW	National Association of Colored Women
SOCAFRICA	Special Operations Command Africa
SOCFWD-NWA	Special Operations Command Forward, North and West Africa
SOF	(U.S.) Special Operations Forces
USPHS	U.S. Public Health Service
WAAC	Women's Army Auxiliary Corps
YMCA	Young Men's Christian Association

Introduction

In the spring of 1941, historian of militarism Alfred Vagts made an impassioned appeal to his fellow colleagues in American academia to commit to the interdisciplinary study of war. War clouds were on the horizon, that much was clear, and Vagts was convinced that, sooner rather than later, the United States would find itself enmeshed in the second global war of his lifetime. Vagts was worried; his experience as a visiting professor at Harvard University only two years earlier had made him aware of a general resistance within the humanities to the study of the military as an institution. "Even now," he wrote, "in the midst of gigantic military programs, leaders of public opinion and education are still reluctant to confront the issue and discuss the relationship of higher education to the greatest problem of the nation today. To them, military studies still appear to be a direct step to militarism."[1] Vagts was dismayed at the disinterest and lack of intellectual curiosity shown by American scholars to this field of inquiry. He felt their liberal ideals had rendered the topic unmentionable, "lest the single syllable, war, prove contaminating to his better nature."[2]

Decrying this intellectual embargo on military studies in a moment of imminent war, Vagts traced this academic resistance to a general distrust of power:

> Arguing from the past, the academic world has denied all justification for the competition for power; disliking the old imperialist competition, including the rivalry of armies and navies in an age when every group in society competed lustily, scholars have extended that distaste to the new competition in arms which has now, alas, become the index of our security. But is this the way to confront the world of dark powers and, to us, questionable values? Do we not at least have to know what we oppose and, through knowledge, strive to end these false powers and values?[3]

Vagts was offended by the charge that those who study war only seek to profit from it. "The theologian who ponders the problem of sin is not necessarily thought a sinner himself," he wrote, "but those who have bothered themselves with military matters have often been regarded as militarists."[4]

He fervently believed that the only way to safeguard democracy was through the civilian control of military power. This, he insisted, could be maintained only by an informed populace engaged in the affairs of its armed forces. Such a responsibility was "more basic than most of the blessings commonly called essential: free enterprise, liberty of speech, fraternity, or the two-car garage. Without civilian supremacy in the state," he contended, "no democratic right or privilege would be safe."[5]

To be sure, Vagts had made his own scholarly investments in the study of military power. More than two decades before President Dwight D. Eisenhower would caution Americans to be wary of the unchecked power of the "military-industrial complex," he had posited a "fundamental and fateful" distinction between what he defined as the "military way" and "militarism". The military way, he argued, was characterized by efficient mobilization of soldiers and materials in order to achieve specific objectives in war "with the least expenditure of blood and treasure."[6] Militarism, on the other hand, rejected the scientific character of the military way. Displaying "the qualities of caste and cult, authority and belief," Vagts claimed that this culture of militarism "may permeate all society and become dominant over all industry and arts"—ultimately hindering and defeating the purposes of the military way.[7]

Yet the theory and practice of militarism was more than an academic enterprise for Vagts. A German company commander during World War I, he was one of a number of refugee scholars who sought exile out of the country during the rise of National Socialism in the early 1930s.[8] As a military historian and a veteran of the first world war, his historiography of militarism was consciously framed by the rumblings of World War II as well as the chronicled hubris of the German military that he had experienced firsthand. In anticipation of this conflict, Vagts proposed a systematic plan for the renewed analysis of the U.S. military within American academia. It was interdisciplinary in structure, preventive in function, and primed to "shake-up . . . the neatly divided and jealously hedged fields of learning."[9] Enlisting the whole of the humanities in this new enterprise, he invited a vigorous "spirit of criticism" into this new field of inquiry, stating plainly that "only an utter reactionary would wish military history to dedicate itself to glorifying all or nearly all that the military have done in the past; a better military understanding would insist, for example, that the Civil War and the world war were not milestones in American history and evolution but simply miles, and would treat them accordingly."[10] Above all, Vagts wanted American academics to take militarism seriously by marshaling the necessary resources to analyze the past, present, and future uses of its power:

> Let history begin and relate how the wars of the past were undertaken; how different they were from one another because of the various societal arrangements of the warring parties as well as because of the changing technology of war. The *then* of former wars will help produce an understanding of the terrific *now* of the war in Europe, Asia, and Africa. Let sociology teach the interdependence of war and society and study the arrangements necessary to secure authority and discipline as well as cohesion in war, inside and outside armed bodies.[11]

Nearly eighty years have passed since Vagts's manifesto cautioned scholars against allowing "a private dislike of the competition for power" to prevent a study of its forces, "which, after all, are seized upon by other peoples passionate for power and for its use."[12] It is not unreasonable to suggest that his grand plan of turning ivory towers into the watchtowers of American militarism through cross-cultural study has yet to come into fruition. Certainly, the stigma attached to military inquiry that unsettled Vagts on the eve of World War II continues to mark research profiles as either radical or conservative in orientation today, limiting what can be generated in both ideological quarters about the military-industrial complex's obdurate presence in modern life. But beyond academia, the ways and means of American militarism continue to hold sway over U.S. national culture. The principled refusal to tote guns in the service of American empire cannot escape the fact the lifeworlds and subjectivities of millions of ordinary Americans—many of them people of color—have been, and continue to be, shaped by the machinations of the military-industrial complex. As a case in point, we would do well to remember that the disproportionate incarceration rate of African Americans in prisons is joined by a similar, if less pronounced, overrepresentation of blacks in the U.S. military.[13] Indeed, the carceral state's appetite for black life has, for some time now, made a similar investment in the recruitment of African American men and women for military service. As complexes in concert with one another, these two industries have left an irrevocable mark upon African American life, history, and culture, and continue to trouble our understandings of race, honor, and freedom today.

Simply put, an analysis of the carceral dimensions of American militarism—and the singular role it has played in transforming black "laborers" into military "craftsmen" in our modern era—is long past due. The pages that follow tell the story of America's military conscription of gender, racial, and sexual difference in the early to mid-twentieth century, examining the embodied use of black military workers in U.S. imperial wars abroad and the discourses of immunity and contagion that followed in their wake. Through the scientifically racist enlistment of African Americans in grunt work, care labor, and medical experimentation, the U.S. military founded models of inclusion and exclusion within a discourse of military respectability—a framework used to conscript people of color, women, immigrants, queers, and transgender persons into military service today. Beginning with the Spanish-Cuban-American War and ending with President Truman's desegregation of the U.S. military in 1948, this study reveals ways in which modern forms of African American gender and sexual identity—marked by elements of freedom and constriction, marronage and control—were produced in concert with the diasporic processes of the U.S. military abroad.

I employ the term "military worker" to highlight both the labor black men and women did while stationed overseas and their subaltern statuses in the segregated American military hierarchy of power. It is vital to note that these workers—the vast majority of whom were male in the contexts I address—were both subjects and agents of American militarism. As such, they vacillated between subaltern and imperialist roles in their interaction with a world globalized by twentieth-century world war. But to only focus upon the overseas service of black men obscures the extent to which American militarism conscripted black womanhood into its imperial project as well—particularly in the untold story of African American fever nurses in Cuba, who believed that their labor and embodied sacrifices entitled them to fair and equal treatment under the law. This book uses the experiences of the black women recruited as yellow fever nurses in America's war with Spain as an intersectional lens through which to gauge the shifting constructions of gender, race, and sexuality during America's imperial ascent. Drawing upon archival research, histories of science and medicine, newspaper accounts, Congressional reports, disease statistics, legal discourse, Army unit histories, literature, music, and cultural theory, *Contagions of Empire* demonstrates how African American military service abroad produced new ideas of racial affiliation, sexual belonging, and global citizenship in the mid-twentieth century, while also illuminating the complicated agency these military workers assumed and exercised through their intense engagements with a militarized world shaped by and through American empire.

Theorizing Immunity and Contagion

The belief that honorable military service and demonstrated sacrifice should grant blacks greater rights of citizenship at home and abroad—what I theorize throughout this project as forms of *immunity*—shaped the opportunities given to and taken by black military workers in America's wars overseas. The historical drift in meanings of the term "immunity" has made the recovery of its older definitions especially pertinent to my project. When used today, immunity is often referred to in its medical sense, such as the kind of immunity one often receives after childhood bouts with chicken pox or the measles; or we think of the word in its legal sense—the kinds of standard exemptions and protections given to foreign diplomats working in international service, and the forms of sovereign immunity that protect municipal actors like police officers or mayors from lawsuits. Within my text, "immunity" is a multivalent term, and I use it to draw attention to the ways black bodies have been central subjects and objects in American citizenship projects like national military service, whereby the corporeal reality of black life is the medium through which discourses of inclusion and exclusion find their practice.

My use of immunity is informed first by the fact that African Americans in the nineteenth century often recurred to the language of the Fourteenth Amendment of the U.S. Constitution in their rhetorical demands for full rights and privileges, or "immunities" as American citizens. While this anachronistic usage of the term animated calls for political and social equality made by African American leadership—especially in the advocacy of Booker T. Washington—it also overlapped with the U.S. government's rationale for using black military workers in America's first imperial wars abroad in the early twentieth century. Black men and women were conscripted for overseas military service for the first time in American history under the War Department's belief that Southern blacks carried an immunity against tropical diseases, making them well suited to labor in the tropical climates of Cuba, Puerto Rico, and the Philippines, and to care for soldiers stricken with yellow fever abroad. To underscore this conviction, the male volunteer military companies were given the name "Immune Regiments," providing the trope of the immune nurse with a masculine counterpart in the figure of immune soldier. Thus, the belief in biological differences between black and white Americans reemerged on the verge of a new century to gild the conditional enlistment of African American nurses and soldiers into care workers and grunt laborers, roles that reflected nineteenth-century beliefs about racial and gender difference.

This historical convergence of meanings about immunity offers a new way to consider the subjectivities of African American volunteers in their sojourns around the world. In one sense, it establishes the scientifically racist origins of black employment in imperial warfare. The belief that black people were immune from yellow fever had flourished in the antebellum era, providing the industrial complexes of plantation slavery an economic justification for the trade in black bodies, and an ideological basis to dehumanize its African workforce. This end-of-the-century endorsement of biological difference became a harbinger of how American militarism would continue to conscript and delimit African Americans through a logic of inferiority. And yet another facet of the term's valence was pursued by black leadership in the United States, who strategically used the valor and sacrifice of black military workers abroad to advocate for greater citizenship rights on the home front. Valiant service and patriotic sacrifice, it was hoped, would endow black soldiers and nurses—and by extension, the black community—with greater citizenship privileges in the United States, granting them, in a sense, immunity from the prejudices and injustices African Americans had long endured. Nevertheless, encounters with black mortality abroad provoked a crisis of citizenship among black troops. Weighing the worth of their sacrifices themselves, nurses and soldiers openly questioned whether they would receive the expanded privileges and immunities for which they had fought, or whether they would continue to be denied social and political equality at home. This crisis, in turn, caused them to reimagine their own relationships to the nation, expanding their prerogatives of citizenship in the newly expanding American imperial landscape.

As black soldiers traveled the world in the early decades of the twentieth century, they experienced a change in the discourse securing black enlistment, and found themselves increasingly subject to novel and quotidian forms of regulation and surveillance by an anxious white military elite. Within this text, sexuality is treated as both an expression of the self and a mode of social control. This perspective, influenced by black feminist thought, gender theory, gay and lesbian studies and queer of color critique, highlights how black military workers—viewed as immune in Cuba— became "contagious" subjects and agents of American empire in the Philippines and beyond. By World War I, white American military officials were afraid that unfettered contact with the French population would inspire dreams of social equality among African American troops and were alarmed at the reports of high rates of venereal disease among black soldiers. These racial and sexual panics produced the rationale used to not only restrict contact between black soldiers and foreign populations but to also conduct medical experimentation upon black men during both world wars.

Military brass viewed black military workers through a lens of contagion. Yet for all the racism and ignorance embedded in that judgment, African Americans stationed in military outposts abroad indeed served as vectors for ideas about citizenship, culture, and freedom. Conceiving themselves as desiring and desirable subjects in the international arena, many black troops found freedom in the sexual commerce that international war engendered—in which venereal disease operated as one powerful sign or "receipt" of exchange—while others took honor in the sexual restraint shown by black soldiers, accomplished through appeals to racial pride, military discipline, and the force of masculine will. Taking note of the ways in which soldiers of color were resistant to, and complicit with, these necropolitical modes of regulation, this book seeks to unpack the longstanding paradox of black military service—why have African Americans continued to fight for a country hell-bent on denying them their rights in civilian society?—and provides a framework for understanding how and why the U.S. military's conscription of racial, gender, sexual difference continues apace.

Historical and critical interest about this emergent moment of black military internationalism has grown in recent years. Rather than offer a formal military history, *Contagions of Empire* examines the ways in which extraordinary moments in the history of American militarism produced a spectrum of exceptional possibilities for military workers of color. This study provides an important counternarrative to canonical histories of U.S. military service that oscillate between the exclusion of black military workers altogether and an understandable need to recover and celebrate them as American heroes and heroines. Because martial honor conferred an exceptional status of citizenship that did not dismantle white American military supremacy but often sought partnership in its hegemony, I also consider workers whose international actions cast them far beyond the boundaries of military respectability. Clubwomen, fever nurses, stevedores, professors of industrial education, dead bodies, and prostitutes all play a role in this transnational narrative, as do grave diggers, band leaders, urologists, truck drivers, and military wives. Recognizing the immunity of these actors—how they exercised their prerogatives of citizenship at home and abroad—offers a new lens through which to examine American militarism's conscription of racial, sexual, and gender difference into its ranks while also charting the intersection of these discourses within the body of the African American military worker, a necessary component of American imperialism since 1898.

As it stands, the contemporary historiography of African American military service has played a vital role documenting the black struggle for civil rights at home and abroad. In so doing, it has helpfully reimagined the black soldier as a *black international*, and has taken seriously the ways race, gender, sexuality, and citizenship have been negotiated within the contact zones of American militarism. Yet I would also suggest that the relative lack of critical inquiry into black military life overseas has fixated upon the freedom dreams of heterosexual men. In doing so, it has inadvertently trafficked in a heteronormative discourse of manhood rights, whereupon the demonstration of a particular form of masculinity (martial courage, for example) entitles the black male subject to rights and privileges of citizenship.

Written at the intersection of African American studies, gender and sexuality studies, and military history, *Contagions of Empire* is invested in deconstructing the hero-citizen discourse that such appeals uphold, however, as such citizenship appeals can unintentionally serve to obfuscate the ideological and material work done by militarism at the global and local levels, while reifying the very norms of race, sex, and gender used to exclude the vast majority of African Americans from expressing their rights as citizens of the United States. The focus on racialized and gendered use of those bodies by civilian and military leadership, and on the diverse ways military workers negotiated modes of regulation and control, serves to open new perspectives on the familiar story of American military intervention abroad.

I should also say something, by way of acknowledgment, about the gendered character of the materials of my project. As you will see, most of the theorists and many of the subjects that I treat throughout my project are, and have been produced by, men. That being the case, it is not only an archive of American militarism that I am studying; it is a *male-patterned* archive of American militarism. This admission is not merely an advance mea culpa from the male writer of this text, nor is it simply a plea for greater gender inclusion in the study of military cultures, at least not on the terms of inclusion for inclusion's sake alone. To be sure, scholars in the humanities have produced a vast literature on masculinity and war. As a contribution to this enterprise, this project argues that by subjecting key moments in the history of the U.S. military abroad to a feminist intersectional analysis—specifically black feminist thought—we see the myriad ways that American military thought is always *already* racialized and gendered, and this allows a new consideration of the instrumental use of categories of difference (such as race, gender, and class) in national projects of inclusion like military service.

Moreover, the "male patterning" of such an archive (and we might begin to consider the conspicuous male patterning of other bodies of knowledge as well) should also signal the biopolitical concerns at the heart of my analysis. American military history is, among other things, a record of race and gender. It is a record of how the management of imperial violence was procured and produced through racialized logics of masculinity, girded by the sovereign right to kill. While the biopolitical and the necropolitical meet in the power of the gun, the stealth of the plane, the wake of the ship, and in the distant hum of the drone, they also intersect in the organization of aid relief, the training of soldiers, the destabilization of local economies, and as articulated in the current mission statement of U.S. African Command, or AFRICOM, the "promot[ion] of regional security, stability, and prosperity."[14]

Beginning with the recent case of an African American soldier killed in Niger, Africa, whose racial difference from his fallen white comrades created contradictory readings of his death in the public discourse surrounding the ambush, the first chapter shows how an enduring belief in black military "refractoriness" shaped nineteenth-century scientific discourses about biological and environmental immunity. Through the examination of graveyard cartography, this chapter also demonstrates how the burial of black American bodies abroad extended Jim Crow logics of white supremacist rule into Cuba, forging a link between blackness, necropolitics, and American militarism during the 1898 conflict.

The little-known history of black women's service during the Spanish-Cuban-American War is the subject of chapter 2. To enlist black women's care labor in the Cuban conflict, army physicians relied on the myth of the plantation nurse, a figure whose biological and thus racial immunity from yellow fever recalled forms of gendered subordination and sacrifice ritualized in U.S. slavery. Archival evidence from newspapers, Congressional reports, and military and civic records suggests that these nurses—including the women who organized them—participated in a project of necropolitical citizenship, wherein the management of sickness and death in quarantine camps abroad was accompanied by the use of that imperiled service in public appeals aimed at securing expanded citizenship rights for African Americans stateside. The gendered and racialized experiences of both organizer and organized offer an intersectional lens through which to consider these subaltern subjects of American militarism as feminine emblems of black immunity, iconic women whose experiences before, during, and after the conflict offer a counterhistoriography of America's first modern overseas war.

In chapter 3 the narrative turns to the life and work of Charles Young. A revered figure in the black community during his lifetime, Young was the third African American officer to graduate from West Point, and the first to reach the rank of colonel. He was the first American military attaché in Haiti, and later became the first African American to serve in that capacity in Liberia. Young's efforts to shatter the myth of the black soldier as an imperfectible beast of burden paradoxically found the black body as a site of self-discipline and social control. Through his quest for leadership in the U.S. Army and performances of martial valor, he enacted a politics of immunity which sought partnership with American militarism, striving to prove by his own example that black people could — if given a chance — excel in the management of violence.[15]

As Young's horizons expanded through his commitment to military imperialism, he became ever cognizant of the forms of racial discrimination that impeded his progress up the army chain of command. Typically reserved in the face of personal insult, in 1906 he began to channel his critique of American militarism into a play he would write about his idol, General Toussaint Louverture. Never published during his lifetime, the five-act drama (which he would complete in 1920, two years before his death in Africa) presented a thinly veiled allegory of antiblack racism in the United States, and remains today as the most pronounced articulation of the emergent Pan-African political awakening of America's first black military imperialist of the twentieth century.

The understanding of the black military worker as a communicable subject and agent of American empire heralded the shift from immunity toward contagion in the historical accounts of African American military service abroad during the two world wars. Chapter 4 examines the contradictory conceptions of African American servicemen that informed American military campaigns against venereal disease during these wars, which were often pursued in tandem with similar campaigns by civilian African American leadership on the home front. While white military doctors depended upon the figure of the sexually infected black soldier made clean in order to prove American technological supremacy through experimental drug treatments, African American intellectual leaders required those same bodies — sanitized in the crucible of modern warfare — to make citizenship claims for the broader African American community in the United States.

The bodies and wills of black men proved crucial to these overlapping projects of modernity and citizenship, regulation and surveillance. Chapter 4 also examines ways in which black soldiers in World War I navigated a discourse of pleasure and danger in route to developing a new consciousness of both race and sexuality abroad. Through a consideration of stigmatized sexual practices, the sexual economy of French brothels, and the movement of African American military bands in France, I show how African American soldiers renegotiated meanings of race and nation in their travels outside of the United States.

Deploying African American men and women overseas during World War II projected U.S. debates about race, rights, and citizenship upon a world stage comprising many theaters, including Europe, the Mediterranean, Africa, the Middle East, Latin America, China, India, Burma, and the Pacific Ocean. The final chapter follows the segregated mobilization of black military workers across this expanded playing field, showing how the black body was once again rendered into a subaltern, contagious, and communicable subject of American militarism. Sex remained an important commodity traded within the economies of pleasure created through U.S. foreign military intervention, and the stigma of venereal disease once again justified the experimental use of prophylaxis drugs upon and within the bodies of African American soldiers.

Even as discourses of immunity and contagion continued to mediate their interactions outside the contiguous United States, black troops encountered a world globalized through technological advances in communication, medicine, travel, and warfare, and this in turn shaped their own ideas about race, sexuality, and citizenship. Viewed in successive historical moments as both contagious and immune, their experiences enabled them to map the contours of a global color line through their military travels, increasing their transnational awareness of colonial policies in allied countries, and granting them a political kinship with the darker peoples of the world.

The epilogue considers the military writings of William Gardner Smith, and the literary reception of his 1948 novel *Last of the Conquerors*. Smith worked as a reporter for the *Pittsburgh Courier* before he received his draft notice to serve as an occupation soldier in Berlin. While deployed, he continued to write for the *Courier* as a special correspondent, detailing the injustices faced by black soldiers abroad under his pen name, Bill Smith. His witness as subject and scribe of the overseas military apparatus offered a counterhistory to America's official military record of occupation, and laid the foundation for what would become the familiar narrative told about black soldiering in the postwar era: that military service in the occupied nation was like a "breath of freedom" for African American troops. These contagious narratives of black military freedom and control influenced successive generations of African Americans to join the service, and produced a possibility that had not been possible until the end of World War II: that black men and women might look toward the military service as a career.

Every empire has its beginnings. As we embark upon this historical study of black military workers abroad, we would do well to consider the insights of Alfred Vagts a final time, as he presciently linked the functions of militarism to those of empire. "With imperialism, as a coeval term, militarism shares the tendency to extend dominion," he wrote. "The former generally seeks size, the latter, strength. Where the one looks primarily for more territory, the other covets more men and more money. The two hardly ever exist by themselves."[16] Since the end of World War II, American military bases have become semipermanent fixtures outside of the United States, and the continued existence of these military-industrial outposts has been criticized by scholars, activists, and former "cold warriors" as manifestations of militarism as well as a new form of empire.[17] Whether one balks at this imperial designation or agrees with it wholeheartedly, the United States has dominated the world through its military power for almost three-quarters of a century, and African Americans played an instrumental role in its foundation and expansion. At turns resistant and compliant, black military workers increased the size and strength of the U.S. military abroad in the twentieth century, yet this fact — easily elided in contemporary political thought — was anything but inevitable. Rather, metaphors of contagion and methods of control militarized the black body for twentieth century service, making it both necessary and at times expendable to the larger project of American militarism. As we will see, the exigencies of modern warfare — along with the bridled agency of black military workers — brought a new chapter of African American life into being through the imperial conscription of racial, gender, and sexual difference.

CHAPTER ONE

We Don't Need Another Hero
Death, Honor, and the Archive of American Militarism

> Just asking but was Sgt La David Johnson and the two Nigerians [sic] running towards or away from the firefight?
> —INTERNET COMMENT, Military.com, 2018

There is still much that remains uncertain about the death of Sgt. La David Johnson, of Miami Gardens, Florida, who was killed in action on October 4, 2017, outside the village of Tongo Tongo, Niger. What *is* known, and what U.S. Department of Defense officials have confirmed as the truth, is that his body, shorn of boots and all serviceable equipment, was found two days after the ambush, concealed under the dense crown of a thorn tree. The twenty-five-year-old member of U.S. Army's Third Special Forces Group had been deployed in a unit to Niger for reasons that were not entirely clear, even to elected members of Congress.[1] This lack of civilian oversight into the specifics of America's shadow wars in Africa contributed to the administrative fog and swirl of rumors that hung over Johnson's death in the days, weeks, and months following the ambush.[2] Seven months after the incident, the Department of Defense released a declassified video to the public that they produced to serve as the official narrative of the event.[3] As the narrator's script attests, "This video is a depiction of the events before, during and after the October 4th, 2017 ambush of a combined force of U.S. Special Operations Force and partner Nigeriens near the village of Tongo Tongo, Niger." Combining file footage with animation, it offers a videogame-like reenactment to relate what is currently believed to have happened to the four Americans, four Nigeriens, and the twenty to twenty-five enemy combatants killed that day outside of Tongo Tongo.

The U.S. military presently directs its operations in Africa from Stuttgart, Germany, through AFRICOM. Together with two lower-ranking command centers also located in Germany, Special Operations Command Africa (SOCAFRICA) and Special Operations Command Forward, North and West Africa (SOCFWD-NWA), AFRICOM extends its imperial shadow over the Maghreb and the Sahel by stationing American soldiers at bases in N'Djamena, Chad, and Niamey, Niger. As of 2017, U.S. Special Operations

Forces (SOF) teams were stationed in northwest Africa to train host-nation partner forces, assist and enhance their security efforts, conduct counterterrorism operations, and carry out joint surveillance and reconnaissance missions with host-nation forces.

According to the narrator, southwestern Niger had become a trafficking route for the Islamic State of the Greater Sahara (ISIS-GS), and on October 2, the U.S. SOF team in Ouallam received intelligence that an ISIS-GS subcommander might be moving into their vicinity. For reasons that remain unclear, the mission plan submitted by the team leader "did not accurately characterize the intended purpose of the mission." Instead of performing a reconnaissance sweep of the nearby town of Tiloa, the mission for which they had received clearance, the team sought to pinpoint the location, capture, and if necessary, kill the Islamic State subcommander in their territory.

This covert mission was manned by forty-six personnel in total. Among them were eight U.S. Special Forces soldiers, two U.S. Special Operations Support soldiers, one intelligence contractor, one Nigerien interpreter, a three-man Nigerien reconnaissance team, and thirty-one members of the Nigerien partner force. Johnson was a special operations mechanic for the mission, driving one of the trucks. Traveling in a convoy of eight vehicles—only two of which had mounted machine guns—the joint American and Nigerien patrol drove to Tiloa, but was unable to locate the subcommander. On their return to base, however, the team received "high confidence intelligence" that placed the suspect northwest of Tiloa near the Mali border, and the convoy turned around in pursuit. The second attempted capture was also unsuccessful, and on the morning of October 4, the team began its trek homeward.

As they stopped at Tongo Tongo so that the Nigerien forces could eat breakfast and get water, the U.S. team conducted an impromptu "key leader engagement" with the village elder. The convoy was only 100 meters outside the village when its tail end came under light small arms fire. The team leader had gone looking for a fight, and now he found it. The joint team stopped, exited their vehicles, took defensive positions, and returned fire.

Believing there were only a small number of enemy combatants, the U.S. team leader and four Nigerien soldiers attempted to outflank their attackers from behind. The video reenactment represents the American and Nigerien forces as blue and green dots, respectively, while the enemy combatants—far more than the team leaders realized—emerge as an undifferentiated, lava-like red miasma slowly growing over the landscape. Stopped in their advance by a body of water, the flanking element engaged the enemy from its position until the commander observed "a larger than expected enemy force moving to his east, which consisted of motorcycles and vehicles with mounted heavy machine guns." Returning to the convoy, the commander issued an order to move south, but three American soldiers closest to the line of fire, Staff Sergeants Bryan Black, Jeremiah Johnson, and Dustin Wright, were killed during the staggered retreat.

Only half of the convoy made the retreat south, and those four vehicles reconvened 700 meters away from the ambush site, creating a second defensive position. Soon after, these soldiers received fire from the enemy combatants. Sergeant Johnson moved to his vehicle's mounted machine gun and fired back. When that weapon ran out of ammunition, he switched to a sniper rifle, and continued to shoot, using his truck as cover.

Michel Rolph-Trouillot has described three processes of historical production: the making of facts, the making of archives, and the making of narratives; all three of these processes are present in what the video shows next.[4] Less than an hour had passed since the initial ambush, and at approximately 12:25 P.M., enemy combatants began to mass on the convoy's second defensive position from the southeast. Flanked by enemy fire, the team commander ordered a withdrawal, and three of the trucks were able to leave the area. However, the overwhelming firepower of the enemy left Sergeant Johnson and two Nigerien soldiers unable to reenter their vehicle. Abandoned by their team leader and the rest of their comrades, the three men escaped on foot, running southwest into the Sahel as the enemy pursued them on trucks and motorbikes.

Suddenly, the video's multimediated narrative pauses. A statement, unaccompanied by narration, flashes upon the screen: "This depiction of SGT Johnson's movement is not based on eyewitness accounts, but solely on evidence recovered during the course of the investigation." This was not entirely true. The institutional fabulation of Johnson's last known moments, a simulated reanimation, if you will, depended not "solely" on the forensic evidence recovered during the investigation. It also drew from a particular history of valor and sacrifice germane to the archive of American militarism, which encompasses the historical production of knowledge about the U.S. military as well the cultural, embodied, and discursive traces left in the wake of this institution in the United States and around the world. From the victory of Mexican forces at the Battle of the Alamo in 1836, to General George Custer's crushing defeat by Lakota Sioux and Cheyenne Indians at the Battle of Little Bighorn in 1876, the "last stand" has been romanticized for over a century of writing on American military defeat.[5] The computer-animated representation of Sergeant Johnson's last stand is perhaps the most modern incarnation of this trope, as a moving blue dot on screen is imbued with valiance, physical excellence, commitment to duty, and courage under enemy fire. This narrative cuts against the reports that emerged in the immediate aftermath of the botched mission, particularly those characterizing the incident as "the worst military fiasco under the Trump administration" and the result of "reckless behavior by US Special Forces."[6]

Sergeant Johnson and his comrades ran for their lives across the arid landscape. Both Nigerien soldiers were killed approximately 400 meters from their truck, their green dots dimming to grey. Yet Sergeant Johnson continued to evade his pursuers. Johnson was well known at home and among his comrades for his athletic prowess. Four years earlier, the then twenty-one-year-old Walmart employee became a local celebrity in Miami-Dade County for riding a BMX bike absent its front wheel back and forth to work, popping a wheelie the whole seven-mile commute to Pembroke Pines. His friends, fans, and Instagram followers nicknamed him "the Wheelie King."[7] Depicted in the video as considerably faster than his Nigerien compatriots, Sergeant Johnson sprinted an additional 560 meters—more than half a mile—until he located the only cover available on the barren plain: a single thorn tree. "At this position," the narrator states, "he continued to fight." The viewer then sees the climatic finish of the battle: a solitary blue dot firing upon an unsurmountable red mass that slowly engulfs the screen and closes upon his position. The video fades to black just before Sergeant Johnson's dot dims, ending the simulation of La David Johnson's last stand.

Six hours after the ambush, American, Nigerien, and French soldiers swept the site of battle in search of Sergeant Johnson's whereabouts, but were unable to locate his body due to the distance he had run from his last known position, and "the density of the tree under which he had concealed himself." From the sky, the tree's spine-bearing branches netted together to form an impenetrable shroud, concealing the location of Sergeant Johnson's body from the god's-eye view of surveillance drones for over thirty-six hours.

On the morning of October 6, Tongo Tongo locals informed the Nigerien military they had identified the remains of an American soldier. The narration here is key: "When Sgt. Johnson was found by Nigerien forces, he was beneath the canopy of a thorny tree. Sgt. Johnson was found lying on his back with his arms to his sides. His hands were not bound. Sgt. Johnson was clothed, though his boots and serviceable equipment had been removed by the enemy. The investigation determined Sgt. Johnson was not captured alive."[8] The viewer is assured by the narrator that although Sergeant Johnson was killed in combat, he died an honorable death—he was not tortured, his body was not desecrated, and he was not taken alive. Bodily integrity and wholeness are emphasized in this retelling, and the deployment of this Christlike narrative by Defense officials contradicts—and works to silence—earlier reports that intimated the opposite: unnamed Nigerien personnel who claimed Sergeant Johnson's body was found bound and stripped naked; the numerous stories reporting "additional remains" were found on November 12 at the original recovery site; and the troubling, emotionally wrenching interview given on *Good Morning America* by his pregnant widow, Myeshia Johnson, who was told by President Donald Trump in his condolence call to her that her husband "knew what he signed up for."[9] Curiously, Mrs. Johnson was prevented from viewing her husband's remains before his burial in Florida on October 21. "Why couldn't I see my husband?" she asked anchor George Stephanopoulos. "Every time I asked to see my husband, they wouldn't let me. . . . They won't show me a finger, a hand. I know my husband's body from head to toe, and they won't let me see anything. I don't know what's in that box. It could be empty for all I know, but I need to see my husband. I haven't seen him since he came home."[10]

In the absence of his body, the speculative reassessment of La David Johnson's last stand has gained new importance, particularly in an unchecked social media landscape where wholly uncorroborated accounts have already depicted him variously as traitor in cahoots with Islamic militants and as a coward who—unlike his three white comrades killed in battle—died running away from the firefight.[11] While such insinuations might be correctly viewed as discomfiting reflections of our current political moment, they are also rooted in a discourse of African American inferiority whose tendrils have historically denied black soldiers claims to citizenship rights. As only the most recent high-profile instance of a black soldier dying in America's wars abroad, Johnson's death in Niger underscored the intense, ongoing contest over how "the political lives of dead bodies" should register within a discourse of American military honor, a discourse founded upon ideals of white supremacy.[12] This chapter reckons with this troubling history in order to trace the contours of Johnson's afterlife in the archive of American militarism, to better comprehend *how* and *why* an African American husband and father of three perished under a thorn tree in Niger, however provisional and incomplete those answers are likely to be. The search for such answers (or perhaps better questions) would benefit from consultation with the work of Achille Mbembe.

Mbembe's "Necropolitics" has been extremely influential in contemporary critical theory and cultural studies. The concept has helped contemporary ethnographers of violent conflict consider how mass graves act as "crucial testimony to the wounds of history," and queer and trans of color theorists have refined the term to account for the ways in which dead trans women of color have become the raw material for rights claims made by LGBT social service agencies.[13] The migration of necropolitics into new arenas of academic thought and activism should not, however, occlude from view the original referent: modern war itself.

War is White: Necropolitics, Race, and the Right to Kill

Initially published in 2003, Mbembe's "Necropolitics" offers at least a partial explanation of the situation on the ground in Niger on October 4, 2017. Over the course of the essay, Mbembe argues that Michel Foucault's concept of biopower, understood as the management of populations into those who may live and those who must die, only begins to account for "the contemporary ways in which the political, under the guise of war, of resistance, or of the fight against terror, makes the murder of the enemy its primary and absolute objective."[14] The scientific and political innovations of modern warfare have produced "technologies of destruction . . . more tactile, more anatomical and sensorial, in a context in which the choice is between life and death."

Mbembe was remarkably prescient in his consideration of the role played by necropolitics in contemporary Africa, wherein the political economy of the continent changed dramatically in the last quarter of the twentieth century.[15] "Increasingly," he states, "war is no longer waged between armies of two sovereign states. It is waged by armed groups acting behind the mask of the state against armed groups that have no state but control very distinct territories; both sides having as their main targets civilian populations that are unarmed or organized into militias."[16] Perceiving a new mode of governmentality at play, Mbembe notes an extralegal form of management in which "populations are then disaggregated into rebels, child soldiers, victims or refugees, or civilians incapacitated by mutilation or simply massacred on the model of ancient sacrifices, while the 'survivors,' after a horrific exodus, are confined in camps and zones of exception."[17]

In Mbembe's insights we can discern something of the methods taken by the Islamic State of the Greater Sahara to cripple an imperialist foe through forms of guerilla warfare. Perhaps more importantly, necropolitics also tells us something about the forms of population management that sent Sergeant Johnson to Niger in the first place.

La David Johnson's mother died when he was five years old, and he was subsequently raised by his aunt. As a child, he was enrolled in 5000 Role Models, a project begun by Florida state representative (and family friend) Frederica Wilson in 1993, in which "at risk" African American boys in the Miami-Dade County area are paired with successful male mentors who "prepare them for college, vocational school, or the military."[18] Viewing minority male children as potential "candidates for society's endangered species list," the program—which has instituted its curriculum into ninety-eight local public schools—aims "to give minority boys hope, as well as the vision of greatness to emulate in their everyday lives."[19]

We might ask: Should mentorship programs like 5000 Role Models be indicted for their role in the militarization of African American boyhood? Rather than celebrate their investment in black male adolescence, should we instead view them as early tracking systems of the great chain of necropolitical being, where black bodies provide the flesh and labor fueling the military- and prison-industrial complexes? Such critiques may find substantial support among progressive activists, leftist academics, and critics of American militarism who might readily fault 5000 Role Models—despite its best intentions—for producing more unnecessary heroes in the ongoing global war on terror. However, this perspective occludes a very long history of African Americans fighting not only for the right to die for their country, but also for the right to kill for it.

As useful as necropolitics has been in providing language to describe the "new and unique forms of social existence in which vast populations are subjected to conditions of life conferring upon them the status of *living dead*," it is vital to note that the foundation of Mbembe's argument turns upon Foucault's historical understanding of the sovereign right to kill, and its relationship to racism.[20] This right, which Foucault argued was indicative of how all modern states function, was rooted in the power of the sovereign to decide whether their subjects lived or died. The power to kill was not limited to the taking of another's life by murder but also included "the fact of exposing someone to death, increasing the risk of death for some people, or quite simply, political death, expulsion, rejection, and so on."[21] As the power of the sovereign retreated and the disciplinary and regulatory powers of modernity advanced, racism began to function as the precondition for exercising the right to kill by providing the moral justification "to kill people, to kill populations, and to kill civilizations" viewed as biologically different than one's own. Foucault believed racism, first developed during colonization, created a "biological caesura between the ones and the others" and made possible the murderous and at times, suicidal functions of the state, because "how can one not only wage war on one's adversaries but also expose one's own citizens to war, and let them be killed by the millions . . . except by activating the theme of racism?"[22] In the nineteenth century, war became much more than a contest between political adversaries; it became a matter of "destroying the enemy race, of destroying that [sort] of biological threat that those people over there represent to our race."[23] Mbembe extends Foucault's argument by examining the legal framework used to wage colonial warfare. European jurisprudence had developed a system of laws for conducting war and concluding peace among similarly situated "civilized" states, but these rules of warfare were suspended in the colonies, since their combatants were viewed as "savages" without such rights. The right to wage war, it follows, was a right enshrined only to white men, rendering the right to kill effectively white. Accordingly, the colonies became the "location par excellence where the controls and guarantees of juridical order can be suspended—the zone where the violence of the state of exception is deemed to operate in the service of 'civilization'" due to the "racial denial" of any human bond between the colonizer and the native. "In the eyes of the conqueror," Mbembe wrote, "*savage life* is just another form of *animal life*, a horrifying experience, something alien beyond imagination or comprehension."[24]

But just as the colonized body was viewed as biologically different, so was that of the African slave. The brevity of Mbembe's treatment of chattel slavery notwithstanding, his understanding of the peculiar institution as "one of the first instances of biopolitical experimentation" hints at how racism and the right to kill coalesced around the notion of biological immunity in the Americas.[25] The belief that African slaves were resistant to contagious disease made them choice laborers in plantation industries often plagued by epidemics of fever. The history of this rationale, much more than its truth in fact, imbued blackness with the qualities of both subhumanity and superhumanity. Not only would it be invoked to employ blacks as fever nurses in the eighteenth and nineteenth centuries, astonishingly, it would help justify the conscription of blacks into subaltern military positions during the Civil War and the Spanish-Cuban-American War.

The practice of American militarism remained entangled with beliefs in white superiority and black inferiority on the eve of the twentieth century and, as a consequence, African American soldiers found themselves fighting for the right to fight on the nation's behalf. The belief that honorable military service and demonstrated sacrifice should grant blacks greater rights of citizenship at home and abroad—what I theorize throughout this project as forms of *immunity*—shaped the opportunities given to and taken by black military workers in America's wars overseas, and continues to shape the legacy of African American military service in our current moment.

To truly understand what Sgt. La David Johnson "signed up for" in our necropolitical present, we must first reckon with our necropolitical past. By refusing a presentist reading of necropolitics that finds it applicable only to contemporary phenomena, we can instead look to "the repressed topographies of cruelty" that Mbembe identified in the plantation and the colony and the ways they produced long-forgotten deathworlds that may appear today uniquely modern.[26] There is a discomfiting continuity in how the employment of African American soldiers abroad unsettles American ideals of honor, patriotism, and citizenship. This holds true, from the U.S. military's originary attempt at charting the gravesites of fallen American soldiers in Cuba in 1898, to its more recent forensic reenactment of the ambush that ended Sergeant Johnson's life in Niger. Through it all, black people have remained instrumental subjects in the growth of the U.S. military-industrial complex and the articulation of American military notions of honor. With the story of Sergeant Johnson's last stand fresh in mind, an examination of the scientifically racist origins of black employment in imperial warfare demonstrates how blackness, as sign and signifier, troubled America's imperial archive abroad from the beginning.

Slavery, Blackness, and Biological Immunity

The belief in black immunity to contagious diseases has a long, contentious, and contradictory history, and continues to be a subject of debate today in the academic disciplines of environmental history and biomedicine. While some researchers have staked their professional careers on the belief that black people have a genetic or inherited resistance to yellow fever, others have just as brazenly opposed that claim.[27] Setting aside for a moment this debate within academia, scholars in both camps generally agree that the *belief* in black immunity—regardless of the truth of its existence—aided and abetted the spin of world economic history in the eighteenth and nineteenth centuries. Armed with the self-cleaning logic of racial capitalism, pro-immunity advocates thought African slave laborers carried an embodied "refractoriness" that made them resistant to diseases that often killed white and indigenous peoples, making their bodies essential to the project of new world slavery. As J. R. McNeill states in his study of ecology and war in the greater Caribbean, faith in racial immunity rationalized the use of black labor in economic terms: "It is among Atlantic history's crueler ironies that in their bodies slaves brought new infections to the Americas—yellow fever, falciparum malaria, and hookworm among them—to which they also carried (inherited or acquired) resistance or immunity, which in turn raised the value of slaves against other forms of labor (such as European indentured servants or wage-earners). *Differential immunity* improved the economic logic of slavery and the slave trade, making it larger geographically, longer chronically, and more intensive than it would otherwise have been."[28]

Portraying enslaved Africans as both infectious and immune, McNeill's research adds an important ecological dimension to the discussion of biological resistance. The environmental changes wrought by large-scale sugar production in the Caribbean plantation economy provided the perfect space for mosquitos to breed, and a sizable population of newcomers upon which to feed. The possibility exists, McNeill asserts, that living in proximity to *Aedes aegypti* for thousands of years exerted "evolutionary pressure" on the immune systems of West and Central Africans bound in the slave trade, giving them a differential immunity Europeans sorely lacked. McNeill qualifies this idea by stating any such inherited resistance "is the result of the disease environment of one's ancestors—not a matter of race or skin color," sidestepping claims of biological determinism that locate difference upon racial bodies rather than natural environments. However, the "difference" in his concept of differential immunity merits further examination, as it implies that the evaluation of black morbidity and mortality rates from yellow fever have little meaning in and of themselves, but must always be contrasted with those of whites to ascertain their relevance. As the invisible center of the discourse, whiteness—specifically white mortality in the wake of yellow fever— served as the normative standard of human endurance. Consequently, the expectation of white death and black survival during fever epidemics marked immunity as a physical quality belonging to a lower order of being. Sheldon Watts, a vociferous skeptic of antebellum reports of race-based immunity, found that "the Sentiment among most laymen and white physicians before and after the Civil War was that blacks were less than fully human: draft animals—horses and oxen—did not die of yellow fever; neither did blacks."[29]

It is through this Manichean comparison of racial disease susceptibilities that modern science has historically gathered data, and the theory of black immunity has drawn its obstinate power. In her critique of this idea, historian Mariola Espinosa argues that shoddy historiography, flawed comparative statistics, and false analogies with malarial resistance colluded to make this narrative so pervasive. Its lore is so powerful, in fact, that over two centuries of recorded yellow fever epidemics among people of African descent have been eclipsed in its shadow.[30] In searching for a reason for this erasure, Espinosa speculates that black yellow fever deaths were systematically undercounted by white physicians in the greater Caribbean, as racial empathy for white sufferers of the disease occluded from view the many black people who perished as well:

> Like native populations under colonial rule, slaves and free blacks in the Caribbean and beyond, of course, were subordinate to whites, and their health only rarely a matter of great concern to white doctors. As witnesses to the horrors of a yellow fever epidemic among their white patients, but removed from the similar horrors these epidemics visited upon black people, these doctors could easily surmise that the latter enjoyed an inherent immunity. Moreover, death rates among the underfed and overworked slaves were frequently staggering even in the absence of yellow fever epidemics. Considering all of these factors, it is not surprising that the lethality of yellow fever among black people was often overlooked.[31]

Espinosa infers that the struggle to save white lives took center stage in the official accounts while black deaths were unremarkable, skewing the statistics from that era with unconscious racial bias. Yet if white supremacy was a hidden factor in the administration of antebellum public health, it also produced states of exception where the need for a reserve labor force of fever workers blinded white Americans to the failures of black immunity. As a case in point, Espinosa cites the 1793 epidemic in Philadelphia, during which members of the white medical establishment explicitly asked African Americans to nurse their fellow white citizens through the fever season. White physician Benjamin Rush published an editorial in the *American Daily Advertiser* meant to drum up enlistment and reassure white Philadelphians wary of hiring black workers. His own cursory research had convinced him blacks were members of an immune race, and as a signatory to the Declaration of Independence, he sought to use his own considerable influence, first to persuade "our white citizens [of] the safety and propriety of employing black people to nurse and attend persons infected by this fever," and second, "to hint to the black people, that a noble opportunity is now put into their hands, of manifesting their gratitude to the inhabitants of that city, which first planned their emancipation from slavery, and who have since afforded them so much protection and support, as to place them, in point of civil and religious privileges, on a footing with themselves."[32]

Black Philadelphians did, indeed, take up the call to nurse the afflicted white residents of the city. Spearheaded by Absalom Jones, Richard Allen, and William Gray—all free black members of the Free African Society—African Americans served the infirmed while close to twenty thousand people, including George Washington, fled the city. However, the widespread belief in black immunity wavered when it became evident that blacks were also contracting yellow fever and dying from it. Rush wrote that "[i]t was not long after these worthy Africans undertook the execution of their humane offer of services to the sick, before I was convinced I had been mistaken. They took the disease, in common with the white people, and many of them died with it."[33] In spite of this reality, black Philadelphians continued to nurse those battling yellow fever, only to be faced with charges of extortion for their services once the epidemic ended in the fall.

In response, Jones and Allen wrote a short tract entitled *A Narrative of the Proceedings of the Black People, during the Late Awful Calamity in Philadelphia* that rebutted those charges while also countering the belief that blacks were immune from yellow fever:

> It is even to this day a generally received opinion in this city, that our colour was not so liable to the sickness as the white. We hope our friends will pardon us for setting this matter in its true state.
>
> The public were informed that in the West-Indies and other places where this terrible malady had been, it was observed the blacks were not affected with it—Happy would it have been for you, and much more so for us, if this observation had been verified by our experience.
>
> When the people of colour had the sickness and died, we were imposed upon and told it was not with the prevailing sickness, until it became too notorious to be denied, then we were told some few died but not many. Thus were our services extorted *at the peril of our lives, yet you accuse us of extorting a little money from you.*[34]

Even when faced with evidence to the contrary, white Philadelphians clung fast to the idea of differential immunity. Historian Jacquelyn Miller has shown their capacity to ignore the truth of black vulnerability was connected to the shrunken labor market on the ground. Black immunity, she argues, "provided them a clear justification for hiring African Americans to perform many unpleasant tasks" linked to contamination, including nursing, house cleaning, and burying the dead."[35] The economic necessity of employing a class of people to serve as the go-betweens between the living, the dying, and the dead helped to forge the idea of blackness as the racial prerequisite for the care labor and grunt work required in fever treatment. In light of the sacrifice the black community had shown during Philadelphia's darkest hour, Jones and Allen decried the charges of extortion levied at them as slanderous. They ended their tract with a proverb that bitterly linked the work African Americans had carried out during the epidemic to the subaltern status historically enjoyed by soldiers during, and after, times of warfare: "God and a soldier, all men do adore, In time of war, and not before; When the war is over, and all things righted, God is forgotten, and the soldier slighted."[36]

Jones and Allen's portrayal of black Philadelphians as soldiers impressed into service was apropos and profoundly ironic. Only a year before the epidemic, in 1792, the Uniform Militia Act became the earliest federal statute to explicitly restrict militia membership to "each and every free able-bodied white male citizen of the respective States, resident therein, who is or shall be of age of eighteen years, and under the age of forty-five years," barring African Americans from the bearing of arms and placing a de facto ban on their service in the military.[37] Despite the fact that blacks did indeed serve during the War of 1812 and later during the Mexican-American War, the Militia Act hindered the general enlistment of blacks in the military for seventy years. This statute would finally be supplanted during the Civil War by the 1862 Militia Act, which allowed the conditional enlistment of African Americans as laborers and soldiers, and the Second Confiscation Act, which freed all slaves in the Confederate South. As precedents to President Lincoln's Emancipation Proclamation, the acts responded to the decline of white Union volunteers, the pressing need for manpower, and the material situation on the ground, where slaves who escaped to Union lines held the status as "contrabands of war." Once African Americans were officially permitted to serve, newly manumitted volunteers and their nominally free brethren encountered, at best, the "civilizing processes" of American militarism, and at worst, the vengeance and indifference of white supremacy.

White northern officers evoked the mantra "From slave, to soldier, to citizen" to convey the hope that the militarization of formerly enslaved blacks might possibly raise them to the standards of nineteenth-century white American manhood. Historian Margaret Humphries has written that abolitionist-minded officers "sought to instill order, discipline, honor, and, at times, concepts of hygiene" among all their new recruits, white and black. "But the black soldier," she argues, "and especially the recently enslaved, required more." If the Negro could achieve the mimicry of white Protestant mores within the "university" of the Union army—then perhaps the former slave might gain a "bridge to manhood."[38] Nevertheless, the historiography of the war clearly shows many white officers continued to view the African American soldier as a degraded subject, whose slave heritage marked him as "quintessentially a person without honor."[39] Among the catalog of insults and abuses they received in Union ranks, black soldiers were paid three dollars less than white troops, received inferior rations, housing, and guns, were subjected to cruel and excessive punishments by their commanders, and—most indicative of their subaltern statuses in the army—were disproportionately assigned to fatigue duty in camp. Most, if not all, African American regiments—including the famed Fifty-Fourth Massachusetts Infantry—spent a good portion of their service employed in backbreaking menial labor, increasing the prevalence of their morbidity and moribundity. Further indicative of how the belief in differential immunity sanctioned their use in the conflict was the propensity which they were used to replace white troops during "the sickly season," leading to their greater proportionate incidence of sickness and death.[40] As historian Herbert Aptheker made clear in his study on black casualties during the Civil War, some white Union officers were disturbed by the racial character of these assignments, and worried that this select use of black troops would hinder their transformation into soldiers. He cited a number of communiqués between generals addressing the practice of employing black soldiers primarily as grunt laborers, with some units forced to "prepare camp and perform menial duty for white troops."[41] One officer, frustrated that the men of his command had been "degraded as simply laborers," lodged a complaint directly with the army's adjutant general. "If they are thus treated in the future, as they have been in the past," he wrote, "we may be sure their morale will be entirely destroyed."[42]

This, arguably, did not come to pass. Despite the worst of such abuses, African Americans saw their participation in the Civil War as a signal moment in the black freedom struggle. Once Union victory was secured and slavery was abolished, blacks viewed their service and sacrifice—including those 37,000 killed during the conflict, and the 8,000 discharged with disabilities—as the moral guarantor of their rights to U.S. citizenship.[43] Yet even after the Civil War concluded, the question of whether the U.S. military could serve as a vehicle for racial progress remained unanswered. Despite the subsequent use of black soldiers in the American Indian Wars—during which four regiments became popularly known as the "Buffalo Soldiers"—West Point would commission its first African American officer only in 1877, twelve years after Union victory at Appomattox. Blacks still found themselves fighting for the right to fight at the end of the nineteenth century, and it would take a confluence of factors—most significantly, the persistent belief in black immunity to contagious disease—for them to be recruited en masse for America's first overseas war.

After the United States declared war against Spain in 1898, black men were mobilized for international combat in Cuba under the War Department's understanding that they carried an immunity against yellow fever and malaria, making them well suited to labor in the tropical climates of Cuba, Puerto Rico, and later, the Philippines.[44] The elapse of a century rife with yellow fever outbreaks in the United States and the Caribbean brought a reprise of the discourse of black immunity in the rationale given for the use of African American soldiers in the Spanish-Cuban-American War, and myths and half-truths about race, region, and disease susceptibility filled the lacuna between educated opinion and the making of facts. Scientists, physicians, and military tacticians—thought to be the most modern Americans of their day—coalesced their thoughts and actions around racial explanations for disease resistance, and the fear that white American soldiers would succumb to yellow and typhoid fevers stimulated public calls for the mass enlistment of black men. To underscore their necropolitical employment, these volunteer military companies were given the name "Immune Regiments." White people in positions of power were not the only adherents of the black immunity thesis, however. For reasons that both dovetailed and diverged with the rationales held by their white contemporaries, African American leaders strategically invested in this logic as well.

War Is Black: Booker T. Washington, African American Soldiers, and the Black Investment in Immunity

The yellow fever epidemic in Cuba served as a watershed moment in the collusion of discourses about race, rights, and immunity in the U.S. military. Booker T. Washington saw the crisis as a vanguard opportunity to augment the fortunes of African Americans through the mass enlistment of black volunteers. With the death of Frederick Douglass three years earlier, Washington had become the preeminent spokesman of his race, its chief war propagandist, as well as white America's trusted ambassador of black popular opinion.[45] In March 1898, one month before the official start of the war, he wrote John Davis Long, Secretary of the Navy, with a petition to use black troops grounded in the discourse of racial and environmental immunity. Well aware of the war fervor sweeping the nation, Washington insisted that service, not sensationalism, had led him to contact Long directly. "In common with all good citizens the Negro race abhors war," he wrote, "but should war be forced upon us I belie[v]e that the Negro is in a position to render a service to our country that no other race can."⁴⁶ Framing his belief in differential immunity as a military advantage, Washington suggested that black Southerners would survive tropical disease environments more readily than white men, especially those from the North. This claim, coupled with an eagerness to showcase their patriotism on a world stage, made African American volunteers choice recruits in the war against Spain: "The climate of Cuba is peculiar and danger[o]us to the unaclimated (sic) white man. The Negro race in the South is accustomed to this climate. In the event of war I would be responsible for placing at the service of the government at least ten thousand loyal, brave, strong black men in the South who crave an opportunity to show their loyalty to our land and would gladly take this method of showing their gratitude for the lives laid down and the sacrifices made that the Negro might have his rights."⁴⁷

In gauging how Washington's sense of political propriety and racial accommodation affected his own editorial vision, it is perhaps important to note an unfinished sentence struck from the final version of the missive sent to the Secretary of the Navy: "In saying this I am not unmindful of the fact that my race has suffered—and still suffer wrongs, but when the welfare and honor of country. . . ."⁴⁸ In this moment of war fever and national pride, Washington struck through his own public mindfulness of the racially specific regimes of punishment, exploitation, and surveillance endured by African Americans—whom he would have barter their immune systems by the thousands—on a chance to perform loyalty to their country through mass military service. By inverting the pathology of difference that had for so long marked African Americans as less than human and undeserving of citizenship rights, Washington presented Southern black men as immune, obedient, and beholden to the legacy of the Civil War, making them the perfect recruits for the overseas military venture. Furthermore, his racial chauvinism guaranteed black hardiness in the face of tropical disease, an assurance which sought to transform the belief in differential immunity into an exceptional political appeal. As the black community volunteered the bodies of their men and women in selfless and perilous service to the nation, the "wizard of Tuskegee" hoped to transmute the sacrifice of black lives in Cuba and beyond into individual and collective rights, or "immunities," for the greater black community in the United States.⁴⁹

In lockstep with Washington's plea, African American newspapers were bullish on the prospect of black soldiers serving overseas. Even so, unlike Washington, whose entreaties towards white bureaucrats were obsequiously patriotic, black press editorials struck a balance between endorsing military service and condemning white supremacy. In an editorial entitled, "Let Afro-Americans Prove Their Loyalty," the *Cleveland Gazette* argued that military service was an obligation of citizenship, and "as much as we abominate the terrible injustice done the Afro-American under his own government . . . we have deemed it our duty that every citizen should respond to the national defense."[50] Blacks could not afford to be passive observers in this war, the weekly maintained, "because however much proscribed and circumscribed in the exercise of his personal and political immunities, his rights *per se* are as sacred and dear to himself as to any other citizen."[51] The *Colored American* was optimistic that the conflict would "bring about an era of good feeling the country over, and cement the races into a more compact brotherhood through a perfect unity of purpose and patriotic affinity."[52] Nonetheless, it also used the language of *political immunity* to address the forms of antiblack racism that continued to divest African Americans of their rights: "With all this, the Negro is not blind to the disadvantages under which he labors. He feels very keenly the humiliating slights put upon him by the unreasonable prejudice against his color. There are times when he is inclined to charge the general government with gross indifference to the rights and *immunities* guaranteed him by the constitution, and to question the integrity of a federal power which fails to protect the lives and property of all its citizens alike."[53]

Even as the black press remained attuned to the issue of civil rights, white mainstream newspapers trained their focus and fascination upon the pathway to military service that differential immunity had created for African Americans. By May 1898, the War Department issued General Order No. 55, a directive that authorized a volunteer force of ten thousand men who, "owing to their origin, the places of their residence, and other circumstances affecting their physical characteristics, possess immunity, or are likely to be exempt from diseases incident to tropical climates."[54] One widely syndicated article did more than just exalt the bravery of a group of volunteers it read as white, it claimed their survival from yellow fever had imbued them with superhuman qualities. According to the author, the intense heat of the fever had driven out "every malarial germ and every latent poison in the body," leaving each soldier "free from every defect of blood and bone."[55] As members of "the only regiment in the world that has been at the gates of death," these men were said to have been reborn by fever, and had gained a tranquility of spirit as well as an invulnerability to other diseases after their physical recovery. "All the evils which he has accumulated in a life time are cooked out of him by the deadly heat and his flesh is as pink, and his blood as pure, as that of a healthy, newborn child."[56]

The *Augusta Chronicle* was less moved by this make-believe portrait, and focused instead upon the incontrovertible fact that no serious outbreak of fever had occurred in the south in twenty years, making even acquired resistance to the disease unlikely. Placing the very premise of environmental immunity in doubt, the paper called bunkum on the entire recruiting enterprise: "It is all humbuggery to talk of enlisting thousands of yellow fever immunes in the south. They are not here to enlist. It is extremely doubtful if two full regiments could be recruited in Louisiana, which contains the city of New Orleans. The south has been gradually getting rid of the disease, and is but little more immuned against it than the eastern or western states."[57] The *New Orleans Times-Democrat* likewise cast its own aspersions on the government's claim of differential immunity. Remarking that five of the ten regiments would be white and the rest reserved for "persons on color," it deduced that the true purpose of the bill was to "give the 'brother in black' a chance": "The Negroes have besieged the President with petitions for an opportunity to show their loyalty and patriotism, and he intends to grant their request outside of the political question involved in this proposition."[58]

The question of whether African Americans would gain commissions as officers in the new immune regiments had politicized the topic of black military service from the early rumblings of the war.[59] While black leadership made this a key demand, the white military establishment believed African American troops needed the paternal authority and supervision of white officers to perform acceptably. Discipline was not their only concern, however. Black officers might also want to *eat* alongside their white peers in the officers' mess hall, a social equation that radically reconfigured the politics of race and power in the military.[60] When it became clear that black officers would indeed receive appointments, albeit in a limited fashion as lower-ranking lieutenants with white superiors in charge, the *Augusta Chronicle* found the prospect of an integrated mess worthy of acerbic opinion. "The question of what makes a negro an immune was not answered until a few days ago in Washington," it wrote. Linking differential and political immunities through the question of racial integration, the *Chronicle* made the sardonic suggestion that black officers' filial acceptance of white supremacy was the ultimate test of military fitness: "Negro officers for an immune regiment were examined when this question was asked: 'In the case you are accepted, will you expect to eat with white officers, or to be on social equality with them?' Those who answered in the negative were directed to be immune and were accepted."[61]

White newspapers' cool reception to African American immune service did not go unnoticed by the black press, which continued to advocate for their troops after the policy had been implemented. To be sure, the broad support of the black community for military inclusion was buttressed by patriotism as well as a belief in national self-determination for Cuba's citizens, especially those Afro-Cuban subjects who had gained their freedom from slavery only twelve years earlier. The *Parsons Weekly Blade* wrote that African Americans were selected to serve because "the African is immune from yellow fever and can best endure the climate" and countered claims that Afro-Cubans were unfit to govern themselves by foregrounding the shared African heritage of Cubans and black Americans. If black men were given the chance to claim honor on the battlefield, the *Blade* suggested, that would prove the latter's fitness for duty and the former's right to nation-build: "It is a fortunate circumstance that the four colored regiments are available at this season. They are related by original ties of race to the [Africans] of Cuba, and as they justified their right to be free Americans, the negroes of Cuba, may be similarly trusted."[62] To the remaining white voices of fair-weathered resistance, the *Colored American* offered a brief yet cutting rebuttal that forecasted grim days in the months ahead: "When the weather gets good and warm down in Cuba," it scoffed, "sundry prejudiced white soldiers will wish immune black men had their jobs."[63] Tendered as a promise and a warning, the mirthless joke aptly foretold the actions black and white regiments would take that summer in Cuba in their efforts to survive the fever epidemic that African American men were expected to withstand.

As specimens of differential and political immunity, black volunteers entered the Spanish-Cuban-American War largely through the advocacy of African American leaders who amplified the antebellum belief that blacks were less susceptible to tropical diseases. With so much riding upon the bodies of black men that summer, however, it is important to note that those inducted under this policy had their own doubts about how effective their alleged immunities would fare on the fields of battle. They expressed their misgivings in the same newspapers that had petitioned for their inclusion, and grew skeptical of the rationale used to secure their service.

Nathanial Bruce, a volunteer in a black North Carolina regiment, took considerable umbrage at how the concept of immunity functioned to enlist black men into wartime service roles regardless of their individual aptitudes.

A professor of Greek at Shaw University, Bruce had fashioned himself in the image of Booker T. Washington, educating himself at Bates College, Harvard, Hampton Institute, and finally Tuskegee, where he studied under Washington himself.[64] No doubt ignorant of his mentor's role in brokering black service through the logic of environmental immunity, Bruce nonetheless rebuked the policy for confirming prejudiced beliefs about African American inferiority. "Some are trying to make excuses for those who are prejudiced and who are unwilling to fight side by side with negro soldiers, by hatching up an idea of 'immunes' to fever, hot weather, foul air, bad stenches, and hard work." To Bruce, immunity was a mode of subaltern classification, a canny way to induct blacks into the lowest ranks of service. As a point of comparison, he noted that there were "hundreds of thousands of 'poor whites' who also live in the hot and sultry and miasmatic swamps of the Sunny South," who could "hold captured islands and endure the hot sun and hard work, not better, but equally as well as their black fellow laborers." Bruce took no pride in this supposed attribute and felt the designation enabled whites to assign blacks to the various forms of menial labor instead of "furnish[ing] men and officers according to their ability and fighting population." He rejected the premise of immunity forthright and the concomitant insinuation of inferiority that lay just beneath its surface: "This plea is false and undignified—only made to deceive and to get negroes into service respected by the other soldiers to begin with as a person respects mules and oxen—only for heat and heavy hauling."[65]

Bruce's cynicism was well warranted. The dawning realization among black soldiers that they would be used primarily as occupation troops long after the fighting ended in Cuba created consternation within their rank and file. Harry Ross, a corporal in the Eighth Illinois Volunteers, enlisted in the war in order to fight for his family and country in gallant combat. "But now that all is quiet," he wrote to the *Indianapolis Freeman* in October 1898, "there is another picture that has presented itself and that picture is disease and death."[66] The true mission of the Eighth Illinois, it seemed to him, was to occupy and pacify the newly acquired territory, which as it turned out, proved equally lethal to black and white bodies. "Sir, when we bade our kind old fathers and mothers, sisters and brothers, wives and sweet-hearts good-bye, we were in the best of health but now it is entirely different for more than four-fifths of our men are sick with the dreaded malaria and fever."

Realizing that they were not immune from the rigors of the Cuban landscape, African American soldiers were shocked by their vulnerability to disease. Instead of finding natural affiliation with the tropical environment,

Ross's unit—enervated by sickness from unknown causes—found the land and the water hostile to human life. The fruit was all "full of fever," the water had to be boiled before drinking, and even the mountain springs ran uncomfortably warm, "for the earth is like a stove."[67] These discomforts of occupation were compounded by a fear of abandonment and estrangement, producing an existential crisis of citizenship for Ross and his fellow soldiers: How would these men, debilitated by disease, be received upon their return to the United States? And if they did perish in Cuba, would their government care enough to repatriate their bodies back to the only homeland most of them had ever known? These material and ideological concerns merged to produce a new imperial state of subjection for the black military worker. In protest and plea, Ross conveyed the mindfulness of a person suddenly and resolutely aware of his place—as agent, actor, and subject—in the caste system of American militarism: "Then comes the trying time, the question is such: we stay here and die or is the good people of our homes going to pray for our deliverance from this country of disease; how can we stay here and die without the hope of our bodies coming home; how can we bear to know that ever should we return we can only present to our sweet-hearts and mothers . . . a wreck of humanity?"[68]

Whether black men were rendered invalid by fever during their time in Cuba or buried and forgotten in a foreign Potter's Field, Ross struggled over what would remain of their bodies after their tours of duty had ended, dulling the luster of the national postwar optimism with a macabre and pragmatic pessimism. And he was not alone. Black troops in Cuba were shaken by the reality of their susceptibility to disease; as an anonymous collective of black soldiers from the Eighth Illinois told the *Illinois Record*, "The much dreaded fever soon sailed in upon us and sad was the day and hour when this monster of human life places a firm grasp upon American white or black. To-day you are ill, tomorrow your sunken cheeks, thin hands, and weak system speak for you, that the bone yard will claim another victim and retire a soul from suffering."[69] George Beard, another soldier from the same regiment, maintained that "If we are kept here a year or two, mothers will not know their sons, wives will not know their husbands . . . for we will be living skeletons."[70] Having borne the onerous brunt of the occupation to that point, black soldiers had little faith that their corporeal bodies, once deceased, would be returned to their families in America to be given the homegoing services they so justly deserved. "When a man dies here," Beard continued, "he is put in a pine box and buried two or three deep in a Cuban grave yard and is soon forgotten by all." "Three Privates" from his unit, who had already

We Don't Need Another Hero

lived down numerous accounts of injustice and deprivations, had given up hope their corpses would be repatriated in the case of their deaths. "I guess we will live to leave our bodies on Cuban soil," they wrote, "for the remembrance of the 8th [Illinois Regiment] who once went to Cuba to make a record for themselves, but were left behind."[71] Though it took nearly two years, most of the dead would, in fact, be repatriated to the United States after war's end. But as the first volunteer tasked to identify and mark the location of the martial graves in Santiago maintained, "only the bony systems of our fallen heroes will rest in home graves. The soil of Cuba retains the sacred remainder, and this fact must continue to give the battlefields of Santiago a peculiar interest and honor, not only to Americans, but to all friends of Free Cuba."[72]

Death, Honor, and Political Immunity

Henry Christopher McCook, a Presbyterian minister and Civil War veteran, made the first field maps of the graveyards in Santiago. Worried that the U.S. military had no system in place to locate the remains of dead soldiers, McCook secured a mandate from President McKinley in August 1898 to mark those sites for future exhumation. The geographical expedition to map the "sacred remainder" of American bodies abroad did more than aid repatriation efforts, however. As simulacra of the ultimate sacrifice made by U.S. soldiers, those cartographies of martial death laid claim to the land itself, thereby justifying the occupation of Cuba by the U.S. Army.[73] Still, both McCook's training as a reverend and his service as a chaplain in the Union army were clearly instrumental in elevating his need to properly honor America's war dead into a moral and spiritual imperative. An antislavery Republican and Lincoln supporter during the Civil War, his own sense of martial honor was deeply inflected with abolitionist sentiments.[74] McCook received a commission as a lieutenant in the Forty-First Illinois Regiment but subsequently declined it after learning his fellow officers took fugitive slaves who had come to them for protection and returned them to their masters for a profit. Military historian Ricardo Herrera has written that "Morality and simple human justice, even if not explicitly stated, informed McCook's sense of honor." The lieutenant's refusal to be part of a regiment where "*slave-trading Officers*" acted with impunity taught him, in effect, that that honor was not the exclusive provenance of white men.[75]

The concept of American martial honor, far from immune from the historical machinations of race, class, and gender, gains its greatest expression through these registers of difference. Death in battle, death from disease, and death through labor carried racialized and gendered meanings within this discourse, and military officials recurred to those categories explicitly in recognizing the performance of black soldiers in life and death. As McCook toured the gravesites of Santiago he took great pains to exalt the heroism and the self-sacrifice of African American soldiers in Cuba, who "acquitted themselves with steadiness, skill and valor that won from all, even the most prejudiced, the warmest encomiums."[76] Given the exigencies of war there was little time or inclination to enact "the spatial segregation of American dead" in orthodox fashion, and most of the dead were buried where they fell, plotted in rowed enclosures or placed in common graves, uncategorized by race.[77] Nevertheless, McCook's own graphic representations of "the rude methods of soldiers to honor and identify the burial places of their comrades" illustrated a blueprint of martial honor drawn from the Jim Crow ideology of the burgeoning white supremacist empire.[78] His sketches, paintings, and photographs of American burial sites in Cuba demonstrate how the interring of black and white bodies in Santiago was organized through the logics of necropolitical citizenship, an honor-bound discourse that, in addition to viewing African American troops as servants rather than soldiers, required the ritual sacrifice of the black body for the very possibility of expanded citizenship rights. The afterlife of honor, made material through memorials, monuments, graveyards, pensions, and parades, finds a curious articulation in the plotting of foreign military cemeteries, and McCook's cartographies of black death in Cuba form a visual and ideological triptych that symbolized American military anxieties about the role of the black soldier, the recognition of black heroism, and the steadfast belief in biological difference between the races.

McCook documented the burial practices of the Twenty-Fifth Infantry upon a plantation south of the village of El Caney. One of four regular units of African American soldiers called up for service during the war, the Twenty-Fifth provided crucial support to the Twelfth Infantry in the eponymous battle there but took significant losses in the storming of the fort. McCook lauded the unit for its gallant service, and noted the care with which its men had attended to the burial of their white commander, and their seven fallen black brothers in arms. Stone, flora, and requisitioned materials had been arranged to render the gravesite into an exemplary scene of Christian sacrifice etched onto the living field of battle. Lt. Harry McCorkle's grave was prominently marked with a headstone and seven large stones that formed a cross atop the length of his buried body (figure 1.1). Iron fences salvaged from Cuban homes enclosed his plot "as a protection from the outside world"

FIGURE 1.1 Drawing of Lieutenant McCorkle's gravesite in Cuba. From Henry Christopher McCook, *The Martial Graves of Our Fallen Heroes in Santiago de Cuba* (Philadelphia, PA: G. W. Jacobs, 1899).

FIGURE 1.2 Photograph of the graves of men from the Twenty-Fifth Infantry near Caney. From Henry Christopher McCook, *The Martial Graves of Our Fallen Heroes in Santiago de Cuba* (Philadelphia, PA: G. W. Jacobs, 1899).

FIGURE 1.3
Painting of tree tablets commemorating members of the Twenty-Fifth Infantry killed at Caney. From Henry Christopher McCook, *The Martial Graves of Our Fallen Heroes in Santiago de Cuba* (Philadelphia, PA: G. W. Jacobs, 1899).

(figure 1.2).[79] In contrast, his men were buried outside of the iron enclosure in a plain, shared mound. Two young trees grew behind the graves, and the names of the "25th Inft. Roll of Honor" had been carved onto the flat surface of their trunks (figure 1.3).[80] "The seven soldiers who sleep at the side of Lieut. McCorkle on Santa Thomas plantation are the silent witnesses of the patriotism, manliness and courage of their race," McCook wrote, venerating the enlisted black men who had been granted a heroic death in the war against Spain.[81] Yet the recognition he bestowed upon the seven black soldiers effectively replicated the social distinctions military officials had tried hard to maintain by keeping the officership virtually white. The burials of Corporal Benjamin Cousins, and Privates French Payne, Tom Howe, John Phelps, John Steele, Aaron Leftwich, and Albert Strother were thus recuperated into a narrative where rank functioned as a metaphor for racial hierarchy, where even in death the men had been positioned as sentries patrolling the gated graveside of their white American commander.[82] For McCook, this gravesite exemplified the possibility of an interracial brotherhood, national reconciliation, and African American perfectibility that could be forged only in the crucible of overseas war. His depiction functioned as a posthumous performance of manhood rights, a sublime appeal for full citizenship that simultaneously extended a Jim Crow discourse of honor into Cuba.

But combat deaths such as those experienced by the men of the Twenty-Fifth were, on the whole, exceptional rather than exemplary. The vast majority of soldiers killed during the Spanish-Cuban-American War—across race and nationality—died from disease. McCook's second mapping of African American burials in Cuba took the men of the Twenty-Fourth Infantry as its study. The Twenty-Fourth had joined the Twenty-Fifth, as well as the Ninth and Tenth Calvary, in distinguished service in the Battle of San Juan Hill on July 1, 1898. Two weeks later, they were assigned guard duty at the yellow fever hospital in Siboney after eight white regiments refused to nurse the mounting number of soldiers ill with yellow fever.[83] It should be said neither the Twenty-Fourth Infantry nor the other three black regular units were deployed to Cuba through the specific logic of differential immunity. However, the environmental rationale used to bolster the enlistment of black men—what Amy Kaplan has described as the Lamarckian argument that viewed them "as though they were physically closer to the terrain, more like the 'natives' than like white Americans"—positioned all African American soldiers who had been deployed in Cuba as grunt laborers whose bodies served as ideological and material buffers between white soldiers and the contagious world.[84]

In the haste of the unexpected epidemic, the hospital at Siboney had become a contagious space of suffering and death, a necropolis in sentiment if not in word, with men dying hourly in its tents and given burial in its cemetery due to lack of proper treatment.[85] When the Twenty-Fourth was asked for volunteers to serve as yellow fever nurses, the entire regiment stepped forward. A day later, forty-two out of sixty men from the first wave of responders became seriously ill with yellow fever or malaria. The regiment was asked again for additional volunteers, and once more, the Twenty-Fourth reportedly volunteered en masse. "The records of heroism in the Spanish-American War, or for that matter, in any other war, present no incident more worthy of commemoration upon the page of history, by the poet's song and by the hands of the sculptor and of painter than this act of the gallant blacks

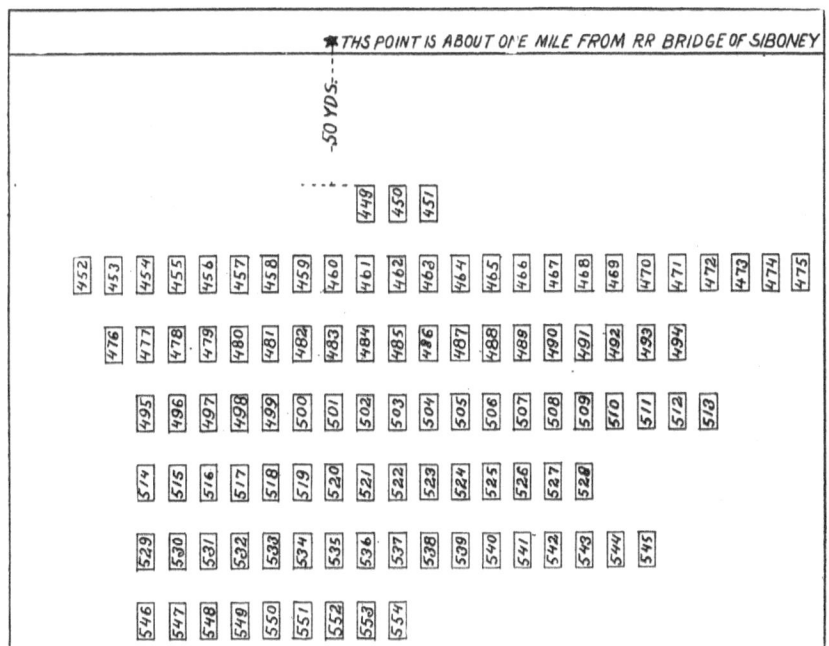

FIGURE 1.4 Map of the cemetery of the General Hospital at Siboney. From Henry Christopher McCook, *The Martial Graves of Our Fallen Heroes in Santiago de Cuba* (Philadelphia, PA: G. W. Jacobs, 1899).

of the Twenty-Fourth Regiment of the United States Infantry."[86] McCook called upon the artisans of public memory to celebrate the sacrifice of men who had survived the battle only to die from disease, "who shirked no duty, whether upon the battlefield or in the presence of the noisome pestilence," and whose deaths marked the material limits of immunity's political gambit. Of the 320 soldiers and officers from the Twenty-Fourth who served at Siboney, 167 men contracted yellow fever, thirty-seven died (including their white commander), and forty received disability discharges.[87] Only twenty-four soldiers escaped Cuban duty unscathed by fever, and even members of this exceptional group were taken by illness during the voyage home or after their arrival at Camp Wikoff.[88]

The general hospital cemetery at Siboney was organized in straight seven rows, and officers slain in duty occupied the first three spots (figures 1.4, 1.5). Out of 105 plots, African American soldiers rested in twenty graves, indistinguishable from their fellow soldiers in every way, if not for the asterisk of difference appended to their names in the list of "Fallen Heroes" McCook compiled as recognition of their "perilous, self-dying" campaign

We Don't Need Another Hero 39

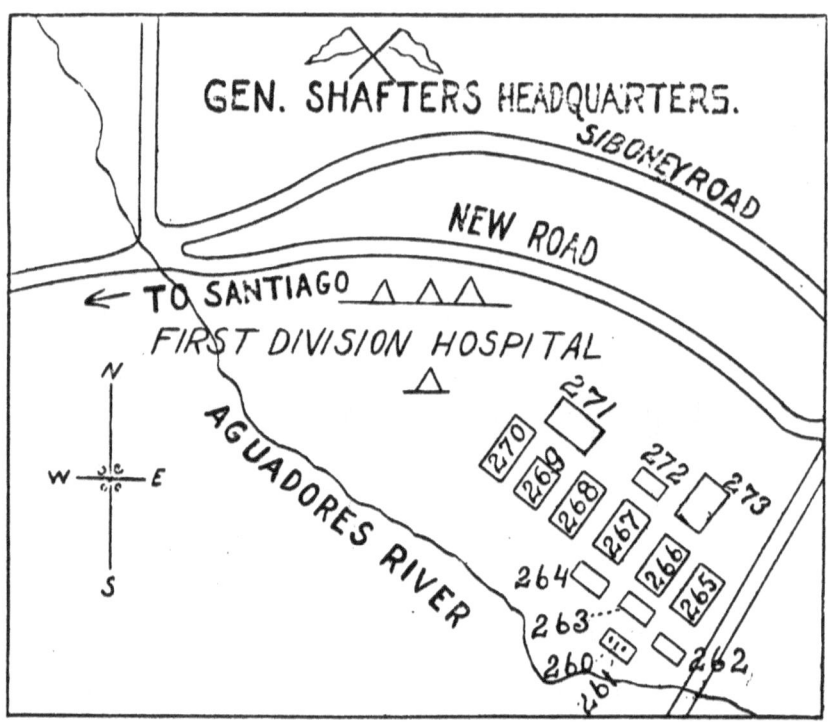

FIGURE 1.5 Cemetery of the First Division Hospital. From Henry Christopher McCook, *The Martial Graves of Our Fallen Heroes in Santiago de Cuba* (Philadelphia, PA: G. W. Jacobs, 1899).

against the pestilence amid the hills of Siboney.[89] The gravesites of at least sixteen soldiers from the Twenty-Fourth were unknown to McCook at the time of his writing, and he speculated they had been buried in the "Unknown" section of the cemetery, or transported to Montauk for stateside interment.

The deaths of these African American soldiers from fever work came as a shock to the many military and civilian officials who had lobbied for their inclusion due in no small part to their belief in racial and environmental immunity against contagious diseases. William Richard Jones was one of the volunteer immunes whose death in Santiago disrupted the certainty of black survival in the midst of contagion. McCook's third map of black death patterns charted his grave in the First Division Hospital's second cemetery among nine other presumably white men, all of whom had died in August and September of that year (figure 1.6). No narrative was provided for the soldier's death, and the information in his service records provides little else to testify to his humanity besides his place of origin upon enlistment (South

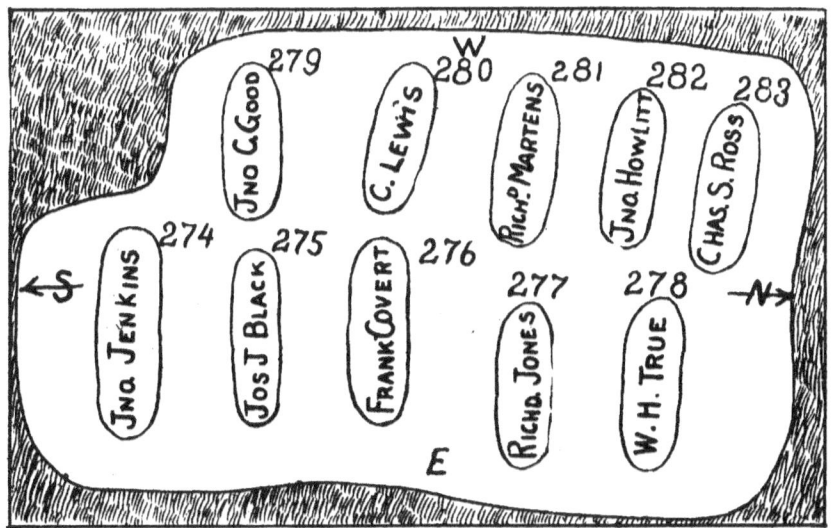

FIGURE 1.6 Drawing of Richard Jones's cemetery plot. From Henry Christopher McCook, *The Martial Graves of Our Fallen Heroes in Santiago de Cuba* (Philadelphia, PA: G. W. Jacobs, 1899).

Carolina) and the captain of his squad.[90] McCook listed Jones as "colored" in the catalog of the dead, but that was not the only qualifier that marked his grave as anomalous among his peers. Buried alongside corporals, sergeants, and privates, "Rich'd Jones" was given the official designation "laborer," a work title that placed him outside the official system of military rank.[91] Working at the First Division hospital, his toils likely included janitorial duty, manual labor, and the burial of the dead. Yet given no ranking in a hierarchy where black men already held one of the lowest positions of power, Jones was located outside the metrics of honor, whereupon his race and class collapsed into one another to signal the emergence of a new subjectivity embodied by men and women: *the black military worker*, a necessary component of American imperialism abroad since 1898.

There is one last detail left to consider in the cartography of Jones's death. In 1899 his body was repatriated to the United States and buried in Arlington National Cemetery (figure 1.7). To this day, the inscription on his headstone reads, "Rich'd Jones, laborer," effectively chiseling his subalternity onto the most hallowed landscape of American martial memory, and transmuting his sacrifice into pure, necropolitical labor (figure 1.8). If military cemeteries are considered to be repositories of martial honor, what kind of honor was available to a military worker like Jones, whose death in labor

REPORT OF INTERMENT							NAME OF CEMETERY Arlington, Va.			
TO: THE QUARTERMASTER GENERAL, WASHINGTON 25, D. C.							EMBLEM (Check one) ☐ CHRISTIAN ☐ HEBREW ☐ OTHER (Specify)			
NAME (Last, First, Middle Initial) Jones, William (Richard)							SERVICE DATA (Company, Regiment, Division, or other organization, and basic arm of service)			
RANK Laborer				SERIAL NUMBER						
STATE				☐ WW I ☐ OTHER (Specify) ☐ WW II						
DATE OF BIRTH			DATE OF DEATH			DATE OF INTERMENT	GRAVE LOC.	DATES OF SERVICE		
MONTH	DAY	YEAR	MONTH DAY YEAR Sept 2 1898			MONTH DAY YEAR	SEC. OR PLOT / GRAVE OR LOT NO. 102	ENLISTMENT	DISCHARGE	DIED ON A. D. / RETIREMENT
REMARKS (Authority for interment, pension, or claim number, disinterment, etc.) originally buried: Santiago, Cuba. Recd NY on Crook, March 30, 1899. Interred as Richard (Wm) Jones. Information taken from old card.							HEADSTONE OR MARKER ORDERED			
NAME AND ADDRESS OF NEXT OF KIN OR OTHER RESPONSIBLE PERSON							SHIPPING POINT FOR HEADSTONE NEAREST FREIGHT STATION			
SIGNATURE OF SUPERINTENDENT OF NATIONAL CEMETERY, OR TRANSPORTATION OFFICER, OR QM OF POST CEMETERY							POST OFFICE ADDRESS			
QMC FORM 14 REV 1 JUL 50			PREVIOUS EDITIONS OF THIS FORM ARE OBSOLETE				SEE INSTRUCTIONS ON REVERSE SIDE			

FIGURE 1.7 Richard Jones's report of interment card. *U.S. National Cemetery Interment Control Forms, 1928–1962* [online database], Provo, Utah: Ancestry.com Operations, Inc., 2012. Accessed via Ancestry.com.

escaped established rubrics for the veneration of military sacrifice while also ruffling contemporary American thought on race, environment, and immunity? The faith shown by civilian and military leaders in differential immunity bore dire consequences for the scores of workers who died in or were debilitated by immune service. Yet these unexpected deaths were not the outliers of this discourse; they were, in fact, constitutive of it, and provided a blueprint for the necropolitical use of black bodies abroad in the century to come.

Graveyard cartography offers us more than afterimages of American military funeral rites at home and abroad; it provides a model for considering how the burial and repatriation of black bodies extended the geographic dominion of America's burgeoning empire. As consecrations of occupation, black military workers were crucial ideological and material figures in the project of political immunity. As useful as they had been in life, so they would be in death.

Only months after the war had officially ended, Booker T. Washington exalted the wartime sacrifices made by African American soldiers in his address at the National Peace Jubilee in Chicago, one of a number of national "peace jubilees" that celebrated American victory against Spain. The invalidation of the immunity thesis had no discernible effect upon his public state-

FIGURE 1.8 Richard Jones's gravestone at Arlington National Cemetery. Courtesy of Anne Cady, photographer.

ments celebrating the endurance of black soldiers and nurses in the postwar period. In a sense, it made his restrained demands for expanded African American citizenship rights more radical, as the suffering endured by black soldiers legitimated the previous claims he made about their patriotism and obedience. "In the midst of all the complaints of suffering in the camp and field during the Spanish-American War, suffering from fever and hunger," he said, "where is the official or citizen that has heard a word of complaint from the lips of a black soldier?" The answer could have been easily provided by any of the of black newspaper editors who regularly broadcast the grievances of African American troops to their readerships throughout the war.

We Don't Need Another Hero 43

Striking through his own mindfulness of such knowledge once again, Washington rooted his commendation of black imperial military service in the same racist discourse that had created its opening. "The only request that came from the Negro soldier was that he might be permitted to replace the white soldier when heat and malaria began to decimate the ranks of the white regiments, and to occupy at the same time the post of greater danger."[92] Washington highlighted the self-abnegation of black soldiers as performances of military respectability, made all the more remarkable in light of the actual fallibility of African Americans to infectious disease. But since the number of American casualties in the Spanish-Cuban-American War was relatively low—especially in comparison with Spanish losses to disease and combat—Washington's political gambit allowed him to valorize the minimal number of dead African American soldiers, while employing their sacrifice as a strategic tool for racial advancement. With characteristic aplomb, Washington made his most strident statement on the political immunities African Americans had earned through their sacrificial service in Cuba through an appeal to the white leadership of the war, those generals and colonels who had observed firsthand how loyal, patriotic, and committed to American imperialism black soldiers had shown themselves to be in the feverish first summer of U.S. military occupation:

> And, if any one would know how he acquitted himself in the field at Santiago, let him apply for answer to Shafter and Roosevelt and Wheeler. Let them tell how the Negro faced death and laid down his life in defence of honour and humanity. When the full story of the heroic conduct of the Negro in the Spanish-American War has been heard from the lips of Northern soldier and Southern soldier, from ex-abolitionist and ex-master, then shall the country decide whether a race that is thus willing to die for its country should not be given the highest opportunity to live for its country.[93]

Dead American soldiers, the black and white bodies still buried in Santiago, served as key rhetorical figures in Washington's most brazen public appeal for racial reunion at the interfaith "thanksgiving service" inaugurating the jubilee. "We have succeeded in every conflict," he chided, "except the efforts to conquer ourselves in the blotting out of racial prejudices." Ever the oratorical master, Washington's use of the phrase "to conquer ourselves" hailed a new American public into being, an inclusive and capacious sense of selfhood that included his multiracial audience in Chicago as well as the black and white readerships throughout the country who later read his speech verbatim in their local papers. "Until we thus conquer ourselves, I make no empty statement when I say that we shall have, especially in the Southern part of our country, a cancer gnawing at the heart of the Republic, that shall one day prove as dangerous as an attack from an army without or within."[94] This American public was at war with itself over race, he claimed, but it might find solemn reconciliation in the martial graveyards of Cuba. "We can celebrate the era of peace in no more effectual way than by a firm resolve on the part of Northern men and Southern men, black men and white men, that the trenches which we together dug around Santiago shall be the eternal burial place of all that which separates us in our business and civil relations." In Washington's metaphor, American cemeteries in Cuba provided an opportunity to bury the history of sectional strife, racial segregation, and political inequality within the newly occupied landscape, transforming the island nation into an opportunity for offshore national reconciliation.

For Washington, the interracial deathbeds in Santiago testified to the historical intimacies that had always bound black and white men together. In a stunning finish, Washington spoke directly to white America, and dared it to reject the truth of this longstanding relationship: "You know us; you are not afraid of us. When the crucial test comes, you are not ashamed of us. We have never betrayed or deceived you. You know that as it has been, so it will be. Whether in war or peace, whether in slavery or freedom, we have always been loyal to the Stars and Stripes."[95]

Washington's Peace Jubilee address received a rapturous ovation from the crowd of sixteen thousand, who had braved the rain to hear him speak in the presence of President McKinley, his cabinet, U.S. military officials, and foreign dignitaries in attendance. The *Chicago Times-Herald* reported "the applause given him made the very columns of the massive building tremble. It sounded more like a roar than cheers and clapping of hands. And it would not cease. Again and again it was repeated."[96] The *Chicago Evening Post* noted how "he moved the audience profoundly by his just claim that the Negro in America has on every occasion that tried men's soul [has] chosen the better part, the part of self-sacrifice and duty."[97] Black editorials across the country were similarly impressed. The *Colored American* wrote that Washington's speech "electrified the country" and "has set an entirely new pace of thought for both races, and struck a keynote destined to establish a loftier and more enduring relation between the Caucasian and the freedman."[98] R. C. Ransom of the *Indianapolis Freeman* suggested that those critical of the orator in the past for not doing enough to combat racial injustice would be forced to reassess their opinions of him. "May it not be that he has proven himself to be wiser than us all? After his splendid deliverances during Jubilee week in Chicago when he plead with such power and eloquence for justice to our race, he never again can be charged with lack of courage, for upon no occasion has his plea on behalf of the race been stronger or braver."[99] Not since the Civil War had the service and sacrifice of black soldiers been so instrumental in a public appeal for expanded citizenship rights, and the columnist viewed Washington's place at the podium as generational shift in accessing power's ear. "Never before within this generation, has an opportunity come to a member of the race, to speak in such a magnificent presence and upon an occasion when he could hold the attention of the country from the President and his cabinet down and get the ear of the world."[100]

But it was Washington's very metaphor of black men and white men lying together in an offshore homosocial embrace that stoked the ire of Southern newspaper editors. They read in his romantic depiction of a deathbed brotherhood endangered by a cancer gnawing at the republic's heart a veiled appeal for social equality among the races. Bemoaning his characterization in the South as an antiracist crusader in sheep's clothing, Washington issued an op-ed brandishing his accommodationist bona fides in the *Birmingham Age-Herald*. "Replying to your communication of recent date regarding my Chicago speech," he wrote, "I would say that I have made no change whatever in my attitude towards the south or in my idea of the elevation of the colored man. I have always made it a rule to say nothing before a northern audience that I would not say before a southern audience."[101] Washington's rebuttal rested on two claims: first, he maintained a firm distinction between ending race prejudice in civil and commercial relations and doing so in "social relations"; and second, there was a vital difference between advocating for the *political* equality of African Americans and their *racial* equality with white Americans. "What is termed social recognition is a question I never discuss. . . . God knows that both—we, of the black race and the white race—have enough problems pressing upon us [for] solution without obtruding a social question, out of which nothing but harm would come."[102] Washington argued that racial prejudice was bad both for business and for the moral constitution of the American self, as it "narrow[ed] and degrade[d]" the soul of black and white alike. Yet its eradication—as foreshadowed by the use of black soldiers in Cuba—would inaugurate a new era of economic prosperity and moral clarity for a newly imperial nation seeking to justify the means and the ends of American militarism. This could be done, he averred, without disturbing the white supremacist understandings of social difference that continued to hold sway at the end of the nineteenth century. The success of both races in this venture would grow in direct proportion to "every manly way they cultivate the friendship and confidence of each other," and chief among these manly modes of cultivation was military service.[103]

Even in a segregated army, Washington recognized military service as conducive to producing the habits he believed would ultimately lead to "the salvation of the Negro," including thrift, economy, honor, educational attainment, property ownership, propriety, and industrial skill.[104] His editorial successfully assuaged his Southern critics and renewed his reputation as a gradualist and pragmatist in the arena of race relations. But always a careful rhetorician, Washington would further edit the archival record of his speech in his first autobiography, *The Story of My Life and Work*, deleting lines that specifically referred to antiblack discrimination and white southern racism.[105]

With his own political immunity restored, Washington continued to trumpet the sacrifices of African American soldiers in his books *The Future of the American Negro* and *A New Negro for a New Century*. In *Working with the Hands*, his sequel to *Up from Slavery*, he also made a fascinating, if flawed, observation about another group of black military workers whose service in Cuba received very little attention at the time: African American women. "The five Tuskegee nurses sent to the front in the Spanish-American war were the only coloured female nurses employed by the Government," he wrote.[106] Tuskegee did indeed provide students to serve as nurses in Cuba, but they were far from the only black women hired as nurses by the U.S. Army. On the contrary, nurses across the country responded to an enlistment call never before granted to African American women. While some had been trained in the few nursing schools open to blacks, others had served as yellow fever nurses during the Civil War. The fact that their service in Cuba received scant coverage made Washington's boast more believable. But even with its faults, his claim shone light upon the little-known fact that African American women had also been recruited for immune service in the Spanish-Cuban-American War. Just as black men were believed to be resistant to the contagions of the environment, black women were thought to be immune from the infections of the body, and these antebellum beliefs facilitated the conscription of African American womanhood into necropolitical service abroad.

What follows is the untold story of the militarization of black women's care labor through the gendered and racialized logics of immunity, and how one uniquely positioned women of color facilitated this vanguard interface between black womanhood and American militarism at the turn of the twentieth century.

CHAPTER TWO

Negro Heroines
Gender, Race, and Immunity in the Spanish-Cuban-American War

> Down in history we find it and in grandest works of art,
> How the men on fields of battle play so well the soldier's part,
> But I come to tell the story of relief from care and pain
> Rendered them by Negro women in the Cuban War with Spain.
>
> —LIZELIA AUGUSTA JENKINS MOORER, "Negro Heroines"

On July 20, 1898, as the swelter of the summer day eased into evening, Namahyoka Gertrude Curtis, a savvy, well-connected black woman of social fame from Washington, D.C., made an urgent appeal to the congregation of First Free Mission Baptist Church in New Orleans. She had been in the city for only a few days, traveling south on special military orders from the Surgeon General of the Army, on a mission authorized by President William McKinley himself. Adopting the initials of her husband for the bulk of her public and professional career, Mrs. A. M. Curtis stood before the black members of First Free Mission Baptist and made her special request: the nation was in dire need of nurses to care for soldiers stricken ill with yellow fever in the ongoing war with Spain, and she was in town to recruit them. Strikingly, this recruiting call was free of gender or racial restrictions—the main qualification was that the nurses must have had the disease previously, thus ensuring immunity. These *immune nurses*, also known as *immunes*, would be sent forthwith to Santiago, Cuba, to care for American soldiers stricken with Yellow Jack.

Outbreaks of yellow and typhoid fevers had compromised the health of the U.S. Army to such an extent that civilian and military officials authorized new protocols to expand its enlistment criteria beyond the commonplace prerequisites of whiteness and manhood. The choice of New Orleans as a recruiting center was a prudent one; the city had a long and virulent history with yellow fever, and there was no better place to find an abundant number of nurses experienced in treating the disease. Black women were specifically sought for this service. Covering Mrs. Curtis's speech, The *Daily Picayune* highlighted this belief, stating plainly, "The colored woman as a nurse is respected throughout the south, for her skill and merit are acknowledged."[1] This respect was founded upon the commonly held belief that southern blacks carried an innate, "natural" immunity against yellow fever, making them ideal candidates for nursing the ill back to health, or, as the circumstances often allowed, preparing dead bodies for burial. As the D.C. matron lauded the moral and intellectual progress of the black race, she heralded the novel and unexpected opportunity now available for African Americans—women in particular. Standing before the congregants in the two-story church on Tulane and Clairborne avenues, Namahyoka Curtis suggested that they too, through their service, selflessness, and sacrifice, might play a role in the race's continued advance.

Curtis was lionized in the national black press as "one of the most brilliant and enterprising young women of the race," and her trip to New Orleans to secure trained immune nurses was understood by the D.C. *Colored American* as a history-making feat.[2] The paper gushed over her efforts, claiming she was "the first woman not of the white race who has been delegated by any branch of the United States government to perform official duties, especially in such an occasion as the present, when there is a status belli with a transatlantic power."[3] An immune herself, Curtis was quite pleased by the response her visit had generated in the city. The numbers of volunteers were great enough that she had to place age restrictions on the women she accepted into immune service. None of the recruits could be younger than twenty-five, since Curtis believed a certain maturity that came with age was required in a war zone, far from home. She also received a number of applications from older black women, described by a reporter as "old black mammies who had nursed the fever in former days."[4] While Curtis turned some of these women away because of their age, she elected to induct others into immune service, some of whom who had nursed since the Civil War.

After completing her work in New Orleans, Curtis had orders to canvas the cities of Mobile, Montgomery, Birmingham, and Tallahassee in search of more volunteers. "I will complete my mission in two weeks," she told the *Daily Picayune* reporter after her Sunday night talk, "and I will then prepare to go to the front myself, leaving my three children in charge of their father and grandfather. I do not want it to be said that I send others where I will not also go. So, therefore, I will be one of the trained nurses that will volunteer to take care of our brave soldiers and sailors who may be stricken with the fever."[5]

The recruitment of immune nurses at a black church in New Orleans opens the story of black women's social and political contract with the U.S.

military abroad through the logic of racial and gender difference. The little-known history of black women's service during the Spanish-Cuban-American War provides the theoretical foundation for an intersectional engagement with race, gender, and American militarism in the twentieth century in the pages that follow.

Through the category of immunity, longstanding prohibitions against blacks and women in the military ranks were supplanted, as antebellum beliefs about the resistant qualities of "negro blood" were used to allow African Americans to serve in military service roles abroad. To enlist black women's care labor in the Cuban conflict, army physicians relied on the myth of the plantation nurse, a figure whose biological and thus racial immunity to yellow fever recalled forms of gendered subordination and sacrifice ritualized in U.S. slavery. Archival evidence from newspapers, Congressional reports, and military and civic records suggests that these nurses—including the woman who organized them—participated in a gendered and racialized project of necropolitical citizenship, wherein the management of sickness and death in quarantine camps abroad was accompanied by the use of that imperiled service in public appeals aimed at securing expanded citizenship rights for African Americans stateside. Blacks often adopted the language of the Fourteenth Amendment in their demands for full rights and privileges, or *immunities*, as American citizens, and Curtis's efforts organizing immune nurses reflected a belief in embodied sacrifice as the price and the cost of citizenship for a disenfranchised people. The national and international mobility displayed by Curtis and her nurses was uncommon for women of color in 1898, an exceptional privilege fraught with the politics of social class, racial advancement, and military imperialism. Cognizant of her privilege, Curtis leveraged her own humanitarian efforts into social and political influence for the rest of her life, becoming a model matriarch of the African American encounter with American militarism at the beginning of the new century. The labor of her nurses, while largely erased in the postwar historiography, nonetheless produced the instrumental rationale black and white leaders would use to establish a permanent nursing corps in the army and to recruit African American male volunteers into subaltern service roles in Cuba, Puerto Rico, and the Philippines. The gendered and racialized experiences of both organizer and organized offer an intersectional lens through which to consider these subaltern subjects of American militarism as feminine emblems of black immunity, icons of sacrifice whose experiences upon the transport ships, in the fever wards, and upon homebound trains aid, abet, and interrupt the narrative of white male supremacy and reconciliation that so often characterizes the historiography of Spanish-Cuban-American War.

Mrs. Curtis's trip to the South to secure immune nurses was officially endorsed by the National Association of Colored Women (NACW), whose membership sent a letter of thanks to President McKinley, "assuring him of the co-operation of this body of women" in support of the vanguard war effort.[6] Ida B. Wells-Barnett, one of organization's founders, lost her parents and her youngest brother to yellow fever in 1878, making it highly unlikely that their leadership put much stock in the certainty of racial immunity. The NACW's support of Curtis's mission was less an endorsement in the belief that black women were invulnerable to the fever but rather an acknowledgment of the volunteers' courage, since some of their most notable members had first-hand knowledge of the lethality of the disease in black southern communities.[7]

During her stay in New Orleans, Curtis was hosted by Colonel James Lewis, a local black politician and member of the interracial Comité des Citoyens (Citizens' Committee) that recruited Homer Adolf Plessy to violate Louisiana's Separate Car Act in 1892.[8] By all extant accounts, her mission was a success—so successful, in fact, that it is unlikely Curtis traveled to Santiago before the fall of 1898, as Surgeon General Sternberg saw her singular value as a recruiter and sent her back into the field to muster more immunes. She inducted over a hundred trained nurses for emergency service, and at least thirty-two are thought to have been African-American women. Despite color bars at most nursing schools in the United States, black graduates from the Tuskegee Institute, Freedmen's Hospital in D.C., Provident Hospital in Chicago, Boston's Massachusetts General Hospital, and the Phyllis Wheatley Training School and Charity Hospital in New Orleans all responded to Curtis's call to enlist.[9] The *Los Angeles Herald* reported she had enlisted 129 nurses by the end of August, and had new orders to accompany her recruits to the disembarking port at Tampa before scouting the South for fifty more nurses.[10]

Port Tampa was the main port of disembarkation for the Spanish-Cuban-War, and over 30,000 men and women traveled through its harbor en route to Santiago. Curtis was needed at the port to better facilitate the process of sending her women off to war, as the very mobility of black women leaving its harbor triggered forms of policing and surveillance that assailed their dignity in transit to Cuba. As one harrowing example makes clear, a *Boston Daily Globe* article headlined the "alleged indignity" that twenty-five immune nurses incurred on their journey from Tampa to Santiago on the transport ship *Michigan*, an old cattle boat hastily repurposed for the transportation of cargo to Cuba. Eleven days after Curtis's appeal in New Orleans, government officials in Florida assigned sleeping quarters for the nurses *below* the deck occupied by mules and horses. The *Globe* reporter noted how race and age marked these women as different, stating that "Twenty of these nurses are negro women, old nurses from New Orleans, and while they submitted it created hard feeling."[11]

The anger and indignation attributed to the multigenerational group of black women volunteers at being "quartered below mules" was a justified response to the conditions under which they were expected to travel to Cuba. Stowed like cargo upon the *Michigan*, the women anchored an inventory list sent by telegram from Port Tampa to the War Department in D.C., which included 175 tons of commissary stores, 300,000 pounds of refrigerated beef, 106 mules, twenty-five wagons, one horse, and about twenty-five paymasters.[12] Moreover, a unit historian for the Second Illinois Infantry, whose regiment was asked to travel aboard the *Michigan* five months later, was unrestrained in his condemnation of the steamer's traveling compartment: "A vessel more absolutely unfit for the transportation of troops can hardly be imagined. Filthy in the extreme, the sickening odors arising from the decks and hold rendered the ship unsanitary to a degree, while the deck on which it was proposed to quarter the troops was situated beneath that on which the mules and other animals were to be carried; and as the decks were by no means water tight, the leakage ran through to the troop deck, causing a state of things easier to imagine than to describe."[13]

The immune nurses who travelled to Santiago upon the *Michigan*, those women who, after overcoming the shock of what had been asked of them, swallowed their hard feelings and consented to sleep on hammocks wet with the excreta of livestock draining down upon them, would have been unflinchingly aware of their subaltern location in the taxonomy of flesh (beef, cattle, human, woman, black woman) floating toward Cuba. Clearly the collective indignity of being forced to travel in animal stowage was not part of the noble sacrifice Curtis had asked them to make in New Orleans. Yet as black women traveling only two years after the *Plessy v. Ferguson* decision upheld racial segregation in public accommodations, few among them could have expected that their movement across Southern state lines and through international waters would be swift, pleasant, or incident-free, even at the behest of a U.S. military at war.

One might question, then, the wisdom of sending a black woman from Washington, D.C., down south to recruit nurses in Louisiana, Alabama, and Florida at the turn of the century, given the local systems of Jim Crow bureaucracy primed to impede her mobility at any stop along the route. In fact, the decision displayed the McKinley administration's deeply pragmatic response to the fact of racial segregation as well as its good fortune to have the remarkable moxie of Namah Curtis at their disposal, since most white Americans, unless alerted to the contrary, received her as a white woman (figure 2.1).

Curtis's fair skin no doubt helped her as she navigated the Jim Crow South. In a family history provided by her daughter, Gertrude, Curtis was described as a "blond, blue-eyed matron of medium height . . . in appearance she was a blond Caucasian."[14] Given the overlapping rash of Jim Crow laws segregating public spaces and conveyances in the Southeastern states she traveled, her complexion likely granted her a privilege that many of the black women she recruited did not possess. Her physical appearance was frequently commented upon during her lifetime; reporters described her as a "woman of culture and beauty" and alternately, as "a woman of mystery."[15] Daniel Murray, the second black assistant librarian at the Library of Congress and compiler of the unpublished *Historical and Biographical Encyclopedia of the Colored Race*, devoted an entry to Curtis, and he suggested that she used the white skin privilege she did enjoy strategically as a tool of racial advancement:

> To the casual observer on first making the acquaintance of the subject of this sketch, he at once classifies her with the Caucasian race, and on a better and more extended acquaintance, through which he learns that she is of African extraction, is disposed to ascribe her splendid intellectual gift to her Anglo Saxon inheritance. Let this however, be as it may, she never leads one long in doubt as to her own identity with the race or people to whose advancement she had dedicated her life and whose material prosperity is her heart's desire. The fact that her relationship to the African race is not readily apparent enables her to learn often the real sentiments of pretended friends, and when so discovered she never fails to denounce their hypocrisy.[16]

Thus, to view her solely at *face* value, as Murray cautions against, to read her efforts to recruit African American nurses as merely the actions of a fair-skinned lackey of a reconciliationist government desperate to stem the yellow scourge impairing its imperial footfalls in Cuba, is to crudely misread

Negro Heroines 53

FIGURE 2.1 Newspaper clipping of Mrs. A. M. Curtis (Namahyoka Gertrude Curtis), *San Francisco Call*, August 27, 1906. Courtesy of the California Digital Newspaper Collection, Center for Bibliographic Studies and Research, University of California, Riverside, http://cdnc.ucr.edu.

the character and comportment of Mrs. A. M. Curtis. Her organization of immune nurses was a highpoint of what the twenty-nine-year-old had already shown to be her remarkable penchant for civil engagement around matters of race and representation. Her administrative prowess, proximity to political power, and willingness to flout orthodoxies of the color line spawned critics and admirers within the black and white communities she lived and worked within, adding to her national renown.

Namahyoka Curtis, Woman of Mystery

Though she was passably white, Curtis staunchly foregrounded her membership in "the colored race" and took special pride in the African American and Native ancestries that entwined her genealogy. Born in San Francisco in 1869, she grew up in a mixed-race community that publicly celebrated the political advances of African Americans and passionately advocated for the expansion of their civil rights.[17] According to Murray, her maternal grandfather, Walter Jackson, was a fugitive slave from Virginia from whom she "inherited a strain of African blood." Stealing his own freedom, he found liberty and love in Philadelphia, marrying Lydia Ann Mason, a German Quaker and devotee of Lucretia Mott's Anti-Slavery Society. They traveled west to California two weeks before the Gold Rush and settled in San Francisco in 1848. Curtis often claimed Jackson was "the oldest colored miner of California."[18]

To be sure, her Native family history was no less impressed with the imprint of race. Her paternal grandfather was Levin Sockum, the first Nanticoke Indian to purchase land in Maryland's land tenure system.[19] In 1855 Sockum was famously tried and convicted for selling gunpowder to a fellow "Delaware Moor," the colloquial term used to describe the amalgam of Nanticoke and Lenni-Lenape peoples who remained in the region and weathered the transition from communal land use to individual property ownership in the eighteenth and nineteenth centuries.[20] Owing to testimony that claimed the Nanticoke community had intermarried with African Americans and thus were technically mulattoes, Sockum was found guilty of violating a state law against selling firearms to black or mixed-raced people. He soon faced another charge of gun possession, and the judge similarly rejected his claim of nonblack ancestry.[21] The court's decision subsumed his Native identity within a brier of blackness, and as a result another member of the Nanticoke nation had been dispossessed of person and property.[22] Worse still, the forty dollar fine effectively left any member of his family subject to the racist whims of Delaware's "black codes," a phalanx of state laws enacted across the South to systematically deprive African Americans, whether free or enslaved, of their rights to bear arms, own property, move freely, vote, and seek fair employment. His family continued to face legal harassment from his white neighbors until the early 1860s, and Sockum ultimately decided to leave Sussex county, selling his property at a loss.[23] Thus the embattled patriarch relocated his mixed-race family to New Jersey. His son, Hamilton, also left Delaware, but his travels took him all the way to the golden coast of California.

In 1869 Levin Sockum's granddaughter, Namahyoka, was born in the city by the Bay. From her birth up until the early decades of the twentieth century, Curtis's racial identification in the census changed four different times, illuminating the porous nature of racial differentiation in America from the Reconstruction period to the beginning of the twentieth century. In the 1870 schedule, she and her parents, Arrena Jackson and Hamilton Sockum, were listed as mulatto in the census. Ten years later, while living with her grandmother, Lydia Jackson, both residents of the household were classified as white. In 1900 the Washington, D.C., census classified Curtis, then a wife and mother of four, as black, but by 1910 she and her entire family were marked mulatto, capping a forty-year period where state registrants used the racial identities of her immediate family members to interpret her own.

Namah Sockum was nineteen years old when she married Austin Curtis, a black medical student from Raleigh, North Carolina. The two moved to Chicago where he completed his M.D. at Northwestern University and she entered public life in the White City. In the early 1890s the couple worked at Provident Hospital, the first medical institution in the country owned and operated by an African American. Austin was the hospital's first intern, and Namah worked as a nurse and solicitor, playing an instrumental role in getting industrial meatpacker Philip D. Armour to provide early start-up funds for the project. Curtis also served a contentious stint as "secretary of colored interests" at the 1893 World's Columbian Exposition, a clerical position critics saw as a transparent effort to placate African American anger at having no representation at the World's Fair. The *Cleveland Gazette* was especially cutting in its critique of Curtis, telling its readers of "Mrs. A. M. Curtis, an Afro-American lady of Chicago, who is styled the 'Secretary of Colored Interests,' but who is really nothing more than a sort of general utility clerk, appointed by the board of lady managers of the exposition . . . to allay as far as possible the 'general dissatisfaction' existing among our people, by this appointment. The scheme is too transparent, however, and will not be worked successfully because of our wide awake and loyal newspapers."[24] Facing criticism within the black community and alienation from the white "Lady Managers" who gave her no autonomy to make decisions on behalf of her constituents, Curtis resigned in quiet protest after only a few months of work.[25]

A year later, Curtis and her family had moved to an apartment on State Street, in the neighborhood that would be known decades later as Bronzeville. Residential segregation held sway in the neighborhood, however, and Curtis was sued by her new landlord for fraud for not stating she had "colored blood in her veins" when she obtained the lease to her apartment.[26] Curtis had signed the lease alone, her landlord claimed, and it was only upon seeing her husband's complexion that his agents realized they had rented to black people. A restaurant owner on the building's first floor complained to the landlord, claiming her business was being "injured" by the presence of the Curtises. The lawsuit made national news, and her hometown paper the *San Francisco Chronicle* wrote that the city's black community was "indignant that education and refinement stand for naught in Chicago and that the color line is drawn so finely there in this day and age."[27] Surprisingly, the landlord's claim that he was "deceived by Mrs. Curtis' fair face" was denied in court, and the forced eviction was not allowed to proceed.[28]

Curtis's victory was sweet. Not only was she publicly vindicated by the court ruling, which absolved her of passing for white in order to obtain a lease, she had also prevailed over a claim of racial fraud reminiscent of the lawsuit that had disenfranchised her grandfather Levin Sockum almost thirty years prior. With this win, the Curtis family became exceptions to the rule of housing discrimination in turn-of-the-century Chicago, undoubtedly fueling the social maven's belief in the efficacy of black political participation on local and national levels.

When the Curtises left Chicago for Washington, D.C., in 1898, Namahyoka Curtis stumped for the Republican Party, becoming the "colored representative" of the Women's Republican Association during William McKinley's presidential campaign. She authored a broadside that implored African Americans to remain faithful to "the party that has remained loyal to [them] in the most trying circumstances" by voting Republican. "This appeal coming from one of our own race," she wrote, "who is always for its advancement and prosperity, I hope will be heeded and we will once again show our *patriotism* which is *Republicanism*, by doing our duty."[29] This stance drew the ire of some black newspapers in D.C. and Chicago, which intimated that her political activism should disqualify her husband's Republican-made appointment as Surgeon-in-Chief at the capital's Freedmen's Hospital.[30]

As a black woman at the nexus of an interracial network of Washington elites on the eve of a new century, however, Curtis had learned to pay the critics no mind. After all, she had met the president several times over and had shaken hands with power. Moreover, the connections she made in her many civic endeavors were instrumental in her selection to enlist nurses in New Orleans. Curtis was nominated chiefly on the recommendation of George M. Sternberg, famed bacteriologist, Surgeon General of the Army, and D.C. resident, who had softened his opposition to using trained female nurses in the war zone due to the typhoid and yellow fever epidemics enervating U.S. forces.

Understood to be a remarkable woman in her own day, Curtis's life and labors — much like the women she worked to organize in the summer of 1898 — have largely escaped historical engagement or cultural retrieval. Sometimes footnoted but rarely featured, Namahyoka Curtis's archival presence is largely cloaked behind the name of her husband, Austin. His own considerable success as being the first intern at the first black-run hospital (Provident Hospital), the first black surgeon appointed to the staff of a white hospital in the United States (Cook County Hospital), Surgeon-in-Chief at Freedmen's Hospital in D.C., and beloved professor of surgery at Howard Medical School has led to biographers of Washington's "aristocrats of color" to largely marginalize his wife's significance as that of a loyal helpmate and member of the Gilded Age's "black 400."[31] But among her contemporaries she was known, respected, and admired. Curtis counted Mary Church Terrell as a close friend and confidant, and regularly hosted her, Mary McLeod Bethune, Booker T. Washington, and Paul Laurence Dunbar at her homes in Washington and Arundel-by-the-Sea, Maryland. Her reputation as a humanitarian grew through her involvement in national relief efforts in Galveston, Texas, after its 1900 hurricane, and especially during the 1906 San Francisco earthquake that reduced her hometown to rubble.[32] In 1912 the *Indianapolis Freeman*, following a trend begun by white suffragists who mounted all-female cabinets to advise the next president of the United States "in the event that women be allowed their full political rights," counted Curtis among eleven race women it thought should fill cabinet positions. Alongside Booker T.'s wife Margaret Murray Washington ("Secretary of State"), Mary Church Terrell ("Secretary of the Interior"), Fannie Barrier Williams ("Attorney General"), and Maggie L. Walker ("Secretary of Commerce and Labor"), the paper appointed Mrs. A. M. Curtis, third on the list, as "Secretary of War."[33]

In 1926 Curtis was among a select few women nurses who petitioned — and received — a military pension for their service during the Spanish-Cuban-

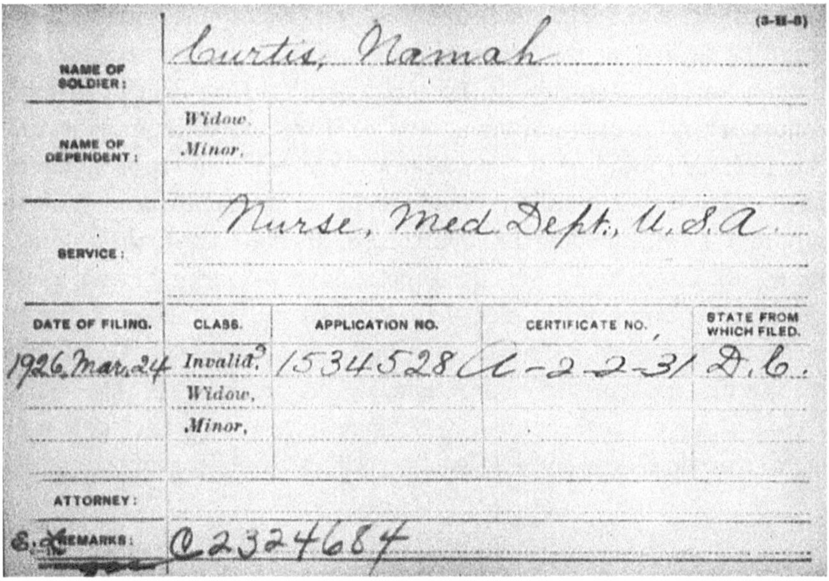
(3-11-8)
NAME OF SOLDIER: Curtis, Namah
NAME OF DEPENDENT: Widow, Minor,
SERVICE: Nurse, Med. Dept., U.S.A.

DATE OF FILING.	CLASS.	APPLICATION NO.	CERTIFICATE NO.	STATE FROM WHICH FILED.
1926 Mar. 24	Invalid	1534528	A-2-2-31	D.C.
	Widow,			
	Minor,			

ATTORNEY:
REMARKS: C 2324684

FIGURE 2.2 Namah Curtis's pension file. National Archives, Washington, D.C., Records of the Department of Veterans Affairs, 1773–2007, Record Group Number 15, U.S. Civil War Pension Index: General Index to Pension Files, 1861–1934, Series Number T288. Accessed via Ancestry.com.

American War (figure 2.2). And when she passed away in the winter of 1935 after sixty-six years of life, she became the first African American woman in recorded history to receive a military burial in Arlington National Cemetery. That this claim has never before been attested, contested, *or* celebrated as a point of pride is an example of the kinds of silences that shroud the histories of black women specifically and black military workers at the turn of the twentieth century more generally. The little that is known about the experimental group of mostly black women mobilized by Curtis on the basis of their alleged immunity to infectious disease engenders the discomfiting irony that at least two and as many as seven of their number died from typhoid fever in their first months of employment.[34] Both Minerva Turnbull, a mixed-race woman from Baton Rouge, and Isabelle R. Bradford, a white woman from New Orleans, thought themselves immune from yellow fever. But in spite of their beliefs, the idea that immunity from one disease should provide resistance to another was a proposition filled with risk.[35] Turnbull's homegoing service happened on a Wednesday, in the intimacy of her sister's home in New Orleans; in contrast, Bradford's first burial was a foreign one, occurring in a Cuban graveyard during the war.[36] In 1901 her body was disinterred and repatriated to the United States, along with thirty-nine other dead soldiers and civilians on the transport *McClellan*, receiving its final rest at Arlington National Cemetery in February 1901.[37] In the drift of history, contemporary historians of women and war have read both nurses as African American; however, two journal articles written in the era list Bradford as white, making Turnbull the lone named black woman to die in immune service.[38] Notwithstanding the importance of this corrective to the historical record, the discourse of immunity—rooted as we will see in the antebellum care practices of enslaved women—effectively marked the military work done by both nurses as black, female, and expendable. Their deaths underscore the fact that the standard metrics for appraising immunity in 1898—race, region, and previous exposure—were imperfect determinants for assessing who would survive and who would succumb to the rigors of fever work.

The Gendering of Racial Immunity

In a postwar Congressional assessment of the role African American immune nurses played in Cuba, Lt. Colonel Benjamin Pope, chief U.S. surgeon in Santiago, described them as "a hardy lot of female nurses—I do not mean lady nurses . . . ," whose services were nevertheless "invaluable."[39] The constraints of "true womanhood" that hampered white women's inclusion into military service abroad were largely absent in military officials' decision to employ black women as military care workers for two important reasons. First, the typhoid and yellow fever epidemics decimating U.S. troops created a state of emergency that softened administrative opposition to using female nurses in an overseas conflict. Second, the assumed immunity of the women and their perceived distance from Victorian modes of propriety as nurses of color meant that their bodies were expendable, freed from certain conventions of gendered subordination in order to serve an overseas military force flummoxed by a viral foe. But the distinction Pope made between "hardy" female nurses and "lady nurses" was racialized as well as gendered, with race providing a historical filter for the gendered relationship between nurse and soldier. It highlighted how the bodies, labor, and aptitudes of black women were viewed as qualitatively different from those of the mostly white women volunteers mustered into emergency service by the Red Cross and the Daughters of the American Revolution (DAR). Dr. Anita Newcomb McGee, the white director of the DAR Hospital Corps and first woman ever appointed Assistant Surgeon of the U.S. Army, had been primarily responsible for training and recruiting women nurses in the event they would be called up for wartime service. However, her stipulation of only recruiting trained nurses meant that the women she inducted into the nursing corps were mostly white. When asked by Congress about the effectiveness of the immune nurses once the war had ended, McGee replied that they were "very satisfactory although the nurses sent to Santiago were not of the same class" as those the DAR had placed into posts in the United States, due to their lack of professional training.[40] What these women did have, McGee conceded, was an embodied resistance to yellow fever, making their unskilled bodies extraordinarily useful in that exceptional time.

The characterization of immune nurses by military officials as hardy but untrained, resilient yet incompetent served to devalue their work and shroud the contributions made by black women during the United States' first imperial war. It also belied the particular history of labor and knowledge of care forged in the crucible of antebellum slavery that had made black bodies singularly valuable in the first place. In other words, the belief that African Americans in general—and black women in particular—held a specific immunity against yellow fever had been centuries in the making. It was, in fact, central to the logics of racial slavery in the Americas, which presumed that the bodies of people of African descent were predisposed to survive the hard labors of servitude, inured to pain, and invulnerable to contagious diseases. Enslaved women, embodying the gendered role of caretakers, nursed black and white patients during the antebellum period, and black and Creole women were especially sought after for their services during yellow fever outbreaks.[41] Some fever nurses, such as the famed Voodoo priestess Marie Laveau, gained great renown for their work during epidemics, while others were viewed with enmity by the white community because they were able to negotiate payment for their services that exceeded established market rates for black labor.[42]

The end of slavery in the United States did little to dispel the common belief that blacks were innately suited for fever work. Even as Social Darwinists proclaimed African Americans members of a frail race on the verge of extinction, they paradoxically asserted a steadfast belief in black immunity to yellow fever. "A negro never dies with it, in any locality, when treated with regard to his ethnical peculiarities," stated an 1868 article in Alabama's *Mobile Register*. "So strong are they in his favor that, even under malpractice, death is the exception and recovery the rule."[43] The discourse of black invulnerability only increased as the germ theory of disease emerged into prominence in the late nineteenth century. The theory, which held that some diseases were caused by organisms too small to be seen with the human eye, provided a new horizon for scientific modernity and medical progress. But even as the world of pathology became less opaque, black and Creole women remained the preferred choice of fever nurse in the postbellum period through the century's end. In 1890 the *Annual Statistician and Economist* admitted that while yellow fever had "lost its terror for the scientist," the best treatment of the disease still lay in the capable and competent hands of black women. "Nursing is everything . . . The nurse does more than the doctor in yellow fever to effect a cure, and in New Orleans nearly all the black 'mammies' are experts in handling the disease, which undoubtedly accounts for the very low mortality in that city's epidemics."[44]

Prominent white southern physicians like Rudolph Matas shared in the sentiment. A pioneer in vascular surgery and professor at Tulane Medical School for forty-two years, Matas had an implacable interest in yellow fever that dogged him his entire life. Born on a sugar plantation near the Bonnet Carre levee in 1860, he was the son of a Spanish doctor who treated yellow fever patients in New Orleans after the Civil War. As a child, Matas contracted the disease during an epidemic but survived to gain immunity. He later entered medical school at the University of Louisiana (later Tulane) and, while there, was invited to clerk for the Yellow Fever Commission, an international group of experts sent to study the disease in Havana in 1879. Matas was selected for his fluency in Spanish, and translated the first article positing the mosquito theory of transmission, written by Cuban commission member Carlos Finlay, into English.[45]

In addition to his interest in the pathology of yellow fever, Matas also took a profound interest in the science of racial difference—what he described as "the study of the comparative pathology of all the races."[46] In 1896 he published *The Surgical Peculiarities of the American Negro*, in which he analyzed the intake records of the Charity Hospital of New Orleans over the preceding ten-year period. Matas worked at Charity as a visiting surgeon, and in contrast with some of his contemporaries, held a less biologically determined view of the surgical differences between black and white bodies, writing that "there are no apparent differences between the races on the operating-table."[47] He did believe, however, that the 300 years of adaptation and acculturation that African Americans had undergone in the United States had "completely modif[ied] the originally acquired and highly differentiated racial peculiarities that the negro brought with him from Africa," robbing him of his previous immunity from certain diseases.[48] The exponential rates of African American morbidity reflected in the Charity Hospital statistics made Matas quite bullish on the black extinction theory, and he concluded that "the colored race is degenerating, if by this we mean a growing inability to resist the causes that are inimical to its existence."[49]

This glum forecast of the future of black people in the United States stood in sharp contrast to his wistful reminiscences of black immunity in the antebellum era, where the work of black fever nurses was a special source of southern pride. Writing in 1905, four years after U.S. scientists uniformly accepted the *Aedes aegypti* mosquito as the prime vector of yellow fever transmission, Matas informed a readership of trained nurses that "The great epidemics of the forties, fifties, and sixties, down to the last great visitation of 1878, marked the golden period, if we may so term it, of the old negro mammy." His romantic endorsement of black women's fever service recurred to a fertile archive of Mammy tropes resonant with nostalgia for the former days of slavery, when black women's care labor was taken for granted and for profit. In those days, he said, spells of yellow fever occasioned an inversion of the paternal order of the household. Matas put it bluntly: "The former slaves then became masters." With the health of the entire plantation at stake, black women were put in charge of the sickroom, temporarily endowing them with the responsibilities of patriarchal power. The sacrifice of black women's bodies in fever work was therefore necessary for the upkeep of the enslaved workforce and the white family proper, whose own survival during fever season depended largely upon the blood and sweat of black women. Guided as much by his own childhood memories of yellow fever in New Orleans as by the medical knowledge of his day, Matas used the concept of immunity to explain the dogged altruism of "[t]he picturesque dark woman with the 'tignon, or bandana kerchief on her head":

> The secret of their success was chiefly due to their relative immunity from the disease, which made them absolutely fearless in their ministrations to the sick. . . . They never forsook their patients and remained with them to the last extremity, no matter what the result might be. When death closed the scene, they remained fearless of contagion to the last and prepared the dreaded remains for sepulture with the same gentleness and respect that had been shown the living. Of course, they were ignorant and illiterate, but the simplicity of their methods, which never invaded the domain of the pharmacopeia, unless by direct command of the physician, was a guarantee of their safety.[50]

Matas's belief in black immunity helped to rationalize the bravery of these nurses, but immunity alone was not enough to explain their actions. "Relative immunity," as a concept, couples biologically essentialist notions of black womanhood to culturalist readings of their care labor. Black women's success in nursing yellow fever was linked to a simpleminded willingness to incur further risk to their own bodies in dutiful and devoted service to the institution of chattel slavery, even when "home"—the site of their stolen labor—was the source of death and disease. As emissaries between the living, the dying, and the dead, black women were, through Matas's logic and life experience, the overseers of the plantation *necropolis*, those entrusted to will the sick back to life or bring deference to the departed when all else had failed. Moreover, their management of the lives and deaths of those afflicted with yellow fever during those epidemics was, from this perspective, one benevolent aspect of the economic system abolished only fifty years prior. As he transfigured the loss of that way of life into the symbol of the black fever nurse, Matas mourned the passing of both: "The picturesque old mammy has now disappeared. She is rapidly passing into history and will soon be relegated to tradition and romance. The black woman with the multi-colored headgear can only be seen occasionally in the household, in the market place, or on the street—very rarely in the sickroom. To see her we must visit the artist's studio, buy the local postcard, or read the romances that tell us of the 'good old Creole days.'"[51]

From his vantage in the opening decade of the twentieth century, Matas believed the growth of professional nursing and the modernization of hospitals in the United States had made black fever nurses obsolete, making them mere footnotes in the bright future of preventive care. Gone were the good old days when Matas's father had visited the sick within the Creole cottages and double-gallery houses of New Orleans, assisted by the head servants of each residence. Yet the repetition of the term "picturesque" in his reminiscences of black women's fever work employs the aesthetic language of nineteenth-century landscape painting in order to romanticize his depiction of care labor as free from the coercive forces of plantation slavery. Just as the American school of landscape artists produced representations of plantation architecture that concealed the violence of bondage behind pastoral and bucolic panoramas, Matas used the picturesque to frame, and thus control, black women's embodied agency during fever outbreaks, reducing them to figures in perspective that served to magnify the scale of the plantation proper.[52] Ironically, the disappearance of the "mammy" from these spaces occurred at the same time as the sickroom—a quarantined zone of treatment within the private sphere—gave way to the hospital as the primary and trusted arena of medical care in American life.[53] As the sickroom changed institutions, it abandoned the paternalistic trappings of slavery—complete with its "picturesque" attendants—and located itself within a postplantation healthcare system that continued to employ black womanhood as a productive subject and object of research and labor.

But if we were to believe, like Matas, that the magic and mystery of black womanhood—fearless, loyal, and so vital in the treatment of yellow fever for over a century—was no longer needed to police the cordon sanitaire within the family home, we would be hard-pressed to explain why the U.S. military saw fit to institutionalize their use in Cuba only a few years earlier in 1898, when white soldiers were unable (and in some cases, unwilling) to care for themselves. Contrary to Matas's assertions, quite the opposite was true. The wartime decision to deploy black womanhood abroad—approved by Surgeon General Sternberg, an original member of the Havana Yellow Fever Commission—successfully militarized their care labor, making a bygone product of black enslavement in the Americas modern, experimental, and above all, useful. Though the modernization of medicine may have led to the disappearance of the mammy in the sick room, her labor remained rooted in black women's cultural practices of care. The presence of African American women in the archive demonstrates that they resisted the prison of historical objecthood the mammy categorization represented, however, even while being characterized as such by white interlocutors. Narratives of their labor in Cuba challenge the myth of the plantation nurse celebrated by Matas by presenting African American women as complex subjects whose tenure in Cuba amplified their senses of patriotism, expanded their awareness of the opportunities and consequences of global war, and underscored their demands for civil rights stateside.

Fracturing Archetypes: Immune Nurses Speak Their Truths

The surviving accounts of Black women's war experiences in Cuba lie mostly within the sensationalist U.S. Spanish-American War reportage that helped to manufacture public consent for the conflict before it began. In the rare newspaper accounts that feature black nurses, they are presented as figures out of place and out of time, but who, when the nation called, proved themselves to be uniquely useful. Journalists, quick to note the Civil War experience of some of the nurses, presented them as unlikely actors whose bodies were overdetermined by the memory of slavery. Because slavery was credited with producing and sustaining the immunity which had been martialed for military use, black womanhood appeared both primitive and modern in the news reports, a Janus-faced creation of race and gender that embodied the ancient mysteries of medical science, the history of slavery and Civil War, and the experimental militarization of gender difference during the United States' first modern world war.

One group of immune nurses who arrived in Santiago in the early days of August were forbidden to disembark from their ship for two days. Despite the fact that they were desperately needed in the army hospitals, the women were confined to the *Olivette* because no provision had been made to house the contingent of American women. Gender difference became a logistical problem for the American military governor of Santiago, who conveyed his worry to Red Cross founder Clara Barton that without suitable protection, the nurses—some of whom were from "good families"—were vulnerable to sexual assault by men in the port city. Barton secured an old marble mansion for lodging and hired travel writer and Latin American correspondent Fannie Brigham Ward to serve as "house mother" to the interracial group of nurses, who included a general's daughter, two Cuban women from Key West, and "several others from various parts of the south, mostly all immunes, recruited for the work by Mrs. Curtis, of Washington."[54] Although her articles mention these women obliquely and never by race, they locate African American nurses as members of her "family" in Cuba, selflessly caring for soldiers and engaging in contact with the local community.

Ward was part of an exclusive group of U.S. white women journalists who covered the war from Cuba, and wrote vividly of her time working with Clara Barton caring for sick and wounded soldiers.[55] She spent much of the 1890s reporting from various locales in Latin America, and had perfected the art of weaving political critique into her quippy travelogues about social life, local customs, and architecture abroad. No fan of the Spanish regime herself, Ward described the housing stock in Santiago as "typically Castilian in character—a brave and beautiful front dwindling to unparalleled poverty and meanness behind the outward showing." She took special issue with the derelict state of her kitchen, as well as the "two Cuban negresses" hired to serve in it, all of whom were, in her estimation, weary testaments to a bygone era of imperial rule. "Our servants match the kitchen to a T," she wrote. "They are elderly negroesses, with families of their own, and, like mother birds, they nightly convey to the home nest every morsel of food on which they can lay hands." By characterizing her Afro-Cuban housekeepers as food thieves and racializing them as black—while remaining virtually silent about the interracial make-up of her own "family" of nurses—Ward displaced anxieties her U.S. readers may have harbored about white and black women living together in a socially equal fashion. Complaining to her readers that the servants were lazy and slow, the syndicated columnist personified the southern plantation mistress sans patriarch struggling to keep both her house and her enslaved workforce in order during the Civil War.

Curtis's recruits would have observed Ward's matronage with knowing eyes. "The immune ladies had come to 'nurse,' not to housekeep," she wrote, as if to convey to her readers her shock and bewilderment at having to acknowledge the black women in the private sphere they shared together as anything other than domestic laborers. But African American women had an intimate awareness of the indignities experienced while laboring in the private spheres of white womanhood. Those who had worked as domestics for white families understood the custom of "pan-toting," or taking table scraps home at the close of the work day, as due recompense for the deprivations of low-wage womanhood.[56] Understanding themselves as part of the Cuban relief effort—and good Christian women to boot—some of the nurses might have looked past the practice or even encouraged it, finding a glimmer of kinship with the women who kept their house in order. Others, whose military service and statuses as American citizens overseas gave them a new sense of entitlement, may have eschewed open displays of solidarity with the housekeepers altogether, seeking instead a strategic alliance with their white American matron based upon mutual feelings of patriotism, sacrifice, and citizenship. Those women, many of whom had doubtlessly lived lives of uncelebrated labor, might have even entertained the opinion that it was nice to have someone wait on *them* for a change.

These encounters would have placed African American women in positions of relative privilege in comparison with their Afro-Cuban contemporaries. Local women—described by Ward as "female pawnbrokers"—eagerly sought out American nurses as active trading partners in the informal economy. "Every day we are visited by mysterious women," she wrote, "some of them evidently belonging to the better class, who wish to buy, sell, or exchange all manner of truck, from a broken-nosed tea kettle to a jeweled sword."[57] Fresh produce was a hot commodity in Santiago, and Ward navigated the grift and thrift of war to supplement the government-issued rations of hardtack, beans, and canned beef with pineapples, onions, and avocados.[58] In those late summer nights, the dinner table offered the nurses a space of repose and contact, where black, white, and Cuban women messed together and reflected upon the day's labors. It was a place to speak about the patients who had died that day and those who had lived; to tell stories about what it was like nursing in the Civil War—how it was different, but similar, too, the loss of life from sickness. The mess table was also a site of culinary invention, where the women suggested different ways to cook hardtack beyond its bland, salt-cracker state—such as soaking it in condensed milk and frying it in bacon fat à la French toast.[59] It would have functioned sometimes as a study, where they could write letters home, which reached their loved ones only after the nurses returned from Cuba.[60] The women may have pondered what the liberation of Cuba from Spain would mean for the Cubans they encountered daily, especially those who kept their house and came to trade with them, and no doubt wondered what they would do with their lives once they returned home to America—if, God willing, they made it through the war unscathed.

Notwithstanding the possibilities of liberal imperial sisterhood that military intervention in Cuba presented for these African American women, existing sources suggest that the circumstances of their housing with Fannie Brigham Ward were rare. Most of the nurses drafted during the first wave of immune recruits lived in tents segregated by race and gender, bivouacking in camps next to the field hospitals to which they had been assigned.[61] In such settings, they had fewer opportunities to have lasting, diasporic engagements with the local population during the foreshortened war, and instead spent the bulk of their service in hastily constructed military encampments alongside white American soldiers and physicians. Mrs. Richardson, a younger nurse interviewed after her unit's return from Cuba, was stationed at a field hospital just outside the line of fire. "Sometimes the bullets would go whizzing so near to us that we could hear them all too plainly, and often expected to feel them," she said.[62] A woman known alternatively in the archival record as "Auntie," "Mother," and "Mammy Cobbs" spoke of living so close to the hospital ward that she was woken by the screams of soldiers caught up in the throes of fever. Nurse Toddy, a black woman from New Orleans, lived in a well-stocked tent with five other women from the Crescent City. But she only consented to be interviewed about her experiences in Cuba on the condition that she first protest against the Jim Crow treatment she and her fellow black nurses received in transit while traveling home via railway at war's end.

The personal accounts of Nurses Richardson, Cobbs, and Toddy offer some of the richest and least-known testimonies from veterans of the Spanish-Cuban-American War. Time in Cuba had, if only for a moment and at great personal risk, broadened the horizon of possibilities available to them as black women, giving them singular roles in the fight against Spain. By the early fall of 1898 the fever season had broken, and the U.S. military decided to send most of its personnel home to prevent new infections occurring among the occupation force. When the immune nurses arrived back in the United States, they were exhausted from the journey but satisfied with the results of their labors: the war was over, the United States was victorious, and they had demonstrated the selflessness, stamina, and patriotism of African American womanhood on the world stage. It seemed only right that such performances of citizenship should entitle them to fair and equal treatment under the law, especially on their trip back home.

Concerned that personnel returning from Cuba might spread contagious diseases to the civilian population, government officials established Camp Wikoff as a temporary quarantine camp on the eastern shore of Montauk, Long Island. As Nurse Richardson and her fellow nurses disembarked there from the transport *Vigilancia*, one local reporter took special notice of the spectacle of their return.[63] "One of the most picturesque nights witnessed since Camp Wikoff was founded was the landing of the twenty-eight colored immune nurses with boxes, bags, and belongings, among which were two parrots, one called Spanish Prisoner, the other Loraine."[64] Like Matas, the journalist saw the black women as picturesque, framing their immune bodies alongside a catalog of the objects they brought back to America, including two animals whose names confirmed their statuses as spoils of war. Not interested only in the things they carried, however, the *Tribune* reporter was quick to note the diverse composition of the group of women themselves. "The nurses were of all ages and complexions, varying in degree from the real old colored 'aunty,' with gray hair and red kerchief, to the up-to-date college-bred trained nurse. Three of the oldest had nursed sick men through the Civil War."[65] The spectrum of black womanhood represented in this passage—in which the nurses' characterization vacillated between old and young, antebellum and modern, dark-skinned and light—exemplified the media's representation of black women during the conflict. And yet, showing an astute awareness of the bias with which American journalism regularly drew its portraits of black people in the United States, the nurses elected one woman, Mrs. Richardson, "a college-bred woman of rare intelligence," to serve as spokeswoman for the group.[66]

Richardson first thanked the chief medical officers of the U.S. occupation in Cuba for the kindness and courtesy they had shown her band of nurses, before detailing the difficult work conditions they had faced caring for fever patients. "We did our best to nurse and care for as many of the sick and wounded as possible, and would cheerfully do it again if occasion demanded. We stood in water ankle deep sometimes while nursing the sick, but did not complain; we knew we were working in war times!"[67] Recounting their humanitarian efforts in Santiago and Siboney, Richardson sublimated the necropolitical horrors of fever work behind a practiced veneer of dissemblance. In so doing, she articulated a form of military respectability that explicitly linked the war in Cuba to the Civil War through the bodies and labor of black women. The embodied knowledge of what it *was* like to work during "war times" gave older black nurses an experiential advantage every bit as useful as the vaunted training received in nursing school.

That experience, filtered through the eyes and ears of white witnesses, shaped the imaginative portrayals penned by the few journalists who chose to cover black immune nurses upon their return to the United States. Cleveland Moffett, a correspondent for *McClure's Magazine* and *Leslie's Weekly*, spent several weeks at Camp Wikoff writing stories about camp life at the demobilization base.[68] One of his features feted a black Civil War–era nurse as beloved as any who had ever served in the Cuban campaign—though at no point in the article does he choose to record her name. Moffett's portrait of the woman, gilded with southern nostalgia, revivified the plantation nurse archetype and militarized it, literally outfitting the mammy trope for war:

> Just an old colored woman standing at the door of a tent in a white dress, clean apron and soldier's wide-brimmed hat, yet this is perhaps, the most famous nurse in the army. This is "Auntie" or "Mother," loved by the dozens of boys she brought through tortured days at Santiago, blessed by scores of fever-stricken soldiers at Montauk. It is from old that "Auntie" knows the happenings of the battle field, for she nursed and cooked through our civil war, and for 35 years since then she has faced all the epidemics of the South, small-pox, yellow fever, typhoid fever, malarial fever, and come out unharmed. Not without reason is she called an immune nurse.[69]

As terms of endearment, the sobriquets "Auntie" and "Mother" were familiar antebellum euphemisms of fictional kinship used by white people to claim ownership of black womanhood in the public sphere.[70] Following this logic of possession, Moffett neglected to disclose the nurse's first or last name; archival evidence suggests, however, that her surname may have been Cobbs.[71] But whether we read Cobbs as a misnamed historical subject, a drawn composite of black women workers who served in Cuba, or a discursive representation of the presence and absence of black womanhood in the field of military history, one fact remains constant: the columnist's description of the nurse articulated the embodied qualities germane to the immune women that Matas longed for years into the early twentieth century—hardiness, selflessness, and devout loyalty to white patriarchy. Clad in her white "fever proof" apron and dress, adorned with a regulation-issue soldier's flat felt hat, Cobbs's choice of uniform challenged the gender norms of the military establishment, marking her as more than a woman but less than a lady—the perfect androgynous and asexual accompaniment to American imperial ambitions abroad. In return, the soldiers she treated saw her as an object of motherly love. In the haze of their fever dreams, her race, gender, and age intersected neatly into a mammy figure that momentarily reconciled the internecine discord of the Civil War and enabled them to claim their own "investments and privations in the national treasury of rhetorical wealth."[72]

Cobbs's testimony differed remarkably from that offered by Richardson and her cohort of nurses, however. While Richardson demurred from discussing the dread goings-on in the fever camp, Cobbs went into gory detail, foregrounding the folly and fragility of white imperial masculinity outside the continental United States. "I have gone through all kinds of sickness. I have seen 500 men killed and wounded in a single day, but I never saw anything like there was in this war."[73] Presenting herself as impervious to the miasma of death and disease in the Cuban fever camps, Cobbs was nonetheless shocked by the filthy and unsanitary state of the military hospitals, which she thought contributed to the suffering of the soldiers. She told of Johnson, the Swede, a soldier whose fever hallucinations caused him to fight the cover from his bed, allowing swarms of flies to infect his bedsores and enter the orifices of his naked body. "A dozen times a day I laid a cloth over his mouth to keep the flies out, but he would throw the cloth away," she said. As a result, the insects ate away at the flesh of his upper jaw "until there was a hole there you could put your finger in."[74] Cobbs also spoke of a doctor in the Second Massachusetts who woke up one night in a delirious rage fueled partly by fever and partly by the overadministration of quinine. In his hysteria, he rushed outside of the hospital tent, naked, and screamed, "The Spaniards have got us; the Spaniards have whipped us! Run, boys; run!"[75] Exposed to the ravages of the Cuban environment, the white male body was plagued not only by tropical fever but also by the insecurity accompanying the American military occupation itself, whose quick victory appeared all the more pyrrhic the longer U.S. troops remained in the shadow of death and disease.

Cobbs's war stories, told through Moffett's editorial hand, served as cautionary tales of the danger of empire building. They also portrayed black women once more as the necropolitical link between two American institutions in crisis: the plantation beset by fever and the U.S. military occupation abroad. As symbols of the former's obsolescence and the latter's emergence, their steadying hand was both a salve and a scold to an imperially minded public. Though the regional split in white American masculinity had been sutured somewhat by the victory against Spain, the new island people under American dominion threatened to infect the U.S. body politic like flies, placing a disfiguring blight upon the face of the fledgling imperial power. Moreover, Cobbs's witness gave war correspondents like Moffett, whose testimony before Congress detailed reports of fraud, ineptitude, and neglect in the medical camps, immunity against charges that they were peddlers of sensationalism.[76]

Nurse Toddy's Protest

Both Cobbs and Richardson told their stories to journalists at Camp Wikoff, but one nurse was granted an in-home interview by her local paper upon her return from Cuba. Nurse Toddy's narrative provides the most historiographically complete account of black women's experience during the Spanish-American War due to its lack of dissemblance, its absence of caustic racial signifiers, its factual accuracy, and most notably, the ability of the subject to dictate the terms of the interview itself. A *Daily Picayune* reporter had tracked Toddy down at her home on Tonti Street between Rocheblave and Palmyra in New Orleans, and discovered that she would consent to the interview only "on condition that she would also express her opinion as to the lack of railroad accommodations, which caused great inconvenience and suffering to the nurses returning to this city from New York after they reached Kentucky."[77] A member of Richardson's corps of nurses who returned to the United States upon the *Vigilancia*, the veteran was incensed by the treatment the women received once they left Camp Wikoff:

> She said that she wanted to protest against the Jim Crow car system, not that she had the slightest objections to being separated from white passengers, but as she had paid the same fare as others she believed that she ought to have had decent accommodations, whereas there were twenty-four nurses, all women, and all colored, in one car that had twenty-eight seats on it, and they were four days in the car without even a place to wash their hands and faces or any manner of sleeping except to get what rest they could sitting up. The worst of it

was that the car was used for a general car for the accommodation of local passengers and all colored passengers riding on the train came into the same car and the men smoked. [At] times the car was jammed with people. The nurses did not go to Cuba for money alone, but had some patriotism and were very much worn out by hard work and the rough sea voyage. They thought that better accommodations were due them en route home.[78]

Speaking at her own house and on her own terms, Nurse Toddy expressed her outrage with the righteous anger of a veteran spurned. In so doing, she fractured the servile mammy caricature that had long characterized black women's fever nursing in the white public imagination. Moreover, her critique of the Jim Crow car system restaged the local and national debates over segregation, demonstrating how the vicissitudes of citizenship can be usefully gauged through the prism of American militarism. To truly appreciate the significance of Toddy's protest against the treatment she and her fellow immune nurses received in transit, we must consider it alongside the failures of the Fourteenth Amendment to protect the legal rights of African Americans at the time, best exemplified by the *Plessy v. Ferguson* Supreme Court ruling two years earlier. While the Thirteenth Amendment (1865) made slavery illegal in the United States, it did not explicitly grant formally enslaved persons the rights of U.S. citizenship. This fact allowed southern state legislators to enact laws and policies—known as black codes—that continued to institutionally disenfranchise African Americans in much the same way slave codes had decades earlier.[79] The Fourteenth Amendment, ratified in 1868, was meant to address that omission, and provided clear language meant to enshrine African Americans with federally protected civil and political rights: "Section 1. All persons born or naturalized in the United States, and subject to jurisdiction thereof, are citizens of the United States and of the State wherein they reside. *No State shall make or enforce any law which shall abridge the privileges or immunities of citizens of the United States*; nor shall any State deprive any person of life, liberty, or property, without due process of law; nor deny to any person within its jurisdiction the equal protection of the laws."[80]

Thus, African Americans looked to the federal government, rather than to those of their states, as the ultimate guarantor of the new "privileges or immunities" accorded them as U.S. citizens.[81] However, when the Supreme Court ruled against Homer Plessy's claims that Louisiana's "Separate Car Act" violated his Thirteenth and Fourteenth Amendments rights, it paved the way for the doctrine of "separate but equal" to thwart federal protections of citizenship through the logic of racial segregation for the next sixty-eight years.[82]

Nurse Toddy's protest, then, was an explicit critique of the Fourteenth Amendment's failure to protect the rights of all American citizens—even those enlisted in federal employment as military workers—from state-based discrimination. She placed the "separate but equal" doctrine under public scrutiny, eschewing its intent and describing its effects upon those women who had answered the call in the nation's time of need. The material reality of riding while black and female on an interstate southern coach in 1898 meant one paid a premium for a substandard and comfort-free service. Riding with white people was the least of her desires; Toddy's point was that the accommodations the returning nurses received were far from the equivalent of those received by nonblack passengers. For four days they had experienced the worst of segregated travel. Cramped into one rail car, the twenty-four nurses slept as best they could with no place to lie down, no facilities for washing up, and no place to recover from their voyage from Cuba. They had, by their very number, converted the space they shared into the designated Jim Crow car, which crowded even more passengers into the already tight quarters. And the men, who paid not the slightest regard to Victorian norms of gentlemanly behavior when in the company of ladies, had the audacity to smoke in their presence.

Toddy's use of understatement elucidates the gravity of her final point: pure pecuniary self-interest had little to do with why these women went off to war.[83] Much like the jaundiced view that saw their care labor as a product of gross sycophancy, the belief that black fever nurses were only motivated by greed trivialized the dangers they faced, reducing their actions to those of mercenaries of hire. Perceived as such, there was no need to bestow upon them the prerogatives of national military service, most notably honor, heroism, and citizenship rights. Rejecting this reading completely, Toddy avowed instead that patriotism animated their actions on the battlefields and in the fever wards, and merited much better treatment than what they received from Kentucky onward. Her assertion of patriotism was an incisive affirmation of citizenship, a public call for the privileges and immunities guaranteed to them by the Constitution, sounded in the city that spawned the doctrine of separate but equal.

At the end of the interview, Nurse Toddy had one parting comment concerning the necropolitical landscape of the Spanish-Cuban-American War. She knew of one nurse from New Orleans who had died in Siboney, an older black woman named Adams, though she couldn't be sure of the name. Toddy was thankful that the rest of the sick nurses she had served with had made it safely to civilian hospitals in the United States, "as Cuba [was] a long way off" from having adequate medical care in the aftermath of war. She had seen so much death in her few months away, and the melancholic scene of American bodies lying fallow in martial graves left a lasting impression in her thoughts. Toddy's intimate knowledge of burying bodies abroad allowed her to ruminate on what might happen when those graves were exhumed, and the fallen military workers were transported back to the states. "It is very sad to die there and be buried in the trenches, by which she meant that they take the dead and wrap them in clothes and put them in the trenches the Spanish had dug for defense, and fill up the trenches, and there the poor soldiers must [lie] until the resurrection, unless the government should some day bring home all the bodies and bury them in one of the national cemeteries."[84] Her witness, like that of Henry Christopher McCook, brought a jingoist U.S. audience face to face to with one of the sublime horrors of modern warfare. Spanish trenches dug to defend the Cuban landscape from American aggressors had been transformed by dint of necessity into burial mounds, plotting the natural landscape with the felled bodies of the invading force. In contrast to the spectacular narratives of American martial bluster that defined the conflict, Toddy offered her grim, matter-of-fact take on how sad a makeshift burial abroad could be.[85]

McCook had himself come into direct contact with African American nurses in his surveys of martial graveyards in Cuba, and he revered the courageous work done by women like Nurse Toddy, whose proficiency in the field validated the experimental use of female nurses in the army. Disrupting the image of the young, white Florence Nightingale–like heroine the American press had fallen in love with in its coverage of women's nursing, McCook instead spoke to the interracial and multigenerational truth of the matter as it pertained in Cuba: "They were not all young and beautiful, nor did they all bear the names of distinguished families. Some were well advanced in years; some were plain work-a-day folks, and some had black skins. But they faced the yellow fever and other contagious diseases with unflinching courage. They bore the hardships and the often shocking and revolting service of hospital duty under the most trying circumstances, and they carried a world of comfort into the hospital tents where our sick lads lay."[86]

McCook would later cite the battle-tested mettle of these women in testimony before Congress in advocating for the creation of a permanent corps of female nurses in the army. His endorsement, alongside a chorus of others, led to the establishment of the Army Nurses Corps (ANC) in 1901. However, despite the excellent example set by black nurses during the Spanish-American War, the ANC systematically excluded African American women from its ranks until World War II, an ignominious truth that diminished their legacy of service and abetted their historical erasure.[87]

Black women were intimate participants of the preparation and burial of American's war dead in Cuba, and the militarization of their care knowledge and labor recalled earlier moments in U.S. history where women of color were conscripted as servants during plantation epidemics. Through the use of their immunities in service to the nation, these women presented themselves as patriotic matrons of respectability whose humility, labor, and embodied sacrifice entitled them to fair and equal treatment under the law. Newspaper accounts and journal articles written after the conflict nonetheless stereotyped them as living anachronisms, antebellum mammy figures whose selflessness, while acknowledged, was purely a function of their historical servitude. Rejecting those limits of necropolitical citizenship, however, black nurses transfigured the logics of heroism to incorporate their own racial and gender difference, representing themselves instead as *citizens in the service*. Their collusion with American militarism thus occasioned their production as "Negro heroines," who were championed as such by Lizelia Augusta Jenkins Moorer in her 1907 collection *Prejudice Unveiled and Other Poems*. The South Carolina–based poet contested the erasure of black women's martial heroism in art and history by dedicating eleven stanzas to the courageous efforts of Namahyoka Curtis's recruits. Personifying prejudice as blind, cruel, and mendacious, Moorer countered the white supremacist propaganda that disparaged black achievement by highlighting the bravery of African American nurses in Cuba, portraying them as subjects "aware of their own vocality" whose bodies filled the dangerous interstice between myths of immunity and the limits of scientific knowledge at the end of the nineteenth century:

> Mrs. Curtis and her nurses have been valiant in the strife,
> May such heroines be favored with a long and happy life;
> In the face of such achievements on the nation's battle field,
> Prejudice is made to tremble, partly too, his lips are sealed.[88]

CHAPTER THREE

Charles Young in Five Acts
Patriots, Traitors, and the Performance of American Militarism

The end of the Spanish-Cuban-American War closed the circuit on the first large-scale military movement of African American men and women overseas in the modern era, bringing black veterans home to a nation that had changed far less than they had. Nonetheless, the black press hailed the return of their soldiers and nurses as heroes and heroines whose service in Cuba marked a new epoch in American history. Just as black military participation had played a signature role in ending slavery during the Civil War, many commentators looked to the peace-time festivities marking the end of war with Spain as a new "day of jubilee" that augured expanded social, political, and economic possibilities for African Americans. However, once the United States signed the Treaty of Paris in December 1898, thereby acquiring Spain's colonial territories, the parades held to commemorate the end of the Spanish-Cuban-American War soon became de facto symbols of imperial expansion and ethnonational exclusion.[1] Unlike the promise held by the racially integrated peace jubilees in Philadelphia and Chicago that autumn—which prominently featured black leaders and African American regiments in their parades—black journalists were outraged to learn the winter jubilee planned in Atlanta would bar black participation altogether. President McKinley had also asked that the name of the southern postwar celebration be changed from "peace jubilee" to "a demonstration of our victorious arms" in an attempt to deemphasize the conclusion of military conflict.[2] By foregrounding the sectional reunion of the North and South through the public omission of black military glory, the segregated jubilee helped the McKinley administration promote its new expansionist policies to a southern electorate wary of imperialism.

Honoring black soldiers was not just a problem specific to the peace jubilee in Atlanta; it foreshadowed the forms of discrimination African Americans would continue to face in the regular army during the opening decades of the twentieth century. Perhaps no figure better represented the paradox of black military heroism than America's first black colonel, Charles Young (1864–1922) (figure 3.1). Widely celebrated as an icon of black manhood

FIGURE 3.1
Portrait of Captain Charles Young (1905). Courtesy of the Ohio History Connection.

within the African American community, Young was racially marginalized by his army colleagues over the whole of his military career. And though he endured systemic modes of discrimination in the officers' corps, Young remained steadfast in his patriotic commitment to race and country, and managed at long last to inscribe his own understanding of honor into the archive of American militarism. The dramatic episodes of his life—which led a son of American slaves to become the highest-ranking black military officer of his generation—exemplified the radical and conservative possibilities present for black military workers in the new imperial moment.

Far from unreflective of these changing times, Young left behind a body of critical and creative writing that testified to his own evolution of thought about race, militarism, and honor, including an unpublished play about his hero, Toussaint Louverture. It is worth noting the propensity with which theatrical models and metaphors have been used both by practitioners of warfare and by literary and cultural theorists of performance. Bringing these two uses of "theater" together to examine the corpus of Young's work, this chapter emulates the dramatic structure of Young's ambitious ode to the Haitian Revolution—which has remained unexamined for more than a century—in order to show how racial difference troubled the performance of American militarism at home and abroad.

Act I: Skin War

> Great men make history, but only such history
> as it is possible for them to make.
> —C. L. R. JAMES

While the McKinley administration recognized that white nationalism was a useful lubricant in civil-military relations down south, the exclusion of black soldiers from the commemorative festivities did not go unnoticed by the black papers. In the *Atlanta Appeal*, one witness to the "white folks' jubilee" registered his contempt in verse. Writing under the pen name "Peter Purity," the author championed the heroic actions of black soldiers in Santiago ("Who won the battle for Uncle Sam? It was the sable sons of Ham"), and expressed his anger at their exclusion in couplets seething with bitterness:

> No negroes were in the jubilee,
> The black heroes we did not see.
> Despite the way they fought so well,
> They kept them out the line like hell.[3]

Another victory parade was planned in the nation's capital in May of the new year. In the months leading up the jubilee, it had become evident to the local African American community that the color line would again circumscribe black participation. The all-white planning committee had little interest in honoring the bravery of black soldiers in the parade, let alone paying homage to the black women from that city who had put their lives on the line to serve as fever nurses during the war. Mindful of their erasure from the planned festivities, the *Washington Bee* called out their recruiter, Namahyoka Curtis, in print, and pushed her to petition for their inclusion at the D.C. jubilee: "There are to be all kinds of representatives at the Peace Jubilee that is to be held in this city May next. Even the white nurses who were employed in the Cuban war will be represented. What is to become of the colored nurses who were sent into Cuba by Mrs. Curtis of the Freedmen's Hospital? Will they not be represented at the Peace Jubilee? . . . THE BEE would suggest to Mrs. Curtis to see to it that her nurses are represented."[4]

Notwithstanding her own considerable influence among Washington politicos, Curtis was no match for an administration resolute in its use of white martial heroism to sell a new war to the American people. The D.C. jubilee program makes no mention of her nurses, and news articles after the fact suggest that neither they nor black soldiers were invited to march in the parade.[5] The sting of this exclusion, while profound, was in some ways a secondary matter; as strident as the *Bee* was in its condemnation of the slight, the commemoration of the Cuban war was old news by then, and black newsrooms had a more urgent story to cover. The Kansas City *American Citizen*, for example, had no interest in featuring another white supremacist spectacle wherein "the white men come marching home to glory" while "the negro marches home to be the subject of ridicule and fall the prey to southern hell hounds and civilized American cannibals."[6] Just as McKinley had intimated in the lead-up to Atlanta's celebration, "peace jubilee" was indeed a misnomer. By May 1899 the United States was a fledgling imperial power, occupying Cuba, Puerto Rico, and Guam, and sending its military to fight a new war of conquest in the Philippines.

Unlike their widespread and largely unconditional support for the war in Cuba, African American newspapers engaged in pitched and acrimonious debates as to whether the African American community should support the imperialist conflict in the Pacific. Like many black periodicals opposing the war, the *Indianapolis Recorder*'s critique of anti-imperialism was both locally and globally grounded. Faithful and self-abnegating military service abroad had yet to deliver the promised dividends to the African American community, which continued to be subjected to racial terrorism and political disenfranchisement in the United States. In particular, McKinley's failure to publicly condemn the lynching of blacks by whites fueled the resentment felt by many editors across the nation. "It is a sinful extravagance to waste our civilizing influence upon the unappreciative Filipinos when it is so badly needed right here in Arkansas," the *Recorder* wrote. "Charity should begin at home."[7] In addition, several papers cited racial kinship with Filipinos as reason enough against the forced annexation of the archipelago into the Union. The *American Citizen* viewed the conflict as "pitting negro against negro," and wrote that "God forbid the sending of a single negro soldier from this country to kill their own kith and kin for fighting for the cause they believe to be right."[8] This perspective was hotly contested, and critics of this opinion ridiculed the invocation of colored kinship across the waters as simplistic and ignorant. The *Indianapolis Freeman*, the loudest and most stalwart advocate for African American military intervention in the Philippines, devoted several editorials to characterizing this position as fallacious. "It is quite time for the Negroes to quit claiming kindred with every black face from Hannibal down," it wrote. "Hannibal was no Negro, nor was Aguinaldo."⁹ Refusing any notion of Afro-Asian solidarity premised on the essentialism of color, the *Freeman* urged its readers to place their loyalty in nation rather than race since "the enemy of the country is a common enemy and . . . the color of the face has nothing to do with it."¹⁰

For the newspapers of the African Methodist Episcopal (AME) Church, however, color had everything to do with the amoral and unethical use of black troops in America's wars abroad. The *Christian Recorder* posed the question of whether the African American soldier, in spite of his demonstrated loyalty in every conflict since the American Revolution, had ever been justly rewarded for his service. As it stood, "Ingratitude, discrimination, humiliation are the only trophies which, so far, he can thank his country's star for." Moreover, the Philadelphia paper asserted that even if he were motivated to fight in hope of future rewards, it would be difficult "for the Negro to fight to deprive others of the things so dear to himself. . . . He knows that the people of the Philippines are struggling for freedom; that they are in their own land; that they are foreign members of his own racial household; that he will get no thanks for being killed himself, or for killing others; that he is only needed because his white comrade cannot stand the fearful odds which daily task his ranks."¹¹

The *Voice of Missions*, the monthly paper of Atlanta's AME Church, aimed to do more than merely trouble the consciences of those participating in the conflict; it sought to stop the enlistment of black men and sow discord in the rank and file by holding them morally culpable as foot soldiers of white supremacy. Since African Americans had no civil, social, political, or judicial rights that white men were bound by law to respect or protect, the broadside lampooned the patriotic investment of black manpower in the current war. "If it is a white man's government, and we grant it is, let him take care of it. The Negro has no flag to defend." The AME Church then turned its attention directly to the "young men of the Negro race," telling them, "if you have a spare life on hand, that you wish to dispose of by sacrifice, for mercy's sake, for honor's sake, for manhood's sake, and for common sense sake throw it away for a better purpose, in a nobler act, in doing something that will perpetuate your memory, to say the least." Under these conditions of white supremacist rule, black military service was not patriotic but pathological, and the missionary department urged the African American ministry to "fight the enlistment of colored men in the United States army, as they would liquor brothels, thievery, breaking the Sabbath, or any crime even in the catalogue of villainy." Above all, the writers of the AME screed lambasted African American soldiers as pitiable members of a scullionized labor class, contemptible handservants of a Jim Crow empire regarded by both white and black people as figures of abjection: "Moreover, the bulk of the white people do not want colored soldiers. Our own governor disapproves of it. The majority of the white press is against it. They regard black soldiers as monstrosities, and we regard them as monstrosities also."[12]

In many ways, the figure of black soldier had become a monstrous amalgam of contradictions at the turn of the twentieth century. Many questioned whether African Americans should continue to invest in the same notion of martial manhood that had, since the Civil War, undeniably played a central role in the struggle for black freedom. While some commentators still believed the future of the Negro was dependent upon his occupation service in Cuba, Puerto Rico, and the Philippines, others launched vitriolic attacks that even wished ill upon his sexual person. "Any Negro soldier that will cross the ocean to help subjugate the Filipinos is a fool or a villain, more fool, however, than villain, we trust," wrote the *Helena Reporter*. "May every one of them get ball-stung is our sincere prayer."[13] Whether written in jest or as punitive denunciation, this curse upon the genitalia of black soldiers was also a symbolic attack upon any notion of Negro futurity premised upon an uncritical investment in militarized masculinity.

Caught within the rancor of this discourse were a fair number of editorials that evinced feelings of regret and resignation at the new use of African American soldiers as imperial toughs in the Pacific. Seeing black troops figuratively caught between the devil of racism at home and the deep blue sea of imperial warfare half a world away, the *Omaha Progress* reluctantly supported their service, remarking, "and since the brave black soldier must fight in this unholy war in the Philippines, let him fight like he can, in such furious onslaughts that nothing but the walls of hell can withstand him; and prove, to those vile creatures who would rob him of his glory and prowess, the soldier that he is, the most courageous, the most enduring, and the finest soldier the world has known."[14]

For one West Point–trained officer of color eager to gain combat experience in America's wars, the chance to fight in the Philippines—complete with its conflicts and caveats—represented a long-awaited opportunity to serve both his race and his country abroad. Charles Young's stint in the Pacific would function as the first act of a storied army career marked by transnational movement, foreign military intervention, and a dissonant relationship between diasporic longing and American nationalism. In time, he would become the most decorated African American soldier of his day as well as America's chief black military imperialist, using his body—and those of the men under his command—to refute the biologically determined beliefs in black inferiority that had occasioned the mass enlistment of African Americans on the eve of the new century. Young's efforts to shatter the myth of the black soldier as an imperfectible beast of burden paradoxically found the black body as a site of self-discipline and social control. Through his quest for leadership in the U.S. Army and performances of martial valor, he enacted a politics of immunity which sought partnership with American militarism, striving to prove by his own example that black people could—if given a chance—excel in the management of violence.[15]

Young's career was, for many years, a prototype of the conditional inclusion of black masculinity into the middle registers of military power, becoming the first African American to achieve the rank of colonel in the U.S. Army in 1917. Indeed, the instrumentalization of his racial difference by military officials was part and parcel of a larger project used to extend American influence into the Pacific, the Caribbean, and Africa, the three regions where he served his longest tours of duty. In the Philippines, he commanded a group of blacks vets that scouted out members of the Filipino guerilla resistance; in Haiti, he became the first-ever American military attaché stationed there on an counterintelligence mission to document Haitian society, language, culture, history, and geography; and in Liberia, he trained African troops and exerted American influence upon a Monrovian government actively courted by European colonial powers. In each assignment, race played either a principal or an ancillary role in his mission objective, and Young—always cognizant of the problems and possibilities created by his blackness throughout the whole of his thirty-seven-year career—performed accordingly. However, upon achieving the rank of colonel he was controversially forced to retire on the eve of U.S. entry into World War I. This decision prevented him from commanding U.S. troops in France and denied him the chance to ascend to the highest rung of the American military hierarchy: a general's promotion.

Often viewed as a tragic denouement to an otherwise brilliant career, Young's retirement effectively radicalized the colonel, pushing him to embrace more critical stances against the army's institutionalized racism in public and in print. And, like thousands of other black soldiers serving overseas in the early twentieth century, his complicity with the technologies of American militarism available to him also occasioned moments of resistance, antiracist critique, and anticolonial solidarity with other nonwhite peoples around the world. Though committed to the tenets of American imperialism in his overseas assignments, Young always understood himself as more than a militarist; rather, he saw himself as a cosmopolitan polymath and nascent black nationalist fashioned in the image of his close friend and confidant W. E. B. Du Bois. Deferential yet driven, he strove to be recognized as one of the preeminent intellectuals of his race, and through the litany of his identities—polyglot, poet, playwright, painter, composer, cartographer, linguist, and scholar—he proved himself to be a consummate performer, producing a broad corpus of literary, scholarly, and creative work that has only begun to be appreciated by military historians and cultural critics alike.[16]

The tactics and strategies of performance he deployed during his career—including the excessive drilling of black soldiers in front of white spectators; committing anthropological, linguistic, and cartographic acts of espionage in Haiti; riding horseback from Wilberforce, Ohio, to Washington, D.C., to prove his physical fitness; and drafting a five-act play about the Haitian Revolution—often exceeded the purely military function of his commission. "It was not enough for him to do well," Du Bois wrote, "he must always do better; and so much and so conspicuously better, as to disarm the scoundrels that ever trailed him."[17] Literally going beyond the call of duty, his excessive accomplishments attempted, as Daphne A. Brooks has written, to "intervene in the spectacular and systemic representational abjection of black peoples," while also to "render racial and gender categories 'strange' and to thus 'disturb' cultural perceptions of identity formation."[18] Caught within this militarized circuit of double consciousness, Young struggled to reconcile the tension between race and nation throughout his entire army career, causing Du Bois to eulogize the life of his friend as "a triumph of tragedy."[19] As such, viewing him as one of the "nineteenth- and early-twentieth century performers who drew from the condition of social, political, and cultural alterity to resist, complicate, and undo racial, gender, sexual, and class categories" requires extending canonical understandings of performance to examine how militarism augmented the performance of race, gender, and citizenship in the inaugural theaters of twentieth-century American empire.[20]

Theater and performance studies scholar Diana Taylor has conceded that war cannot be conceptualized without the use of theater models and metaphors "that prepare politicians, soldiers, and the various publics to imagine, rehearse, and participate in militarism."[21] But while such militaristic scenarios normally reflect state-sponsored viewpoints, they can in fact "rehearse other worldviews. Ordinary people can take them back, as Augusto Boal tried, to envision more liberating outcomes."²² As one such scripted scenario meant to counter dominant beliefs in black military incompetence through an historical reenactment of revolutionary liberation, Charles Young's *Toussaint L'Ouverture: A Negro History Drama in Five Acts* (1910) is among the rarest artifacts of black popular performance found within the archive of American militarism. Both in its disappearance from canonical history and its reemergence during our present "archival turn," the play troubles the temporal stability of the archive, challenging its white supremacist repertoire of honor through its heroic depiction of the Haitian Revolution. As such, Young's drama "allows for an alternative perspective on historical processes of transnational contact and invites a remapping of the Americas, this time by following traditions of embodied practice."²³

Written in multiple theaters of American empire, *L'Ouverture* is a work of staggering breadth and scope. At just over 160 manuscript pages in length, the play might readily be categorized into the "Post-Bellum-Pre-Harlem" era of African American literary and cultural production that preceded the so-called Harlem Renaissance — an overlooked period marked by "high aesthetic dynamism and political dynamism" — if not for the stubborn fact of its lack of publication and performance history.²⁴ Yet beyond a need to burnish Young's credentials as an unheralded, early twentieth-century African American intellectual in search of canonical inclusion, there exists more potent rationales for analyzing this reenactment of one black revolution, unthinkable to some, unforgettable to others.²⁵ In other words, if we believe Michel-Rolph Trouillot's claim that formulas of erasure and banalization worked to silence the Haitian Revolution in Western historiography, we must also contend with Jeremy Glick's understanding of the successful rebellion as "the grand refusal to forget," since the event "continues to be an inspired site of investigation for a remarkable range of artists and activist-intellectuals in the African Diaspora."²⁶

In this sense, Young's play rightfully belongs to a genealogy of twentieth-century dramatic works — black radical tragedies, to be precise — that constitute "a field ripe for speculative thinking on the interrelationship between Black radical pasts, presents, and futures, as well as the continued relevance of leaders and masses in Black revolutionary struggle."²⁷ Though Young's portrait of Louverture largely conformed to the hagiographic image of the man he had long idolized — a man reminiscent of himself — it presented the most radical and sustained comment on the legacies of slavery, colonialism, and warfare he would make during his lifetime. Offering the clearest testament and most pronounced articulation of Young's incipient Pan-African political awakening, the 1910 working draft presented a thinly veiled allegory of antiblack racism in the United States, a witnessing of white supremacy's failure as a military strategy, and—in the absence of his own published autobiography—a prophetic memoir whose narrative arc of ascendance, dismissal, radicalization, and exile tied the colonel's future to Louverture's past. Through its "critical fabulation" of a tragic hero, Young's Negro history drama prophesized his own eventual banishment to Liberia, where he—like Louverture—would die in exile, away from the country he had pledged his life to serve.[28] Inarguably, the fatal flaw that augured doom for both character and author was an obdurate belief that white men, once presented with evidence of black excellence, would view them as brothers in empire; as a consequence, both figures became martyrs in the name of equality. What follows then, is a reading of a play within the drama of Colonel Young's life, a performance of black radical tragedy marked by the betrayal of the loyal black subject, whose concept of honor is forever riven by the nation state's refusal to accept him as a citizen; and yet, through the pain of this betrayal, loses a nation and gains a Pan-African consciousness.

Act II: Children of the King

> At times, war seems to meld seamlessly with performance.
> —DIANA TAYLOR

By the start of the Spanish-Cuban-American War, Young had waited nearly a decade to test his mettle on the battlefield and to prove his competency as a leader of men. His father had served as a Union soldier during the Civil War, a fact that influenced his decision to attend West Point in 1885. Alienated from his classmates because of his race, he spent much of his time at the nation's oldest military academy in isolation. "No one ever knew the truth about the Hell he went through at West Point," Du Bois wrote. "He seldom even mentioned it. The pain was too great."[29] Though he struggled socially and, at times, academically, Young graduated from the institution in 1889, only the third African American to do so. After receiving his commission, he spent much of the 1890s strategically assigned to positions that removed the possibility of him either commanding or serving alongside white men.[30] He performed garrison duty with the Ninth Cavalry in Nebraska and Utah, and later taught at Wilberforce University in Ohio as a professor of military science. There he would meet Du Bois, a newly minted Harvard PhD hired to teach classics, beginning their lifelong friendship.[31]

When war against Spain was declared four years later, Young received a wartime promotion to major and accepted the command of the Ninth Ohio Battalion, a unit of black volunteers from his home state. In fierce anticipation of joining American troops in Cuba, the major mustered in a battalion of sixteen officers and 314 men, and traveled to Camp Alger, Virginia, for training.[32] Young gained a reputation for exacting discipline. He earned the nickname "Dynamite" among the men he hoped to transform into soldiers, and drew crowds of white people fascinated by the spectacle of their precision drill. Yet as the summer wore on and it became less and less likely the Ninth would ever see action in Cuba, some of the volunteers grew weary of the constant drilling and the audience of white onlookers. Once the brief war ended, soldiers went public with their criticism. Taliaferro Miles Dewey complained to the *Cleveland Gazette* that Young pushed his troops much harder than the white commanders did theirs, particularly when in front of white folks. "We are frequently compelled to go through bayonet exercises, hand, foot and body exercises for the edification of the crowds of white people who come for the purpose of seeing the show. We are applauded and praised but that does not make us feel any less tired."[33] Responding to Dewey's letter in the *Gazette*, Winslow Hobson accused Young of being in thrall to the white gaze, and explicitly resisted the racist implications of having to perform as such. "We have worked hard since being in service and we need a well-earned rest," he wrote, "but will never get it as long as there are any white people to see us drill." Not to put too fine a point on the matter, Hobson clarified his use of racial descriptors in his critique. "I say white people because the major does not try as hard to please his colored visitors as he does the whites. We hope our friends will help us out of this."[34] A month after his first letter, Dewey wrote to his hometown paper again and doubled down on his original allegations, and claimed Young's need for white approval had led to the demoralization of the Ohio battalion overall. "It is true that he takes pains to gratify the curiosity of white people to the neglect of our race. Whenever there is a large crowd of white people on the grounds, we can be expected to be 'drilled to death' as the boys say."[35]

If the testimonies from Young's volunteers are to be believed, the major had a penchant for showing off his well-drilled battalion specifically for white spectators. Some felt he exhibited their performances of physical fitness and group synchronization in order to impress a white public skeptical of competent soldiers and officers, while others thought he did so to further his own military career. Although he vehemently protested these charges, asserting "We are trying to make soldiers out of these boys, and the yellow journals are trying to turn them back into tin soldiers," the production of soldiers under Young's command occurred in a petri dish of public opinion; and while both whites and blacks anxiously watched the all-black battalion's progress, white spectatorship was required for validation and valorization.[36]

Young was deeply frustrated the Ninth Ohio was not called to service in Cuba. In addition to not having the chance to lead his men into battle, he was unable to make use of his unique linguistic dexterity, which offered proof of his academic legitimacy at West Point. A true polyglot, Young had excelled in languages at his alma mater, had taught French and German at Wilberforce, and was also proficient in Latin and Spanish.[37] Far from the only African American soldier adept at speaking foreign languages, however, African American troops displayed what was, for many, a surprising facility at intercultural communication in Cuba and later, in the Philippines. Ironically, the myth of racial immunity that the War Department promoted through their enlistment made way for the fear of *contact* between them and the foreign people they encountered in their imperial sojourns around the world. U.S. military commanders feared that their black soldiers, who were deeply familiar with the social and political violence underpinning U.S. regimes of segregation, would find racial and social affinity with those they met while serving the U.S. empire overseas. Indeed, they had good reason to worry. Despite the difficulty black soldiers faced in acclimating to Cuba's environment, many of their letters home spoke about the affable relations between themselves and Cuban nationals. George Beard noticed how African American soldiers developed proficiency in Spanish, making the assumed barrier of language difference permeable. He wrote that soldiers acted as interpreters for their non-Spanish-speaking comrades, and noted with considerable zeal that "If the people in Springfield could hear corporals Morgan and Ross talking to these Cubans they would think that they had studied the language at some college; they talk so fluently."[38]

The acquisition of Spanish in Cuba by African American soldiers no doubt aided them when all four black regiments were redeployed to the Philippines in 1899. C. W. Cordin's participation in language exchanges with Filipinos was complicated by the desires of the denizens themselves. "I like to talk Spanish so that I can add to my store. But they want to talk American for the same reason."[39] Richard Johnson of the Forty-Eighth Volunteer Infantry had some success in learning some of the different languages indigenous to the country, though the frequent movement of his regiment kept him "pretty well mixed up.... I picked up a few words of Tagalog which they spoke in Manila, but this became useless when we moved to La Union where they spoke Illocano [sic]. While I did better than some in learning the native language there were others who did far better in this.... A few showed a remarkable aptitude for these dialects, and strangely enough these were generally the less educated ones."[40]

U.S. war correspondent Stephan Bonsal noted that the surprising linguistic facility of black troops in foreign lands "came to be regarded as anything *but* a subject for congratulation." African American soldiers had "got on much too well" with the "little brown sisters" as evidenced by the number of marriages occurring between black men and Filipina women. The idea that African American soldiers might become "united" to the Filipino population "by the tenderest of ties" stoked fears among white American officers that African American soldiers were in closer sympathy with aims of the native populations than they were with those of their white leaders and the policy of the United States."[41] Propaganda campaigns by Philippine forces targeting black troops heightened these anxieties by hailing them as racially abject subjects instrumentalized by their "white masters" to secure American imperial ambitions that would hasten their own extinction through the labor of conquest.[42] Michael Robinson of the Twenty-Fifth Infantry noted how they had "been warned several times by insurgent leaders in the shape of placards, some being placed on trees, others left mysteriously in houses we have occupied, saying to the colored soldier that while he is contending on the field of battle against people who are struggling for recognition and freedom, your people in America are being lynched and disenfranchised by the same who are trying to compel us to believe that their government will deal justly and fairly by us."[43] One pamphlet, allegedly written by Aguinaldo himself, had been addressed to the men of the Twenty-Fourth Infantry directly. Several hundred copies of the tract had been captured by the Thirty-Sixth Volunteer Infantry before distribution, and referenced racial extinction and the lynching of Sam Hose in Georgia in its plea for black soldiers to switch sides: "'To the Colored American Soldier.' It is without honor that you are spilling your costly blood. Your masters have thrown you into the most iniquitous fight with double purpose—to make you the instrument of their ambition and also your hard work will soon make the extinction of your race. Your friends, the Filipinos, give you this good warning. You must consider your history, and take charge that the blood of . . . Sam Hose . . . proclaims vengeance."[44]

Sam Wilkes, chronicled in the historical record as Sam Hose, was a black farmhand in Georgia lynched by a white mob in April 1899. Hose had killed his white employer in a dispute over wages, and was tortured and burned alive in front of two thousand white onlookers, some of whom fought over his body parts as souvenirs.[45] The necropolitical use of his body by Southern newspapers like the *Atlanta Journal Constitution* inaugurated a reign of lynch law in Georgia, reifying his torture in lurid descriptions meant to serve "as an example to members of his race who are said to have been causing the residents of this vicinity trouble for some time."[46] In the Philippines, the re-emergence of Hose in Aguinaldo's appeal to African American soldiers also employed the desecrated black male body as a spectacular proxy for white supremacy, racial terrorism, and labor without recompense. Equivocating between insult and solidarity, such a loaded propaganda tract would have undoubtedly received a mixed reception from the majority of black occupation troops in the Pacific theater. As the soldier tasked with burning these placards told the *Cleveland Gazette*, "Colored Americans are just as loyal to the old flag as white Americans and it will always be so."[47]

Though most of these anticolonial appeals went unheeded, some appeared to have their intended effect. Black desertions did take place, and none was as sensationalized as the case of David Fagen, who defected from the Twenty-Fourth Infantry in November 1899 and fought against U.S. forces for at least two years as an *insurrecto* officer in the Philippine national army.[48] Infamous for its audacity, Fagen's rebellion has been recovered by contemporary scholars who view his rejection of U.S. racial imperialism as a demonstration of anticolonial resistance and a harbinger of Afro-Asian solidarity. Concurrently, we might also understand his actions as a modern form of *marronage*, as the term invokes the historical practice of enslaved Africans escaping their plantations in order to form independent settlements and communities in Jamaica, Cuba, Puerto Rico, and Brazil, as well as the figurative "deformation" of servile notions of African American identity that literary theorist Houston A. Baker argued presaged "the very flight, or marronage, to the urban North of millions of black folk," fomenting the birth of the "New Negro" as a modern subject during the Harlem Renaissance.[49]

A year and a half into Fagen's campaign against the U.S. Army, Charles Young received orders to rejoin the Ninth Cavalry in the Philippines. Bearing the rank of captain—the first African American in the regular army to do so—Young traveled to Luzon before being dispatched to Samar Island, where he commanded a smaller band of American soldiers and Filipino camp followers conscripted to aid the U.S. Army. Two men from his regiment,

Privates Edmund Dubose and Lewis Russell, had already been charged with deserting their camp, requisitioning weapons, and defecting into enemy lines, making the once unthinkable action of marronage plausible. Dubose and Russell remained on the run for four months before returning to their company on Samar Island. They claimed they were cajoled into capture by Filipino nationalists and had not taken part in any actions against U.S. forces. Unconvinced by their story, a military commission found them both guilty of desertion and sentenced them to death.[50]

During the time of their defection, Captain Young had taken troops into the interior of Samar, fielding off attacks from guerilla forces and establishing a temporary base for soldiers and war refugees in Matuguinao.[51] Given the size and terrain of the island, it is highly unlikely that Young's forces encountered the same nationalist groups that harbored Dubose and Russell, or for that matter, Fagen, who was thought to be located on the larger island of Luzon. But the very idea of black men committing treason within the U.S. Army—regardless of provocation or rationale—could not have sat well with the captain. Given the onus of racial representation, Fagen's marronage imperiled the larger project of African American military inclusion and threatened Young's own ambition to become the first African American general in the U.S. Army. While the white press derisively referred to turncoat commander as "General Fagen," black newspapers—sensitive to the negative representation of African American soldiers in the media—were reluctant to give his exploits much coverage at all. Yet his iconicity as the foremost traitor to the U.S. state during the conflict unquestionably cast a shadow over the actions of other African American soldiers serving in the Philippines, some of whom were discharged for fraternization with the enemy, while others—like Dubose and Russell—were executed for desertion in the wake of his actions.[52] This additional stigma may explain, in part, why so few of his former comrades commented about Fagen during and after the war, even as mainstream newspapers celebrated his alleged capture and killing by Philippine scouts in December 1901.[53]

While few extant sources exist to confirm it, Young would have been resolutely aware of Fagen's exploits, and likely understood himself as being part of a broader mission to bring in the rebel dead or alive, if given the opportunity. Similarly, Young's stature as the only black West Point officer in the regular army would have made Fagen cognizant of the captain's ascent of the army chain of command. Given the underground propaganda networks that targeted black soldiers, it is probable he would have learned about Young's arrival in the Philippines. Positioned at ideological and militaristic loggerheads, the two men—the officer and the revolutionary—represented radically opposing performances of black martial masculinity at the onset of the twentieth century: one forged in the crucible of military complicity and the other in the fires of anticolonial resistance. The two Buffalo soldiers had taken different paths toward self-determination, and for seven months they operated on different islands of the Pacific archipelago but always in proximity of the *idea* of the other. Young's determination to serve both his race and his country as an officer emulated the view attributed to his army forebear, Martin R. Delany, who believed "when he entered the council of kings, the black race entered with him."[54] Fittingly, due to his heroics in the jungles of Samar, Young's men would give their commander a new nickname: "Follow Me."[55] In contrast, Fagen—a noncommissioned veteran of the war in Cuba—renounced his allegiance to the United States, and with it, his dispossessive investment in the nascent dominion of white American militarism. Even in death, his act of armed resistance rejected the faith placed in political immunity to transmute the fortunes of black soldiers and black communities at home and abroad. Fagen abandoned the same racial futurity that Young had pledged his life to uphold, and his myth grew in infamy until he came to represent the new American century's first turncoat revolutionary, a symbol of the unruly and unforeseen consequences of black soldiers' contact with the world abroad. As we will see, the memory of Fagen remained with Young long after his first Philippine tour, and time and personal experience would augment his estimation of the revolutionary.

Act III: Conflicting Torch-Bearers

> I wanted to write a romance that exceeded the fictions of history—the rumors, scandals, lies, invented evidence, fabricated confessions, volatile facts, impossible metaphors, chance events, and fantasies that constitute the archive and determine what can be said about the past.
> —SAIDIYA HARTMAN

In the autumn of 1902 the Ninth Cavalry was recalled to the United States, and Captain Young was rewarded for his stellar performance in the Philippines with a choice assignment at the Presidio, the former Spanish fort in San Francisco. The next summer he served as the superintendent of the Grand Sequoia National Park, building roads to make its magisterial trees more accessible to tourists, before returning to the heart of the city in order to marry his fiancée, Ada Mills, in 1904. Charles and Ada Young left

San Francisco that May to begin the former's highest-profile assignment to date: he had been stationed on the island of Hispaniola to serve as the American military attaché to Haiti. There he was expected to furnish the army's Military Intelligence Division (MID) on the mainland with information about the culture, topography, and military readiness of the country as well as its neighbor, the Dominican Republic. Discretion and assimilation were key to the mission's success, and as such, Young operated as both an intelligence officer and a diplomat in the role of the first-ever American attaché sent to Haiti, as well as the first African American to occupy such a position in the army's history.

In his study on the history of military attachés, Alfred Vagts explained that those chosen to serve in this capacity "have nearly always been chosen on the basis of superior qualifications, and only occasionally for extraneous reasons (to reward a political favorite, or to exile an officer who had become too 'awkward' to keep at home)."[56] Young's West Point pedigree, as much as his service in the Philippines, played a key role in garnering him the prestigious diplomatic post. In addition to being an accomplished linguist, his portfolio sketches from the academy showed great aptitude in drawing and cartography, essential skills needed to document his "country of residence based on military considerations . . . including the whole country's offensive and defensive aspects, its important military positions and posts and the most promising method of making war on it."[57] But the fact that he was the highest-ranking black officer in the United States Army was chief upon the "superior" qualities considered in making the appointment. According to the *New York Times*, Young was selected for the position because "in addition to his professional qualifications, it is believed by the President and Secretary Hay, that Capt. Young, being of the negro race, will increase his usefulness and efficiency in that country."[58] President Roosevelt's decision to appoint Young followed an established practice of appointing African American diplomats to Haiti in the late nineteenth century—including Frederick Douglass, who served from 1889 to 1891.[59] Beyond the prestige of the post, Young's desire to serve in Haiti was fueled by his adoration of Toussaint Louverture, the former slave turned leader of the Haitian revolution whom he saw as the most important military figure in modern black history.[60] Years earlier, he had told his company clerk, Private H. W. Nicholas, "Nick, someday I am going to be a Black General, a Toussaint Louverture," making his assignment to Haiti a prophetic step in his own path toward greatness.[61]

Relieved of the day-to-day responsibilities required in leading soldiers, Young turned his time in Haiti into a research sabbatical and entered one of the most creative and productive periods of his life. He and Ada arrived during the centennial year of the nation's independence from France, and Young was received in state at the National Palace by President Pierre "Tonton" Nord-Alexis, who held a champagne reception in his honor.[62] Referred to in the local papers as a "beau noir . . . with correct and distinguished poise," "Capitaine Young" charmed the Haitian elite immediately, who were enamored with his spit-polished good looks, charisma, and knowledge of French.[63]

With his entry into society thus secured, Young began his work in earnest, compiling comprehensive studies of Haitian culture, geography, and language, all with an eye towards gauging the country's present and future military capacities for the MID. He spent two years traveling Haiti on horseback, making frequently excursions to the Dominican Republic in order to produce accurate maps of the region. Taking his surveys into some of the most remote areas of the country, Young's mounted traverses produced some of the earliest modern topographic surveys of Haiti.[64] In addition, he spent many days researching at the College of St. Martial and produced numerous reports detailing the politics, government, and history of both Haiti and the Dominican Republic, resulting in a 284-page monograph on the former.[65]

Young put his incisive ear for language to work as well. In a letter home to his friend, poet Paul Lawrence Dunbar, he wrote gleefully, "God bless you, boy you would be in clover down here if you once got to the informal Creole. It is wholly unworked field (tenor cognita), full of surprises, cockroaches, and revolution."[66] Taking his own advice, Young published the *Little Handbook of French Creole, as Spoken in Hayti* (1905) a year later. Despite his humble assertion that "no attempt to treat this subject from a scientific or linguistic standpoint is herein made," the text is likely the first Haitian-French-English-Creole dictionary of its kind, preceding the first linguistic study of the language by three decades.[67] Containing rules on basic grammar, pronunciation, verb lists, common phrases, conversational Creole, regional proverbs, and literary excerpts from the works of Georges Sylvain (*Cric? Crac!*) and Justin Lhérisson (*La Famille des Pitite*), the handbook also offered his own opinions about how the Haitian tongue was shaped by the legacy of colonial slavery. "It is well to remember from the start in learning the Creole that it consists of one-half words, one-quarter gestures, and one-quarter grunts and exclamations," Young wrote. "Apropos of these grunts and exclamations they show their slave origin and are relic of the dark days when the negro dared not express his feelings for the injustice and cruelty received from his master and when a gesture or an 'oh!' varied from a surprise to a prayer or mild protest." Far from ridiculing this verbal trait as reflective of "a kind of monkey-jargon[,] a make-shift of ignorant negro slaves trying to express themselves in French a language too difficult for them to speak in its purity," Young found the characteristic endearing and indicative of the performative repertoire of Creole, whose phonology and phonetics embodied the memory of slavery.[68] "The Creole has not lost its charm and forcefulness in this regard after 100 years of freedom. There are many educated and refined Creole women to-day who pride themselves on their ability to express every shade of feeling by a single gesture or interjection."[69]

Young's appreciation of Creole was an extension of his reverence for Haiti's history. But while he admired the linguistic history of the Haitian people, he was reportedly shocked at the lack of public memorials in Port-au-Prince built to honor the leader of slave-led revolution, General Toussaint Louverture. With the ongoing centennial celebration of Haiti's founding as the world's first free black republic in the modern era, Young found this absence especially pronounced, stimulating his desire to create his own tribute to his idol.[70] Hence, alongside his general intelligence-gathering efforts, Young began to conduct research for a historical drama he would write about the slave rebellion that changed the world, with Louverture at its center. This project, begun in the libraries and archives of Haiti, would take him years to complete. It went through several iterations as he changed duty stations and advanced in his career, and its unfinished status would nag him for more than a decade until its completion in Liberia in 1920.[71] The play was never published or performed during Young's lifetime, and an early draft is now housed at the National Afro-American Museum and Culture Center in Wilberforce, Ohio.

There is no record of the exact sources Young used to shape *L'Ouverture*, but the form and content of the play suggest he was deeply influenced by the work of two nineteenth-century British abolitionists: Harriet Martineau's historical novel *The Hour and the Man: A Historical Romance* (1841) and J. R. Beard's *Toussaint L'Ouverture: A Biography and Autobiography* (1863). Beard's compendium likely served as the play's historical source text, and Young's script adopted many of the fictional family relationships and subplots conceived by Martineau—such as the love affair between Toussaint's daughter and his nephew Moïse—in order to sentimentalize its narrative for the stage. More than just a pastiche of these texts, however, *L'Ouverture* brought an original eye and an ethnographer's ear to the role played by voodoo in its depiction of Toussaint's life story. Within the play, voodoo is the prophetic power that chooses the leader of the revolution as well as the cultural practice that marked the dividing line between black and white gods, savagery and enlightenment, Africa and Europe. That the plot of *L'Ouverture* turns so sharply upon Toussaint's initial rejection and subsequent embrace of voodoo makes Young's previous anthropological studies of the religion noteworthy. He regularly encountered ritual ceremonies during his travels in Haiti's interior, and while generally agnostic in his relationship to Christian religion, he developed an appreciation of voodoo's African roots—even becoming an initiate at his own request.[72] Later, in *Military Morales of Nations* (1912), his comparative ethnic study of militaries worldwide, Young touted Toussaint's military use of voodoo as a morale booster during the Haitian revolution, when "slaves were encouraged to carry on their religious rites, and when under its wildest excitement they were dashed against their oppressive masters, believing that if they met death in Haiti, they would be animated again free in their beloved Africa. . . . History records that even Toussaint Louverture himself, good Catholic, great, humane, capable, and intelligent as he was, could not ignore the important morale that the native religion gave to his slave comrades."[73]

L'Ouverture's first act, "Skin War," opens on the day of fete in northern Haiti in the port of Le Cap, with the country's multiracial citizenry celebrating news of Louis XVI's overthrow in France. With the sounds of the "Marseillaise" playing in the distance, a series of potted vignettes establish the revolutionary mood as well as the racial stratification of the society. Three white plantation owners toast the downfall of their former king while protesting mulatto attempts to secure full citizenship rights in Paris, taking special umbrage at their pretensions toward equality with whites. "Does the president of the Assembly believe," the first planter asks, "that because these men of color are equal in numbers and partake of the commercial and territorial wealth of the island with their white superiors whose manners, culture and civilization they ape, that such a bastard and degenerate race can ever become a part of the French nations?" The men then turn to discuss their divergent views of enslaved black population, seeing them "humble unaspiring, safe, and submissive," as well as "lascivious, passionate, and lazy".

Yet there was one individual who stood out to the agriculturalists as a singular, enigmatic example of a dutiful and obedient "pure-blood black": Toussaint Breda. "I have never seen a better slave nor a more trustworthy overseer," the third planter says. "He is polite to his superiors; even in his humility, sympathetic toward his master, taking a lively interest in his welfare." However, his alleged literacy and intellectual acuity raised disconcerting questions among the trio. "They tell me that the Negro, Toussaint, actually reads and loves Epictetus, Socrates and Plutarch; and that he studies and understands the military works of the world's great captains. Why pray?"[74]

The planters' conversation is interrupted by the arrival of a march of mulattoes and freemen, who have just received word that the General Assembly has granted full rights of citizenship to all free persons of color in the colony. A fight between the mulattoes and white planters breaks out, and one of the black bystanders is killed in the melee. Toussaint's stage entrance reflected the very selfless qualities that the grand blancs found worthy of note. In the aftermath of the riot, rumors of a three-way race war abounded, and Toussaint had come to the Cape to whisk his family members away to safety in the mountains. While there he finds his father, Gaou-Guinou, and implores him to retreat with him. But Gaou-Guinou, dressed in a "semi-African costume having a haver-sack of an animal's skin at his side and long staff in his hand," has other plans. When asked where he is going, Gaou-Guinou responds, "I'se gwine at whah I'se gwine at, dahs whah I'se gwine at; and I'se doin' de tings dat all good Africans should be doin': I'se huntin' foh Freedom."[75] As one of the few characters drawn completely in dialect verse, Gaou-Guinou plays the first-generation African foil to a second-generation son besotted by French nationalism, a flaw that ultimately leads to his son's undoing. Young's substitution of Southern black dialect for Gaou-Guinou's Haitian Creole tongue followed his belief in the language parallels between the two; he wrote in his dictionary that "The point to be first understood is that Creole is a French dialect, just as the dialect of the Southern negro of the United States is a dialect of the English. Altho(ugh) the union is not nearly so intimate."[76] His choice to portray Toussaint's father in this manner was also a literary tribute to his friend, noted dialect poet Paul Laurence Dunbar, who died in Ohio during Young's assignment in Haiti.

Though free himself, Gaou-Guinou has chosen to fight alongside the enslaved blacks, and came to recruit his son for the cause. Toussaint rebuffs his offer with a bible verse. Unshaken by this initial refusal, Gauo-Guinou implores his son to forgo the white man's religion and honor his native gods by attending a voodoo ceremony with him the following evening. Toussaint again refuses, telling his father, "Never will I join hands with that unholy cult, dealers in charms and witch-craft and sometimes in more terrible things! My heart has left that degrading belief for a region of blue air and sunshine where dwells the Spirit of the Christian's God."[77]

In the midst of their exchange, the music of a voodoo procession draws near, and Gauo-Guinou begins to sing in Creole, "Dambala waydo tocan / Ai-i-do waydo tocanyo / Do-si-lo Waysan Dagay!" The members of the procession, clothed in "carnival costume of Africa," stop to pay homage to Gauo-Guinou, and continue to sing and dance. Young's stage directions mark this moment in the script as a signal event in Toussaint's mythic origin story: "A mamaloi (priestess) possessed by the frenzy of the drum-beat leaves the crowd, approaches Toussaint, wipes his face with a red bandana handkerchief and calls him 'Liberator'—'The man from the Mornes'—'Deliverer of the people'—'First of the Blacks.'" Though intrigued and clearly affected by her prophesy, Toussaint remains resistant to its call. Gaou-Guinou attempts to sway his son's conscience once again:

> GAOU-GUINOU: Do you not heah what these my people say ob you, Toussaint Breda? You shall be a "Deliverer" you shall be "First ob de Blacks";—and you would rather stay a po Niggah slabe, dan to lead all dese willin ones into de Light of Freedom, my son?
> TOUSSAINT: I cannot with good conscience listen to the words of sooth-sayers.
> GAOU-GUINOU: Then you had better listen with bad conscience; for I tell you, Toussaint Breda, dat dese, even the lowest ob dese slabs hab heahd de Lion of Liberty roah within their own breasts and dis sound once heard by sleeping men, they will neber sleep nor be the same again![78]

An entranced child grabs Toussaint's hand and calls him "Son of de Dusk and de Morning Star," and Gaou-Guinou and the procession leave him to choose his fate. Recalling the prediction made by Abbé Guillaume Thomas Raynal that foretold of a black Spartacus coming to liberate his people in bondage, he questions whether he is, in fact, that figure of prophecy. "My God, I'm weak, sinful and my heart has imagined a vain thing: forgive me, O God!—But Abbé Raynal has predicted that a 'Deliverer' will come. I have felt the need of such a savior. . . . Why should not I, Toussaint Breda, descendant of powerful kings, (and fine black Africans they were) be ordained to lead to liberty and manhood and honor the blacks of St. Domingo and carry this selfsame light to my brothers beyond the wave in that sunny African Land?"[79]

This question is answered in act 2: "Children of the King." Toussaint chooses to attend the "Voodoo service" upon Morne Rouge, and Young's stagecraft envisioned a large palm-thatched "tonnelle" under which the ceremony was held, decorated with garlands of flowers and red bows, "thus giving the whole a barbarous but picturesque effect."[80] Seated at the center of the stage, the Papaloi and Mamaloi participate in a frenetic call-and-response with the large ensemble of dancers, musicians, and worshippers awaiting the declaration of war against the whites and the anointing of the revolution's leader. Before Toussaint arrives, however, the high priestess has a premonition about the Deliverer's fate that augurs the drama's tragic structure as a whole. In a halo of golden light, she sees a white-clad figure on a mountaintop, "pure of soul, pure of thought, pure of body," whose crown of wild olives is then stolen by an eagle.[81] By so clearly foreshadowing Toussaint's ascendance, military brilliance, and betrayal by Napoleon—the "eagle" who "pounces upon him" and "carries off the crown," leaving him to fade into the "purplish gloom" of the prison in Joux—Mamaloi's prediction gave Afro-Caribbean religious traditions a clairvoyant edge over Raynal's enlightenment prophecy.

When Toussaint appears, he once again refuses the call to serve. But upon learning that his friend Lafitte had been the innocent bystander killed in the earlier riot between whites and mulattos, he chooses to lead the revolution. Still, he doubts his ability to effectively militarize the formally enslaved group of fighters, stating, "There are too many fierce, desperate, and undisciplined men here to submit to the measures that I would take to mould these ignorant men into decent soldiers that might accomplish something looking toward their final freedom."[82] Yet even after accepting the call to be the Deliverer of his people, Toussaint remains beholden to Catholic dogma, epitomized by his repetition of the maxim throughout the play, "to bear and forbear; to return good for evil and tolerate no retaliation."[83] This organizing principle in his approach to warfare, diplomacy, and honor would, in the end, be his greatest character flaw, undoing the faith that his fellow white countrymen would ever treat him as military and intellectual equal.

For the remainder of act 2, Toussaint displays his remarkable skill as a military leader. In addition to transforming men into soldiers at a training camp in the mountains, he establishes a hierarchy of delegated power—naming several of his friends as generals—and establishes a code of military justice whereby violators of his prime directive are executed. After fifteen months of fighting under the flag of Spain, Toussaint receives word that France has abolished slavery in Saint-Domingue, and he decides to switch his allegiance to France. In tears, he tells his spiritual confidant, Abbé de la Haie, "I'm free—free, do you hear Father? And the object I cherished for my race and people is about to be realized. In this decree I see a rift in the rock that barred us to the door to liberty and manhood. I shall make the opening and those may follow who will. I force no man's conscience."[84] After personally delivering a letter to General Hermona informing him of his decision,

Toussaint then escapes on horseback while pursued by Spanish guards. Watching him flee to safety, a crowd of black soldiers shout, "L'Ouverture! L'Ouverture! Vive! Vive! See! [*Pointing*] He is safe! Safe! Vive freedom!"[85]

Act 3: "Conflicting Torchbearers" chronicles Toussaint's attempt at forging a tripartite coalition between himself, General Étienne Laveaux, Commander-in-Chief of the French Forces, and André Rigaud, mulatto commander of the Forces of the Department of the South. The first scene begins at Toussaint's headquarters at Dondon, with Laveux and Rigaud standing in admiration before a large military map of Saint-Domingue. "Look, Rigaud, here is the best military map of St. Domingo that I have seen," Laveaux says, leading Rigaud to verify it was drawn by Toussaint's hand. "I have heard it said that in imitation of the Great Commanders, Alexander and Caesar, he gets his information of a district, with its topographical descriptions from those who have lived there, verifying it by questions from others, and from these data he draughts his maps."[86] Extolling Toussaint as an aficionado of military history and a talented mapmaker, Young gave a subtle nod to his own cartographic prowess, shirking his own characteristic humility to interpolate his experience as an attaché in Haiti into his mythic portrait of Louverture.

Toussaint arrives, and after a moment of mutual admiration, he and Rigaud share a private conversation conceding the difficulties racial difference presented in holding their multiracial coalition together. Aware that many in Paris eagerly awaited the day when slavery would be reestablished and the rights of men of color could again be restricted, Rigaud tells Toussaint frankly, "Blood is stronger than water and in my rashness, I sometimes think in this clash of interests that, as a rule, no white man will be so unselfish as to sacrifice the claims of the whites that justice and equity may be done to people of darker hue."[87] As a commander of black and mulatto troops, however, experience had taught him that "mental and moral instruction for all [his] men" was the key to running a multiracial army. "It pays," Rigaud said. "It has shown me the capacity of black men for all kinds of instruction and their ability to think and reason."

Rigaud's intentions are less than transparent, however, as it is later revealed that the mulatto elite have no interest sharing equality with the blacks, and have hatched a plot to assassinate Toussaint. Still, his endorsement of race-relations training within the institution of the military is another moment in the text that bears Young's authorial imprint. Spoken through the mouth of his character, this proposal was a provocative and prophetic suggestion for the highest-ranking African American officer in a segregated army to make in 1910. In fact, more than sixty years would pass—two decades after the desegregation of the U.S. military—before the army would begin making such programs mandatory for its troops, operating under the belated recognition that they help "maintain the highest degree of organizational and combat readiness by fostering harmonious relations among all military personnel under Army control."[88] Instrumentalizing his fictional characters in much the same way he had been used by military officials throughout his career, Young intended the spirit of Rigaud's proposal to impinge upon then contemporary army policies of inclusion and training.

Rigaud and Toussaint end their meeting amicably, with the former portraying himself as a mulatto intermediary between blacks and whites "to help bridge this chasm of selfishness on one side and ignorance and fear on the other," thereby winning the latter's trust "in heart as well as in mind."[89] Meanwhile, the proprietors of color, concerned that their primary workforce has been freed, conspire to reenslave the blacks and force them to return to their plantations, while placing themselves in position to rule Saint-Domingue. "The whites must submit or be made to leave," one character says to the assembled caucus, "and the Negroes must be kept in servitude." When asked how they can accomplish the latter task with Toussaint in power, the plan to assassinate him is divulged: "Lay the lion low and the cubs do not dare to show their teeth. Our women weave the web for Toussaint."[90] The mulatto elite, spearheaded by Rigaud's fiancée and mother-in-law, are incensed that a former slave is held in higher esteem than their mulatto commander, as he was "from every standpoint head and shoulder above the black." Yet given Rigaud's sympathies toward the cause of racial equality, they concede he must be "bent to our way of thinking." Worried less about the color line than their bottom line, mulatto slaveowners took a pragmatic approach toward the question of social equality, proclaiming that "Our cast needs slavery worse than it does civil rights and equality with the whites. The former is our life, the latter only a means of enlarging that life."[91]

Young leans quite heavily upon the trope of the tragic mulatto to explain the motivations of the proprietors of color, who attribute their passionate convictions to the fact that "the mulatto has the ability to carry the world away by storm, he cannot wait—therein we differ from our white half-brother."[92] In the next scene, Elvire Ogé seduces Rigaud into ending his partnership with Toussaint and Laveaux. Making a rapturous appeal to the superiority of their bloodlines, and baiting Rigaud with the line, "You place an ugly nigger above my love!," she secures her betrothed's consent in the treacherous scheme.[93]

Rigaud returns to the Cape, where the mulatto elite have assembled in the town square to enact their plan. They choose him as leader of the new mulatto conspiracy, and in a complicated scene that abridges several historical events into one, Rigaud sends guards to arrest Laveaux in preparation for sending him away from the island. Just then, Toussaint enters the town square with troops in tow, fresh from his victory over the British. Seeing Rigaud, he extends his arm in a handshake, to which a voice in the crowd men of color shouts, "No, no, never, Rigaud!"[94] Retracting his hand, he struggles to explain his abrupt change in sentiment. Toussaint, surprised, inquires whether Laveaux shares his feelings of ill-will. Another voice from the crowd rejoins, "Tell him, André, that it matters not what Laveaux things now. That mulattoes are going to rule here as in the South. Tell him no mulatto has ever nor is ever going to play second fiddle to a Negro slave."[95] When he learns that Laveaux had been imprisoned on Rigaud's orders, Toussaint promptly sends his men to free the colonial governor, and places his former ally under arrest.

Affronted by the idea a black man would dare detain him, Rigaud's response occasions one of the play's most intriguing moments of racial resignification. "What do you mean?" Rigaud asks incredulously. "That a nig—that I'm about to be put in arrest?" "Say the word and relieve yourself, general!" Toussaint responds. "Yes detained, if you want to say it, by a 'nigger.' Remember the 'Niggers,' as you deridingly and contemptuously term them, are not ashamed either of their antecedents nor their color."[96] Toussaint rejects both the ontological worldview that sees blackness as abject and the sedimented meanings that have accrued around the epithet "nigger," and refuses to be ashamed of his heritage or skin color. "My father, Gaou-Guinou, will tell you that among many of the tribes of our motherland, Africa, black is a very fashionable and esteemed color; that tribesmen pride themselves in having it as you do your infiltration of white blood!" Characterizing whiteness as a pollutant, Toussaint undermines its ideological hegemony, positing instead his own African-descended blackness as a point of pride: "Believe me, the black blood will, if it commends itself to history by battling for liberty and a fuller life, take away the taint that you in your short-sightedness deem to be the cause of your debasement. The men of color must see that I labor for their elevation as well as our own. This alone is the desire of my life and efforts. Even your word 'Nigger' shall yet be made honorable by us!"[97]

In the future, Toussaint avers, the term "nigger" will lose its taint of abjection and thus be reclaimed as a term of endearment and title of honor. Daring to imagine a new regime of meanings attributed to blackness—where, one day, nigger might become synonymous with honor—Toussaint's radical resignification of the axiology of race was, of course, a product of Young's imagination. Known for keeping a steely reserve in the face of racial discrimination, Young could—through the proxy of theater—stage controversial ideas he had long harbored in private, such as inverting the logic of inferiority associated with "nigger" through the silver tongue of Toussaint. Without a doubt, the character of Toussaint stirred feelings of negritude and black pride in Young, expressions that contrasted sharply with his public persona as a figure of military respectability, on one hand, and a race-effacing exponent of American militarism, on the other. While the epithet had circulated within transnational cultural productions of his day—most notably during the "coon song" craze of the 1890s—Young's early twentieth-century reclamation of "nigger" as a term of endearment would have been unprecedented, had the play ever been produced.[98]

The third act ends with discovery of the assassination plot, and a prototypical example of Toussaint's forbearance. The general holds a dramatic religious ceremony performed atop a hillside crowned with large crucifix, and grants clemency to all the major players in the mulatto conspiracy, including Elvire Ogé. Broken by the shame of Toussaint's absolution, Elvire goes into "cloister life," while Rigaud takes exile in Paris, where he might "fight this bloody monster, this ungrateful wretch, this black devastator of St. Domingo, by other means!"[99] In act 4, "Under the Eagle's Eye," Commander-in-Chief Louverture puts the finishing touches to a new constitution for the colony, one that, in addition to naming him governor-general for life, also "protects liberty and gives equality to all the people, sanctions religion, encourages agriculture, provides for succession in government, recognizes the sanctity of marriage and makes commerce free."[100] Though proud of this accomplishment, Toussaint desperately seeks its approval by Napoleon Bonaparte, the first consul of the newly installed French consulate. He not only idolizes Napoleon but sees him as the white version of himself. Early in the play, during his soliloquy about whether to accept the call to lead, Toussaint anticipates C. L. R. James's later claim that slaves in Haiti had heard of the French Revolution but "had construed it in their own image: the white slaves in France had risen, and killed their masters, and were now enjoying the fruits of the earth."[101] He remarks, "There is another in France now of humble Corsican origin who has risen, they tell me, to the highest seat in Government; curbed the relentless wrath of the giant Revolution; and carried the nation to glory and honor. Bonaparte has made himself the first of the whites, moving under his 'Star of Destiny.' . . . (And thus may I not become the First of the Blacks as presaged by those seers of the fate of all men?)"[102]

Toussaint had, in fact, caught the spirit of the thing, though his hope for a future relationship with Napoleon based on mutual admiration was, as James might have said, gravely inaccurate. His fantasy of national inclusion—such a driving motivation for this black military worker—blinds him to a series of French maneuvers meant to depose him and retake the recalcitrant colony. Later in act 4 Toussaint watches the French naval fleet gather in Semana Bay. Surrounded by his chiefs of staff, he succumbs to a rare moment of panic: "We must perish, Henri; all France is coming to Saint Domingo! France has been deceived and comes to take revenge and re-enslave the blacks, Christophe."[103] Just as the ships break up into squadrons to attack multiple fronts at once, he quickly devises a spirited defense, vowing to "never permit the viper of slavery to reraise its venomous head upon San Domingan sod."[104] This recognition of betrayal thus engenders the play's most resonant evocation of Pan-African unity. Though the odds are long, Toussaint urges his commanders to remember that they fight for "the pride of Negro rule," their own freedom, and that of their families, after which his "brothers in arms" expand the scope of his freedom dreams to spread the fight against slavery to the greater West Indies, then Africa, and finally the United States:

> CHRISTOPHE: We will demand of these French at their coming an account of our brethren in Cayenne, in Martinque (sp!), and in Guadaloupe (sp!) where they have decreed the perpetuation of slave bonds.
> DESSALINES: We will demand also of them an account of our brothers on the Coast of Africa.
> TOUSSAINT: Africa! ay our brothers in Africa!—they too have lain very heavily upon my bosom, and if God will, they shall be my business *at some future day.*
> LA PLUME: And our brethren on the main-land of America must not *in that day* be forgotten.
> CHRISTOPHE: *May God speed that day!*
> ALL: —*That day!—Amen!!*[105]

Crucially, it takes Toussaint's joint chiefs to help him see beyond his feelings of injured nationalism and bruised ambition to imagine a more capacious project of black freedom, one that sought to break the chains of slavery for once and for all. They know that he is the key to turning the tide of the triangular trade, *to turning the Atlantic black*, and for a moment, their collective dream of a free Haiti is eclipsed by the promise of a Pan-African empire.

America becomes the final front in Toussaint's war against racial capitalism, and at some future day, it too would be his business. "I took arms for the freedom of my color, which France alone proclaimed, but which she had no right to nullify," he says. "Our liberty is no longer in her hands; it is our own. We will defend it or perish!"[106] As the heroic zenith of the play, this moment of protoblack nationalism, understood as the quest for "a black nation-state or empire with absolute control over a spatial geographical territory, and sufficient economic and military power to defend it," was surely meant to jolt Young's African American audience into a new diasporic awareness of the history, if not the practice, of black radical resistance.[107]

Toussaint's last stand is rewarded with the return of his sons, "dem darkplumed birds wid de foreign fedders" educated in France and held as hostages in the fleet.[108] Their preceptor hands him a letter from Napoleon, instructing him to submit control of Haiti to the French in exchange for his sons and the first consul's grace. Aware of the plan to reenslave the colony, Toussaint refuses and prepares for war, placing his faith in the immunity of his men to withstand the hazards of the Haitian environment. He has secret intelligence that General Leclerc, the commander of French forces, is sick with yellow fever, and believes the best strategy is to wait and let nature take its course: "Then heat, hunger, thirst and finally fever will aid us mightily until August when the dread angel of pestilence will spread its black mantle over them and all will be finished."[109]

Unable to best Toussaint militarily, Leclerc proposes peace with the commander-in-chief, swearing to "respect the liberty of the people of St. Domingo."[110] He heartily accepts Haiti's reincorporation into the French empire, and vows to take no other honors than his general's retirement. This will not come to pass, however, as the treaty is all part of a grand scheme to betray Toussaint in route to the reoccupation of the island. The fourth act ends with Toussaint's capture inside his own home. Shocked, shackled, and stripped of his father's ancestral sword "Acpassi," he tells his French captors that "The justice of Heaven will avenge my cause."[111] Before Toussaint and his wife and children are taken to the *Creole* to be shipped to France, GaouGuinou seizes the sword from the guards, cursing, "What, you dare to touch Acpassi, white man? May your hand wither!" Drawing the blade from the scabbard, he shouts, "Aia bombaia bombé! — My son, we warned you to watch dat dese white men would tie your hands."[112] A stoic Toussaint begs his father to drop the sword. "Put it up, Pere Gaou-Guinou, they may seize me and carry me off, but in France I shall have a fair trial. Justice is all I ask." Ever the patriot, he makes his final statement on Haitian soil: "They have only felled the trunk of the tree of the Freedom of the blacks; branches will sprout for the roots are numerous and deep."[113] Taken to the ship under guard, Toussaint waves a last adieu to the people weeping on the shore. Gaou-Guinou drops his son's sword, which had been blessed with the God-spirit Dambala, into the sea. He asks of it one final request: "Acpassi, conqueor, go! Let your sperit wander wide until he returns to dis lan dat he hab redeemed. I too follow! Aiya bombaia Bombé! Go!"[114] Then, amid the wailing lamentations from the people left ashore, he offers his own body as sacrifice to the God-spirit, and "precipitates himself into the sea."[115]

Act IV: Under the Eagle's Eye

> What sort of body is the officer corps?
> What sort of man is the military officer?
> —SAMUEL P. HUNTINGTON

When Charles and Ada Young traveled to Haiti together under American military orders in the first decade of the twentieth century, the newlyweds quietly became the first African American military family to serve abroad. Historian Donna Alvah tells us military families had lived in U.S. overseas territories since the beginning of the early twentieth century, and as one of the first black couples, the Youngs had to negotiate the hazards of the color line as they traveled the globe together and lived among white American military families. Apparently, news of their marriage caused an uproar among the white officer wives of the Ninth Cavalry as protocol required that they call on Ada and invite her to post functions.[116] Due to these constraints, military postings in foreign countries gave them singular privileges normally reserved for white American families of similar rank, without the same degree of social anxiety created by U.S. racial segregation. Little has been written about Ada's life in Haiti, but Brian Shellum imagines that, given her middle-class upbringing in Oakland, life in "the squalid capitol of Port-au-Prince" would have been a drastic change from her "comfortable and orderly San Francisco."[117] While this may be true, evidence also suggests that Ada operated with a fair amount of independence in the city. Charles's cartographic surveys of Haiti regularly took him away from the capital for two weeks at a time, during which periods Ada would have been expected to keep house in his absence. David Kilroy notes that the couple was intellectually well suited, as they shared "a passion for music and literature, and a penchant for foreign languages and culture, which drove their mutual ambition to live out their retirement years in Europe."[118] Assuming that she, too, spoke French, the *Little Hand-Book of French Creole* may also offer a glimpse of the independence and privilege she experienced as an American military wife in Port-au-Prince. Its translation of useful, everyday phrases—controlled for the gender norms of the day—suggest that Ada as much as Charles likely haggled with the local grocers ("We have very good meat for you today"), had furniture made ("Here is a sofa to match the chairs"), interviewed domestics ("Do you know how to serve a table?"), rented apartments, ("I want a furnished one"), sent out the laundry ("The shirts are not well ironed"), and contracted with seamstresses ("I have some sewing for you").[119]

What is known about Ada's time in Port-au-Prince is that she tragically suffered a miscarriage a year into their assignment. In a letter to his friend and mentee, Benjamin Davis, Charles wrote that he hoped Davis would be "more successful with children than I, as I have lost one before its time, due to the hot climate here doctors say."[120] When Ada became pregnant again, she traveled back to the United States to live with his mother, and on Christmas Day 1906 their son, Noel, was born in Ohio. Young would spend the rest of his time in Haiti mired in a local diplomatic scandal that had international implications for the U.S. government's relationship with Port-au-Prince. Local politicians had grown suspicious of the major's horseback reconnaissance missions, and rumors circulated that the major was gathering information on the government and sketching fortifications for a future invasion.[121] Young's tour was cut short, however, after his Haitian aide broke into his office and stole several confidential documents, including his draft monograph on the Dominican Republic. Though his aide was caught and the papers were recovered, the State Department recommended he be recalled from his position, as his safety and security had been compromised.[122] Young was cleared of any wrongdoing and the incident had no discernible effect on his career. After he returned stateside in May 1907, he spent a year at the MID office in D.C. debriefing intelligence officers on what he had learned in Haiti.[123] Young returned to the Philippines a year later, this time with Ada and Noel in tow, and in 1909 their daughter, Maria Aurelia, was born abroad.

The Young family spent the next two years stationed at Fort D. A. Russell in Wyoming, and it was there that Charles wrote the surviving draft of *Toussaint L'Ouverture: A Negro History Drama*. A consummate perfectionist, Young was dissatisfied with that version of the script, and for the rest of his career, he brought drafts of the drama with him on his stateside and overseas assignments, always planning to get back to it. It came with him to Monrovia, Liberia, in 1912, where he had his second posting as military attaché. During his three-year tour in a position Booker T. Washington urged he take, he used his status as the leading African American military imperialist in Africa to reorganize the Liberian Fighting Force, oust corruption from the Americo-Liberian elite, and ward off the political influence of European colonial powers.[124] Young also spent time in the Liberian interior, building roads into the bush, and engaging in skirmishes with local tribes—through which he suffered his only physical battle wound.[125] His creative life appears to have continued unabated, as he wrote the majority of the score for W. E. B. Du Bois's musical pageant *The Star of Ethiopia* while in stationed in Monrovia. The five-act extravaganza earned rave reviews for its soundscape from theater critics, who noted its music was "extremely weird, thrilling and full of savage characteristics."[126] Of course, Young remained dutiful to his primary mission objectives, which he carried out in automatic fashion: he prepared detailed intelligence briefings on his host country. In fact, those members of the Americo-Liberian elite who resented the major's intrusion into their spheres of influence had good reasons to distrust his motives by the end of his first tour, when 330 U.S. marines—armed with the intel provided by Young's maps of Haiti's coastlines—arrived on the shore of Port-au-Prince in July 1915, beginning the nineteen-year U.S. military occupation of the country.

Young returned to the United States the following autumn, and in 1916 he was awarded the Spingarn Medal from the National Association for the Advancement of Colored People (NAACP). He was just the second winner of the award meant to honor "the man or woman of African descent and of American citizenship who has made the highest achievement during the year in any field of elevated or honorable human endeavor."[127] Young spent the rest of the year into the next stationed at Fort Huachuca in Arizona, where he helped to hunt Pancho Villa in Mexico during the "Punitive Expedition." Although U.S. forces were unsuccessful in this venture, his performance in the field earned high praise from General John J. Pershing, who sat on the board that promoted him to lieutenant colonel.[128]

These were high times for Young. Here, at the pinnacle of his success, his sterling example had brought him ever closer to reconciling the tension between race and nation by exemplifying his love and duty to them both. And, with America's entry into World War I on the horizon, it also made Young's goal of becoming the U.S. Army's first black general a virtual certainty. He had a positive working relationship with Pershing, who was named commander of the American Expeditionary Force (AEF), and his demonstrated fluency in foreign languages would be critically useful in the field and in the headquarters in Europe. He had seen combat in the Philippines, Liberia, and Mexico, and while proud of his black heritage, he had proven himself, as Toussaint says in *L'Ouverture*, "above partiality of race" and firmly "under the Eagle's eye."[129] In his patriotic devotion to American's interests at home and abroad, Young thought he had proven himself worthy to wear a general's star.

This would not come to pass. During his medical exam for promotion to colonel in May 1917, military physicians discovered he had symptoms of high blood pressure and albuminuria. While they were tempted to waive their findings based on his otherwise good health and their need for capable officers in Europe, they were ordered to seek a second opinion. The exigencies of war would not shake army doctors from their original findings, and Young's bid to reenlist was rejected. Their final diagnosis—advanced Bright's disease—concluded that strong physical exertion would threaten his life, thus assuring that he would see no time in France.[130]

Crestfallen by the decision, Young vigorously petitioned military and government officials to waive the medical recommendation and allow him to serve in Europe. He made appeals to former president Theodore Roosevelt, who had overseen his work in Haiti, and General Pershing, whom he had recently served under in Mexico, all to no avail. David Kilroy has convincingly argued, however, that Young's forced retirement was engineered in the main by white officers loath to serve under a black superior. They had taken their complaints to their Mississippi state senator, who consequently raised their concerns with the Secretary of War.[131] Young's diagnosis provided an expedient solution to the problem caused by his rapid ascendance up the military hierarchy. Whether they were unwitting implements or directly complicit, army medical officers found themselves defenders of the white supremacist assumptions that lay beneath two canon-forming questions, posed by Samuel P. Huntington in 1957, that would later animate the study of twentieth-century military history: "What sort of body is the officer corps? What sort of man is the military officer?"[132] Despite his evident qualifications to excel in the management of violence in Europe, Young's racial difference—so instrumental in his career up to that point—had finally rendered him unfit to lead American troops abroad.[133]

Rather than go silently into retirement, Young continued to fight for the right to serve in World War I. In an effort to prove his physical fitness, the cavalry officer undertook a publicized 497-mile horseback ride that began in Wilberforce, Ohio, and ended in Washington, D.C. According to his itinerary, the trip took sixteen days to complete, with Young averaging thirty-one miles a day.[134] This final spectacle of masculine exertion and excess, while appreciated by the black community, had little if any impact upon the decision to keep him out of France. But the controversy surrounding Young's removal from active duty did stem efforts to retire him outright. Stuck in the doldrums of the appeals process at home in Ohio, the forlorn colonel contemplated returning to work on his play. Kilroy suggests he remained intrigued by its potential in a time of world war but passed on it because he remained stymied in his belief, articulated in his stage notes from 1910, that "the great number and constantly shifting scenes would preclude the possibility of its representation."[135]

These bouts of writer's block notwithstanding, Young refused to languish at home. His felt experience of racial discrimination in the army served to radicalize his critique of the U.S. military in particular and American life more generally. In public and in print, Young spoke freely about the discriminatory treatment faced by African American soldiers, and made the pragmatic case that racist beliefs about black aptitude impeded mission effectiveness. He joined the board of the NAACP, and spent the summer and fall of 1919 giving public talks promoting the association as having "the biggest patriots of America today" because its members "realize that prejudice must be destroyed."[136]

Young also responded to an editorial written in the *International Military Digest* that asserted African American officers were inherently inferior to white officers. Grounding its claim on a continued belief in biological differences between the races, the editorial argued that "the leadership of Negro troops by Negro officers was a failure," and though there were isolated cases of black excellence in the officer corps, those officers were not "Negroes" but "mulattoes."[137] Young replied with a letter to *New York Evening Post* that ridiculed the racial calculus the assumption rested upon, which had left many African Americans perplexed as to what, in fact, made one a Negro. "According to the editorial, any man that evinces leadership and capacity as an officer, be he white, yellow, brown or black as the ace of spades, is a mulatto," he wrote. But since nine-tenths of black people in American had "mixed blood," and "for the purpose of achievement claim the mulattoes in their own racial group," Young surmised that "the Negro problem is solved as pertaining only to the one-tenth."[138] Furthermore, the fact that numbers of black soldiers returned from France with Croix de Guerre and Distinguished Service medals on their breasts refuted the logic of black inferiority in the present, much as had been already been done in the past. Too humble to use himself as a reference, he instead cited three historical examples of "pure Negroes" who had achieved military distinction in the acid test of war:

"History tells us that Toussaint L'Ouverture, with a leadership that no man ever surpassed and who routed the best troops of Napoleon Bonaparte, was a pure Negro, and a slave until after fifty years old. Major Martin R. Delaney was a pure Negro. 'Fagan' and others that can be mentioned were pure Negroes."[139]

Toussaint's inclusion in this list is a no surprise, nor is Delaney's, an incredibly complex figure whose political trajectory, as maintained by cultural theorist Paul Gilroy, "through abolitionisms and emigrationisms, from Republicans to Democrats, dissolves any simple attempts to fix him as consistently either conservative or radical."[140] But the addition of David Fagen to this Pan-African lineage of racial militarism, in light of Young's forced retirement, represented a public reappraisal of how the latter viewed the renegade soldier. Fagen, like Toussaint and Delaney, was part of the history of black military service being reduced to tales of incompetence and servility in the public imagination, and though only twenty years had passed since his revolt in the Philippines, the quotation marks enclosing his name suggest he had already achieved mythic status as a profile in black self-determination. His recovery signaled the potential use of his radical legacy in even the most conservative campaigns toward military service, as well as Young's creative and scholarly attempts to chronicle black history in his own writing. "*Ex parte* judgments will not go in the future history," he wrote, "for the black man will not only act his history, but he will write it, and be it said that he knows history methods, and that with him they are not those which come from the heat of prejudice and a direct and concerted attempt to discredit any group of American people."[141]

Though denied his general's star, Colonial Young spent the most of 1919 coming into his own as a public intellectual. His speaking tours around the country drew crowds, and he remained an inspirational figure in the African American military community, even in retirement. His time in the public eye would not last long. In November he received word that he had again been selected to serve as the American attaché in Liberia, effectively revoking his bully pulpit. While biographers have not posited a causal link between Young's activism and his African assignment, it is worth considering that his public talks also attracted the attention of the army's military intelligence officers, who had been monitoring potentially "disruptive" groups and individuals within the black community since 1917. In this program of racial reconnaissance, the MID used black operatives to observe and document African American political activity. Containing reports on both radical and centrist black organizations, the "Negro subversion" files compiled information about charges of racial discrimination made by African American soldiers and civilians, and "kept abreast of the state of morale of black troops at camps in the United States and the American Expeditionary Forces overseas."[142]

A month after Young received his orders for Monrovia, the MID reported on a talk he had given to the National Urban League about "the progressive movements among the Negro people in America." According to the report, Young rebuffed government calls for a monument to black soldiers, and argued instead that "the Congress of the United States give them the thing for which they fought—liberty and full democracy." Of particular interest to the agent attending Young's lecture at St. Mark's Church in Roxbury were his statements attacking the American policy of discrimination, segregation, and lynching, as well as his anthropomorphic suggestion "that the Race stand on two legs, one economic and the other political." And while the agent knew the colonel was soon sailing to Liberia, they made a point to note the political leanings of his associates. "We have information to the effect that Col. Young is a staunch friend of the editor of the 'Baptist World,' Rev. Moses, who is radical anti-British, also of Dr. DuBois, head of the National Association for the Advancement of Colored People."[143]

More than any of his friends, Du Bois tried hardest to make Young reconsider accepting his assignment in Liberia. Young telegrammed Du Bois on Halloween to tell him the news, and said his acceptance was the only chance of saving the attaché position "to race," implying perhaps that if he declined, the next American attaché in Liberia would be white. Du Bois dismissed these concerns, and wrote that if he refused the State Department's request something in New York would open up. He ended his return telegram brusquely: "Advise strongly against Liberia."[144] Du Bois also wrote directly to the Secretary of State Robert Lansing to question the wisdom of sending Young back to Africa. "Colonel Young is a man that always does his duty regardless of his personal advantage or disadvantage," he wrote, "but as one of his friends I know that his former stay in Liberia was very near fatal." During his first Monrovian tour Young had almost died from kidney failure brought on by blackwater fever, a severe malarial infection. Du Bois pointed out the government's hypocrisy in retiring him during the war because of high blood pressure and activating him now without the same regard for his health: "If his disability was so great as to keep him from France is it fair to send him (to) Africa where his life will certainly be jeopardized?"[145]

Despite Du Bois's entreaties on his behalf, Young would not relent in following the call of duty to Liberia. The fifty-five year old again brought an imperialist's passion and a missionary's zeal to his second assignment in Africa, and his belief in the benevolence of American militarism allayed any personal concerns he had about his health or the possible exploitation of Liberian resources by American interests. Five years had passed since Young's last tour, and he was dismayed by the state of the country upon his return. Liberia was in desperate need of investment, its military was in shambles, and some of the American officials on the ground were unfit for their positions.[146] But Young's own history as a military attaché had begun to hamper his influence in Liberia, as news spread in the country that his maps facilitated the invasion and occupation of Haiti. An article in *The Crisis*, reprinted in a local paper, claimed U.S. Marines had "sailed into the harbor of Port-au-Prince under cover of darkness and assisted by charts and sketches drawn by Colonel Young, Military Attaché to the American Legation under President Roosevelt; charts and sketches which had been filed at the War Department."[147] In a letter to Du Bois, Young voiced his complaint that the article might hinder his ability to serve Liberia effectively: "I send you some of the local paper by this same wail to let you see how the wind blows. 'Is Young a spy here drawing maps and plans for the U.S. to take us over as happened in Haiti?'—This is the cry of the man in the streets egged on by Liberian politicians, English and French. So that one cannot turn a wheel for good here."[148]

Young was, of course, in Liberia doing the very things that led to Haiti's loss of sovereignty—drawing maps, compiling dossiers on Liberian history and culture, and offering his assessments on its capacities for the future. But time in Monrovia also gave him the time and inclination to return to his creative pursuits. He sent Ada over one hundred poems and song lyrics for prospective publishing in London, where she had taken residence while her children attended boarding school in France, and he also contemplated writing new dramas on Montezuma and the life of abolitionist John Brown.[149] Significantly, Young finished a draft of the Louverture play—since lost to history—and had even contracted with African American actor Clarence Muse to turn the script into a film on Blue Ribbon Pictures, which was never released.[150]

In the absence of either of these finished treatments of Louverture's life, the surviving draft of his Negro history drama offers prophetic insight into the final years of his military career. While stationed on the plains of Wyoming a decade earlier, Young may have dreamed but could not know that his professional aspirations would take him to Africa twice, nor that his bid to be the army's first black general would be thwarted by a conclave of white civilian and military bureaucrats. But in 1910 he did fabulate a comparable betrayal of military honor in the final act of *Toussaint L'Ouverture*, ending his folk history of the Haitian revolution with a tale of white jealousy, black martyrdom, and Pan-African sanctification.

Act V: Two Men of Destiny

> I tell you this as a brother who has been over the whole road.[151]
> —CHARLES YOUNG

During his two-year post at Fort D. A. Russell, Young was still in the dramaturgical process of transmuting his research on the Haitian revolution into a playable theatrical production. Though the draft of his play was nearly complete, he appended the title of page of act 5, "Two Men of Destiny" with a handwritten parenthetical addendum, "For Reading Only," which suggests that this final act had yet to be fully rendered into script form. As the climax of the quintessential "closet drama" his play has come to be, the conclusion relies heavily on the actual letters Toussaint wrote to Napoleon while incorporating Young's conception of voodoo as a redemptive and emancipating force into the narrative.

The act opens in the Tuileries Palace in Paris, where Napoleon's aide, Cafferelli, debriefs the first consul on Toussaint's capture and arrival in France. The prisoner had been separated from his family and stripped of "every insignia of his former position," and was made to share a cell with his servant, Mars Plaisir, in order to "take the stiffness out of the neck of the 'Big Negro.'"[152] While pleased by Toussaint's capture, Napoleon remains bewildered by the absurdity of the situation; after all: "The Negro's place is a St. Domingo cane-field and not the Cabinet or Council Board."[153] The idea that he would ever enter into diplomatic negotiations with chattel was inconceivable. Affronted by the overtures made by the "insolent and obstreperous black revolter" to style himself in his "brother in destiny and glory," Napoleon delights in Toussaint's downfall, as it has broken the back of the rebellion and created a path for the reestablishment of slavery in Haiti. "This black ogre shall repent and beg me in vain for every spark of ambition. His heart shall be made to bleed by my hand."[154]

The perfect foil to Toussaint's heroic characterization, Napoleon is a covetous and cunning representation of white military power affirming its ethnonationalism and reasserting its supremacy through the purge of racial difference. Eager to keep his prisoner out of the public eye, as "he is too dangerous to ever have his liberty again," he orders Toussaint to be remanded to "the most dreary, coldest, and fear-inspiring" prison in France, the ice-bound prison in Joux.[155] Napoleon redeploys the logic of environmental immunity to enact the necropolitical death of Toussaint, whose black body is not expected to withstand the rigors of the frigid climate: "The winter winds and the ice of the Alps will be hell to a Negro used to the tropic sun throughout sixty years of his life."[156] He also conscripts Mars Plaisir in a plot—revealed upon pain of his life—to extract the location of Toussaint's buried treasure, a rumored stash of millions that Napoleon thinks have been earmarked for the future "redemption of his native Africa."[157]

The play's final scenes are set within Toussaint's cell in the prison at Joux, a sparely drawn thirty-by-twelve foot dungeon with bedding, a fireplace, and one small grated window that afforded silvers of light to the room. Toussaint and Mars Plaisir are led into the space, and the general is shocked by the cold temperature. "Are we underground?" he asks the guard, as "the grave is warm in comparison to this place." Watching flakes of snow and ice fall from the window, Toussaint takes stock of the peril that awaited them. "Why man, do you not know that the Negro is a child of the sun and that ice and dark are his poison? If you are ignorant of it, your master, the First Consul, is not—He means to murder us!"[158] Toussaint's belated recognition that Napoleon's concept of honor in no way extended to him was spirit-crushing. He had held fast to a belief that as a citizen of France he would receive his day in court. Alas, there would be no trial, and he would have no chance to defend himself; fictions of imperial brotherhood had blinded him to the fact that Napoleon did want him dead. Excluded from French prerogatives of justice, Toussaint became a witness to his own disappearance, and his death by degrees was all but assured in the dungeon of Joux.

Intuiting Napoleon's scheme to use Mars Plaisir to reveal the hiding place of his supposed riches, Toussaint waits for his servant to fall asleep before reflecting upon his halcyon days of Haitian rule. "Far more precious than Mt. Gibao's gold are the treasured memor[ies] of other days," he says, pausing in reflection, "of liberating my race; of raising the colony to the greatest height of prosperity; of duty well done; of injuries forgiven; these lie buried where Bonaparte can never reach." He wonders if the revolution is still ongoing, and whether his comrades Christophe and Dessalines continue to fight for the freedom of Haiti.[159]

The fervor of his reverie dims once he turns his thoughts to the fate of his family, occasioning his sole moment of emotional vulnerability in the entire play. Realizing he will never see them again, he rises from his chair, buries his face into his hands, and falls forward onto his rude table, consumed with grief. And here, the critical fabulation of the lives of these two men of destiny—Toussaint Louverture and Charles Young—finds its most propitious opening for assessing the black military exile's relationship to race, nation, and honor. Characteristically reserved, Young rarely expressed his anger and agony in public; as Du Bois maintained, "only now and then behind the Veil did his nearest comrades see the Hurt and Pain graven on his heart."[160] This anguish is evident, however, in his written response to a young black man from Cincinnati who considered following his path into West Point a year before he left for Liberia. Young spent little time on pleasantries. "My advice is, don't think of it. If you put one-half of the time, patience, diligence and 'pep' in any other profession or vocation, you will succeed and get rich but if you go thru the Military Academy it means a dog's life while you are there and for years after you graduate, a pittance of a salary as a subaltern and in the end retirement on a mere competence, which does not pay if you have a little girl in view that wishes to wear diamonds."[161]

Based on his own life experience, Young offered what at first appears to be a largely deracinated, fiscally conservative rationale for foregoing officer training. Yet his next sentence signaled his lifelong commitment to the cause of racial uplift, and his belief in Negro futurity. "I tell you this as a brother who has been over the whole road." Looking back on his military career, his attempts to prove to the white body of the officer corps he belonged had been an enervating waste of time and effort. Had he channeled his love of environmental conservation and natural aptitude for languages into more speculative business ventures like agribusiness, chances were strong that he'd be a wealthy African American expatriate entering retirement "instead of a Colonel on the scrap heap of the U.S. military."[162] Sent from his desk at Camp Grant, Illinois, where he commanded a training unit for laborers and stevedores in the interregnum between the end of World War I and his second Liberian tour, the letter reflected the cumulative disregard he felt as a black man who had given thirty years of his life to Uncle Sam. Here he was, at the apex of his career, overseeing the transformation of black men, not into officers, but into *workers*. It was all too much to take. Over the course of three decades Young's reputation among the military brass had depreciated from "colored patriot" to "Negro subversive," and he viewed his forced retirement as a racist betrayal, proof positive that the Veil that delineated social and political power in America extended into its military as well. Once an instrumental player in "the baton change from the Old Army to the new, and from the Buffalo Soldiers and the pioneering black officers of the Reconstruction era to those Black soldiers and officers who would live to see an integrated army," Young had found himself, by the end of his life, fairly expendable to the larger project of American militarism.[163]

As such, reading his choice to accept his assignment in Liberia as a form of exile, far from being a radical interpretation of military history, allows for a final consideration of the spectrum of possibilities available to the black military worker in the opening decades of the twentieth century. Consider the fact that in his defense of black officers, written one month after he labored to dissuade another black man from following his road, he cited three men—Delaney, Louverture, and Fagen—whose practice of racial militarism fractured the bonds and bounds of national citizenship. His new appreciation of their examples of Pan-African militarism provided the blueprint for his voluntary exile, and indicated his willed refusal to live the remainder of his life behind the American Veil.

Young remained in Liberia almost two years before his fateful trip to Nigeria in November 1921, where he had been sent to compile a report on the country's political, cultural, and ethnic identity.[164] While there, he indulged in the chance to see the ancient walled city of Kano, whose thirty-foot-high and fifteen-foot-thick walls had been first been built in the eleventh century to fortify the city against invasion. Young made the 500-mile roundtrip journey into the Nigerian interior to see the marvel a week before Christmas.[165] He fell seriously ill on his return to Lagos, however, and was taken directly to Grey's Hospital, where he was diagnosed with acute nephritis.[166] Young remained in the hospital for thirteen days before finally succumbing to kidney disease and cardiac failure on January 8, 1922, at the age of fifty-seven.[167] He was laid to rest a day later in the European section of Ikoyi Cemetery, itself a site of colonial consecration, and was given full military honors in ceremony conducted by British colonial officials. Young's body remained under African soil for over a year before being repatriated to the United States in May 1923.

A month after Young died, Du Bois wrote an editorial in *The Crisis* excoriating the U.S. military for its complicity in the colonel's death. While in Liberia, Young had twice requested leave to return to his family in Europe and have dental work done; the June 1921 request was denied, and the second approved to start in April 1922, pending the successful completion of his official duties.[168] "Steadily, unswervingly he did his duty," Du Bois wrote. "And Duty to him, as to few modern men, was spelled in capitals. It was his lode-star, his soul: and neither force nor reason swerved him from it." Such willful neglect by military officials was but one example among the litany that proved to Du Bois, beyond a shadow of a doubt, that the army had sent him into exile to die on his own sword. "His second going to Africa, after a terrible attack of black water fever, was suicide. He knew it. His wife knew it. His friends knew it. He had been sent to *Africa* because the Army considered his blood pressure too high to let him go to *Europe!* They sent him there to die. They sent him there because he was one of the very best officers in the service and if he had gone to Europe he could not have been denied the stars of a General. They could not stand a black American General."[169]

Du Bois believed the idea of a black American general leading U.S. forces in Europe was too much for the army officer corps to bear, and this racist rationale facilitated the necropolitical abandonment of the colonel in Liberia. He would repeat this charge a year later, when Young's body returned to the United States and was given an elaborate funeral service in the amphitheater of Arlington Cemetery in June. "They knew that there was not a single white officer at the front who was Young's superior as a military man," he wrote in the July 1923 editorial, "and very few were his peers. They knew what Young could have made of the 92nd division."[170] Du Bois was angered by the hypocrisy of Young's former classmates and fellow officers, whose public tributes in the wake of his homecoming extolled a love for him never shown in life. With his legacy regulated and checked, the white military establishment welcomed Young home as the docile patriot they thought they knew, and some even went as far as to deny he had ever faced hazing and isolation at West Point because of his race.[171] Du Bois called out the efforts to sanitize the military historical record as "Caucasian propaganda" at its finest. "And unless we, who know the truth from Young's own lips, contradict these conscious and unconscious lies, the propaganda will go down in history and children will grow up and believe that merit is recognized at West Point whether clothed in black or white."[172]

Yet even as Du Bois thoroughly castigated the U.S. military for its racist treatment of Young, his scathing critiques were confounded by a contradiction: How could he righteously defend a man who was complicit in his own demise? It pained Du Bois to acknowledge that the man he loved as a brother had been trapped and twisted by his twoness, inevitably caught in the Möbius logic of double consciousness. The two men had known each other for most of their professional careers, and Young's life was a figure study of Du Bois's theory applied to African American military service. In every effort he made to mollify white America, in every excessive drill of black soldiers he conducted in front of white spectators, in every mission he accomplished beyond the call of duty for race and country: Young was a man plagued by the contradictions of American militarism. From Du Bois's close vantage, his pal from Wilberforce too often sought the validation of his white peers. He had taken to viewing his self-worth through the eyes of others, always exceeding the highest standards of military honor while the white officer corps—whose aggregate undoubtedly believed "Negro officer" was a contradiction in terms—looked on in contempt and pity.[173]

Nevertheless, Du Bois's defense of Young downplays what I continue to suggest was a deciding factor in his return to Liberia—his engagement with the ethos of Pan-African militarism. First theorized by John Henrik Clarke as "military Pan-Africanism," Young's thought and creative practice emulated the belief that nineteenth-century wars against slavery and colonialism provided a useful genealogy of military resistance against white supremacy worldwide. If we remember the distinction Vagts makes between "militarism," which desires influence over all society, and the "military way," the legitimate practice of violence used to achieve military objectives, we might close the semantic distance between Clarke's and Young's theories of Pan-African warfare. Clarke's conception of military Pan-Africanism is anti-imperialist and antinational; after all, the goal of turning the Atlantic black was about freedom from, rather than collusion with, European colonial powers and New World slavocracies. It would take Young a lifetime—and in the end, his very life—for the career military imperialist to arrive at the same conclusion. Like Clarke, he came to see military Pan-Africanism and intellectual Pan-Africanism—the building of new cultural and religious institutions—as concurrent projects, and each had the legacy of Haitian independence to thank for its emergence. As Clarke explained, "Haiti, with its then recent revolutionary tradition, became an inspiration and a spiritual and political haven for a large number of Black Americans who were searching for a place where they could feel whole again in a nation that had fought and won the battle against slavery. This longing for a home with other people where they had a sense of nationality was the basis of the Black American-Caribbean connection in the nineteenth century. This is a sadly neglected aspect of Pan-Africanism."[174]

If the memory of the Haitian revolution as military victory spurred African American diasporic thought and practice in the nineteenth century as Clarke suggests, we should also note that the black embrace of militarism, Pan-African or other, has often ended in tragedy. His observation concerning the spiritual and political utility of Haiti allows for a final consideration of *Toussaint L'Ouverture*, whose tragic ending depicts what he might have recognized as the performative "creation myth" of modern Pan-Africanism, rewritten by Young for an early twentieth-century audience.

Left to rot in Joux, Toussaint grieves the loss of his family, his homeland, his citizenship, and soon his life, becoming a witness to his own political erasure in the fight to free Haiti. At the nadir of his despair, he receives a moment of compassion: the prison warden charged with enforcing the draconian conditions of his imprisonment travels to Paris for four days, and in the interim, a new officer sympathetic to Toussaint's plight takes command of the prison. Captain Calomier offers, and the entire audience witnesses, the small mercies granted an old soldier at the end of his run: a touch of coffee, news of the revolution, better food, extra firewood, and a sympathetic ear "that feels deeply your wrongs, General Louverture."[175] Toussaint avows, and Calomier affirms, his mistreatment at the hands of Napoleon and Leclerc; only racism could explain these deviations from the established rules of war: "General Leclerc employed toward me means which have never been employed towards the greatest enemies. Doubtless I owe that contempt to my color; but has color prevented me from serving my country with zeal and fidelity? Does color of my body injure my honor or courage?" "Not a bit!" Calomier responds, finally providing the audience with a redeemable white character in the figure of an honorable French officer.[176] He promises to do what he can to reach the ear of Napoleon and effect Toussaint's request for a military tribunal, but fears the general's continued imprisonment is a foregone conclusion. The best he can offer Toussaint is a temporary reprieve from the harsh treatment he had come to know.

The next scene opens a week later as Toussaint awakens to the beginning of spring. "Mars Plaisir! Mars Plaisir! Awake the spring has come! See the sun has even found its way into our window! But where is Mars Plaisir?"[177] Toussaint is alone. In his slumber, his servant had been removed to reveal the secret location of Toussaint's wealth to Napoleon. Grateful for the privacy it afforded him, Toussaint also realizes his stock of firewood is empty. His calls for more wood go answered, and he understands, finally, that his end has come. "So this finishes it! They steal my servant and leave me with a loaf of bread and a jug of water and without wood! — It is meant that I should be a martyr for Negro freedom to put God's solemn seal upon its perpetuity."[178] Rather than increasing his desolation, Toussaint's acceptance of his fate induces feelings of contentment and peace within him. "I was hungry, I was cold a moment ago, but both have left me. My work is finished! And now it is time for Old Age to wrap me round with the winding sheet of peace — and sleep!—Sleep!" His serenity is supplanted by a manic burst of energy—"New life doth fill my soul!"—that precedes his full break from the reality. In a dying effort, Toussaint stands and hallucinates that he is back in Haiti, re-enacting the command of his generals from the mountains overlooking Samana Bay. "Let loose upon the tyrants, Christophe!—No retaliation Moïse—spare the priests, old people, women and children, you doughty Dessalines!—Yes we will fight to the last to avenge the death of these brave blacks, for our own liberty and to reestablish tranquility and order in the colony!"[179] Through his reverie, Toussaint relives both his greatest military victory against Leclerc and his Pan-African awakening, two moments of self-making that transformed Toussaint Breda into the embodiment of black radical manhood.

Before he dies, the chorus of voices in Toussaint's head desire a final word from him on the war against transatlantic slavery. In his last soliloquy, he insists that neither the armaments of man nor abandonment by God will brook their desire for freedom. Rejecting the religion of his oppressors, he completes his radical exegesis and "swoons from this final effort," dying in his cell in Joux:

> What's that? Ah! Let the white oppressors prepare their ships for their slave chattels! Let them make their muskets and let them choose the conscienceless scum of earth to man their ships and shoot their guns! Let them forge their chains; let them break the native's heart and kill his body, stifle the breath of this soul, withal; still though they may forget, there is an unforgetting God. Even should God forget or abandon our liberty and sink into nothingness, we will say: God, thou art our Father not our master; still will we battle to break the tyrant's chains![180]

And here, in the wake of Toussaint's death, is where Young's folk history of the Haitian revolution takes its strangest theatrical turn. After the prison warden returns to Joux, the audience discovers that, contrary to what they had previously been shown, no one had provided for Toussaint during his four-day absence, as the key to his cell had purposely been taken to Paris. When the warden summons Calomier to accompany him on a check on the prisoner, his actions reveal that the previous scene showcasing his empathy toward Toussaint never actually happened, but was, in fact, the first of the general's hallucinations.[181] The audience must now contend with the discomfiting knowledge that Toussaint received no mercy before his death. This original interpretation of Toussaint's mythic end deviated sharply from the canonical narratives Young had used as inspiration for his play, particularly those intended to aid the cause of abolition. In Young's treatment, Toussaint had been abandoned to suffer his final days alone, and even the inclusion of a requisite white savior character could grant him no respite in his time of greatest need.

The prison officials enter Toussaint's cell and discover his lifeless body upon a pallet. Calomier raises Toussaint's head, and a flake of ice falls upon the torch lighting the room, "leaving only the pale light of the lantern upon the face."[182] After the men leave, an apparition of Christ appears on stage and weeps above the corpse. It fades instantly, and in its place the sword "Acpassi," sent by Gaou-Guinou, is suspended in mid-air. The sword is then "grasped for by a multitude of brown and black arms and hands bound in union by a huge Python, 'Dambala'; this being a prophecy of Negro freedom to be achieved by the war-like ardor and the indomitable will of the Haitian people moralized by the religion of their ancestors."[183] As the union of black and brown arms reach for the hilt of Acpassi, the Haitian national anthem, "La Dessalinienne," plays and the curtain falls on the stage.

Young's play ends with the beatification and canonization of Toussaint as an icon of Pan-African militarism. Though sacrificed in the struggle for black freedom, his redemption by Dambala augured more than a free Haiti; it provided a diasporic origin story of the black radical tradition in the Pan-African world. Young wrote what was, in some ways, a fairly conventional tragedy meant to inspire racial uplift through the veneration of a beloved hero; but after his service in Haiti, his own life emulated the drama's unfinished narrative of black martyrdom, a mimicry that vacillated from parable to prophetic memoir. As a closet drama read more than a hundred years after its creation, the play endures as a cautionary tale fiercely critical of the belief that faithful military service will grant African Americans greater rights, even as it reenacts a performance of racial militarism that celebrates the birth of a black radical hero. Young's racial hagiography fractured the circuit of double consciousness that tethered black freedom to dreams of national inclusion, and presented his audience with an urtext of black radical manhood freed from its imperial restraints. The play's final vision, black and brown arms united at the hilt of Acpassi, returned the spirit of Toussaint to his beloved Haiti while also prophesizing victory against colonialism and transatlantic slavery. Young named the sword after the Akpassi, now Isha, people in modern-day Benin, which served as one of the centers of the Yoruba diaspora and a main source for Haitian slaves. As such, Acpassi's appearance in the dungeons of Joux brought the ghosts of colonial slavery back to the metropole to finish what Toussaint had started, a revolutionary performance that inspired a son of American slaves a century later to reach unprecedented heights in his career as a soldier, motivating his quest for citizenship, and establishing his sterling ideal of racial manhood.

As his biographers make exceedingly clear, among all the extraordinary experiences that define the life and legacy of Charles Young, it was his time in Haiti that left the greatest impression upon the black military hero. There were low points, to be sure; he was unquestionably affected by the loss of his first child, and the circumstances surrounding his removal from his first diplomatic post frustrated him greatly. However, the time he spent in Port-au-Prince began one of the most productive periods of his professional and creative life. Not only had he excelled in gathering actionable information useful in the event of a U.S. invasion of the country, he completed literary and cultural works that testified to his competence as a linguist, scholar, and cartographer. But Young left Haiti with a memento that cemented this adoration of Toussaint Louverture as a personal icon, and presaged his prophetic emulation of the revolutionary leader himself. Alongside the English-language sources he read while researching his drama, he also read Haitian historian Joseph Saint-Rémy's *Vie de Toussaint-L'Ouverture* (1850), whose frontispiece features a lithograph of the General in full regalia.[184] When Young returned to the United States, he brought back an eight-by-seven-inch self-painted watercolor of Toussaint inspired by Saint-Rémy's image. Adding vibrant colors to the former's black-ink print, he depicted Louverture in a blue grenadier uniform, trimmed with a gold sash and opulent epaulets, and a gold-trimmed black bicorne hat that curved athwart a handsome face. To the right of his profile is a short, illegible quote written in French and/or Creole, along with the signature, "Toussaint L'ouverture." Beyond the coloration of the image, Young's profile differs from Saint-Rémy's in the angularity of its bone structure and the fullness of its chin. Given the historical debates concerning the use, truth, and meaning of Toussaint's iconography in the nineteenth and twentieth centuries, one might be forgiven for seeing in Young's portrait something more than a need to counter purportedly racist caricatures of Louverture that portrayed him with a pronounced, lower jar.[185] They might, in fact, discern a striking resemblance between the watercolor and Young's own chiseled visage, as his 1905 studio portrait bears a remarkable likeness to his painting of the Pan-African icon. Viewed side by side, the two images favor one another, sharing the same full lips, similar square chins, and, set beneath alert brows, penetrating eyes that look forward into an unbridled future.

CHAPTER FOUR

Contagious Immunity
Race, Sexuality, and the Black Venereal Body Abroad

Charles Young is not the only figure from this study of black military immunities to appear in the army's World War I Negro subversion files: Namahyoka Curtis, the army's indefatigable recruiter of black nurses during the Spanish-Cuban-American War, was featured in a 1919 report as well. Major W. H. Loving, an African American officer working in the MID, sent a report to the director of military intelligence in Washington, D.C., describing a mass meeting of "Ex-Soldiers, Sailors, and War Workers" held by the League of Democracy at the Howard Theatre in June, held to rebut charges made by a white colonel from the Ninety-Second Division that black troops were "cowards," and were "dangerous to no one except themselves and women." Though Curtis's name was not listed on the circular advertising the meeting, it was listed in the report alongside two others—Lieutenants Osceola McKaine and Charles Lane—whose comments attracted the attention of Major Loving. Loving failed to give a direct quote from any of the speakers, deciding instead to include an unattributed excerpt from one of their speeches: "Until we have colored officers commanding white men we do not want white officers commanding colored men. If satisfaction cannot be had from the Secretary of War we will go to Congress. We own no special allegiance to a government that discriminates, segregates, and permits lynching and burning at the stake."[1]

While we cannot know whether these specific words critiquing discrimination, segregation, and lynching were uttered by Curtis, it is clear that army intelligence officials viewed her as someone whose political activism on behalf of African American officers in the postwar period threatened military order, making her worthy of surveillance. This was a sea change in how she was formerly viewed by the army, which had treated her as the quintessential military matriarch since the days of the Cuban war. Twenty-one years had passed since her own military service, and in that time she had become a fixture among Washington's black social elite, remaining committed to the cause of racial uplift through two decades of local and national acts of political advocacy and humanitarianism. Her local papers continued to follow her political activism as well as her social calendar over the years, reminding their readers that "while she is an enthusiastic woman, she is a thorough race worker."² In 1904, the *Washington Bee* made the assertion that Mrs. A. M. Curtis was the "only female canvassing for the Republican party" in the presidential election; four years later, the *Indiana Freeman* suggested she would likely be asked to speak for the Taft and Sherman ticket in Indiana, Kentucky, Ohio, Illinois, and out west in Colorado, Utah, and California, "where her influence is especially strong."³ During the 1906 San Francisco earthquake, she managed the Red Cross distribution of relief aid in the city, and the branch vice president sent "appreciative thanks to the National Board for sending this loyal, unselfish daughter of California to assist in alleviating the dreadful suffering of her own people."⁴

Curtis continued to promote African American history and culture through the medium of "the world fair." Reprising the role she had played in Chicago, she advocated for greater black representation in the St. Louis and Jamestown expositions, and served as the fiscal agent in the latter.⁵ When faced with familiar charges that the expos discriminated against African Americans, she resigned from the first post, and threatened to leave the second.⁶ Curtis was also active in civic debates concerning the control of the Washington, D.C., school board—punctuated by the dismissal of Anna Julia Cooper from her position as principal at M Street High School in 1906—and earned a reputation as a troublemaker. "Some irresponsible person may say as it has already been said, that Mrs. Curtis is a meddler," the *Bee* wrote, scoffing at the insinuation. "Why doesn't some one else meddle on the same line that she is?" Indicating the deep gender bias directed toward black women like Cooper and Curtis in positions of power, the paper recommended that "some of the so-called representative colored men go before the Senate Committee and tell what they have done to uphold corruption in office and then compare their work with that of Mrs. A. M. Curtis."⁷

The *Bee* continued its fond coverage of Curtis into the next decade. In 1913 it made the exaggerated claim that "Mrs. A. M. Curtis is perhaps the only female politician of note among colored women of this country."⁸ Hyperbole aside, it was news to many in the black community that Curtis had declined an invitation to work for the Red Cross in Europe during World War I, "on account of pressure of domestic duties and for personal reasons," but by 1914, the forty-five year old had retired from her role as humanitarian aid worker.⁹ She would, however, continue to advocate on behalf of African American and women's empowerment and inclusion in civic, national, and military politics in her own inimitable way. In 1917 she addressed the Woman Wage-Earner's Association, an organization of clubwomen cofounded by her friend Mary Church Terrell to assist the numbers of black women migrating north for work.[10] And one year before she was placed under military surveillance, she began a "Smokes for the Boys" campaign to raise money to buy cigarettes for black soldiers shipping off to France.[11]

So, while we cannot know exactly what Curtis said at the League of Democracy that led to her inclusion on the list of "Negro subversives," it is more than likely she announced to the audience her own stake in the treatment of black officers: all three of her sons—A. Maurice Jr., Arthur, and Merrill—had been commissioned as first lieutenants in the army during the war. As the male scions of her family lineage fought in France—surely with her blessings—the mother-of-four's commitment to ending racial discrimination in the military became a highly personal affair. Her sons were emblematic of modern black manhood—new Negroes in a new century—and the future of her family might be made or revoked through their entanglement with American militarism. As patriot and mother, Curtis's heteronormative investment in the discourse of Negro futurity, once so compatible with army policy, abraded military intelligence's efforts to assign a standard typology to Negro subversives, whose characteristics ranged from the patriotically indignant to the radically seditious.

Yet even under this umbrella of political generalities, the Negro subversion files reveal covert attempts made by the white officer corps to identify a distinct racial difference among African American soldiers—to prove, in a sense, that black people were biologically and culturally inferior, and thus unfit for military service. On October 21, 1918, the MID sent out a secret bulletin for intelligence officers entitled, "Special Bulletin: The Negro Problem in the Army." The document stated at the outset that its purpose was not to make recommendations on the best practices for handling black troops; rather, MID was on a fact-finding mission about the habits, conduct, and complaints of the soldiers of color under their command. "If, incidently [sic], we set forth some of the features of the negro problem which have come to our notice," it said, "it is only to try to clarify for I.O.'s [intelligence officers] the enquiry in which we need their help."[12]

The prologue of the bulletin gave a potted history of African American service, stating that the handling of black troops in the old regular army was "of comparative simplicity," since those soldiers were in the army by choice, not conscription. Now, with the draft, the government had asked "the entire colored population to take a full share in the war. Their men, their money, and their devotion are needed, to the greatest possible extent." As a result, it argued, "prominent negroes have raised, even more than in civil life, the question of "equality" of the negro, and agitators have made what capital they could of the situation. "'Why should we fight for America?' they ask. 'What has she done for us? Are we still Jim Crow in the Army?'"[13]

These posed questions went unanswered for the time being, as the bulletin shifted to outlining a full taxonomy of "the drafted negro" with Darwinian precision. In the beginning, it argued, the transition from civilian to military life is greater for him than for the white man, primarily for reasons of hygiene. "He is seldom so accustomed to personal cleanliness or general sanitation. The mere requirement of having to take a bath may seem an intolerable burden." The drafted negro, especially in the South, was also characterized by his lack of discipline, his laziness, and his mental ignorance, which increased the isolation he felt being away from home. "In the army he is more cut off from home associations than the white man, because the act of writing letters, if he can write at all, is a mental and physical strain. He does extraordinarily little reading of newspapers, but takes in his information through the ear." These traits worried MID officials, who claimed "the reason that enemy agents and agitators have had good success in proportion to small effort among the negroes, is found in this isolation and this gullibility."[14]

Though seen as largely ignorant and gullible by the officer corps, the drafted negro might still have his qualities of being effectively utilized, as his "habitual easy-going docility may prove either an asset or a liability according to how he is handled." As such, military commanders were asked to complete a "Questionnaire Concerning Colored Troops," which would result in an aggregate depiction of the black military worker to give MID "greater precision" in solving the problem at hand. In answering the survey, commanders were cautioned to be objective in their assessments and to not be swayed by any previously held beliefs they had about black people: "Please be careful *not to be influenced by any prejudices or views you may have inherited from civil life*. Look at the questions presented with absolute impartiality, and solely with a view to the army, remembering that all we are concerned with is the production of the highest possible efficiency and morale."[15]

The forty-three-question survey covered a range of topics, all meant to offer a better taxonomy of the newly conscripted black soldier and his capacities for military use. In the stateside responses to the questionnaire—the majority of which were authored by white officers—one trope recurred in the correspondence that signaled a widespread belief in the biological and moral inferiority of conscripted African American troops: the figure of the sick and sexually infectious black soldier. The term "venereal," as an adjective and a noun, was used to typify black men as morally degraded, physically unfit, and contagious; therefore, modes of exclusion, confinement, and control were implemented to segregate "venereals" from the rest of the healthy population in camp. However, the imperfect practice of these modes of control made it possible to view all black men as sexually infectious and unworthy of military service. Contributing to the already existing beliefs about black immune bodies forged in slavery, these memos reveal that the anxieties catalogued in the Negro subversion files were sexual as well as racial.

The sexuality of black men, considered an untrammeled domain of vice and ignorance to many military officials, provoked feelings of resignation and disgust in the officers who responded to the questionnaire. At Camp Grant in Illinois, one officer wrote that the condition of one of the battalions under his command "is such as to detract from the efficiency and moral of all men therein." He claimed at least 75 percent were "venereals" and, accordingly, could do no work: "But for the greatest part of the day these men do absolutely nothing but sit around on their bunks, indoors or out, where they talk, or sleep, or shoot craps behind the officers' backs."[16] Seven months later, a different officer wrote "the great number of venereals among the colored soldiers at Camp Grant have caused them to be regarded as a menace to the community and accordingly they are not welcomed," which resulted in a policy of not letting "venereals" go out on pass.[17]

The conditions at Camp Grant were seen as a microcosm of a larger problem of mustering black men into service around the country. To that end, Major Loving went on a tour of camps in Kentucky, Arkansas, Alabama, Georgia, South Carolina, North Carolina, New York, and Virginia, to personally attest to conditions of morale among black recruits, and to make suggestions based on his findings.[18] He found a culture of indifference regarding the health of black soldiers and neglect in their care. This was especially pronounced in the "development battalions" established in 1918 either to retrain unfit men for duty with combatant or noncombatant forces, or "to promptly rid the service of all men who, after thorough trial and examination, were found physically, mentally, or morally incapable of performing the duties of a soldier."[19] At Camp Humphreys in Virginia, Loving wrote that while most of the men in the development battalion were suffering from some kind of venereal disease, others had been rejected from overseas duty "because of some physical defect," and the two groups of men ate and slept in the same tents. "The venereals also mingle with other soldiers in the Y.M.C.A. tent and participate in games and sports therein," he said, "to the detriment of the health of the well soldiers."[20] He also recounted a story of meeting a visibly sick soldier sitting alone on a bench, suffering from an advanced case of syphilis. "He could scarcely walk. I also found this man to be sharing the tent with three other soldiers who are not suffering from any venereal diseases."[21]

Loving was troubled by the overall laxity shown in the control of black soldiers in venereal stockades, and worried about the physical and ideological effects of housing sick and well soldiers together. Beyond this, he found the medical treatment received by sick soldiers woefully negligent, and highlighted the case of Camp Zachary Taylor as prime rationale for "the urgent necessity of colored physicians to care for colored soldiers, and especially for venereal cases among colored soldiers."[22] His Kentucky example was unique in that while the camp could not be surpassed for discipline and cleanliness, and the relationship between black and white soldiers was "very cordial," the men in the service and labor battalions received no military training at all. The soldiers were required to perform all manual labor in the different parts of the camp, "which seems to occupy all or the better portion of their time." Camp Zachary Taylor had its own development battalion of quarantined men, and its single unit housed soldiers suffering from lameness, rheumatism, and venereal diseases. It was the neglect shown toward the last group of men by white physicians that alarmed him, and gave credence to his direct appeal for more black doctors to be commissioned as officers of black battalions. "The white physician is alright so far as his ability is concerned," he wrote, "but he cannot and will not take the interest in these different venereal cases as the colored physician will." Loving was explicit in identifying the underlying factor he believed was behind the negligence shown to black men diagnosed with sexually transmitted infections and diseases: interracial genital anxiety.

> In the first place, [the white physician] is not accustomed to treating colored patients, and especially in cases of this kind where he must actually handle the privates of colored men in order to get results. The fact is that they do not do it, but leave it to the hospital attendants, and the men are consequently neglected. In many cases men are discharged from the hospital before they are thoroughly well. If these men perchance be member of the labor battalion it would be to their detriment to do laborious work. Therefore, I recommend colored physicians for colored troops. I consider this to be absolutely necessary for the good of the service.[23]

While it was perhaps indecorous for Loving to state in print, there was no greater symbol of the problem of black futurity for white doctors and black leaders during World War I than the black penis.

What follows offers an examination of how anxieties around race and genitalia produced the logics for two parallel and at time overlapping projects of black masculine perfectibility and restraint within the U.S. military at home and abroad. The presence of sexually infectious black soldiers provided the rationale used by white army doctors to enact novel and conventional modes of sexual control in their efforts to discipline the bodies and desires of black servicemen stationed overseas. While some of these physicians would go on to claim the experimental regulation of black male sexuality as a technocratic success, African American leaders touted the "clean" body of the African American soldier—sanitized in the crucible of war—as a matter of masculine will rather than medicine. Since the stigma of sexual infection troubled the heteronormative discourse of Negro futurity and imperiled the project of political immunity, internal and external debates about the sexual health of black soldiers gained greater significance in the ongoing quest of national inclusion. By critiquing and contesting the discourse of the black venereal body in professional journals, making direct outreach efforts to black troops stateside and abroad, and deploying a discourse of racial hagiography in black periodicals and memoir, leaders of the African American professional class employed the trope of a sanitized black soldier during and after the war, brandishing his sexual restraint in their broader claims for citizenship rights. In all, the ringing charge of venereal subversion transformed black male bodies into sites of discursive battle and medical experimentation by the end of World War I.

Prepping for War: Race, Prophylaxis, and Social Hygiene

Evaluating the sexual health of African American recruits was not Loving's primary reason for making his tour of stateside training camps, but he was confronted with overwhelming evidence of carelessness in their medical treatment, and ignorance among the soldiers themselves. He had no problem admitting the truth of what War Department statistics had presented as a damning fact: the dramatic proportionate difference between rates of venereal disease among black and white soldiers. In 1917, 63,586 servicemen were hospitalized for venereal disease. Over 59,000 were white and four thousand were black, creating a rate of 109.1 per 1000 for white troops compared to 310.5 for black soldiers.[24] Far from viewing these statistics as a permanent indictment of black manhood, Loving believed that proper education of soldiers and effective treatment by physicians would bring the black venereal rate down to acceptable levels. In the vast number of camps he visited, however, these guidelines were imperfectly implemented, if at all. Army policy held that all suspected venereal subjects be quarantined until they were cured and ready to return to active service. Loving believed in the principle of quarantine, and took efforts to explain its military rationale to soldiers he met on his tour, who viewed it as an extension of the larger system of racist control they were experiencing. But in his view, white officers were less interested in protecting black soldiers from one another, making quarantine procedures null and void and creating an undue stigma on black soldiers as a whole.

Eradicating this stigma became a point of activism for black community leaders, who engaged modes of advocacy and outreach in their efforts to remove the venereal taint from black soldiers during World War I. Writing in black newspapers, professional journals, and memoirs, these men and women expended considerable energy rebutting arguments made by white health practitioners that black bodies were morally suspect and prone to disease, thus making African Americans unfit to serve in the war effort. A particularly strident voice within this discourse was that of physician A. Wilberforce Williams, whose weekly column on "Preventive Measures, First Aid Remedies, Hygenics and Sanitation" ran in the *Chicago Defender* from 1913 to 1929.[25] Prompted by a report from the Surgeon General's office that showed a high incidence of venereal disease among recently examined African American recruits, Williams penned a guest editorial for the journal of the National Medical Association, the oldest national organization representing African American physicians in the United States.[26] While imploring black physicians to do more to reduce high rates of venereal disease in the larger community, he criticized the less-than-scientific methods used to characterize those rates as normative for and endemic to the race as a whole. "It has been the custom and practice since the [Civil War] in many sections of this country," he wrote, "to examine and see a few colored patients, at the various public clinics, city or country hospitals, and, although these patients are the most ignorant and most neglected and of the lowest strata of the colored race, the *whole colored race* has been charged with *being a venereal race*."[27] Williams addressed the question of whether "the race" was a "venereal race" again in his August 1919 *Chicago Defender* column. Using a class-based politics of resentment to rebut those charges once more, Williams also used the occasion to indict white sexuality as historically venereal, thus rendering VD cases among African Americans into vestiges of the colonial sexual encounter of transatlantic slavery as well as modern instantiations of interracial sexual contact. "The venereal diseases know no color line," he attested, and almost as an aside, subsequently mentioned that, "in fact, the venereal diseases are white men's diseases [and] the Negro was free from these vile sex diseases when he first came to America. This fact does not concern us now, but these diseases are amongst us. Let us eradicate them. While it is distributed in both races, it is not working the havoc with the white race that it does in the Colored race, because first, being a primitive white man's disease, he has acquired more or less immunity against it."[28]

Another black physician, Charles Victor Roman, also criticized venereal disease rates among black soldiers as statistically inaccurate and "undoubtedly tinged with prejudiced" based on the testimony of black doctors within and outside the army ranks. Much like Williams, he believed that "higher incidence must be admitted" and active outreach by black and white physicians alike must be undertaken to spread the principles of social hygiene among the larger African American population.[29] In September 1918 the War Department appointed a prominent group of black surgeons and physicians—Roman chief among them—to mount a stateside campaign against venereal disease in and around the cantonments where black troops were stationed in significant numbers. While the bulk of these camps were located in the South, the War Department also stationed thousands of African American soldiers in the Midwest and Northeast in order to "prevent concentration of over-large contingents of colored soldiers at any one camp."[30] The "VD tours" gave African American health practitioners occasion to spread the gospel of social hygiene through lectures, educational pamphlets, and slide-projector presentations especially prepared to "meet the special needs" of even those troops who could not read.[31] Roman's bombastic appeals were reportedly heard by over 22,000 persons alone. His lectures couched Victorian codes of sexual morality into patriotic *cris de coeur*, imploring soldiers in Illinois, Georgia, and Virginia "to extend the influence of our flag and to widen the borders of freedom" while refraining from sexual activity.[32] The broad strokes of his rhetoric painted simple yet involved homilies of social hygiene that often employed crass comparisons between the intelligence of Man and the brute behavior of animals. "There are three ways by which we may use up our powers of life," Roman wrote. "We can use it [sic] up in thinking and thereby accomplish our aims and purposes in life. We may use it up in eating and become a glutton or a hog. We may join the donkey and the guinea pig and spend our life's energy in sexual dalliances."[33] Though imbued with free sexual will, Man faced the spiteful wrath of a feminized Nature who "set her stand [sic] of disapproval on sexual promiscuity by fixing venereal disease as penalty for prostitution."[34] Roman's personification of Nature as a sexual martinet subverted the germ theory of disease that had come to define the contemporary discourse of disease transmission, and imbued it with punitive and sinister intentionality. "The sexual act has but two purposes or places in an honorable life. It is a generative act and an expression of love. Sexual congress is the creator's high seal of approval upon the marriage vow. Sexual congress between people who do not love each other is brutal passion degrading human reason. Nature has made no provision for prostitution. Gonorrhea and syphilis are but expressions of her disgust."[35]

After showing his audience slides that demonstrated "what King Pox and Madame Clap have done for mankind," Roman concluded his lecture with a progressive nod toward the technocratic success of prophylaxis. "Remember those around the throne had on robes that were white not because they had never been soiled, but because they had been washed. If you fall in the ditch, call for help—apply for the prophylactic treatment."[36]

The prophylactic treatment promoted by black social hygienists in their stateside road shows was conceived and administered by two white American doctors who had left a necropolitical imprint on the regulation of black male sexuality during the war. In 1917, Hugh Hampton Young and George Walker, professors of urology at the Johns Hopkins Medical School, had joined the ranks of civilian doctors who actively sought and received commissions to serve as medical officers in the AEF. Many American doctors had been prompted to service by the lectures and speeches of Colonel T. H. Goodwin of the British Medical Army Corps, who called for "one thousand well-trained surgeons" to help shore up severe losses British doctors had taken at the front.[37] Young and Walker had taught at Johns Hopkins since before the turn of the century. Only a year apart in age, the late forty-something doctors were both well respected in the practice and research of genitourinary surgery. Young was from San Antonio, Texas, and Walker hailed from Yorkville, South Carolina. Both men traced their bloodlines through proud Confederate histories of resistance during the Civil War.[38] Each went on to have celebrated careers after World War I—particularly Young, who is regarded to this day as the "father" of modern American urology. As the first president of the American Association of Genito-Urinary Surgeons said of him, "the prostate makes most men old, but it made Hugh Hampton Young."[39]

Upon enlisting in the U.S. Army's Medical Corps, Young secured passage to France on the same steamer that ferried General John Pershing, commander-in-chief of the AEF, to the war zone. Young used his opportunity upon the S.S. *Baltic* to bend Pershing's ear—as well as those of his officers—toward the necessity of guarding against venereal disease throughout the war. As James G. Harbord would later write, "One of the new Medical officers [on the ship] was Hugh H. Young, a professor in Johns Hopkins, an authority on social diseases. He gave several rather terrifying lectures on his specialty."[40] The voyage aboard the *Baltic* with Pershing and his chiefs of staff provided Young with a unique opportunity to link his personal and professional concerns as a specialist in urinary diseases to the broader war effort, as he persuasively argued that a fight against venereal diseases had to be waged in order for America to win the war. "General Pershing sat in the front row, and at the end of the hour thanked me for 'a very interesting talk,'" Young wrote. "He said he considered venereal disease one of the most important problems confronting the Medical Corps, that he personally was greatly interested in the subject, and while in Mexico had adopted extraordinary measures to prevent venereal infection among his troops."[41] The measures Pershing alluded to (taken during his 1916 American expedition along and across the Mexican border to capture Pancho Villa) included a regulated system of military prostitution, whereby women were corralled into barbed-wire enclosures and were regularly inspected for venereal disease by one of Pershing's doctors. Though these measures were said to have drastically lowered the rate of disease acquisition among U.S. troops, Pershing would not officially sanction military prostitution during World War I. In fact, convinced in no small part by Young that social vices (via prostitution and the consumption of alcohol) were greatest causes of venereal infection, Pershing would eventually issue General Order 77, which placed brothels and bars off limits to all American soldiers in France.[42]

Young was not only an advocate of Pershing's quest to make the AEF "the cleanest Army in the world," he quickly became one of its primary architects. After reaching Europe he was appointed director of the Division of Urology, which placed him in charge of all urological and venereal disease work for the AEF. He undertook a comparative study of the venereal disease treatment programs of other Allied countries, criticized the French method of regulated prostitution as unhygienic, and adopted the New Zealand practice of giving condoms and "chemical prophylaxis" to soldiers for AEF-wide use.[43] Chemical prophylaxis was an experimental method of curtailing venereal infection after possible exposure through the direct application of chemical "preventives" on the genitalia. At special "prophylactic stations," solutions of 2 percent protargol or 10 percent argyrol (both silver compounds) were injected into the patient's penis through the urethra and held for five minutes; afterwards an ointment of calomel (mercury chloride) was rubbed over the external genitalia for three more minutes.

Based on his research, Young compiled a manual of military urology—the first of its kind for the AEF—which outlined the use of chemical prophylaxis among U.S. troops. He also requested that staff urologists trained in his methods be appointed to every division in France. A colleague from Johns Hopkins, George Walker, was placed in charge of the seaport bases, which had experienced a spike in venereal disease rates owing to the social proximity between shore-bound soldiers and French prostitutes.[44] Another strong proponent of chemical prophylaxis, Walker followed Young as Urologist-in-Chief for the AEF in early 1919, and would pen the definitive history of America's crusade against venereal disease in France, *Venereal Disease in the American Expeditionary Forces* (1922). Walker theorized that the administration of prophylaxis had both therapeutic and behavioral effects upon the sexual conduct of soldiers, writing that "much of the glamour and romance of illicit 'love' will be lost if men can be impressed with the necessity of prophylactic measures after each exposure. . . . For by so doing, the association of the act with disease—gonorrhea, syphilis, chancroid is established and once an idea such as that is planted, it is apt to grow and keep the individual constantly face to face with the sordid danger of venereal infection and all of the degradation and suffering it may cause not only him but to those who are dear to him."[45]

Walker's appeal to rationality by way of imbuing both sexual acts and prophylactic treatment itself with disease-related stigma substantiates Allan Brandt's argument that the fight against venereal disease in the AEF was a moment in which Progressives "looked to the instrumentalities of social engineering to insure the efficiency and order that the twentieth century required."[46] Having served as chairman of the Maryland Statewide Vice Commission before his military commission, Walker bridged the gap between military and civilian modes of public health.[47] He argued forcefully for the use of prophylaxis among the wider American population at war's end, believing that technology had brought the world closer to the complete eradication of venereal disease. "For what this science accomplished in war," he wrote, "it can accomplish in peace, and will accomplish if given a fair trial."[48]

As evidence of their technocratic victory over venereal disease during the war, Walker and Young cited the reduction of high rates of venereal disease among African American stevedores stationed at Saint-Nazaire, France, and later, in the port cities of Brest and Bordeaux, through the use of chemical prophylaxis. Saint-Nazaire was the first seaport base expropriated for American use during the war, and its medical officers were aware as early as October 1917 that its men were contracting high rates of venereal disease.

Impressed with what they had heard from the French Medical Corps about *réglementation de prostitution*, American medical officers in Saint-Nazaire drafted a "Proposal to Have Houses of Prostitution for the A.E.F.," a document that Young lampooned as "one of the most noted and amusing literary productions of the army." While never approved for official use during World War I, the document posed a number of questions concerning the successful regulation of bodies involved in the proposed sexual service, including whether women involved should contract their sexual labor via military or civilian agencies, how long their length of service would be, and what responsibility would befall the American military government in the case of temporary or permanent disability or death. Acknowledging the necropolitical use of women's bodies in the sexual service of American militarism, the proposal also asked whether there will be "any race distinction made among the applicants for service or will 'Jim Crow' principles be applied and receive official recognition?"[49]

Despite the rejection of this proposal, Jim Crow principles would find official recognition in the subsequent proposal to reduce the venereal disease rate among African Americans working as stevedores on the docks of Saint-Nazaire, whose off-duty activities were believed to include sexual encounters with French civilians. In evaluating the racial and sexual logics at play in crafting this proposal, it should be noted that Young was unabashed in his opposition to sexual congress between black men and white women. In his autobiography, he recalled a visit to the Ninety-Second ("American Negro") Division headquarters in Bourbonne-les-Bannes, where he met with its medical officers to discuss "venereal problem." To his surprise, he discovered that all the doctors, lieutenants, and captains were black. Young used this opportunity to make his thoughts about interracial sexuality known: "I talked very frankly about the unsurmountable [sic] barrier between the two races, the necessity of leaving white women alone, and their duty as officers to impress these facts upon their men. I heard afterwards that my remarks did little good and that most of these Negro doctors became engaged to French girls."[50]

In an exasperated tone, Young complained that "French women apparently had no aversion to colored troops, and the contacts of each Negro soldier were frequent."[51] Walker likewise found in his own investigation that large numbers of black soldiers "were slipping away every chance they got from their work on the docks to spend the night in the city" and that "under the cover of darkness, [they] got away and had intercourse with white women in adjacent fields and houses."[52] In response, Young recommended a number of measures, implemented in December 1917, which specifically restricted the movement of African American soldiers in the port city. A barbed-wire stockade was built around the stevedore camp, and guards were placed at the entrance, "affording complete control of the men themselves."[53] Whenever a soldier left the confines of the camp for any reason he was required to take a prophylactic treatment upon his return.[54] The effects of compulsory prophylaxis were "magical," according to Walker, "and gave results which were not dreamed possible":

> The records show that the rate fell from 625 per thousand to 110 per thousand! One organization of 1,800 men recorded only 2 cases in one month; whereas their former rate had been about 50.
>
> In Brest, the rate dropped from 480 to 48, and remained between 40 and 50.
>
> In Bordeaux, where it had been about 300, it was reduced to 60, and for seven weeks was even as low as 20 per thousand per year.
>
> Such brilliant success was due almost solely to compulsory prophylaxis, for the men were allowed to go out from 5:30 to 9:30 and do whatever they pleased.[55]

Young agreed, writing in his autobiography that compulsory prophylaxis had an "instantaneous" effect on the venereal rate, rapidly reducing it "until it was as good as or better than that of the white troops." He then followed this statement with an anecdote that hinted at the side effects compulsory prophylaxis had upon the genitalia of African American dockworkers, implying that the material gains made by this process of control did not come without pain for those involved:

> The colonel commanding one of these camps was approached by his Negro orderly, a regular who had been with him for some years. The orderly calmly announced that he wanted a change of station. Whereupon the colonel said: "Corporal, you've never had an easier job. I simply send you on errands, ten or fifteen within the camp, and perhaps fifteen or twenty outside the camp every day. You certainly can't object to such an easy job as this." "No, Colonel, the work ain't hard, and I don't mind how often you send me on errands inside the camp. It's them errands outside, because every time I comes back they takes me to the prophylactic station, and I'm getting awful sore."[56]

Young was known by his colleagues for his "off-color humor."[57] The joke he told within his memoirs — that the Negro orderly's penis was made sore from repeated injections of silver compounds into his urethra and the continuous application of mercury chloride upon his genitalia—made light of what was, in theory, an eugenicist mode of social control, and in practice, a systemized form of torture endured by black soldiers in France. Using humor, Young reified a belief that black men were immune from pain, intellectually inferior, and inured against instruction; as such, their regulation during the war required reiterative modes of punishment that sought to make their bodies remember what their minds could never be expected to comprehend.[58]

Young and Walker received considerable notoriety from their time spent overseas in the AEF. Inducted as majors, both men earned promotions to colonel by war's end. They both returned to Johns Hopkins as victors in the crusade against venereal disease, and Walker's book received a favorable review in the *British Medical Journal*, which asserted, "It is evident that much can be done both in the way of prevention and cure when men are under discipline and the medical officers capable and energetic."[59] Not to be outdone, Hugh Hampton Young achieved a success that endures till today. One of John Hopkins's most celebrated surgeons and researchers, Young is commonly referred to as the "father" of American urology due to the numerous innovations he made in the field, including research and surgery upon intersex people. This patriarchal designation arguably puts him in league with nineteenth-century surgeon J. Marion Sims, considered by some as the "father" of modern gynecology. But when we remember that Sims achieved fame—and contemporary infamy—for perfecting a treatment for vaginal fistulas through his experiments upon enslaved African American women, we might give pause to consider the ways in which the experimental use of black male soldiers in World War I merged modes of military and medical knowledge production in a successive modernity that also found the sexual bodies of black persons dependable objects of analysis.[60]

And yet, an important question remains: How effective *was* chemical prophylaxis? As the senior consultant in urology for the AEF, Walker conducted a study that compared two groups of venereal contacts. The first group had contracted syphilis, gonorrhea, or chancroid after using prophylaxis, and the second group had contracted one of these ailments without taking prophylaxis at all. Comparing the two groups, Walker found that the rates of acquisition of the three diseases were nearly the same.[61] In addition to the insignificant differences between the two sets of data, it should be noted that using chemical prophylaxis possibly increased the chances of contracting chancroid by 6 percent. Walker (and the subsequent AEF historians who would cite his study) would arrive at a different conclusion, however: "These relative proportions among men who had contracted venereal disease after using prophylaxis and among men who neglected to use prophylaxis being about the same, indicate that the prophylaxis as used by us in the American Expeditionary Forces was equally effective against the three diseases."[62]

While this study does not necessarily dispute claims made by American doctors that chemical prophylaxis was effective in treating sexual infections, it might compel us to consider additional reasons for the "magical" and "brilliant" success of reduced rates among African American soldiers in France. What seems most apparent is that the intense restriction of movement placed on black soldiers in port cities—complete with a punitive method of sexual control—limited the access those soldiers had to the sexual commerce the war engendered, in which venereal disease operated as one powerful sign or "receipt" of exchange. Adriane Lentz-Smith cites evidence of this restricted movement in an unpublished letter to *The Crisis* written by a sympathetic white captain in Bordeaux, who was astounded to learn his company of black stevedores had received only two days off in six weeks of dockwork—with those on the nightshift working up to fourteen hours without food.[63] Arthur Barbeau and Florette Henri also point to the fact that when military officials placed French brothels off limits to all American soldiers, the rate of venereal disease quickly fell for both black and white troops. Once the restrictions were lifted, the white rate began to climb again. However, because of the compulsory prophylaxis of black soldiers—which again, entailed not only mandatory treatment but also a restriction of movement—the black rate continued to drop until it hit a low incidence rate of 30 exposures per 1000.[64]

White army doctors who treated African American soldiers during the Great War were instrumental in institutionalizing the idea of the "Negro venereal" within medical and military discourse. They authorized their experiences and opinions in medical journals and at professional conferences once the war had officially ended and they were returned to their civilian lives. George H. Day, a physician who treated patients at Camp Pike (Arkansas) and Camp Alexander (Virginia), said at the seventy-first meeting of the American Medical Association in 1920, "It is my belief practically all negroes are venereals. Why this is true is quite easily understood. Furthermore, it is my belief that comparatively few are ever cured of venereal disease. When an occasional one is cured, he betakes himself to his usual haunts to become quickly reinfected. I am convinced that the majority of negroes do not respect the moral code or honor the sanctity of wedlock; so the endless chain of infection and reinfection goes merrily on."[65]

But now, a century removed from the statistics themselves, we might consider these venereal disease reports in slightly different terms. Draconian measures had been taken to discipline the bodies and desires of African American soldiers, making the medical apparatus of the U.S. military a vital mediator of the overlapping taxonomies of race, class, gender, and citizenship in the army. While the intersecting stigmas of race and sexuality gave credence to the belief in the black venereal body, we might also view increased venereal rates among black troops as acts of marronage, albeit less grand than Fagen's. Indeed, understood as "petit marronage," these disease acquisition rates might be understood as small escapes made against the ruling military orthodoxy as well as the politics of respectability espoused by African American leaders on the home front, who utilized the figure of the "clean black soldier" in order to secure citizenship rights for larger black community in the United States.

Protecting Black Manhood: Sex, Respectability, and Racial Consciousness

While the specific causes of lowered rates of venereal disease among African American soldiers in France during World War I remain historically uncertain, it is clear that those contracted figures gave rise to contrasting and competing interpretations within the American intellectual discourse of the day. In the United States, leaders of the African American professional class continued to ally themselves with the social hygiene movement in order to safeguard the health and morals of African American troops. Arthur B. Spingarn, white chairman of the NAACP and chairman of its legal committee, wrote articles in *The Crisis* as well as the *Journal of Social Hygiene* during his World War I service as a captain in the Sanitation Corps. He encouraged civilian organizations to partner with the War Department in repressing vice around army camps as "the prevalence of venereal disease in civil life, as shown by the drafts, has made it evident that civilian facilities and activities cannot be neglected without failing to protect the army."[66] In this regard African American periodicals served as important discursive outlets in offering a view of black soldiers as clean, courageous heroes in the war effort. War letters reprinted in black newspapers functioned as compelling pieces of positive racial propaganda that brought private missives between soldiers and their loved ones into public discourse. For example, Private Arthur E. Williams's account of a company inspection by General Pershing in France illustrates how racial pride could be produced through the rhetoric of social hygiene during the war. Upon finding out the "fine-looking bunch" hadn't had a case of venereal disease in six months abroad, Pershing showered praise upon those soldiers and shame upon the "white organizations" in camp that had not attained such a record.[67] "'That is certainly fine; a Colored organization, six months overseas, and not a case of venereal disease. I am proud of these men, and I am NOT proud of some of the white organization [sic] that have been in this camp, and I shall hold this company up as a model for the entire A.E.F.' Some class to that compliment, eh?"[68]

Perhaps no black periodical played a greater role in promulgating the trope of the morally and physically clean black soldier hero than *The Crisis*. Among the numerous causes Du Bois championed during the war, he was particularly concerned that the contributions and sacrifices made by African American soldiers in France would suffer historical erasure. Attendant to his goal of "fix[ing] in history the status of our Negro troops," Du Bois's editorial vision employed modes of racial hagiography that turned the figure of the African American soldier into an aspirational model of courage, sacrifice, cleanliness, and social critique.[69] The publication of Roscoe C. Jamison's poem "The Negro Soldiers" in the September 1917 issue of *The Crisis* announced the circumscribed archetype that would mark much of Du Bois's commentary during the Great War:

> These truly are the Brave,
> These men who cast aside
> Old memories, to walk the blood-stained pave
> Of Sacrifice, joining the solemn tide
> That moves away, to suffer and to die
> For Freedom—when their own is yet denied!
> O Pride! O Prejudice! When they pass by
> Hail them, the Brave, for you now crucified!

Considered "undeniably the finest contribution in verse to the Negro's participation in the war" by literary critic William Stanley Braithwaite, "Negro Soldiers," with its thematic mix of martial heroism and Christian imagery, derived much of its poignance through its depiction of black soldiers as martyrs. The poem was republished at least twice in *The Crisis*, ritualizing its message of sacrifice, and Du Bois continued to run features that depicted black soldiers as Christlike figures in uniform. He would also employ the rhetoric of sacrifice to underscore the link between heroism and hygiene. Du Bois used his November 1918 "Men of the Month" column as an opportunity to highlight the clean life and cleansing death of a teenage private killed in France. The brief memorial to Kenneth Lewis, "a clean, fine young man of only eighteen years," reprinted a letter of condolence from his battalion captain to his bereaved mother. "He lived up to my expectations in every way and conducted himself as a good, clean man and a soldier," the officer wrote, assuring the mother of her son's moral and physical purity. "What can his country do for such sacrifice?" Du Bois asked his reader. "It can make itself as clean and unselfish as he."[70]

The Crisis also published Florence Lewis's "A Negro Woman to Her Adopted Soldier Boy," in which Lewis employed the trope of the military matriarch in order to fabulate a penpal relationship between the speaker and an anonymous black soldier stationed in France. The narrator, who has never met the soldier, believes they share "a real kinship of the spirit—whose souls have met in an union which transcends that of flesh and blood."[71] Imploring her overseas soldier to "Cease thinking in persons, in races, in cities and countries" and to instead "Think in worlds," the spiritual "Mother" proclaims that the African American soldier's ability to endure insult and injury in relative anonymity makes him "the most heroic figure in this war." Seeing her soldier as a "super-man," the speaker then gives him advice on how best to protect his manhood while fighting in France:

> Let me repeat what I have so often written, my dear soldier. Your courage and strength are unassailable as long as you keep your Vision. Heads up and eyes straight forward is required spiritually as well as physically in a true soldier. Let no happening distract you from the great thing to which you are called. When you have wiped out error in one shape, other forms of it will fade away. Such is the contagion of Good. Try to make those friends of yours get this higher view and you will be helping them to a greater happiness and a higher manhood.[72]

The presence of African American women as matriarchs in France was rare, but two clubwomen followed in the footsteps of trailblazers like Namah Curtis and Ada Young to lead relief efforts and health outreach among African American soldiers overseas. Addie Waites Hunton and Kathryn Magnolia Johnson were two of only nineteen African American women selected to perform YMCA camp service in France, and detailed their experiences in their memoir *Two Colored Women with the American Expeditionary Forces*. Over 380,000 African American soldiers were stationed in France during World War I, and at times the ratio of black soldiers to black female YMCA workers ran two hundred thousand to three.[73] Hunton and Johnson, clubwomen from New York and Ohio, respectively, served as surrogate "mothers, sisters, and friends" for the "thousands of men" funneled through the seaport bases during and after the war, and bore witness to the waxing and waning morale of black men in camp.[74]

Here, it is helpful to consider historian Chad Williams's notion of a "mobilized diaspora" in theorizing the transformation of racial and sexual consciousness experienced by black military workers in World War I. By considering the mobilization of people, material, and ideas marshaled in the conflict, a broader historical understanding of how militarism contributed to the production of the modern African diaspora is gained. "The war set millions of descendant Africans in motion through the demands of combat and labor," Williams writes, "bringing them into contact with one another and fundamentally transforming the demographic, ideological, and imaginative contours of the diaspora."[75] As female witnesses and participants in this circulation, Addie Hunton and Kathryn Johnson recounted seeing French colonial troops, Chinese laborers, and injured French soldiers upon their arrival at Bordeaux, and had a particular reaction to the sight of African American soldiers guarding German prisoners. "Somehow we felt that colored soldiers found it rather refreshing—even enjoyable for a change—having come from a country where it seemed everybody's business to guard them."[76]

While primarily tasked to help keep up the morale of homesick soldiers (which often involved letter writing and teaching literacy skills), the women, under YMCA sponsorship, also worked "to promote clean morals among the men, by the free distribution of booklets, tracts, and wholesome pictures."[77] They organized Sunday evening "Quiet Hours" in which they "spoke to the boys and urged them to keep themselves clean for the sake of the good women back home."[78] Serving lemonade, hot chocolate, macaroons, and cake in the YMCA canteens, Hunton and Johnson became convinced of the sexual continence of the African American soldiers they encountered in France. "Because they talked first and talked last of their women back home, usually with glory upon their faces," they wrote, "we learned to know that colored men loved their own women as they could love no other women in the world."[79] One night the women recollected watching a news reel of a Red Cross parade on Fifth Avenue in New York City. When a group of uniformed black women were shown marching on the screen, "the men went wild. They did not want that particular scene to pass and many approached and fondled the screen with the remark, 'just look at them.'" Sometimes black soldiers would come up to Hunton and Johnson for no other reason than to stare at them. "Lady," one fellow said, "I just want to look at you, if you charge anything for it I'll pay you—it takes me home." Looking into the eyes of black men, the women had all the evidence they needed to reject the claims of higher venereal rates among African American troops, and, the even more unmentionable charge, that they had developed a sexual taste in white women. "Hundreds of incidents gave evidence of the love of these men for their women," they wrote, and connected this transnational longing for black heteronormative affection to the birth of a new racial consciousness: "We learned to know that there was being developed in France a racial consciousness and racial strength that could not have been gained in a half century of normal living in America. Over the canteen in France we learned to know that our young manhood was the natural and rightful guardian of our struggling race. Learning all this and more, we also learned to love our men better than ever before."[80]

The production of new understandings of race and identity fostered in the crucible of modern warfare might be thought of as an unexpected by-product of America's military engagements abroad. Moreover, while warfare and white supremacist rule clearly had an irrevocable impact on how African American soldiers understood themselves in relation to the world, it should be remembered, as Adriane Lentz-Smith rightly reminds us, that "black soldiers in World War I shaped their understanding of manhood in relation to the ideas and activism of black women, through the expectations of the civilian community, and through interactions with foreigners."[81] For Hunton and Johnson, the YMCA canteens run by black women provided spaces for black soldiers not only to take respite and find repose, but also to reimagine and renegotiate the meanings of race and nation outside of America. These were also sites in which the politics of racemaking cohered with an attendant politics of sexual respectability. Black female YMCA workers—often by their very presence in camp—served as reminders of the African American world the soldiers had left behind. While seeking to assure their readers that "colored men loved their own women as they could love no other women in all the world," Hunton and Johnson believed that keeping soldiers occupied with in-camp activities was the best way of steering them clear of the sexual economy that lay just outside the gates. "The Armies of the Allies had won the war," they wrote, "but there was a moral conflict for the war-weary men hardly less subtle and deadly in its effects than the conflict just ended."[82] Hunton and Johnson's concern over the sexual proclivities of African American occupation troops underscored the importance that sexual propriety played in the larger project of racial uplift championed by leaders of the black professional class during World War I. It also demonstrated that the racial consciousness reportedly manifested by African American soldiers over

French canteens had been accompanied by a new and potentially dangerous sexual curiosity.

Dangerous Pleasures: Petit Marronage, Venereal Disease, and Community Stigma

The fear that sex with French women might change the sexual identities and thus the moral constitutions of American troops abroad was not limited to African American race men and women. This anxiety also effected larger efforts made by the YMCA and the AEF to dissuade any sexual contact from happening between American troops and foreign women in the first place. Hunton and Johnson would have no doubt been aware of the great lengths to which their white colleague, Elizabeth Bain, had gone in an attempt to keep "the chippies" away from American soldiers. Over a six-week period, and between the hours of 8 P.M. and 2 A.M., Bain approached some 2,700 American soldiers seen with "street women" along the Grand Boulevard in Paris, and convinced more than a third of them to part ways with their overnight paramours.[83] George Walker endorsed Bain's methods in his record of venereal disease in the AEF, though he admitted "it naturally required a woman of great deal of tact and a peculiar personality to carry it out."[84] As it turned out, stemming female prostitution as the primary source of sexual contagion among U.S. troops was only one of his objectives in France. In his book, Walker also found time to comment upon the role he believed French prostitutes played in the "transmission" of sexual practices presumably unknown to American soldiers. During his time as Urologist-in-Chief of the AEF, he came upon evidence of what he termed "abnormal or perverted relations" occurring between French prostitutes and American troops, with *perversity* referring to the practice of oral sex. "[W]hatever the origin of the twisted impulse," he wrote, "it creates but one effect, a subtle state of demoralization that is far more dangerous to society as it is at present constructed, at least from the Anglo-Saxon viewpoint, than mere immorality could ever be."[85]

Tucked away in the penultimate chapter of Walker's larger venereal study of the sex life of the army abroad are the results of 237 interviews conducted with women in France—most of whom were considered prostitutes—that tended to affirm the American soldier's "new" affinity for fellatio.[86] While the American soldier was "no namby-pamby individual when he arrived in Europe," he was in Walker's estimation largely ignorant of the "sad knowledge of the scope and diversity of Nature's vagaries where the human mechanism is concerned."[87] Moving beyond a concern for disease transmission, the Johns Hopkins trained physician believed fellatio—in its practice and reception—threatened the fabric of American manhood. The sexual pleasure it produced, divorced as it was from the act of conception, fit the definition of perversity coined by Richard Krafft-Ebing, who was wont to differentiate between vice (which was understood as perversity) and disease (which was understood as perversion) in his book *Psychopathia Sexualis*.[88] The knowledge of fellatio had wound its way into the American trenches, however, and threatened to produce an affective shift in American sexual mores once the doughboys returned home. "When one thinks of the hundreds and hundreds of thousands of young men who have returned to the United States with these new and degenerate ideas sapping their sources of self-respect and thereby lessening their powers of moral resistance," Walker wrote, "one indeed is justified in becoming alarmed."[89]

Walker did have a point. His idea that oral sex might change the sexual behaviors of American troops, and thus transform the sexual script of American culture, has been pursued by sexual moralists like himself as well as less reform-minded commentators. Notwithstanding his unintentionally droll tone, his impassioned harp against fellatio belied the eroticism evinced in his own chronicle of how this particular sexual practice dared to impinge on the sexual identities of the hundreds of thousands of young men returning stateside from France. He culled seventeen interviews from the 237 he received, and allowed nineteen women to speak generally about the American soldier's fondness for fellatio while also offering post–World War readers a window onto an international zone of sexual contact replete with players and names. Apparently working some of the same street corners as Elizabeth Bain, Walker's anonymous interviewer—chosen especially for this "disagreeable and delicate task"—catalogued both the bodies and the responses of women he met in the public spaces of Paris, Bordeaux, Grenoble, Nantes, and Saint-Nazaire.[90] He introduced America to the plainly dressed yet very pretty "Pierette," who said "that Americans were very different from French when they first landed, but now they have changed, for they have been to school in France, to the school of love, and have learned to make love . . . like the French."[91] The short, plump, and blond "Raymonde" seized the interviewer's arm and "offered to make love in any way I liked. Said if I wouldn't go with her I could go with her friend, or the three [of us] would make love together."[92] The good-looking "Henriette" walked two blocks with the interviewer, telling him she was "walking to seek my fortune in the light of the moon." He responded that "that was a very poetical way of putting it," and she answered back that she was, indeed, a poet.[93] Juliette and Andree, a pair of very dark and good-looking sisters of Algerian extraction, were thought of as "unusually educated" in that they spoke French, Italian, and Spanish. "They were in love with Americans and were going to America as soon as possible. They said they practiced perversion a little. They begged me to indulge with them."[94] Few were as decisive in their opinions as slender Marie from Nantes, who sat alone at a café before being solicited by the interviewer. Marie had known many Americans from the time they had first landed. "They are all perverts," she said, offering a contradictory assessment of from whence the soldiers learned their "new" sexual knowledge.

The fear that "perversion" would end the American republic as George Walker knew it is not my primary concern here; though to be sure, linguist D. W. Maurer argues convincingly that American sexual discourse did change upon the return of U.S. soldiers from France after World War I. Maurer found that "all varieties of oral sex were thought of as French and were so named. French became an adjective, a noun, an adverb, and a transitive verb. All French women were believed to be uncontrollably erotic; French novels were known to be saturated with raw sex, and anyone saying a taboo word or phrase was likely to preface it with, 'excuse my French but. . . .'"[95]

The shift in American discourse that saw "French" become a marker for all manner of modern erotica read France (and particularly its city of light, Paris) as a recurrent site of possibility, pleasure, and desire. Likewise, as it gained a foreign affect upon its publicization within the American social sphere, the blowjob became symbolic of the new lingua franca American soldiers had picked up abroad. Writer Christopher Hitchens, delivering his own take on the popularity of fellatio within American culture, argued that the "idea" of the blowjob was "re-exported" to Europe and beyond by way of American global military engagement. Its preference as the "beau ideal" of American soldiers lay in two interrelated functions. "It was a good and simple idea in itself. It was valued—not always correctly—as an insurance against the pox. And—this is my speculation—it put the occupied *and* the allied populations in their place. '*You* do some work for a change, sister. I've had a hard time getting here.'"[96]

In Hitchens's formulation, fellatio became a shared performance of gender and nation, power and place in the new imperial order of things; and had become, as the title of his essay suggested, "as American as apple pie." What Walker believed to be a danger to Anglo-Saxon society was revised by Hitchens as a right of American military occupation, a just—if unequal—exchange for services rendered in the line of overseas duty. My interest lies, however, not in the veracity of these opposing origin stories of oral sex in the twentieth century, but rather what these stories intimate about the official observation that American soldiers—and black men in particular—were being irrevocably altered by their time in France. Whether demonized as licentiousness or celebrated as liberation, sexual freedom was perceived as a threat to progressive notions of manhood as well as the fixity of the color line. Sexuality became a site of struggle, negotiation, and agency, and its institutional acknowledgment by army officials produced modes of control that also created possibilities for self-determination. As such, the affective shift in American sexuality that is alternatively feared and lauded by these commentators in their appraisal of a sexual practice must be located in relation to, and seen as constitutive of, the coeval shifts of gender, race, and class wrought by world war. Moreover, I would also suggest that this discourse of pleasure and danger cannot be fully comprehended without including the perspectives of African American soldiers themselves, whose narratives of sexual expression and racist control complicate the stories we tell about the sex life of the American military in France.

In this regard I turn now to the autobiography of Elisha "Ely" Green, a self-described "half-white bastard" who served as a noncommissioned officer in charge of other African American stevedores in France. Green notes with clarity that the stigmatization of black sexuality by military officials began long before they set sail for Europe. Born in Sewanee, Tennessee, to a black mother and a white father, Green joined the military convinced that fighting in the war was the only way black men could attain manhood, "instead of being a nigger or a Negro to American soil."[97] While waiting to embark for France at Camp Stuart, Virginia, the red-headed recruit and his barrack mates received a visit from a chaplain who gave them a physical demonstration on the evils of venereal disease. "The Chaplain came bringing with him three venereal subjects that had been in France and made a show of them. Then he advised us not to indulge in sex relation with the white woman of France. This will be your reward. Like these men. I had no idea that this was the beginning of a segregation move that would confront us when in France."[98]

Proving at the very least that war has many theaters of engagement, the chaplain's venereal show cast the white women of France as conduits of venereal disease, and the three men on display as hapless victims of their own immoral desires. While Green is does not specifically racialize the "venereal subjects," the point can be made that the spectacular use of American soldiers disfigured by sexually transmitted infections in this modern morality play gestures toward longer traditions of the use of conscripted black bodies to confirm and maintain hegemonic understandings of race, gender, and sexuality—both in the aforementioned cases of Sims's experimentees and in the life and labor of Sarah "Saartjie" Baartman, otherwise identified in the historical record as the "Hottentot Venus."[99] Green's response to this performance is striking in that he, as spectator, actively refuses the hail of pathology—on the contrary, he clearly reads this display of "venereal subjects" as a racist ploy to stop black soldiers from having sex with white French women.

Still, Green was caught within the ambivalent space generated by his own subalternity. As an African American noncommissioned officer, he was in charge of a number of longshoremen in Saint-Nazaire, working the same docks that had been placed under venereal quarantine by Walker and Hampton Young. Offering an important counternarrative to their official medical histories, Green was witness to the intense racial and sexual restrictions placed upon himself and the men under his supervision, yet was also responsible for making sure his men received prophylactic treatments after the rare occasions on which they received liberty passes.[100] His authority, dispersed as it was through a segregated and white supremacist army, was far from autonomous. Green was both a subject and an agent of American military power, and vocally criticized the very policies he was tasked to implement. In so doing, he articulated and practiced a politics of survival. In one instance, after a "tall mulatto" sergeant shot and killed a black soldier over a loaf of bread, Green gave an impassioned speech in order to quell a riot brewing among his men. Recognizing that while most of the white American fighting force was armed with guns, "all we have are cargo hooks. . . . To survive we are going to respect all the laws that [are] forced upon us."[101] He offered to fight any man who disagreed with his orders rather than report them to the "brutish wolves" in the military police, whose white Northerners regularly beat and tortured black soldiers in the guardhouse. Neither choice would change his belief that they were "just slaves here." Occupying the interstitial role of foreman, Green elaborated the infrastructural obstacles his men had to navigate in order to survive their tours of duty in France. "We have one street in all of St. Nazaire and one block that we can walk. We are guarded to work, and from, and while we work and sleep. These white people have formed a [traditional] program over we Southern Negros so as to keep us in control. So when we go back home we will be under perfect control. Now you can see why I say I am from now on fighting for survival."[102]

Green's caution was founded in his knowledge that a number of race riots had broken out stateside during the war, and black soldiers participating in the skirmishes had received disproportionate and retributive sentences. The most notorious example of this occurred in Houston, Texas, in the summer of 1917, when a riot between armed black soldiers and white policemen and armed civilians led to the execution of thirteen of the soldiers.[103] In this context, it is significant that only a sentence later in his plea Green makes an explicit link between the struggle for survival as black men in a racist army abroad and his concern for the sexual health of the men under his command. "Please remember this. Any time I find a man suffering from venereal disease I [will] report you, so God help me, because of your health and our family back home."[104]

That the death of a man over a loaf of bread should serve as catalyst for a discussion about community survival and sexual health demonstrates the intersections between sex, race, and power at play in Saint-Nazaire. Green's promise to refer VD-infected soldiers for treatment differs in intent, I would suggest, from the many examples that have been covered in my analysis thus far. In the private discourse engendered through an unjust act indicative of the brutality of military conscription, Green differentiated between the need for sexual continence (as advocated by black and white hygienists alike) and the debilitating impact of social stigma that might lead a soldier to hide his medical condition by appealing to their shared need to survive. Pershing's crusade against venereal disease politicized infection rates at all levels of the AEF hierarchy, in that a total unit's performance could be rewarded or penalized based upon their incident rates. Thus individual actions carried larger ramifications, making every soldier's sexual choices potentially reflective of their entire unit's welfare and morale. Green described an inspection given to his men by their new commander, a white first lieutenant who was proud of his clean record. "No doubt you have [the] cleanest record of any Co. in the entire A.E.F.," the lieutenant said, and told the men their common goal was to make it back to the U.S. to see their "Lucy" free of venereal disease. "We are all going to see Lucy together. The only ones that we will leave here are those who goes on pass and don't pursue the prophalactic [sic] treatment and finds himself with a pencil with no lead in it. Venerel [sic] disease is the only thing that will rob you of pencil writing. Of course Lucy wouldn't want it if it didn't write."[105]

After the speech, the commander significantly relaxed the restrictions the company had worked and lived under during their time in Saint-Nazaire. By having white officers to vouch for the authenticity of their claims, as well as utilizing the same kinds of statistics medical men George Walker and Hugh Young championed as proof of America's technocratic victory over the black venereal body, African American soldiers also employed the archetype of the clean, black soldier to gain political redress within a racist system of military control. Redress in the immediate sense was measured in the relaxing of rules confining the movement of African American soldiers to the routes between base camps and work sites, allowing them temporary access to the economies of pleasure engendered by the war. Green provided a rare glimpse of African American soldiers' engagement with this economy during World War I, and highlighted the problematics and possibilities contained therein. After weeks of continuous hard labor on the docks and shipyards of Saint-Nazaire, Green and his men were given a liberty pass to explore the nightlife of France. There was only one block of bars that had been made available to African American soldiers, and as Green approached one such "honky-tonk," a large white woman stood at the door shaking a club, yelling: "Blanco, allee tout suite" (White man, go away).[106] It was not until Green's men convinced the woman that, in spite of his fair skin, their sergeant was indeed a black man that she relented and quickly invited them into her establishment. Pushing Green across the dance floor and to the bar, "Big Mama with the Meat Shaking on the Bones" began to speak fluent English. She told Green all his drinks were on the house, and that she only spoke French to white American soldiers so she could feign ignorance at their English-based request to enter her bar.

Green was accompanied by over twenty men, and as their sergeant, he held on to everyone's money. After he doled out five hundred dollars to his soldiers, Big Mama asked him how long they would be on pass, as she had only six girls in the place. Learning they were on liberty for six hours, she hurriedly left her club and came back with "beaucoup Mademoiselles"—twenty-five at Green's estimate—who wore short dresses and had "ribbon laced legs." Green wrote that "Many of these men hadn't as much as shaken hands with a white woman, not to think of being entertained by one," and thus were quite shy. After consulting with Big Mama briefly, the women approached the men and asked them to dance, and "the party was on. Soon quick lunches were brought in. The girls were drinking champagne."[107] While Green never explicitly says that Big Mama's honky-tonk was not only a bar and club but also a brothel, all signs point toward its having being utilized as such. Green took his men to Big Mama's place once a week for six weeks, making sure to usher them out and back to camp by their eight o'clock curfew. At the very least it is clear that there was a monetary exchange for goods and services rendered inside the honky-tonk.

I should state here that my project has no stake in romanticizing sex work—particularly the modes of sexual labor that are generated in the wake of military conflict. Feminist theory and practice have shown that militarism affects different bodies differently, and contemporary scholars—led in large part by political theorist Cynthia Enloe's corpus of work—have endeavored to show the differential effects this power has had upon women's lives. With this very much in mind, I would nevertheless also suggest that, following theoretical cues set by Samuel R. Delany in his discussion of the sexual culture of the Times Square movie houses in the 1970s and 1980s, and by Robin D. G. Kelley in his treatment of black working class "spaces of pleasure" in the early to mid-twentieth century, we read the problematics and the pleasures arrived at in Big Mama's brothel as carrying the possibility of interclass, interracial, and international contact—perhaps even solidarity—as negotiated within a militarized discourse of pleasure and danger.[108] Like the YMCA canteens, Big Mama's brothel also allowed African American soldiers to renegotiate meanings of race and nation outside of the United States—and I would add that it helped produce the figure of the African American soldier as both a desiring and *desirable* subject in the international arena. Both black money and black bodies had purchase within these economies of pleasure, and despite a lack of archival evidence to attest to all the details of what happened within the honky-tonks, a broad understanding of what constitutes "sex" allows us to code under that rubric what we do know to have occurred in those contact zones, among those shy soldiers and the ribbon-laced Frenchwomen, between those quick lunches and champagne. If segregation produced "congregation" for southern blacks, as argued by historian Earl Lewis, then we might imagine both the limits and possibilities made available to African American soldiers frequenting the racially segregated spaces of the French honky-tonk, where white soldiers were kept away both by guile and by military rule of law, and where black bodies might be celebrated as "instruments of pleasure" rather than "instruments of labor."[109]

Given that such practices of marronage were self-consciously designed to elude the materiality of the archive, it is important to reflect upon the role music would have played in these social gatherings, both for its use as a social lubricant in the interactions between French prostitutes and African American soldiers and for its function as a medium through which soldiers could participate in the ongoing, transnational processes of black cultural production. Importantly, music invited a kind of "open source" appropriation that often flouted the boundaries of race, class, and nation, a phenomenon made evident in the fact that the white English proprietor of the establishment frequented by Green's men derived her name from a popular American blues song of the day whose singer proclaimed:

I'm a big fat mama, got the meat shakin' on my bones
I'm a big fat mama, got the meat shakin' on my bones
And every time I shake, some skinny gal loses her home[110]

Green's memoir might lead us to presume that the blues was the primary kind of music played and appreciated in the French brothels catering to African American soldiers. Yet the multitude of black musical styles in development in the early twentieth century—which were enriched and diversified by differences of region, class, and technique—make any assumption premature. Narratives written by African American musicians during this period attest to the influence that prostitutes had upon the music played in their places of work. W. C. Handy, writing of his stint playing in a red-light district called the "New World" in Clarksdale, Mississippi, mentions that "these rouge-tinted girls, wearing silk stockings and short skirts, bobbing their soft hair and smoking cigarets [sic] in that prime era, long before these styles had gained respectability, were among the best patrons the orchestra had."[111] Ferdinand Joseph "Jelly Roll" Morton cut his musical teeth playing piano in the notorious red-light district of Storyville in New Orleans. According to his contemporary, trumpeter Buck Johnson, Morton played music that "the whores liked."[112] And that music was ragtime.

Let the Rhythm Hit 'Em: Music, Mobility, and Metaphors of Contagion

Writing in his influential work of jazz criticism, *Blues People: Negro Music in White America* (1963), Amiri Baraka (LeRoi Jones) described ragtime as a commercially viable and hybridized American musical product formed through a series of abstractions and appropriations, akin to "the picture within a picture within a picture, and so on, on the cereal package."[113] Situating it as a pre-jazz music popularized by African American musicians working in the northern United States, Baraka argued that ragtime developed from a "paradox of minstrelsy insofar as it was a music that the Negro came to in imitating white imitations of Negro music."[114] He wrote:

> Ragtime was a Negro music, resulting from the Negro's appropriation of white piano techniques used in show music. Popularized ragtime, which flooded the country with songsheets in the first decade of this century, was a dilution of the Negro style. And finally, the show and "society" music the Negros in the pre-blues North made was a kind of bouncy, essentially vapid appropriation of the popularized imitations

of Negro imitations of white minstrel music, which, as I mentioned earlier, came from white parodies of Negro life and music. And then we can go back even further to the initial "steal" American Negro music based on, that is, those initial uses Euro-American music was put to by the Afro-American. The hopelessly interwoven fabric of American life where blacks and whites pass so quickly as to become only grays![115]

Baraka's disdain for ragtime as an inauthentic mode of black cultural expression and more of an amalgam of interpretations by black and white musicians is frequently expressed in his text. As a "composed music" it had more in common with European, "legitimate" modes of performance than "the vocal origins of Negro music" he held in high esteem.[116] Baraka's critique was no doubt influenced by the culture of exploitation that emerged in the age of the mechanical reproduction of music (first via transcription and later by phonographic pressing), which served to enrich the coffers of white producers and distributors of the blues, Dixieland, and jazz, while the African American originators and innovators of these forms rarely shared in their profits. Despite his strong criticism of ragtime, however, he could not deny its popularity, and cited its historic rise as a cautionary tale against black artists engaging in cross-cultural appropriation. "I mention ragtime here because it seems to me important to consider what kind of music resulted when the Negro abandoned too much of his own musical tradition in favor of a more formalized, less spontaneous concept of music. The result was a pitiful popular debasement that was the rage of the country for almost twenty years."[117]

Among the artists Baraka held responsible for ragtime's twenty-year reign was James Reese Europe, who, as a lieutenant in the 369th Infantry Regiment, was credited with bringing its infectious melody to France. Born in 1880 in Mobile, Alabama, Europe moved to New York City at the turn of the century to study music and to become a professional musician.[118] By 1910 he had gained considerable acclaim as the first president and conductor of the Clef Club, an organization of African American musicians, singers, and dancers. The first of its kind in New York City, the Clef Club's 125-piece orchestra became the first group of African American musicians to play Carnegie Hall in 1912. The Clef Club also had an economic function in that it served as a way for African American musicians to network and find paying gigs, often through the white patrons of New York's hotels and cafes.[119] Europe became quite successful as a band leader, so successful in fact that his friend and colleague Noble Sissle was genuinely shocked when he told him he had had joined the Fifteenth New York National Guard Regiment in September 1916. Over Sissle's protests that there was too much work to be done managing his musicians, Europe urged Sissle to enlist as well, arguing that service in the National Guard would provide them with a rare opportunity to enhance their race and class statuses in Harlem. Due to the "clannish" nature of New York City, and the fact that they, as musicians, worked mostly at night, Europe thought they had little chance of meeting influential members of the city's elite. Explaining to Sissle "that our race will never amount anything, politically or economically, in New York or anywhere else unless there are strong organizations of men who stand for something in the community," Europe felt enlisting in the war effort in the early going was an important way for African American men to marshal economic and political power—political immunity—to be used to serve the greater black community in Harlem. "Now," he said, "some of the most influential men of our race, in Harlem, are going to join this regiment, as they realize the moral effect it will have, being promoted, financially, by the biggest men on Wall Street. It will eventually mean a big Armory where the young men can have healthful exercise, swimming pools, and athletic training, and it will build up the moral and physical negro manhood of Harlem."[120]

After convincing Sissle to enlist, Europe was approached by his regiment's white commander, Colonel William Hayward, who wanted him to develop and lead a regimental band. Europe then set out assembling what he hoped would be "the Best Military Band in the World."[121] With plans to increase the standard size of the military band from twenty-eight players to forty-four or more, he worked diligently to recruit musicians to serve in the regiment. In addition to taking out advertisements in national black newspapers, Europe traveled to Puerto Rico specifically to recruit woodwind players (since he thought there were few great black reed instrumentalists in New York) and brought thirteen musicians back with him to enlist in the New York National Guard.[122]

On December 13, 1917, Lieutenant Europe, Private Sissle, and the rest of the Fifteenth Regiment sailed to France on the U.S.S. *Pocahontas* transport ship. Writing in his unpublished biography of James Europe, Sissle described the journey across the Atlantic in ways that illuminate Paul Gilroy's theorization of ships as "microsystems of linguistic and political hybridity" as well as "distinct mode[s] of cultural production."[123] Military hierarchy maintained that lower-ranking men sailed in the bottom ship holds, while officers stayed in quarters closer to the surface. This structure effectively compartmentalized

African American performance practices and musical traditions by rank and class. Sissle noted that men on deck often "[cast] longing glances to the west—homeward." Yet when he made inspections "way down in the lowest hold, below the water line," he encountered a "chorus of voices singing with all the religious [sic] of a Georgia Camp Meeting." Their plaintive renditions of spirituals such as "Steal Away, Jesus" swept "from one side of the hold to another" and resonated up through the hatchways, their disembodied voices invoking the experiential conditions of the Middle Passage transatlantic slave ship journey.[124] On the upper deck of the ship, officers in the first- and second-class cabins sat in the dining salon in complete darkness, and listened to Lieutenant Europe improvise at the piano. Sissle's description of the scene links the rhythm of Europe's piano playing to the motion of the *Pocahontas* crossing the Atlantic, with both his melody and the ship's movement cloaked in darkness so as to not betray their position to German U-boats patrolling the depths: "The rhythm was as steady as the rise and fall of the Pocohantas [sic] as she rolled over the sea. Weird and blue were his melodious modulations as he would extemporize and weave from key to key, reflecting his wandering thoughts into wandering themes—like a ship without a rudder—finally, when he was able to get his, what seem to be unmanageable emotions under control, he would suddenly and softly strike a chord and request the quartette to sing a certain number."[125]

The "weird and blue" extemporaneous song that emanated from Europe's piano, played upon the deck of a ship whose insides echoed with the sounds of African American spirituals, transfigured the *Pocahontas* into a chronotope (to employ Gilroy's theoretical model) for the very blues tradition Baraka worked so diligently to historicize; a tradition he, ironically, took great pains to exclude Europe from.[126] Through Sissle's narration, the *Pocahontas* became a "blues" ship, transformed through its transportation of a "blues people" away from the only land many of them had ever known as home, and whose base of black suffering impinged upon the superstructural production of African American culture abroad.

The *Pocahontas* reached the port of Brest on New Year's Day in 1918, making the Fifteenth Regiment the first African American combat unit to set foot in France. Welcomed at the port by French soldiers and sailors, Lieutenant Europe and his band disembarked from their ship and responded in kind with a syncopated rendition of their allies' national anthem, "La Marseillaise." Emblematic of the amalgamated mode of production that rankled Baraka, the "ragged" version of the anthem was not immediately discernible to the assembled crowd. Yet upon recognizing the altered arrangement of the European march, "there came over their faces an astonished look, quickly alert snap-into-it-attention and salute by every French soldier and sailor present."[127] If we consider the port of Brest as a "contact zone," a modern "space of colonial encounter, the space in which peoples geographically and historically separated come into contact with each other and establish ongoing relations, usually involving conditions of coercion, radical inequality, and intractable conflict," then we might better understand Europe's musical arrangements as one of the originary sounds of the contact zone created by and through American militarism in the twentieth century.[128] The arrival of the blues ship *Pocahontas*—and particularly the blues men who emerged from her hull to play for those French crowds on January 1, 1918—announced a significant expansion of the instrumental use of soldiers of color during the war. Europe and his men would soon find themselves in the roles of musical emissaries, becoming the representative sight and sound of the American military abroad.

Ironically, it took two white veterans of the American stage to convince military officials in France that the Hellfighters should tour throughout the military theater. Actor E. H. Sothern and theater director Winthrop Ames had been sent by the YMCA to "see exactly what amusement the boys in khaki wanted" and witnessed Europe's band perform.[129] Ames was particularly impressed with their performance, writing: "no sooner had they begun to play than it became obvious that we were not listening to the ordinary army band at all, but to an organization of the very highest quality, trained and led by a conductor of genius."[130] Ames and Southern recommended to General Pershing that the Fifteenth Regimental Band perform at the opening of a winter resort in Aix-les-Bains requisitioned by American troops as a recreational leave area. On February 10 the band received its orders and soon began its journey through the French theater in route to Aix-les-Bains.[131] The band found itself playing for the French and American audiences it encountered along the way, making the three-day trip to the rest station a tour in itself. As documented by Arthur Little, the white battalion commander of the 369th, the Hellfighters played a private concert for an American general at his chateau in Tours. While appreciating the band for its musical excellence, the general underscored the diplomatic importance of their mission: "He explained that where we were going, no American soldiers had as yet been; that, according to the impression left by us upon the minds of the French population of the great territory through which we were to pass, so would rest the reputation of American soldiers in general." France had no color line, the general said, and begged the men not to be the cause of one, as their mission held strategic importance beyond mere entertainment. "He told the men that they were not merely musicians and soldiers of the American Army but that they were representatives of the American nation. The eyes of France would be upon them; and through the eyes of France, the eyes of the world."[132]

The privileged movement that the Hellfighters enjoyed in France was secured in no small part due to the low rates of venereal disease among their men, a fact which positively impacted their chance of being one of the few African American regiments to see time at the front during World War I. In helping draft a letter to Pershing requesting combat troop status for the 369th, Little made sure to mention that the Hellfighters hadn't had a case of venereal disease in three months.[133] We might rightly begin to understand the role played by these African American and Puerto Rican musicians in France as providing the originating archetypes of the "jazz ambassadors" who would tour many parts of the Western and non-Western world during the height of the Cold War, and whose contradictory experiences of modernity overlapped with those encountered by Europe and his band members more than thirty years before. As chronicled by historian Penny Von Eschen, the State Department–sponsored tours, which employed jazz luminaries such as Louis Armstrong, Duke Ellington, and Dizzy Gillespie, were meant to project an image of America as freedom-loving, democratic, and antiracist, despite the fact that the lives of the black artists involved "had been molded amid the quotidian terror and humiliating constraints of segregation."[134] The Hellfighters band would, indeed, have the "eyes of the world" trained upon them during their time in France; yet in the tradition of black transatlantic performance practices articulated by Daphne Brooks, Europe and his men would use this rare opportunity to fracture the relationship between spectator and performer by *looking back*. Following Von Eschen's suggestive reading of Ralph Ellison's *Invisible Man* in her theorization of the significance of the State Department tours on mid-century jazz historiography, we might say the that the Hellfighters "slipped into the breaks" afforded by their French tours and effectively altered their own understandings of race, nation, and subjectivity.[135]

In the summer of 1918 Noble Sissle wrote a special report for the *St. Louis Post-Dispatch* that gave his description of a band performance in Nantes.[136] Framed by the newspaper as a "study of the effect of Yankee ragtime on French audiences," Sissle's observations were meant to supplement the many accounts he had read concerning the use of American bands in the war effort, which mainly reflected upon their role in keeping up the morale among

American soldiers fighting in France.[137] If the ragtime and jazz melodies played by Jim Europe's band had been good enough to make the most lonesome doughboy long for home, Sissle wondered how they would affect a population unaccustomed to the sound and swing of their syncopated tunes. The opportunity arose earlier that February when the band performed a concert to mark Abraham Lincoln's birthday in a packed opera house in Nantes. No Americans besides the Hellfighters were present, and Sissle was sure the "greater part of the crowd had never heard a ragtime number." They began their program conservatively, starting with a French march before moving to vocal selections from their male quartet. By the time they had played John Philip Sousa's "The Stars and Stripes Forever," the house was "ringing with applause." Next, they played an arrangement of so-called "plantation melodies" before unleashing upon the audience what he referred to as "the fireworks": W. C. Handy's "The Memphis Blues."

While a number of critics have been fascinated by this moment in Sissle's dispatch, few have highlighted the sensuality of his description in ways that actively engage the tropes of pleasure and danger that I am arguing are crucial to understanding the sexual consciousness of black and brown soldiers abroad. Waiting for the drop of Europe's baton, the horn players "blew the saliva from their instruments, the drummers tightened their drumheads" and Europe himself twitched his shoulders to be sure his "tight-fitting military coat would stand the strain." The representative body of America in France tightened and swelled in anticipation of the destabilization of time, space, and social location obtained by playing Handy's signature ode to Memphis, a song written in 1909 for the mayoral campaign of Edward H. "Boss" Crump, whose refusal to enforce state prohibition laws allowed prostitution and gambling to thrive on Beale Street.[138] Both conductor and musicians "seemed to forget their surroundings; they were lost in scenes and memories" while the assembled French officers started to "pat their feet," temporarily losing their "style and grace." Sissle wrote that "'Lieutenant Europe' had once again become 'Jim Europe,' who a few months ago rocked New York with his syncopated baton." His body bobbed and swayed in "willowy motions" and his trombone players waited impatiently "for their cue to have a 'jazz spasm' and they drew their slides out to the extremity and jerked them back with that characteristic crack."

While both jazz and ragtime had been notionally linked to sexuality through their associations with music played in barrel houses and speakeasies, some etymologies of the word "jazz" explicitly trace its origin to its turn-of-the-century use as a verb referring to sexual intercourse.[139] By 1918 jazz was still a relatively new term whose origins were up for debate, however, allowing the "jazz spasms" spoken of by Sissle to circulate within the public discourse—and particularly the black and white communities in St. Louis served by the *Post-Dispatch*—without explicitly denoting coitus or ejaculation. Yet within the contact zone of American militarism, the sounds of the Hellfighters band produced demonstrable and pleasurable effects among the French audience not at all unlike those experienced through sexual intercourse: "The audience could stand it no longer; the 'Jazz germ' hit them, and it seemed to find the vital spot, loosening all muscles and causing what is known in America as an 'Eagle Rocking Fit.' 'There now,' I said to myself. 'Colonel Hayward has brought his band over here and started ragtimitis in France; ain't this an awful thing to visit upon a nation with so many burdens?'"

"Ragtimitis" should be understood as more than a humorous neologism coined to describe the French public's embrace of American syncopated music during World War I; it was also an attempt to signify upon the metaphors of contagion that marked the popularity of African American performance practices in the public domain. To be sure, Europe had made earlier statements that likened the impact of ragtime's success in pathological terms. In 1909 he had been one of five "young and successful colored composers" asked to respond to the claim made by John Philip Sousa that the vogue for ragtime had died due to its oversaturation of the marketplace.[140] Much of Europe's initial musical success came from his creative association with Vernon and Irene Castle, an internationally renowned white ballroom dance team who had popularized the Maxixe, Tango, and Fox Trot dances in the early twentieth century.[141] His response to the music critic was that there was no such thing as "ragtime"; "ragtime" was the term given to an already extant musical practice, a nickname "given to Negro rhythm by our Caucasian brother musicians many years ago." Europe understood "Negro rhythm" as the root of ragtime's appeal, and "in these days of theme famine, many eminent Anglo-musicians have become inoculated with that serum—Negro rhythm ('ragtime')."[142] Performance studies scholar Barbara Browning has argued artists of the African diaspora have been known to "recuperate the notion of African 'infection' by suggesting that diasporic culture *is* contagious, irresistible—vital, life-giving, and productive. The life-giving plague redeems the very qualities Western stereotypes have scorned, especially sensuality."[143] Within a military context, Sissle's use of "ragtimitis" allowed him to appropriate the discourse of sexual infection that read African American soldiers as venereal bodies in an effort to project the Hellfighters as global, mobile, international figures performing on the world's stage. And while the Hellfighters were perhaps the most decorated African American band to play in France, they were certainly not alone. Historian Emmett J. Scott listed at least nine other notable black regimental bands that also saw service in World War I, giving particular praise to Philadelphia's 350th Field Artillery Band led by Lieutenant Tim Brymn and his seventy-piece orchestra, known as both "The Black Devils" and "The Overseas Jazz Sensation."[144] These military bands provided an archetype of black military performance whose influence would extend temporally and geographically into new theaters of war produced by American military conflict in the twentieth century.

The Harlem Hellfighters Come Home

Ragtimitis, syncopation, Negro rhythm: working in the shadows cast by American militarism abroad, African American soldiers made the most out of their subaltern positionality, navigating the shoals of pleasure and danger presented by World War I in their sexual and expressive traffic across France. After the Hellfighters returned to the United States at the end of World War I, the band members committed their brand of ragtimitis to wax in their cover of the hit song "How 'Ya Gonna Keep 'Em Down on the Farm (After They've Seen Paree')?" The popular song questioned whether the returning American soldier would be content with returning to his humdrum, quotidian day-to-day lifestyle associated with agricultural labor after experiencing the pleasures and delights of wartime service in France. As a number of commentators have noted, the song gained a political charge when performed by African Americans in the immediate postwar years, and gestured toward the transformations in black masculinity that had become a hallmark of the conflict.[145] Invoking the sights of Paris and the streets of New York City, and employing the newly minted term "jazz" as an active verb that simultaneously described states of movement, improvisation, excitement, and uncertainty, the song imagined an American soldier whose tastes and desires had been forever altered by the excesses afforded him in overseas service. Father Reuben, the song's main speaker, intimates that vice spawned in the wake of the war found traffic among the boys yet to return to the farm:

> Mother Reuben, I'm not fakin'
> Tho' you may think it strange
> But wine and women play the mischief
> With a boy who's loose with change[146]

Posited in a syncopated pop song, Father Reuben articulated the very serious anxieties military and government officials harbored about the return of American soldiers to the mainland. American social hygienists and moral reformers hoped that the end of World War I would provide the impetus for the construction of a new American society, a nation whose victories in warfare and disease prevention abroad signaled a new era of social and sexual morality on the home front.[147] George Walker's hope—that the experimental success of containing the spread of venereal disease among soldiers of questionable characters might find large-scale implementation in civilian life—depended in no small part upon the proper conduct of soldiers returning stateside. To foster this larger goal, U.S. military and civilian authorities produced tracts and pamphlets that spoke directly to the homebound soldier waiting for departure in a French seaport. One pamphlet in particular, *When You Go Home: Take This Book with You*, implored the reader to teach "the folks at home" the government's doctrine on venereal disease, and to complement that with "what you have seen with your own eyes":

> We've talked to you a lot since the war began about gonorrhea and syphilis. We've given you the straight facts as simply as we could and tried to show you why it is dangerous to go with loose women.
>
> We've probably tired you at times, but you've listened, and you've made a record both you and the country can be proud of.
>
> Our army is the cleanest in the world. You've made it so. You've made it ten times cleaner than the country. Now, we want the cleanest country, too, and we're counting on you to get it.[148]

While the date of first publication is unknown, the pamphlet would have been printed after the Armistice to end hostilities on the Western front was signed on November 11, 1918, and distributed to soldiers in the USO huts they frequented in their free time. Alongside other titles such as *Nurse and Knight*, *Out of the Fog*, *When a Man's Alone*, *The Spirit of a Soldier*, and *A Square Deal*, *When You Go Home* was almost certainly among the reading materials furnished to the men at Camp Pontanezen, France, which gained the designation as the main embarkation base for American soldiers returning to the United States in December 1918.[149] Located in the port city of Brest, the base was important in that its deepwater harbor allowed large transport ships to move troops and supplies to and from France; 791,000 soldiers arrived in the city during the war and nearly a million embarked from the port by the first half of 1919.[150] Addie Hunton and Kathryn Johnson traveled there to "join in the great 'Battle of Brest'—the battle for the morale of the tired, anxious soldier waiting for transportation back to home and native friendships."[151] They were there for six weeks in the summer of 1919 and estimated that fifty thousand black soldiers funneled through "the mill" during that time.

The main function of embarkation camps like Pontanezen was to prepare American troops for stateside arrival through systematic cleaning and delousing of the body. Benedict Crowell and Robert Wilson described the processes of a similar camp at Bordeaux, and paid particular attention to the way in which men, soiled by the dirt of war, were cleansed and thus transformed into ideal specimens of American manhood. "The Bordeaux mill ground swiftly, yet ground exceedingly fine. To it came the raw material—dirty, ragged, weary humanity. It reached out for this material, whirled it into its machinery, and a little while later delivered from the other end its finished product—clean, well-clothed, deloused, and comfortable American soldiers, their service records compiled up to the minute, American money in their pockets, and a mighty self-respect swelling in their chests."[152]

More than just an extended metaphor for the production of one mode of American masculinity at the end of World War I, Crowell and Wilson's description of the embarkation camp deftly articulated the technological processes involved in the transformation of the doughboy (back) into a civilian. Like Bordeaux, Camp Pontanezen served as a highly regulated detention center for incoming and outgoing American soldiers. Pontanezen was unique, however, in that it also contained a quarantined area for the isolation of men with infectious diseases; by July 1919 "all the venereals from the Army of Occupation" were received there, requiring extensive additions to the camp to be made.[153] Isolated from the rest of Camp Pontanezen on its northernmost extremity, the quarantined area billeted close to 1,400 soldiers at a time. It segregated soldiers racially as well as by medical status—"venereal suspects" were separated from those who had received definite diagnoses of syphilis, gonorrhea, or chancroid.[154] Its treatment facilities were able to treat four thousand cases of gonorrhea in an hour and a half, and had its own YMCA hut and canteen. Pontanezen's quarantine was a site for the disinfection, reeducation, and moral redemption for American soldiers seeking medical clearance before being allowed to sail for the United States. "Educational classes were maintained, instruction in hygiene, citizenship and other lines given, and a general friendly attitude maintained. This attitude was reciprocated, and a good morale was shown to be possible among the unpromising material which an aggregation of venereal patients furnishes."[155]

Given the bias of the race- and class-based readings of disease acquisition offered by most military sources during the war, it may be surprising to note that during some months the officers among Pontanezen's venereal aggregate scored the highest rates of venereal disease. In 1919 the officer VD rate per thousand was higher than that for enlisted men for every month from March to July, with a five-month average of 1.32 exposures for enlisted men to 2.34 for officers.[156] This fact would ultimately go unnoticed in most of the post–World War I narration of disease and warfare, however. The thresh of Pontanezen's mill ended for most African American soldiers on August 3, 1919, when the last YMCA hut for "colored Americans" in France closed.[157] As the new Negro citizens produced through the machinery of the embarkation camps journeyed home, the specter of the black venereal would continue to haunt their cleaned, well-clothed, and deloused bodies throughout the interwar period, shaping civilian policy on the home front as the U.S. Public Health Service transitioned its war-directed efforts into broader health campaigns for the American public at large.[158] The transformation of black minds had preceded the demobilization of their bodies, however, as black troops came home to a nation that had, once again, changed much less than they had. Armed with a little money and the new rhythm that Father Reuben had warned Mother about, African American soldiers returned from France with a new consciousness of race, sexuality, and power.

In 1898, myths of immunity secured the overseas employment of African American military workers; by 1917, military medical discourse viewed black men serving in the European theater as flagrantly venereal. Punitive attempts by U.S. military officials to discipline the bodies and desires of African American soldiers indicate that the idea of the "Negro venereal" had consolidated within the civil-military discourse with all the coherence of a species. This stigma merged two contradictory ideas—immunity and contagion—into the figure of the African American military worker, and played a central role in the technical, biological, and political regulation and containment of black soldiers abroad. And yet importantly, the necropolitical management of African American soldiers in France was far from a totalizing project; black soldiers' own practices of marronage signified upon the trope of venereal subversion by appropriating the discourse of contagion that rationalized their regulation and control. Though viewed as subaltern actors in the European theater of operations, men like Ely Greene, Noble Sissle, and Jim Europe made their own temporary escapes from white supremacist surveillance as well as the politics of African American respectability in their travels across France, asserting their racial difference and whetting their sexual curiosity in the contact zones produced by global conflict.

As these soldiers returned to the United States at the end of World War I, ragtime's twenty-year reign gave way to the ascendance of jazz in the American popular imagination, a shift accompanied and accelerated by unprecedented advances in the reproduction and distribution of musical sound via the phonograph and the radio. While some veterans of African American military bands became major players in the jazz age of the next decade, ragtime's most significant ambassador did not live to witness the Roaring Twenties. On May 10, 1919, James Reese Europe was killed in Boston when a disgruntled member of his band stabbed him in the neck with a penknife, ending the life of the internationally renowned, allegedly infectious, and self-avowed carrier of African American culture abroad.

CHAPTER FIVE

Communicable Subjects
African American Soldiers Trip the Global Color Line

The characteristic rancor that divided African American public opinion on the Spanish-American War was also present in the political discourse spawned by black intellectuals during and after World War I. In the context of unchecked racial violence in the United States during the span of the conflict, black public opinion on military service in France was as fractious as it had ever been over the war in the Philippines, if not more so. As the United States fought in France, many members of the black professional class held tempered expectations that African American soldiers would gain greater rights and immunities through their military exploits abroad. While they advocated for the rights of black soldiers at home and overseas, African American leaders continued to criticize U.S. national policy for the duration of the conflict, and pressed for President Wilson to enact antilynching legislation.[1] The groundswell response against W. E. B. Du Bois's infamous editorial call for the black community to "forget our special grievances" and "close ranks" with white America in war against Germany in the July 1918 *Crisis* demonstrated that community advocates were no longer content to wait for tales of black military glory to transform the material conditions of black life stateside.[2] Moreover, once it became public that Du Bois was himself seeking a position in army intelligence—creating the appearance that his editorial was written quid pro quo to secure that commission—members of the NAACP and the progressive black left accused him of brazen treachery.[3] Deferring their criticisms against white supremacist rule was an unthinkable position to take for Niagara Movement veterans William Monroe Trotter and Byron Gunner, who argued instead that the war occasioned "the most opportune time for us to push and keep our 'special grievances' to the fore. This we should do for the very best interest of the democracy for which the war is being waged."[4]

Left, Right, and Center: Black Oppositional Politics during the Interwar Period

Chandler Owens and Asa Philip Randolph, founders of *The Messenger*, went further in their critique of American foreign policy than did most black leaders at the time, drawing the ire and interest of the Department of Justice, which arrested them under the Espionage Act, in part for publishing the article "Pro-Germanism among Negroes." The article—printed the same July in which Du Bois published "Close Ranks"—offered a satirical response to a warning given by an army intelligence officer at a recent NAACP convention, who interrupted the proceedings to declare that antiracist critiques, particularly those "complaining of the race prejudice which American white troops had carried into France," had brought them "under suspicion" of having been affected by German propaganda campaigns. "In keeping with the ultra-patriotism of the oldline type of Negro leaders," Randolph wrote, "the N.A.A.C.P. failed to grasp its opportunity." Randolph's petty dig at Du Bois rebuked an older generation of black activists for their continued reliance upon models of military immunity to augment the fortunes of the African American community. Instead of capitulating to the intelligence officer, the organization "might have calmly and frankly informed the Administration representative that the discontent among Negroes was not produced by propaganda, nor can it be removed by propaganda." In truth, the "deep and dark" causes for black discontent had little to do with German disinformation campaigns; rather, "Peonage, disfranchisement, Jim-Crowism, segregation, rank civil discrimination, injustice of legislatures, courts and administrators—these are the propaganda of discontent among Negroes," he claimed. "The only way to remove this general unrest and widespread discontent among Negroes is to remove these cankerous causes." After offering these suggestions for further consideration, Randolph cut to the heart of his critique: there continued to be a vexing contradiction between American militarism's rallying cry of democratic freedom abroad and America's treatment of its black citizens at home. "The only legitimate connection between this unrest and Germanism is the extensive government advertisement that we are fighting 'to make the world safe for democracy,' to carry democracy to Germany; that we are conscripting the Negro into the military and industrial establishments to achieve this end for white democracy four thousand miles away, while the Negro at home, though bearing the burden in every way, is denied economic, political, educational and civil democracy."[5]

July 1918 proved to be a hot month in the printed discourse of African American militarism. Another document circulating that month in Tennessee illustrated that some of the most pointed and threatening critiques of the American mode of militarism practiced during World War I came from black soldiers themselves. Pvt. Sidney Wilson of the 368th Infantry sent the following letter to the chairman of the draft board in Tennessee as well as to the editor of a white newspaper in Memphis:

> Dear Sir,
> It afoads to the soldier boys wich you have sint so far away from home a great deal of pledger to write you a few lines to let you know that you low-down Mother Fuckers can put a gun in our hands but who is able to take it out? We may go to France but I want to let you know that it will not be over with untill we straiten up this state. We feel like we have nothing to do with this war, so if you all thinks it, just wait until Uncle Sam puts a gun in the niggers hands and you will be sorry of it, because we is show goin to come back and fight and whip out the United States, because we have colored luetinan up here, and thay is planning against this country everday. So all we wants now is the amanation, then you all can look out, for we is coming.[6]

Mincing no words, Wilson foretold of a return of Atlantic blacks from France with much more to show from their time in Europe than a new rhythm, a few fancy dance steps, and an expanded sexual repertoire; he portended revolutionary retribution against white supremacist rule in the United States, evoking a legacy of Pan-African military resistance that ran from Toussaint Louverture to David Fagen. This, to be sure, was not an inconsequential threat. As told by historian Mark Ellis, once Wilson was identified as the author of the expressive missives, he was sentenced to ten years hard labor, received a dishonorable discharge, and forfeited all pay due.[7] But regardless of whether Wilson's threats were actionable, civilian and army officials were unsettled by the *nerve* of the prophecy itself, and were no doubt troubled by the pleasure taken in its conception.

Such sentiments inevitably fed into a postwar War Department assessment that the use of African American soldiers in the conflict had been a failure, and their employment in any future war should be restricted to labor battalions. Using the peacetime drawdowns as rationale, army officials effected a de facto disbanding of the army's four black combat regiments, winnowing their troop levels and placing them in small detachments as "housekeeping troops" at several bases.[8] While organizations like the NAACP continued to petition for greater military inclusion for black soldiers in the interwar period, other black radical actors like George Padmore railed against the black worker's collusions with militarism. In his book, *The Life and Struggles of Negro Toilers* (1931), Padmore gave a comparative analysis of the race- and class-based oppression faced by an estimated 250 million "Negro workers and peasants" of the world, arguing that the conditions under which they lived "form one of the most degrading spectacles of bourgeois civilization."[9] Building on insights gleaned and resolutions adopted at the first International Conference of Negro Workers held the previous year in Hamburg, Germany, *Negro Toilers* linked the practices of lynching, peonage, Jim Crowism, political disenfranchisement, and social ostracism found in America to equally restrictive and punitive modes of social and economic control practiced by colonial powers in Africa, the West Indies, and Latin America. He was particularly pointed in his critique of African American leadership, cautioning black American toilers to be wary of two types of "American Negro" reformists: the petty-bourgeois, embodied by Du Bois, "who are merely office-seekers and demagogues paid by the ruling class to befuddle the Negro masses in order to direct their attention away from revolutionary struggle into reformist channels"; and the trade union lackey, represented by Randolph, who Padmore accused of having bankrupted the Pullman Porters Union, leaving it a "largely a dues-paying organisation and sick and death benefit society" controlled by the American Federation of Labor.[10]

Padmore believed another "imperialist war" loomed on the horizon, and he cautioned black workers the world over to take notice of the "increasing armament race" going on between nations purportedly pursuing peace.[11] In his chapter "Black Soldiers of Imperialism" he described the transnational conscription of black soldiers by different imperial powers, placing the United States in the league of European colonial empires of old. While indicting France for having the most developed system of colonial conscription, Padmore was insistent in his belief that "all imperialist powers are also training black soldiers for future wars. This applies especially to the United States, Great Britain and Belgium."[12] Though the United States had no compulsory military service, he railed against the ways industry and government colluded to militarize African Americans by coercing them to enlist in "Citizens' Military Training Camps," which were military summer camps for young adults.[13] "Through this method of industrial terrorism," Padmore argued, "thousands of Negro youths are being trained to take their place in the trenches to fight for their capitalist exploiters."[14] He also claimed that historically black colleges and universities—including his alma mater, Howard University—were using Reserve Officer Training Corps (ROTC) programs and War Department instructors to prepare the "sons of the Negro bourgeoisie to lead the workers and peasants of their race to slaughter."[15]

Padmore hailed the African American officers produced via these civil-military apparatuses as the subaltern agents of U.S. imperial power, lackeys

Communicable Subjects 169

of an international racket that by 1930 had created military contact zones in over twenty countries and territories. Admittedly, the actual number of African Americans soldiers who fit the officer description given by Padmore in 1930 would have been quite small. While France's policy of "militarising Negroes" under Senegalese politician Blaise Diagne may have created an enfranchised buffer group that could be used "as the direct tools of the imperialist to foster their sinister aims," the form of race oppression that Padmore found to be most pronounced in the United States had conspired to exclude African American officer commissions in the regular army after World War I concluded.[16]

In a later analysis of the postwar enlistment patterns of black officers, William H. Hastie, the former dean of Howard University Law School, found that those officers who wanted to maintain their active duty status in the Officer's Reserve Corps during the twenties and thirties faced intractable obstacles that caused many of them to go inactive. Writing in a special issue of the *Journal of Negro Education* devoted to the Negro soldier in 1943, he said that fewer than ten African American officers from the world war were in the active reserve in 1940. The War Department held tight to its belief that the experimental use of black officers had been a mistake, and much of the bias they faced was built upon the prejudicial judgments white officers made against them during the Great War. "In France," Hastie wrote, "the vilification and slander of the Negro officer by other American officers in their contact with the French people was notorious. The Negro was pictured as an unintelligent, diseased, half human degenerate."[17] Just as seditious threats made against white military hierarchy offered proof of the African American soldier's treacherous nature, the specter of his diseased venereal body continued to haunt the rationales used to exclude blacks from the officer corps. As a representative case in point, the number of black officers commissioned through the ROTC, the Citizens Military Training Corps, the National Guard, and direct appointments made from civilian life totaled approximately 500 persons at the beginning of World War II. If we consider that the entire Officers' Reserve Corps totaled 100,000 at the same time—with blacks constituting one half of one percent of that total—it is clear that America's black military bourgeoisie played a severely limited role in the articulation of U.S. foreign policy during the interwar period.[18]

Padmore's prediction that more African Americans would be conscripted as officers in the U.S. military did come to pass, however, only eleven years after the publication of *Negro Toilers* announced the growing militarization of people of African descent around the world. In fact, African American women, who until World War II had only aided the U.S. military as civilian actors, were among the first class of officer candidates of the Women's Army Auxiliary Corps (WAAC). Out of an entering class of 440, forty black women enrolled at the WAAC officer candidate school in Des Moines, Iowa, in July 1942.[19] Due in no small part to the efforts of black leaders like Hastie and his assistant Truman K. Gibson, working on the inside of the military bureaucracy, combined with the lobbying pressure of activists in the civilian world like A. Philip Randolph and the NAACP's executive secretary Walter White, African American men and women saw increased opportunities for officer training during World War II.[20]

White also contributed an article in the same *Journal of Negro Education* issue that featured Hastie, and he relayed a cautious optimism that modest gains had been made regarding the treatment of black troops in the U.S. military. He too cited the opening of officer candidate schools to persons "irrespective of race, creed, color or national origin" as a decisive factor improving race relations between white and black members of the armed services.[21] In addition, White spoke of the "picturization" of the African American soldier in media produced by the War Department, the Office of War Information's Bureau of Motion Pictures, and other government agencies as having a pronounced effect upon the general public's feeling about black military service. "Time after time," he wrote, "theatre audiences have remained silent when white troops or factory workers are shown on the screen only to burst into applause or other audible approval when Negro soldiers or workers are seen."[22]

Two archival films from the period portray the contrasting archetypes of immunity and contagion that I have argued are hallmarks of African American military service in the twentieth century. *Wings for This Man*, a newsreel highlighting the Tuskegee Soldiers, and *Easy to Get*, a venereal disease prevention training film, are public and private representations of racial and sexual anxieties that plagued the "picturization" of black military masculinity, depicting the black soldier as a figure who was, on one hand, hardworking, honorable, and rights-bearing, and on the other, contagious yet perfectible, and in need of sexual regulation. Just as courageous images of African American soldiers in newsreels raised the morale of the black community and garnered their support for war, depictions of sexually infectious troops of color attempted to tamp the prurient desires of black men in their military travels at home and abroad.

Wings for This Man and Easy to Get: Picturing Black Military Masculinity in World War II

White made two trips to Hollywood in 1942 to implore movie producers to improve their depiction of African Americans on screen.[23] *Wings for This Man*, produced by the First Motion Picture Unit of the Army Air Force in 1945, typified the positive representation of the African American soldier that White thought created "a distinct advantage in the present conflict on the matter of race and racial relations."[24] Narrated by Ronald Reagan, who served as a captain in the Army Air Corps and acted in military educational and training films during World War II, the film lionized the Army Air Force's first African American fighter pilots, the Tuskegee Airmen. Formerly part of the 332nd Fighter Group of the Army Air Corps, the airmen were the products of a civilian-military partnership between the War Department and Tuskegee University. After flying with distinction as bombing escorts over Germany and Italy, the pilots of the 332nd were represented as the quintessential black American heroes of the war.

Wings for This Man extolled the virtues of Tuskegee's soldier-students as well as the bootstrap advocacy of the school's first president, Booker T. Washington. Over forty years had passed since Washington pledged to recruit ten thousand black men to serve as immune soldiers in Cuba; and on the eve of World War II, an experimental flying school for black airmen had been built on the site of his institutional legacy. One might argue that the Wizard's long-term investment in the logic of immunity had suddenly begun to pay titular dividends. Both Washington and Tuskegee operate as powerful rhetorical figures in a propaganda short meant to introduce the American public to a new historical moment in which black men might serve as both soldiers and pilots in the war effort, with Reagan's voiceover attempting to allay national qualms that black men were mentally incapable of becoming aviators.

The film is replete with images of black soldiers training for military service. One scene in particular shows a field of black men performing synchronized scorpion push-ups before cutting to a P-51 Mustang aircraft in flight. Speaking over Beethoven's Symphony No. 9's "Ode to Joy" finale, Reagan's narration links the physical preparedness of the airmen to the excellent aeronautical instruction they receive at Tuskegee:

> He trains his muscles down here very close to the ground, but he'll use the same sense of balance and coordination in the skies above Tuske-

gee. For this job of flying is never easy, and sometimes it's very, very tough. But he's learning how high and how fast and how far he must go to reach the enemy. Pilotage, dead reckoning, theory of flight, radio code. Yes, he's getting muscles in his mind. He's getting hard, keen, quick. He's coming into the clear. Here above the warm familiar hills of Alabama, these Americans are learning to fly in the most tight flight formations they'll use someday to hunt down the German and Jap above his own cities. . . .

Here's the answer to Adolf and Hirohito. Here's the answer to the propaganda of the Japs and Nazis. Here's the answer: Wings for this man. Here's the answer: Wings for these Americans.[25]

Reagan gives the viewer a campus tour of this factory of black masculinity, where black men are transformed into fighting, thinking machines—hard, keen, quick allies with white America in the fight against fascism. Physical fitness and mental acuity are the keys to the production of patriotic bodies, and the narrative of the film portrayed a government embrace of black men as fighter pilots, smoothing over the history of racial exclusion in the Army Air Corps and the intense lobbying efforts needed to put wings on black men.[26]

Yet the heroic specimens of manhood celebrated in this propaganda short were radically different from the image of black manhood the army employed in its efforts to stem the spread of venereal disease among African American troops. In 1944 the United States Army Pictorial Service Signal Corps produced a training film exclusively for black soldiers fighting in World War II entitled *Easy to Get*. As an educational aid, the film was meant to instruct new black recruits in ways to protect themselves against venereal diseases, which had been shown to be the leading cause of sickness and "lost time" among American military personnel in World War I.[27]

Easy to Get was the result of a number of collaborative efforts made by American military and civilian authorities to address anticipated and actual outbreaks of venereal disease among American soldiers during World War II. During the mobilization for war, the U.S. Public Health Service (USPHS), the American Social Hygiene Association (ASHA), and the War Department produced integrated venereal disease programs that emphasized education, improved treatment facilities, and suppression of prostitution in areas surrounding military encampments. Codified within the Eight-Point Agreement of 1939, this interagency collaboration explicitly addressed itself to the well-being of the nation, in terms that explicitly reflected a concern for healthy masculinity. In 1941 Dr. Millard Hanson, addressing a regional conference on social hygiene and national defense less than a year before the United States officially entered World War II, framed his talk with the following anecdote: "Several years ago a large sequoia tree fell mysteriously. Having survived the rigors of storms for more than a century, the tree was destroyed by a tiny insect that could have been crushed between one's thumb and forefinger. The insect had eaten away at the vital structure of the tree. Venereal diseases are a menace to the physical and economic life of our nation, and imperil our well-being at a time when the National Defense Program necessitates the unimpaired resources of our man power."[28]

Hanson's phallic metaphor quickly extended into a national and sexual conceit: the felling of hardy American manhood by the menace of venereal disease threatened to jeopardize the physical and economic livelihood of a nation preparing for war. Warren F. Draper, assistant to the Surgeon General of the USPHS, articulated this idea in more material terms. Speaking at the same conference, Draper cited a study of 120,000 men examined for syphilis by Selective Service boards to argue that both soldiers and defense workers were especially susceptible to venereal disease. "Venereal disease ranks high among the factors which cut down a man's ability to produce," amounting to "a considerable loss in the national strength needed for the 'all-inclusive defense' asked by the President."[29] The burgeoning American military-industrial complex had to be protected from the "sabotage of syphilis and gonorrhea" that was the leading cause of "lost time" among soldiers and workers. With the rapid expansion of the defense industry and the attendant migration it was expected to spawn, Draper predicted prostitution would play an active role in transmitting venereal disease among both populations. "All this means a great movement of workers into expanding industrial areas—a movement paralleling that of the armed forces into military areas. Such shifts of population create an Interstate Commerce in venereal diseases. Some workers may carry infections into the areas involved, but the greater hazard lies in their exposure to sources of infection fostered by boom-town conditions. These conditions are accompanied by influxes of prostitutes. Prostitution, in one form or another, is the greatest spreader of venereal disease."[30]

As is the norm with most studies of venereal disease during both world wars, the deviant female body—rather than that of the American soldier—is singled out by Draper as the primary vector of disease and contagion, thereby making sex workers a threat to the social and economic order of the nation.[31] Yet in explaining that prostitution is one by-product of boomtown economies, Draper offers an important insight for studies of twentieth-century migration. What scholars of American history and culture have come to understand as the "Second Great Migration" of African Americans to urban centers for work in defense industries was accompanied by a parallel movement of men, women, and materiel into military theaters of war. Of the sixteen million American soldiers serving during World War II, 73 percent served abroad.[32] With a thirty-three-month average tour of duty, nearly twelve million American soldiers traveled throughout North America, Europe, the Mediterranean, Africa, the Middle East, Latin America, China, India, Burma, and Pacific Ocean nations during the course of the war, intermingling with the bodies they encountered along the way. The "commerce" in venereal diseases Draper speaks of was not only interstate but also transnational, and those unequal exchanges—framed within the context of sex and war—continued to make venereal rates among American soldiers a discursive indicator of the sexual circulation of U.S. troops around the world.

The practice of using race as an instrumental category in the recording of venereal statistics continued in World War II, and the difference in disease acquisition rates sharpened the distinctions army officials made between black and white soldiers. The numbers showed that American soldiers in general and African American soldiers in particular incurred high rates of venereal disease stateside and overseas. Structured in a comparative black/white binary in the civil-military discourse, the statistics for white soldiers set an institutional norm from which black soldiers deviated.[33] Despite the collaborative efforts of the War Department, USPHS, ASHA, and various state and federal health departments, data on transmission rates in the U.S. "Zone of Interior" showed that some 145,000 soldiers had been exposed to syphilis by the time of separation from the armed forces in World War II.[34] Because the Wasserman blood test for syphilis was known to produce false positive results in reaction to the presence of other diseases (including malaria and tuberculosis), this figure was understood to be inflated.[35] Thus it was officially reported that closer to 26,000 soldiers needed follow-up treatment for syphilis upon separation from the armed forces, and that another 11,000 had previously been in treatment before leaving the service.[36]

This reframing of the overall data functioned to reassure the American public that the military was not releasing large numbers of syphilitic soldiers back into the civilian population. However, no such reevaluation of numbers due to the Wasserman test's failings figured in even the most sympathetic readings of black soldiers' venereal disease statistics. The same military preventive medicine document that explained how tuberculosis and malaria complicated VD tests noted that African American VD rates were consistently eight to twelve times higher than the rates for white soldiers—without ever questioning the validity of these statistics in light of the widely held belief that black soldiers were more than twice as susceptible to tuberculosis as were whites.[37]

In a section titled "Special Problems of Control among Negro Troops," high rates of venereal disease among African American soldiers were blamed on several factors, including socioeconomic conditions in the black community predating army enlistment, insufficient recreational activities and an excess of prostitution in communities surrounding the segregated training sites of black soldiers, the inadequacy of venereal disease education programs designed without black soldiers in mind, and "the presence of a defeatist attitude on the part of many commanding officers with respect to venereal disease prevention among Negro troops."[38] This final point is given further emphasis in Ulysses Lee's book *The Employment of Negro Troops*, produced through the army's Center of Military History (CMH). Lee's study remains the most thorough reference work on the experiences of African American soldiers during World War II. An African American officer himself, Lee served as an education officer and editorial analyst in the field during the conflict, and was the military history specialist on African Americans in the army in the CMH for seven years afterward. In addition to producing *Employment* for the CMH, Lee also submitted a portion of it as his dissertation in the history of culture from the University of Chicago.[39] Lee wrote that the stigma of venereal disease adversely affected relations between the majority white officer corps and enlisted blacks. "The presence of venereal diseases bulwarked personal prejudices in the training and use of Negro troops. No amount of instruction in the nature of transmission of these diseases could overcome completely the aversion of most noninfected men to venereals. Nor did the circulation and posting of reports detailing the high rates of infection occurring in many Negro units aid in dispelling the notion, often alluded to in officers' letters requesting transfers, that Negro troops were personally careless and dirty."[40]

In evaluating the use of media to indoctrinate black soldiers into following the standards of military hygiene, army medical officials rated existing venereal disease education programs as inadequate, and found the standard cache of films produced by the USPHS and the ASHA to be ineffectual. The filmstrips tended to take the forms of military medical lectures (1942's *Sex Hygiene*), ideological appeals to (white) race and nation (1941's *In Defense of the Nation*), triumphalist narratives of scientific progress in the diagnosis and treatment of venereal disease (1939's *With These Weapons*), or cautionary tales of the perils of illicit sex (1941's *Know for Sure*). Very few of these films featured black characters as anything other than stock caricatures, such as *Know for Sure*, which cast Etta McDaniel—sister of Academy Award winner Hattie—as a maid in a brothel.[41] Recognizing that racially specific media might have a better effect upon the sexual behavior of black troops, the War Department, Signal Corps, and the Venereal Disease Control Division collaborated in the conception and production of *Easy to Get*, a training film they hoped would successfully stem the high rates of venereal disease clocked among those soldiers at home and abroad.

Easy to Get follows the travails of two black sad-sacked soldiers stuck in the VD dispensary, both of them clueless about how they caught their venereal cases. Corporal Baker, "a smart, clean-cut guy [and] a good soldier," met a wholesome young woman at the drugstore while home on leave. A fair-complexioned beauty, she looked "like a girl a guy could go for, not just for the fun but for keeps." Baker and his new girlfriend go the movies, eat ice cream sundaes, and smoke cigarettes under the canopy of trees. "She put the finishing touch to Baker's furlough and made it wonderful." It is not until Baker returns to camp and uses the latrine that he suspects something awry.

> *Scene 1: The dispensary.* A white officer pulls up from his microscope. He enters the next room and sits down at his desk. Corporal Baker sits on the other side.
>
> "You got Gonorrhea, Baker."
>
> "Gonorrhea?" Baker responds, wide-eyed. "Why I don't know how I—"
>
> "I do. You had a dirty woman."
>
> "No sir," Baker objects, "Girl back home. She wasn't any prostitute."
>
> "Have you known her long?"
>
> "I—I met her the day I got home, sir."
>
> "On the street or in a bar?"
>
> "I don't mess around with street walkers," Baker says with a chuckle of disbelief. "I met her in the drug store."
>
> "Was she a pickup?"
>
> "No sir, I just met her, that's all."
>
> "And you had her that night?"
>
> "No sir," Baker says. He lowers his eyes. "The next night."
>
> "And you didn't use a rubber?"
>
> ". . . She was afraid of them, sir."

"Or a Pro-kit?"

Baker shakes his head. "No sir."

"And you didn't go to a Pro-station."[42]

"She looked clean sir, she looked clean all over."

"Not on the inside, Corporal. Where you touched her she was filthy and diseased. That girl of yours was just a pick up."

The film cuts to the crippled knees of a former star athlete and a close-up of a penis with a condensed milk-like discharge before introducing the next man waiting for treatment at the dispensary, Private Anderson. Anderson, we are told, is quite the playboy. "But he's not a bad soldier. He's just out for the laughs, and the more of them the better." A week earlier he had had a good time at a lively juke joint. There he met a woman whose allure even caught the narrator off guard: "*Mmmm. Damn sight better looking than anything he expected to find in a place like this.*" A black woman in a skin-toned bodice and printed skirt drapes her arm over a pinball machine. Bored by the game being played, she looks up to see Anderson watching her from across the room of black dancers. Their eyes lock. "Sure, he knew she was a whore, so what?" the narrator asks. "Whores are supposed to keep clean, aren't they? Don't lots of places even have laws to make them keep clean?" Played by black actress Muriel Jones, veteran of Broadway's *Carmen Jones*, the woman takes Anderson's hand and leads him up the stairs of the juke joint. Beneath them, sailors and other "good-time girls" jitterbug the night away.[43]

The film segues to a close up of Anderson in postcoital satisfaction, still lying in the woman's bed. He knows "it was time to take a Pro, because it's no good unless you take it right away." The woman's hand enters the screen and puts a cigarette in his mouth. "But Anderson didn't exactly feel like leaving. Not when he could lie around and have a smoke and . . ." She lights his cigarette. "Then maybe for another two bucks. . . . Well, he was out for a good time, wasn't he?"

Scene 2: The dispensary. The white officer is back at his microscope. Anderson stands to his side.

"What made you think she might be clean, Anderson? She was a prostitute."

"Well that's it, sir. I figure if being a prostitute was her job she'd have to keep clean."

The officer sits Anderson down, preparing him for the bad news.

"You know, you might have stayed well if you'd gone to the Pro-station."

"I will next time, sir."

"There won't be any next time for quite a while, Anderson. You've got syphilis."

"Sweat it out, Anderson," the narrator says, as a symphony punctuates the medical officer's revelation. "But if it's any comfort to you, you're lucky. Some men aren't smart enough to go to a doctor when they get a case." The scene dissolves to a shot of a black bed-ridden veteran from World War I. "This man for example: he was a hero in the last war. But the wounds that have kept him in and out of the hospital ever since 1918 weren't from combat. He caught syphilis from a whore overseas and never went on sick call." The fictional embodiment of the black venereal body is shown in a hospital bed, his face sunken and drawn, awake yet immobile as he stares into space. Presented as a victim of his own indecorous appetites, the black war hero lost his honor through violating the taboo against interracial sex in France, and came home an invalid as his reward.

Scenes of syphilitic men proceed in succession, each man's story representing different stages of the disease's progress. One asymptomatic man dining at a luncheonette counter keels over into his plate of food from an apparent heart attack; another convalescent, who sometimes "runs wild and has to be held in bed with straps so he doesn't hurt anyone," slurs his speech and is shown to have lost his short-term memory. The terms "syphilis" and "gonorrhea," as well as their colloquial namesakes—"bad blood," "pox," "lues," "a case," and "dogs" for the former, and "the clap," "a strain," "the running range, and "a dose" for the latter—flash upon the screen. The narrator reiterates that you can catch these diseases only one way: from a woman. "It doesn't matter if she's a high school girl or a juke joint girl," the viewer is warned. "Inside her may be sores, full of crawling little germs . . . that stick to your skin like molasses." The speaker then advocates the use of prophylaxis as a means toward disease prevention, both mechanical (i.e. condom-based) and chemical. This film promoted the army's new "Pro-kit," a new mobile form of self-administered chemical prophylaxis meant to be taken after sex. Eliminating the need for physicians handling soldiers' genitalia, the kit contained a presoaped washcloth, and an ointment based on calomel (a mercury derivative) and sulfathiazole, allowing the soldier to take the matter of prophylaxis into his own hands.[44]

Beyond promoting the army's newest technological advances in public health, *Easy to Get* was unique among the anti-VD media produced during the war in its bold attempt at using race as a fulcrum for behavioral change and disease prevention. At the time the film was produced, military officials agreed that "the present training aids used in conjunction with venereal disease education lack maximum value because they are aimed primarily at the white soldier." In response, they recommended that "psychological appeals for the avoidance of venereal disease" should be used in media directed toward black troops. Among those appeals were racial pride, competitive spirit, and patriotism.[45] Using sports as an analogy for excellent sexual health, the film shows black boxer Joe Louis beating "Hitler's boy" Max Schmeling in their 1938 rematch as a testament to Louis's "clean" health and physical fitness. "Keeping clean means keeping healthy," the narrator says, "and it was good health that beat the Germans before the war even started." Scenes from the 1936 Berlin Olympics are shown next, and the narrator sings the praises of black American athletes such as Jesse Owens and Ralph Metcalf, "who all knew the value of good health and staying clean." Turning venereal disease into a metaphor for the Axis powers, U.S. military authorities hoped to galvanize both race pride and patriotism as effective preventives against it.

The film's final moments are startlingly explicit. Two penises, cauliflowered with warts, are given close-ups before the narrator relays a cautionary tale of congenital syphilis. "And this man: He had to pay a terrible price for catching syphilis. He married the girl he loved and passed the germs on to her. Pretty soon she had a baby. It had syphilis, too." The camera shows the disfigured face of a newborn baby, looking up through thickly lidded eyes, who is missing one of its nostrils. "It would've been better dead." As a symbol of black infant mortality and social death, the syphilitic child—made monstrous through no fault of its own—is a potent reminder of the sins of the black venereal body and its place in the necropolitical order of being. To end the film on such a dour note, however, risked alienating those soldiers patriotically invested in fighting for race and nation, and whose labor was necessary for military operations. Instead, the propaganda piece closes with a stern lecture administered by actor, entertainer, and activist Paul Robeson.

Introducing the public of black soldiers to a man respected all over the world for his talent as an athlete, singer, and performer, the narrator declares, "Mr. Robeson has done as much good for our people as any man alive. Listen to him." Seated behind an executive desk, Robeson likens the movie the soldiers have been watching to the lectures on sexual health he received from his football coach twenty years past, before they had "pictures like this." "He gave it to us hot and heavy and we took it," he says, "because if you want to play football you've got to have a healthy body." Robeson then admits that this particular film—with its graphic depiction of genital deformities and bodily diseases—is indeed frightening, but not as frightening as the War Department statistics he's seen on black rates of venereal disease. "We've got to do something about this," he implores, "and we have the answer." Speaking both as an elder statesman and a "race man," Robeson chides the newest generation of African American soldiers to remember the lessons of prevention described in the film for themselves, their families and their communities. He ends his broadside simply: "We must defeat VD."

Easy to Get was considered one of the best training films of the war by American military authorities.[46] It represented a measured and calculated attempt by the U.S. military to use "race psychology" as a tool in the psychological operations of the war effort. Appeals to African American racial pride became common rhetorical devices in VD media, becoming one of the ideological tools used to regulate the sexuality of black men. By producing educational aids featuring African American figures, army officials hoped pride in race would lead to pride in nation, engendering a new sense of sexual responsibility among African American troops. Ulysses Lee noted that "One post bulletin, announcing a venereal disease campaign slogan contest for Negro troops chided, '. . . the Negro has excelled in every phase of warfare except the control of V.D.'"[47]

Yet the kind of sexual control military officials hoped to engender in African American soldiers through the dissemination of race-specific media was only the most recent twentieth-century attempt to curb what had been understood and quantified by military doctors as a socially constructed and biologically determined predilection toward sexual excessiveness.[48] *Easy to Get*'s cast of characters—the callow corporal, the promiscuous private, and the paternalistic white doctor—were pliable archetypes drawn from the World War I interface between African American soldiers and white American officers serving in France. While it had been modernized for contemporary recruits, the specter of the black venereal body continued to animate differences observed in the disease acquisition rates of black and white soldiers with racial and sexual stigma. The recitation of these statistics—which spurred even a known communist sympathizer like Paul Robeson to national action—functioned to produce (and maintain) racial difference through the perceived sexual deviance of African American soldiers.[49] As film scholar Thomas Cripps observed in his cogent reading of *Easy to Get*, "The message was clear: The army was really two outfits, the one, black, hedonistic, Dionysian, and *sick*, the other white, Apollonian, and healing."[50] In the span of two world wars that marked the discoveries of penicillin and sulfa drugs as curatives for syphilis and gonorrhea, respectively, the medical discourse on venereal disease and black bodies shifted from one of biological difference to pathological recidivism. Notwithstanding the culturalist leanings of the latter view, the Army Medical Department was transparent in acknowledging the social factors complicating effective treatment of black troops in the United States, one that nonetheless circumscribed black soldiers in a web of pathology:

> It was apparent throughout the war that the high Negro venereal disease rate was only one facet in a complex social and economic problem and that, without a solution of the fundamental underlying factors, efforts to control venereal disease in Negro troops by films, directives, schools for noncommissioned officers, disciplinary action, and other measures could not be successful. These measures could only influence the fringe of an enormous problem. The failure to control venereal disease among Negroes in the Army was, at least in part, a reflection of the failure of society through individual and governmental efforts to develop a satisfactory race relationship between the white and Negro populations.[51]

This discourse of pathology followed black men as they left the borders of the nation state en masse through the overseas deployment of American troops in World War II. African American soldiers would again face charges for their disproportionate share of venereal disease and in response, a largely white officer corps subjected them to novel medical and sociobehavioral experiments in the treatment. Through the experimental use of sulfa drugs and the exhibition of live human bodies, the national discourse linking black pathology to the social and economic disparities of black life in America would now attempt to contend with the transnational awakenings of the black soldier abroad.

Closing Ranks Again

Walter White took a special interest in the service of black troops overseas, and he was especially keen on a number of pocket travel guides produced by the War Department for the use and education of American soldiers traveling in foreign countries. Written for what might be understood as a "universal" American soldier, the travel guides were for White important contributions toward "decent and intelligent" race relations in the army, as they avoided American racial prejudice while acknowledging racial and cultural difference.[52] He had collected pocket guides to New Zealand, India, China, Egypt, North Africa, New Caledonia, Australia, and Syria, and took a sustained interest in the guide to West Africa. Interspersed with maps, pictures, and unattributed "African" proverbs such as "Without powder a gun is nothing more than a stick," the thirty-nine page booklet gave a brief survey of the customs, religions, habits, and histories of the inhabitants American soldiers were likely to encounter during their tours of duty.[53] From its first sentence, the guidebook explained that American soldiers were stationed in West Africa to guard supply lines to North Africa, Egypt, India, Russia, and China; as such, they were part of a "world-wide strategy to smash Hitler and the Axis."[54] In addition, the document warned against any public exhibition of white or American supremacist sentiments soldiers might hold against their "brown, yellow or black allies," and White hoped similar guides might be quickly made available for dissemination stateside.[55]

The West Africa guidebook also showed some of the explicit ways American soldiers were indoctrinated as agents of an imperial worldview invested in protecting U.S. interests in foreign lands. For instance, it advised American soldiers to be constantly aware that they were representatives of the United States and should conduct themselves in ways that curried favor with their West African allies. "Good will towards America is a valuable asset and you will want to protect it. You will understand that not only you as an individual but also your nation will be judged by how *you* act and what *you* say. Even this brief introduction to West Africa, its people, and customs may aid you in avoiding anything that might stir up suspicion or even hatred of Americans—and thus serve Hitler's cause."[56]

The guidebook advocated a mix of soft diplomacy, individual responsibility and national pride as guarantors of an Allied victory during World War II. American troops were asked to do everything possible to befriend both the Africans and the Europeans they encountered in West Africa, reminding them that "All of you will have to be good diplomats as well as good soldiers."[57] Soldiers were told to expect to meet few white men in their travels—only a smattering of colonial officials, traders, missionaries, and fewer, if any, white women. The Africans they would meet—particularly the young, educated ones—were proud of their race and their countries, and were "somewhat more sensitive to slurs and insults than others; it's best not to discuss political issues with them."[58] Dealing with black West Africans was expected to provide the biggest challenge to negotiating diplomatic relations on the ground, and American soldiers were urged to maintain a united code of silence against interfering in colonial affairs: "While many of them also hold grievances and suspicions, some just and some unjust, against their present white rulers, you—don't forget—are *not* going to West Africa to settle internal problems. When such subjects arise, listen—and say nothing. You won't be well-enough informed to discuss these problems anyway, and you are bound to offend someone if you do."[59]

As a matter of operational security, American soldiers were ordered against commenting on West African race relations for fear of stoking anticolonial sentiments that might imperil U.S. objectives in Africa. The fear that American troops would violate this "prime directive" of noninterference in the political affairs of their host nations was characteristic of the diplomatic dilemma of stationing individuals racialized in the United States abroad. American soldiers were cautioned that while the African was valuable as a friend, he was useless or even dangerous as an enemy. West Africans were fully aware of Hitler's new colonial designs on African people and resources, the guidebook stated, and exhibiting racial prejudice against Africans or African Americans could damage mission effectiveness. "Everyone is entitled to his own prejudices, but it would be only sensible for those who have them to keep them under cover when such high stakes as the war and men's lives are on the table."[60] A sensible racist kept his mouth shut around the natives—not because supremacist thoughts were invalid in themselves, but because the public announcement of such beliefs might compromise mission readiness.

West Africa (understood by the War Department to include the colonial territories of French West Africa, British West Africa, and Portuguese Guinea, as well as Liberia) was only one of the geographic theaters serving as a backdrop for the militarized articulation of U.S. race relations in Allied territories during World War II. This was a key difference between the first and second world wars, and contributors to the *Journal of Negro Education* issue on the American Negro in the two world wars all cite the greater transnational playing field as raising the stakes of black military service. Civil rights attorney and legal luminary Charles H. Houston wrote the volume's summary, and argued that the global character of the current war had made it impossible for colonial and imperial white persons to maintain the same kind of hold upon racial power. Because of that, "white American colorphobes" were in a panic. "World War I was a European war. World War II is a global war. World War I was a struggle to see which coalition of European nations should dominate the earth. World War II is fundamentally a struggle of hemispheres. In World War I the political supremacy of the 'white' race was not challenged. In this war, in spite of Churchill, it is doomed to inevitable defeat. The best the white race can hope for out of this war is partnership. The non-white peoples are rapidly taking their places at the head table."[61]

Houston, a World War I veteran who, as dean of Howard University Law School, had attempted to make Howard University a "West Point of Negro Leadership," is a singular voice in the discourse of African American militarism I have traced thus far.[62] His position as a civil rights lawyer, NAACP advisor, and mentor to future Supreme Court Justice Thurgood Marshall would seem to place him squarely in the line of "American Negro petty-bourgeois reformists" George Padmore critiqued in *Negro Toilers*. Though Padmore may have dismissed him solely as a proponent of black militarization, Houston provides a counter reading of the war's radical aftereffects on global affairs. For him, the increased militarization of the black working class had not stopped the revolution; it had fomented it. The question for white American supremacists was no longer about how to win the war, Houston maintained, but to whom to lose it:

> They lose if Russia emerges from the war politically dominant and military impregnable. They have already lost Asia, whether China or Japan wins the military decision. They consider they will even lose the United States if by his service in the war the Negro comes into full possession and enjoyment of his citizenship. The result is they have launched a determined offensive on the home front to impress on the Negro in the armed forces that wearing the uniform of his country does not improve the segregated subordinate status he carried into the service from civilian life.[63]

As Houston noted, the increase of racial terror borne upon black bodies stateside during the war — particularly those wearing military uniforms — had created a moment of reckoning for American militarism. It was clear to him that the United States could never fight another war of this scale, "or carry a dominant role in a militarized world," without increasing black participation in its armed forces, yet the violence of antiblack racism in military and civilian life imperiled the material practice of total warfare and hemispheric struggle.[64] "No one knows how long this can continue without a major explosion taking place, to the disgrace of this country in the eyes of the world," he wrote. "Negro soldiers would get the worst from such an outbreak, but when men have been abused and cuffed beyond human endurance, they reach the point that they do not care."[65] As such, the future of the black military worker could not be foretold, but would be determined "by the plexus of international conditions rather than by the conscious will of the leaders of state."[66]

More than solely a question of manpower, however, the deployment of African American troops in Allied countries during World War II stirred up the dogged question of "Negro patriotism" within African American political discourse, as a newer generation of black intellectuals looked critically at black leadership's acquiescence in American militarism during World War I. As proof, the *Philadelphia Tribune* cited Du Bois's editorial stance calling for African Americans to "close ranks" with white America in the previous conflict. This generational clash elicited a direct response from Du Bois, who dismissed the charges as bad history as well as reflective of the arrogance of youth. "Each generation faced by the horror of war is disposed to think that its attitude is wiser and braver than that of generations gone."[67] Reflecting upon the recent Japanese attack on Pearl Harbor, Du Bois's Valentine's Day editorial for the *New York Amsterdam Star-News* outlined the traditional arguments used to debate the question of black patriotism in every American conflict since the Revolutionary War. "There are always two extreme attitudes: One, perfect acquiescence in whatever the white nation says, thinks or does; the other, open rebellion against taking up arms for the United States. Few, of course have followed either of these two paths."[68]

Twenty-three years had passed since the publication of "Close Ranks." After rereading his editorial, Du Bois felt "no desire to change a word. We shall stand ready to fight shoulder to shoulder for democracy with soldiers of any race or color and for a democracy of all men."[69] He reminded those critical of his earlier endorsement of American militarism of what had preceded it: the wholesale efforts taken to enact antilynching legislation, the support of black officers in the AEF, the defense of black soldiers prosecuted in the Houston riot of 1917, and the fight to keep Colonel Charles Young "from being summarily retired from the Army."[70] While unbowed by the criticism he received for endorsing black participation in World War I, Du Bois was frank in his acknowledgement that African Americans had received limited rights and immunities as a result of that conflict's aftermath. "We may sadly admit today that the First World War did not bring us democracy," he wrote. "Nor will the second." Regardless of the outcome, Du Bois believed African American men and women had to do their part as soldiers in this war, even if that meant fighting for the right to fight. He predicted that if Hitler won the war, Africans and Asians would be subjected to a caste system resembling modernized slavery.[71] For him, the stakes were just too high. "We close ranks again but only, now as then, to fight for democracy and democracy not only for white folk but for yellow, brown and black."[72] Du Bois had weathered the blows his reputation had taken in World War I, and had urged

African Americans to close ranks again, this time for the future of people of color around the world.

Deploying African American men and women overseas during World War II projected U.S. debates about race, rights, and citizenship upon a world stage that included many theaters. Those zones of performance and contact included Europe, the Mediterranean, Africa, the Middle East, Latin America, China, India, Burma, and the Pacific Ocean. Reflecting on the travels of African American soldiers abroad, Walter White would claim after the war that the ultimate payoff for black soldiers was not restorative citizenship rights in America but rather an increased transnational awareness of colonial policies in allied countries—a political kinship, he argued, that they now had with the darker peoples of the world:

> World War II has given to the Negro a sense of kinship with other colored and also oppressed peoples of the world. Where he has not thought through or informed himself on the racial angles of colonial policy and master-race theories, he senses that the struggle of the Negro in the United States is part and parcel of the struggle against imperialism and exploitation in India, China, Burma, Africa, the Philippines, Malaya, the West Indies, and South America. The Negro soldier is convinced that as time proceeds that identification of interests will spread even among some brown and yellow peoples who today refuse to see the connection between their exploitation by white nations and discrimination against the Negro in the United States.[73]

The movement of black soldiers beyond the borders of the U.S. nation-state again rendered the black body into a subaltern, contagious, and communicable subject of American militarism, and discourses of immunity and contagion mediated its contact with the world outside of the contiguous United States. Despite the public lauding of all-black units such as the Tuskegee Airmen, more than half of the 900,000 African American soldiers on active duty during World War II served in support (i.e., noncombat) capacity in engineer or quartermaster units, and their labor often placed them in direct contact with the foreign allied populations of their host countries. Sex remained an important commodity within the economies of pleasure created through U.S. foreign military intervention, and venereal disease statistics gathered by the military units abroad again saw a strong trend of disease among black soldiers in the different theaters of war in which they were stationed. The high rates helped justify the experimental use of a new preexposure prophylaxis upon African American soldiers, much like what had happened over twenty years before in France. Army doctors issued experimental doses of sulfathiazole and penicillin to these modern immune regiments sent overseas to construct airfields, build roads, guard pipelines, drive trucks, unload ships, man ports, stock ammunition, transport supplies, and in the case of the black women in the Women Army Corps, sort mail.[74] These kinds of experiences allowed black soldiers to map the contours of a global color line through their military travels, creating a counter discourse of African American internationalism produced through the machinations of the U.S. military and enabling the offsite production of African American identity and culture. The military case histories of African American soldiers in Africa, India, and the Middle East demonstrate that, although subordinated through hierarchies of race, class, and gender, African American soldiers wielded a certain amount of agency—often manifested in their contacts with black, brown, and yellow peoples during World War II—owing to America's military and economic power.

Working on the Color Line

One of the unforeseen problems involved in deploying African American soldiers overseas during World War II was finding allied countries that would willingly accept them as temporary residents. Brigadier General Dwight D. Eisenhower, working as the liaison between the War Department and the State Department, admitted he had found no foreign country where black troops would find welcome. By March 1942 this unforeseen difficulty had, in the words of historian Ulysses Lee, "assumed an air of high international intrigue" as a number of foreign governments sought guarantees against deploying black soldiers in their countries and a promise to relocate those already sent.[75] While fears of miscegenation animated many of their concerns, there was a larger issue of interest to countries with colonial possessions. The presence of African American soldiers abroad, it was argued, threatened to disrupt the racial and economic caste systems of many of the countries and territories in general support of American intervention during World War II. British administrators in Bermuda, Trinidad, and St. Lucia feared their colonial authority might be "disturbed by the arrival of well-paid and well-clothed American Negro troops."[76] The Australian government, whose "White Australia" racially restrictive immigration policy had been in place since 1901, was extremely wary of the prospective deployment of African Americans to its territory. Australian officials amended their policy only after General Douglas MacArthur assured them he would "do everything possible to prevent friction or resentment on the part of the Australian government and people at the presence of American colored troops," which included moving them away from population centers.[77] Representatives from Alaska, Panama, Chile, and Venezuela made similar requests.

In response, the War Department produced two policy papers in June 1942 debating the use of black soldiers overseas. One dealt with the Caribbean theater and the second was a general survey of the attitudes of other Allied nations. Recommendations against using black soldiers in the Caribbean and the whole of Latin America were again connected to issues of economic and racial power, as white foreign troops would almost certainly receive less pay than African American soldiers. This would disturb the colonial order since "the local authorities try to keep the native populations contented with a low standard of living."[78] Yet this rationale was ultimately ignored as most military theaters had yet to absorb their proportion of African American troops, and it was thought black men would be "peculiarly adaptable to tropic as opposed to more rigorous climates."[79] In addition, the Caribbean theater was not seen as a major arena of war; sending black troops there would free up white units for use in more active theaters.

The general survey revealed a wider range of opinions of how native populations in various Allied countries worldwide would receive African American soldiers. Canada, Newfoundland, Great Britain, and Northern Ireland were thought to have no problems with black troops, while Greenland and Iceland—believed by the Americans to dislike all foreigners—might be unreceptive. Stationing black soldiers in Hawaii, Alaska and Ascension Island was not recommended, as the proximity of cohabitation with white American soldiers would likely exacerbate existing racial tensions. British India, whose "political difficulties . . . are of an especially complicated and grave nature," should receive black troops only through the acquiescence of its colonial government.[80] New Zealand had no distinct "color line" between whites and the indigenous Maori; it was thought the presence and segregation of African American soldiers might effectively create one. Stationing black soldiers in the Middle East would be fine, though placing them in parts of Africa would depend on their colonial controllers. British West and East African colonies (including Sierra Leone, Ghana, Gambia, parts of Nigeria and Kenya) were thought to be hospitable, while French Equatorial Africa (Gabon, Central African Republic, Republic of the Congo, and Chad) and the Belgian Congo might pose difficulty given the strictness with which their white officers treated African soldiers. Similarly, sending African Americans to South Africa seemed unwise to American military officials since "the appearance of American negro troops would undoubtedly further influence the very ticklish political situation in this dominion." But Liberia, "being a colored nation," should have no objection to African American troops broaching its shores. Sending them to China, however, was not recommended. "While the Chinese are not race-conscious, their Government is ready to exploit politically any action which can be distorted to appear discriminatory. They will undoubtedly complain of any Negro combat troops sent to China as second rate and will seek to make a political issue of the matter."

Despite the sense of pessimism that marked many of the survey's findings, the report was not a wholesale condemnation of African American soldiers going overseas. Their labor—particularly as members of quartermaster companies—was being vastly underutilized in the war effort owing to restrictions placed upon their movement abroad. Additionally, members of the African American press advocating black soldiers' deployment abroad formed an odd coalition with U.S. congressmen whose constituents had seen large numbers of white soldiers and few black troops sent overseas. Regardless of whether countries welcomed or resisted the presence of African American soldiers, the report argued, "The military situation alone should decide whether negro troops should be accepted in any specific area."[81] Taken together, the two policy papers represent politically calculated theorizations of the possible consequences of African American military contact with an allied world at war.

As expected, the deployment of black soldiers abroad created operational problems during World War II. On August 29, 1942, an Oklahoma-based quartermaster truck regiment of African American soldiers arrived at the seaport of Matadi in the Belgian Congo. Sent there to help build a southern trans-African ferry route, only two days passed before Albert De Vleeschauwer, the Belgian government-in-exile's Minister of Colonies, began to petition for its transfer. Two weeks later, the commander of the company, Captain James V. Harding, requested an immediate change of station, noting that the white Belgian residents of Matadi were openly hostile to the presence of his African American soldiers:

> Racial restrictions are extreme, and no consideration is given our Colored troops above that of the Native Negro by the local white population. . . . There are no places where our troops may go to be served food, or drink, in contrast to the freedom which is enjoyed by our white troops. . . . The Native villages are 'off limits' to all American troops due to sanitary conditions and safety precautions, and this

effectively precludes any possibility of correcting the situation. . . . Our men are accorded the same pass privileges as White troops in the area, but exhibit no desire to avail themselves of such privileges as they state that a general outward and bold exhibition on the part of the populace showing Colored soldiers' presence and services are not wanted makes their status very obvious. . . . The condition of the Native population is exciting considerable comment among our men who are rapidly becoming to feel that the things they are fighting for are [a] fallacy.[82]

Arguably, more than national pride fueled the negotiations between the American military and the Belgian government operating in exile. While Belgium had been invaded by Germany during World War II, its colony remained loyal to the exiled government in London. The resource-rich Congo played a vital role in the Allied war effort through the export of rubber, copper, uranium, cotton, and vegetable oil. In fact, its Shinkolobwe mine provided the uranium ore used to create atomic bombs used in the Manhattan Project.[83] The recognition of the need for good relations with a valuable ally seems to animate Harding's request for troop transfer as much as his care for the treatment of African American soldiers, whose presence in the Congo disrupted the Belgian colonial order. Despite claims by the Belgian Information Center in New York that "The Belgian Congo is open to men of goodwill and ability whatever their nationality, and the closer ties that are developing between the Congo on the one side and the British Empire and the United States on the other are of a lasting nature," it was made clear to the Americans in Matadi that the politics of race trumped those of nation, and any lasting camaraderie would have to acknowledge and play by the rules of those politics.[84] Soon after Captain Harding's letter went through the appropriate military channels, the company was transferred to the friendlier host nation of Liberia, where the history of African American settlement and American economic investment (via the Firestone Rubber Company) ensured a much warmer reception.[85]

As their encounters with different regimes of international military power showed, African American soldiers were contested subjects in the discourses of democracy and colonialism espoused by allied countries. World War II provided the context for competing interpellations of African American subjectivity around the world, and one of the ways in which black soldiers responded to these hails was through epistolary address. Through writing letters to the African American press, national leaders, community organizations, and the War Department, black soldiers continued to create a public discourse critiquing their experiences within the U.S. military stateside and abroad. Phillip McGuire discovered a number of these letters in the National Archives soon after they were declassified in 1980, and reprinted them in the collection *Taps for a Jim Crow Army: Letters from Black Soldiers in World War II*. In its foreword, historian Benjamin Quarles suggests the letters might be read as a "literature of liberation" produced by a subaltern counterpublic of African American soldiers, who had carried on a tradition of antiracist critique begun by their black military forebears at the turn of the twentieth century.[86]

McGuire begins his chapter "Jim Crow Goes Abroad" with a letter written by African American soldiers in India in December 1944. Addressed to "The Afro-American Newspapers," the letter railed against the imposition of white supremacist racial norms that resulted in black segregation:

> Dear Editor:
> We are writing you enlisting your aid concerning segregation of Negro troops in India and we would like you to take an appeal to the NAACP.
>
> First off on the ship a lecture was given by Dr. Paul D. Lindbergh and he asked the Negro troops not to mention racial prejudice in the States. And right on the ship we weren't allowed to drink from the cool water fountains.
>
> Then the first thing we encountered in India is segregation. American, British, Indian, Chinese and Negro troops, all attend the same show and the Negroes are piled in a huddle right in the rear.
>
> The boys are getting plenty fed up of being troddled on when they are giving their lives for America. And when a complaint is taken to an officer the only answer we receive is, "I'll see about it tomorrow."
>
> And we would greatly appreciate you giving this letter to the NAACP and let them see if they can do anything concerning it. We would also like for this to get in some Negro paper.
>
> Yours with thanks,
> Negro Troops in India.[87]

Not only does the letter petition against the racist treatment of African American troops from shore—to ship—to shore, but it also testifies to the witnessing of a new colonial ordering of humanity experienced at the intersection of race and nation. Even in the China-Burma-India theater of war, black troops had to huddle in the rear of the show.

Many of those "Negro Troops" seeking political redress likely traveled to India on the U.S.S. *General William Mitchell*, which embarked from Newport News, Virginia, in August 1944 and arrived in Bombay on November 7 that year. The U.S.S. *Mitchell* carried five thousand soldiers of different army units, including a group of fifty detached service engineers.[88] The bulk of the black soldiers spoken about in the aggregate would have worked as engineers in the construction of the Ledo Road, a 271-mile land route from the border city of Ledo in Assam, India, through Burma (now Myanmar) and on to Wanting, China. Nicknamed "Pick's Pike" and "Stilwell Road" after the generals leading its construction, the road was an important supply route to China after the Japanese occupied Burma and closed the Burma Road, "700 miles of dirt highway that represented China's last overland link with the outside world."[89] Construction on the road began in December 1942 by two black units, the 45th Engineer General Service Regiment and the 823rd Engineer Aviation Battalion. Alongside Chinese, Indian, and Burmese laborers, fifteen thousand American soldiers came to work on Ledo Road, and 60 percent of them were African American.[90] Despite this fact, their presence has been marginalized to the point of erasure in accounts generated from the time of its creation up until our current historical moment. In a February 1945 newsreel meant to congratulate generals Stilwell and Pike on the completion of the supply route, the narrator all but erased black labor from his account: "Bumper to bumper they roll, and service is well organized all along the route. Here's a gas station in the middle of the wilderness, a land of towering mountains, swift, tumbling streams and dense jungle never before traveled by white men."[91]

In recent years, journalists, historians, and community activists have worked to recover the experiences of these military workers, which were relegated to the footnotes of American military history for more than half a century.[92] According to a report by the American Forces Press service, the first public recognition those soldiers received was during a 2004 Defense Department Black History Month observance at Florida A&M University.[93] At that time the Defense Department was able to locate only twelve living African Americans who had worked on Ledo Road. Mose J. Davie, who died on July 24, 2008, was one of the recognized road builders. He was drafted in 1941 while a senior at Tennessee State in Nashville and served as sergeant major of the 382nd Engineer Construction Battalion. "I lost three years of my life working on that road," he said. Recounting his journey to India, Davie articulated in material terms the experience of ship racism described in the

"Negro Troops" letter. "It got so hot they had all the black people in the hull of the ship below the water level. They had a white guard on the doors in the event that a torpedo hit the ship. I took a job running a mimeograph machine on the top deck to keep from going down into that hole."[94] Davie slept on the steel floors of the ship deck instead. While white sailors enjoyed access to better food, black soldiers on board ate hardtack and cold pork and beans for breakfast. "They picked up some Indian cooks in Calcutta, but when the train stopped for you to eat, you got some hardtack full of bugs and weevils out of the boxcar. You couldn't eat it in the daytime. You waited until night so you couldn't see what you were eating."[95]

Building Ledo Road was a backbreaking endeavor, requiring the removal of more than 100,000 cubic feet of earth every mile. Yet the belief that black bodies were immune from the ravages attending labor in tropical climates continued to find acceptance in the China-Burma-India theater. In a study on African American war correspondents during World War II, historian John D. Stevens found that the army, "with its mystical belief in the special adaptability of blacks to jungle climates, turned to black laborers, as the army had turned to them for garrison duty in yellow fever-infested Puerto Rico in 1898."[96] If the employment of black immunes in the Caribbean had been a tragedy, then the reemergence of that rationale to secure Ledo Road's completion was a farcical ruse to secure military labor in light of the evidence of black morbidity and mortality in both historical moments. Due to the seven-day workweek and poor living conditions, Davie lost a third of his body weight over his three-year tour. As he recalled, malaria was a "man killer over there" and many men died from it, leading to the saying that the army had lost a man a mile building Ledo Road.[97] Sadly, this was a grievous undercount. In all, 1,133 Americans died during the construction of the military engineering miracle.[98]

Drugs, Sex, and Foreign Women: Regulating Othered Bodies Abroad

The myth of immunity that helped to justify the use of African American labor on the Ledo Road and elsewhere throughout the zones of World War II continued to work in tandem with the discourse of contagion, which constituted black soldiers as crucial subjects of scientific study at home and abroad. American civilian and military doctors and researchers persisted in their efforts to develop a so-called "magic bullet" to eliminate the scourge of venereal disease once and for all. After World War I, Hugh Hampton Young, the celebrated urologist of the American Expeditionary Force in France, developed the antiseptic *mercurochrome* for use in genitourinary infections. He remained an avid champion of the product during the interwar period, despite the fact other researchers had run clinical trials that cast doubt on its effectiveness. According to medical historian John E. Lesch, "Young established an early commanding lead over his evidence, and never lost it."[99] In his autobiography, Young acknowledged that mercurochrome had yet to be generally adopted by the medical profession because the antiseptic dye had to be administered intravenously. He did, however, cite the success his research team at Brady Urological Institute had had in experimenting with a new class of drugs that could be taken by mouth.[100] *Sulfanilamide*, introduced to the market as *Prontosil* in 1935, created a "therapeutic revolution" in the treatment of bacterial infections, and provided the impetus for the vast expansion of the international pharmaceutical industry.[101] German chemical industries began to test the pharmaceutical use of their products in the 1880s and 1890s when companies like Bayer realized coal tar derivates and synthetic dyes held antiseptic properties. In the postwar period, the United States, France, and Britain were forced to recognize their dependence upon Germany for fine chemicals, and the 1920s and 1930s saw an expansion of pharmaceutical manufacturing and research in those allied countries. The success of Prontosil and the start of World War II spurred the production of sulfanilamide worldwide and made way for a "larger and more truly international pharmaceutical industry in which the United States had replaced Germany in a leading position."[102]

Sulfa drugs, also produced as sulfathiazole, represented the next phase in the U.S. military's quest for an effective prophylaxis against venereal diseases. Because they could be taken orally, they were hailed as an important advance over the invasive application of silver compounds and mercury chloride during World War I. African American soldiers, used as experimental subjects in venereal disease prevention during that war, were also part of significant clinical trials of sulfathiazole in World War II. In March 1943, Captain James A. Loveless and Colonel William Denton, both of the U.S. Army's Medical Corps, published the results of a study on the oral use of sulfathiazole as a prophylaxis against gonorrhea in the *Journal of the American Medical Association*. Approximately 5,400 African American troops at Fort Benning, Georgia, were participants in the experiment, with 1,400 in the test group and 4,000 in the control group.

Much like World War I, the administration of sulfathiazole in Loveless and Denton's study was linked to soldiers leaving and returning to the fort on their liberty passes. As an advance upon the earlier era's use of prophylaxis, however, members of the Georgia test group were ordered to take their drugs *before* leaving camp. They received two grams of sulfathiazole whenever they left Fort Benning; if they left without taking prophylaxis, they were required to take two grams of sulfathiazole upon their return, and two additional grams in the morning. Using a pre- and postexposure method, Loveless and Denton recorded the gonorrhea acquisition rate for the test group at 9 per 1000 per year versus the control group that charted 171 per 1000.[103] This study, alongside a similar experiment conducted by Armored Forces in Fort Knox, Kentucky, pioneered the use of sulfathiazole as a prophylaxis against gonorrhea and chancroid by the U.S. military.[104] The success of these experiments stateside encouraged U.S. military doctors to employ liberal use of sulfathiazole in the different theaters of World War II. In the United Kingdom, "three typical Negro organizations" were part of a three-month trial of sulfathiazole by mouth for the prophylaxis of gonorrhea and chancroid in May 1943, and the "encouraging results" produced through the experiment further advanced the use of sulfa drugs overseas.[105] Soon sulfa drugs would also be used in tandem with penicillin to treat venereal infections, and by 1944 the Chief Consultant in Medicine to the U.S. Army would state that "from a military standpoint no more important development in therapeutics has occurred than in the field of venereal diseases."[106]

Rates of venereal disease among African American soldiers were proportionately higher than those of white American soldiers in the European theater, with their disease-acquisition rates measuring a 4.5 times greater average. This ratio of racial acquisition rates also held true in Egypt, Central Africa (including parts of French Equatorial Africa, the Belgian Congo, and Kenya), Liberia, Iran, Australia, the Philippines, and India. It should be noted, however, that American soldiers across race incurred the highest rates of venereal disease in the Mediterranean theater (which included Italy and North Africa) at a rate of 90.5 exposures per 1000 per year.[107] The problem was especially acute in Naples, where the rate of acquisition among white combat troops rose to over 100 per 1000 per year in December 1943.[108] The U.S. military's preventive medicine report on venereal disease control in the Mediterranean was quick to explain the rates as being the result of ineffective governmental systems of regulated prostitution in the region, and lack of access to antivenereal drugs, both of which had led to a "large reservoir of venereal infection in the civilian population."[109] While gendering that reservoir of disease as female, the report attempted to shield white Italian womanhood from venereal stigma by arguing war-induced poverty had turned many Neapolitan women toward prostitution, thus making them vectors of contagion. "It was not lust, but necessity, not depravity of the soul but the surge of instinct to survive which led numerous women into the ranks of the amateur prostitutes on whom regulatory legislation had little or no effect."[110] As if to underscore their point, the Mediterranean report included a photograph of suspected Italian prostitutes whose caption read, "Destitute and desperate, many women in Naples turned to the streets."

Wearing worn, salvaged coats and dresses, the women were given a reprieve from their complicity in the wartime sexual economy—and thus in the transmission of venereal disease—through a discourse of helplessness that absolved them (as well as their white American johns) from culpability. This discourse becomes all the more legible when read against the decidedly unsympathetic reports on venereal disease controls in theaters where African American soldiers incurred the highest rates of disease. The War Department's guidebook to West Africa had attempted to inculcate a sense of cultural relativism, respect, and relatedness into the minds of American soldiers stationed in Africa. In spite of these efforts, the U.S. West African Service Command's preventive medicine report characterized the population in the theater as "illiterate and primitive in dress, manners, and customs. Their homes were crude huts of thatched grass; their towns were dirty, lacking in sanitation, and generally uninviting."[111] The high rates of venereal disease between West Africans and African American soldiers were explained in terms of a diasporic, monoracial communicability. "The native of this region was racially the same as the American Negro soldier," the report stated, "and friendships were begun from the time of the first arrival of U.S. troops." This, coupled with a belief that "sexual promiscuity was more or less universal among the natives" explained the 429.2 per 1000 per year rate of exposure for African American troops in September 1942.[112]

The venereal rate recorded in other regions of Africa paled in comparison with those reported among African American soldiers stationed in Liberia. Stationed at Roberts Field near the capital city of Monrovia, African American troops had been sent to Liberia largely to protect the Firestone Rubber plantations, which provided a rare and valuable source of natural rubber for the Allies. Former U.S. Secretary of State Cordell Hull noted the strategic importance of Liberia during World War II in his memoirs when he wrote, "With Japan's occupation of the rubber producing areas in the Far East, Liberia became of greatly increased importance to us as one of the few remaining available sources of natural rubber."[113] The acquisition rate of venereal disease among black soldiers at Roberts Field hovered at 650 per

1000 per year from August to November 1942, and the U.S. military doctors recurred to a discourse of racial communicability to explain the high rates of contact. "The natives were, again, all Negroid, similar to those in Central Africa, and had similar ideas as to sexual promiscuity. The U.S. troops in this area were nearly all Negro engineers, and there was no want of companionship. The physical attractiveness of native women was not unlike that of women the Negro soldiers were accustomed to in the United States, and, furthermore, there were no color or social barriers to their seeking companionship and sexual gratification."[114]

In contrast to the photograph of the Neapolitan women featured earlier in the preventive medical report, a "group portrait of Liberian girls" was included to underscore the writer's contention that those naked, painted, female Negroid bodies were promiscuous, contagious, and—much like their African American brethren from across the pond—in dire need of sexual regulation. These women were among the 600 women housed in American military regulated brothels adjacent to Roberts Field, known by the local villagers as "Smell-no-Taste" since they could smell the foods cooked and consumed on the American military base but were never offered any to eat.

In September 1942, U.S. military officers met with representatives from the Liberian Health Department and the medical director of the Firestone Rubber Company to address the high rates of venereal disease circulating among the black men in camp and women outside.[115] The result was the creation of two medically regulated "women's villages" named Paradise and Shangri-La.[116] Women who sought admission as prostitutes were examined for venereal disease, "particularly for evidence of venereal ulcers or vaginal discharge," and those found free of disease were photographed, tagged, and permitted to enter the villages. There they could purchase thatched homes, or "palaver huts," at the price of fifteen dollars for a three-room cottage complete with a community sanitary facility provided by the Liberian government.[117] Women deemed infectious were removed to a quarantined area under military guard called "Idylewilde."[118] Anthropologist Charles L. Briggs's has argued that the discourse of epidemics produces "sanitary citizens" and "unsanitary subjects" as objects of analysis and knowledge caught in the multiple, competing, overlapping, and shifting spheres of communicability.[119] As representative of this phenomenon, a report on the Liberian brothels produced for U.S. Surgeon General Thomas Parran Jr. in December 1942 described the process of "tagging" by which the Liberian women were known, named, and classified as either sanitary or unsanitary by virtue of medical examination:

The residents of the women's villages are examined weekly. Any woman showing any evidence whatsoever of infection has her tag taken up and is treated until all signs and symptoms have disappeared. The tag is then returned and she is again permitted to enter the women's village. The tags, in addition to showing that the women have been examined and found free of obvious venereal disease, serve as means of identification. Wherever it is apparent that several soldiers may have acquired infection from the same woman, she is removed from the village irrespective of the results of physical examination.[120]

To be identified as a source of venereal infection was to be removed from Paradise and Shangri-La and to enter the Idylewilde quarantine. Even with these controls in place, many soldiers continued to contract venereal diseases, presumably from women outside of the village brothels. With the permission of the Liberian government, U.S. military officials examined all women within ten villages of Roberts Field for venereal disease, and used sulfathiazole to treat those infected with gonorrhea.[121] And in a fashion similar to the methods used by Loveless and Denton, African American soldiers going on pass from Roberts Field were given two grams of sulfathiazole by mouth and were told to apply an ointment made from mercurous chloride and sulfa powder to their genitalia after sexual exposure. If a man returned from pass without having used either method of prophylaxis, he was given four grams of sulfathiazole. After these control measures were introduced, the disease acquisition rate fell from 715 to 470 per 1000 per year.[122] Frustrated by the only modest reduction in venereal disease, U.S. military doctors in Liberia argued their prophylaxis efforts were hampered by the publicized "quick cure" of gonorrhea by use of penicillin, the removal of pay forfeiture as a penalty for contracting disease, and the "frank carelessness, laziness, and disregard of health and regulations" displayed by those men infected.[123]

The brothels regulated by the U.S. military in Liberia offer important examples of how it both succeeded and failed in the offsite biomedical regulation of sexual contact occurring between its own subaltern subjects and the foreign, feminized, and racialized bodies they encountered during World War II. Owing to its need for rubber, the United States had reestablished its colonial relationship with Liberia, extracting its natural resources from above and below, and used an enfranchised buffer group of African American soldiers to do so. The comfort women of Liberia trouble the discourse of African American militarism that I have thus far rooted in themes of subalternity, immunity, travel, and contagion during the early to mid-twentieth century. Much like the Korean *kijich'on* prostitutes conscripted into sexual service on and around U.S. military bases during and after the Korean War, the "Liberian girls" of Roberts Field represented the literal and figurative booty of war for African American soldiers sent abroad to protect rubber plantations and construct, control, and operate military airfields near Monrovia.[124]

A similar instance of the regulation of foreign female bodies by the U.S. military occurred in the Persian Gulf Command, where U.S. soldiers helped build and maintain highways, railroads, and airfields needed to convey supplies from the Gulf ports of Iran to the Caspian Sea and the Soviet border.[125] The preventive medical report for the command claimed that venereal diseases were "rife among Persians of all ages" and estimated 80 percent of the population was infected with syphilis or gonorrhea.[126] Venereal control officers in the theater blamed the large number of African American motor transport and engineering units for the spike in disease acquisition. Like the medical officers in Liberia, they too bemoaned the introduction of penicillin as well as the ending of pay forfeiture as lessening soldiers' inhibitions against contracting venereal disease. Racial communicability was not invoked to explain the high rates of disease acquisition in this theater, perhaps since the military guidebook to Iran stated that the "Iranis . . . belong to the so-called Caucasian race, like ourselves, despite the dark color of the skins of many of them."[127] In November 1944, the regional commanders took what they admitted was "the drastic measure of presenting a demonstration of venereal disease using infected native prostitutes from Andīmeshk, Iran, as exhibits."[128] Similar to the display of venereal subjects Ely Green had witnessed over twenty-five years earlier during World War I, the prostitutes were the highlights of a "lecture-demonstration" given to several commands in the region, and were said to have voluntarily admitted themselves for treatment, observation, and exhibition at the Nineteenth Field Hospital in Iran. The preventive medical report for the region explained the logistics of the lecture in detail:

> The post commander opened each period with a talk on military aspects of venereal disease, passing on the desires of the district commander in this respect. The chaplain followed with a short talk on moral and religious aspects of bodies free from venereal disease. Then medical officers gave short but thorough talks on various venereal diseases, stressing the correct and exact use of prophylaxis. The medical officers then exhibited the native prostitutes to the personnel

of the command with explanations relative to each prostitute's disease, prognosis, and health hazard to the community. Each session ended with a question-and-answer period. The immediate reaction of the men to these demonstrations was that of shock and revulsion.[129]

The description of this lecture-demonstration shows how the technical, biomedical, and ideological regulation of African American soldiers abroad necessitated a similar regulation of the foreign and often female bodies they encountered overseas. This spectacular use of Iranian prostitutes illustrates how the discourse of pleasure and danger that I have previously suggested is a hallmark of African American militarism in the early twentieth century had, by World War II, been powerfully refracted through discourses of colonialism and Orientalism. As of yet, we have no documents such as Ely Green's account of the use of venereal subjects during World War I—no evidence of African American counter discourses that actively contested the interpellating hail of the official U.S. military medical narrative in this later moment, which cast the "Persian" body as an unsanitary subject of American empire. Donald H. Connolly, U.S. commanding general of the Persian Gulf Command, was so impressed by the lecture-demonstration that he gave orders to take the venereal show on the road, with the added provision of using males with visible genital lesions if women could not be obtained. In a January 1945 summary of the program, an officer reporting to Connolly wrote about the lecture-demonstrations in glowing terms. "It should be one of the finest educational demonstrations of its kind that the majority of troops have ever had the opportunity to attend. Those to whom we have given a lasting impression to remember throughout their life-time will be better, wiser and happier men for having seen these cases. It was an opportunity for them to both hear and see the truths about venereal disease at one time, an opportunity rarely offered the average citizen-soldier."[130]

Yet in spite of the enthusiasm shown by the U.S. military brass in the Middle East, the preventive medical report admitted that the effectiveness of this program was never really evaluated.[131] African American acquisition rates, which had been lowered from a high of 482 per 1000 per year in March 1943 to 105 in the summer of 1944, climbed steadily to 361 by the spring of 1945 and soon reached the original levels of peak infection.[132] Theater surgeons argued that allied victories in Europe in May and Japan in August contributed to the relaxation of sexual morals by American troops, which contributed to a spike in venereal disease—an aftereffect of demobilization U.S. social hygienists had long feared.[133]

Through the biomedical use of their bodies and the physical extraction of their labor, African American soldiers served as key ideological subjects in the articulation of American military supremacy during World War II, reprising a role that had been played by black military workers since the Spanish-Cuban-American War. After the Allied powers claimed victory against Hitler, Hirohito, and Mussolini, a new need arose for American soldiers to serve as occupation troops in Germany. Their presence in the defeated nation would help oversee the denazification, demilitarization, deindustrialization, and democratization of the German land, people, and industry. As the United States, the Soviet Union, Great Britain, and France occupied and vied for strategic control of the former capital of the Third Reich, African American soldiers would become pivotal subjects and agents in the post–World War II sexual and racial politics of Berlin.

Keep On Trucking: Black Mobility, White Resentment, and the Racial Occupation of Germany

In the waning summer months of World War II, victorious Allied leaders met in the city of Potsdam on the outskirts of Berlin to hash out plans for the partitioning and reconstruction of Germany. "Like heirs coming together in the house of the deceased warily to oversee the division of goods," as cultural critic Wolfgang Schivelbusch characterized the Potsdam Conference, "the victorious powers planned to convene in the capital, Germany's former center—and now vacuum—of power."[134] President Harry Truman, Premier Joseph Stalin, and Prime Minister Winston Churchill agreed in principle to decartelize, demilitarize, denazify, and democratize Germany's land, people, and industry by dividing the country into four occupation zones. While Berlin technically lay in territory granted to the Soviets during the 1945 scramble for Germany, it was agreed that an Allied Command, or *Kommandatura* (as it would come to be known), would establish quadripartite rule of the former capital of the Reich. Although each sector retained its own autonomy, the Allied Kommandatura made collective decisions on matters affecting the whole of Berlin. This included stemming the outbreak of venereal disease that came in the wake of Germany's demobilization. As historian Annette F. Timm explains, the rape of women in the city provided the "jump start" for the elevated rates among the German population: "One out of every three women in Berlin was raped or coerced into sexual contact after Soviet troops invaded the city in April and early May 1945. Berlin health authorities estimated that at least 10 percent of rape victims contracted V.D. In the month after the city's fall, they tested 34,000 Berliners for sexually transmitted diseases. Sixty children, 3,946 women, and 608 men were found to be infected with gonorrhea or syphilis."[135]

By September 1945 U.S. military officials identified rising rates of venereal disease among American soldiers as well as persons displaced by the war as a major problem plaguing the U.S. occupation. To effect immediate change, "fraternization," or social and sexual interaction between American troops and the occupied populace, was prohibited. The vast literature on fraternization in occupied Germany chronicles the U.S. military's initial attempt to ban all forms of communication between American soldiers and German nationals during the occupation, and its subsequent realization that the ban was impractical, unenforceable, and contrary to mission effectiveness.[136] Radio spots on the nonfraternization policy aired on the American Forces Networks in Europe, and as early as March 1945, American and British military radio stations broadcast virulent anti-German propaganda as a means to dissuade Allied soldiers from consorting with the enemy:

> A German girl might be as good to look at as English girl but she has a different way of thinking. She's been taught the Nazi way and the Nazi way is to hate. Steer clear. Don't fraternize.
>
> A pretty girl is like a melody. But a pretty German girl's melody is the death march . . . for you. She hates you . . . just like her brother who fights you . . . just like Hitler who speaks her thoughts to the world. Don't fraternize.[137]

Though this discourse of the morally dangerous German woman was firmly in place by the end of World War II, and despite the widespread evidence showing the elevated presence of venereal disease in Germany in the war's aftermath—especially among persons displaced by the conflict—African American soldiers were vilified for having the highest rates during the occupation period. U.S. military officials linked venereal disease to excessive fraternization, and argued that out of all American troops, "the American Negro soldier embraced fraternization with enthusiasm and with little bitterness for the enemy":

> If a surviving influence of Nazi racial doctrines made the Negro soldier less acceptable socially than in the other European countries that he had already visited, this barrier was soon broken down. The generosity of the typical Negro soldier opened doors for him in Germany, just as in other European countries. Germans were quick to sense that

Communicable Subjects 203

there were, on the whole, greater material advantages to be gained from fraternization with Negroes than with white troops. It is reported that, in some localities, German women would not accept the clothes of white soldiers to launder when there were Negro soldiers stationed nearby.[138]

Fraternization predictably took on a taboo charge when white American officers and enlisted men witnessed African American soldiers interacting with German women. A number of commentators have noted the bitter irony in the fact that the U.S. military—tasked to democratize Germany—exported Jim Crow racism to the American sector, effectively foisting a color line upon the German people.[139] White American military police frequently stopped German women in the company of black soldiers and brought them into custody for VD checks, creating a stigma that, as historian Heide Fehrenbach explains, "negatively affected the views of local populations toward them and caused respectable women, out of fear for their reputations, to disassociate themselves increasingly from black soldiers."[140]

It should be noted, however, as cultural historian Tina Campt reminds us, that antimiscegenation discourses had been in circulation in Germany since long before the American military's efforts at antiblack indoctrination. The term "Rhineland Bastard" had been used since 1919 to define and disenfranchise German citizens fathered by African colonial troops occupying parts of Germany during World War I.[141] Campt writes that the term itself served as a discursive site in which fears of race, gender, sexuality, and disease intersected to create an early and enduring image of the Afro-German population. "As part of the deployment of the 'Rhineland Bastard,' the children of Black soldiers were also depicted as carriers of the infectious diseases of their fathers—in particular, sexually transmitted diseases. Sexuality played a critical role in the campaign against the Black troops, for the representation of Black soldiers as a sexual threat [in German newspapers] provoked the most vehement popular reaction."[142]

In a successive historical moment, black U.S. soldiers' sexual activity with German women became the source of serious enmity between white and black American troops in post–World War II Germany, and led to a number of public confrontations (from insults to fist-fights, riots to murder) as well as private machinations among the white American military elite to restrict and exclude African American occupation service in the country. The loudest salvo in this battle for the hearts, minds, and bodies of the German people arguably occurred not in the segregated beer halls of Berlin but rather in the senatorial chambers of Washington, D.C., in the summer of 1946. On August 14 of that year, Colonel Francis P. Miller, former executive policy officer for the Director of Intelligence at the U.S. Office for Military Government in Germany (OMGUS), testified before the Senate's Special Committee to Investigate the National Defense Program to the widespread misconduct occurring at all levels of the military government in Berlin.[143] During his testimony Miller spent considerable energy railing against the conduct of African American troops, as he feared that "for generations to come, the German people will remember what undisciplined, uncontrolled Negro troops have done to them."[144] He claimed that high rates of venereal disease among black troops were the result of a lack of discipline, and added that "It was the common habit of a Negro company to have 20 or 30 whores, prostitutes living off in the woods somewhere, clothed in American uniforms and eating American Army rations."[145]

Miller's sensational testimony prompted a number of investigations, and none would gain more national attention than the inquiry launched by the committee's chief counsel, George Meader, who then toured American military installations in Germany on a fact-finding mission. His findings, known as the Meader Report, were released in November 1946 and received extended commentary from the mainstream U.S. as well as the African American press well into the new year.[146] Diplomatic historian Kevin Ruffner's rich treatment of this army scandal frames it as a colony-metropole political firestorm initiated by the actions of one spurned army intelligence officer on leave from his post in Berlin, whose own phobias concerning the conduct of black troops and persons displaced by the war created an international controversy that threatened to cripple America's standing among the occupation governors. The episode troubled General Lucius Clay, then governor of the U.S. Occupation Zone in Germany, who said in a November 1946 meeting with senators stateside that "the Soviet press and the German press in the Soviet zone utilize every opportunity to criticize and discredit not only the American but also the British military government"; thus, he maintained, any consequent congressional investigation would hamper his ability to negotiate with the Russians in Berlin.[147] Significantly, the report had much to say about displaced persons, or "DPs," the terms given to the millions of mostly Eastern Europeans—many of them Polish Jews—displaced by the war and held in camps in the occupied zones of Germany awaiting repatriation to their home countries.[148] Meader insinuated that DPs were ringleaders of the black market, and identified them (alongside black troops) as a primary cause of crime in the American zone. While many African American newspapers and black politicos like Walter White were critical of the "vicious and unverified charges against Negro troops in Europe and against Jewish displaced persons in the American zone of occupation," satirist George Schuyler, writing in his regular column in the *Pittsburgh Courier*, found "nothing to get excited about in it":

> Meader said that the Negro troops in Germany, like their white comrades, were shacking up with German girls and swiping Government rations to aid their play. This happens wherever soldiers have unlimited authority in conquered countries, and Negroes are little different from whites in such matters. All Allied troops, especially the Russians, have been guilty of rape, black market operations and general arrogance. All of them with any sense and initiative have shacked up with the more personable frauleins. I would have done so under such circumstances and so would Walter or any other fellow not paralyzed who was 4,000 miles from "God's Country." It is no smear of Negro soldiers to assert this. The fact simply proves that, as Kipling says, "Single men in barracks don't grow into plaster saints" and that "Men are as a like as a row of pins" regardless of color.[149]

While Schuyler dismissed the importance of the report summarily, as did the Senate, which ultimately rejected Meader's recommendation for further investigation for a lack of evidence substantiating Colonel Miller's charges, it did have the demonstrable effect of galvanizing opinion among the U.S. military elite to severely restrict African American opportunities for service in Germany.[150] Given his matter-of-fact tone regarding the spoils of warfare, Schuyler would have perhaps been nonplussed to read an internal Third Army report of operations, drafted the same month as his editorial, materially linking the alleged black market activities of displaced persons with black soldiers serving in quartermaster and supply units:

> There are increasing indications that United States soldiers, especially Negro troops, are actively participating in black market enterprises. Arrests during this period clearly depict a chain of supply of American scrip to a Displaced Persons gang, who in turn make resale of scrip either to Displaced Persons or German civilians at scandalous prices (13,000 Reich marks for a hundred dollars). Evidence of sale of United States property on the black market such as tires (selling at 1,000 marks each) was also uncovered during the period. There are sections of the Displaced Persons and Civilian population continuing to sell schnapps to United States soldiers for cigarettes, candy, or scrip,

which are then bartered on the black market for any other items which the individuals may deem essential.¹⁵¹

These kinds of reports increasingly drew the ire of white American unit commanders like the Third Army's General Geoffrey Keyes, who believed that the "Integration of colored troops should not be carried out as an experiment in the occupational zone of Germany."¹⁵² American forces in the theater had already drawn down from a troop strength of 1.6 million in May 1945 to 135,000 by mid-1947, with black soldiers constituting roughly 10 percent of the latter figure. By 1948 the number of African American soldiers in Germany had fallen to ten thousand.¹⁵³ Economist John Willoughby's reconstruction of the paper trail white officers left in their attempt to remove black troops from their postwar German commands demonstrates the U.S. military's desire for its occupation to be viewed as racially white.¹⁵⁴ For the Americans, public health was as much about perception as it was about praxis, and some officials believed it was easier to disappear black troops from occupation service than to deal with the disciplinary problems they were said to pose.

The prejudice against African American servicemen was so extreme that General Lucius Clay reportedly believed the best use of African American soldiers in Berlin would be as parade troops. "We are going to dress them up, and if it works out as I think it will," he said, "we will send them around to other colored troops in the [German states] as an example of how colored troops could look and act." In July 1947 the general's wish was fulfilled, and the 7800th Infantry Platoon was organized and assigned to Berlin as Clay's personal honor guard, one of the last racially segregated units consciously organized as such by the U.S. Army.¹⁵⁵ One of the scant references to the all-black drill team extant in the historical record today comes from Frank Howley's memoir. They appear in his description of the Russian and American propaganda battles waged after the Soviets broke from the Allied Kommandatura on June 16, 1948, beginning their blockade of the Western Allies' railway and road access to Berlin in order to force them out of the city. Howley claimed that among the different propaganda campaigns the Russians adopted to sway the German public toward Soviet currency reform, the "oppression of minorities" line held much appeal. It was here that Clay's honor guard would find their ultimate use value as visual negations of antiblack U.S. propaganda produced by the Soviets. Similar to the Buicks, Fords, and Chevrolets shipped to Berlin to counter chatter of American economic collapse (prompting one German to remark to Howley, "If this is American economic collapse, then Germany certainly would like to have a lot of it"), the soldiers of the 7800th Infantry Platoon served their time in Berlin as representatives (and representations) of modern American progress:

> Germans were told at length of the terrible conditions under which the American Negro lived. Soviet-licensed newspapers blandly used material from old American books on slavery as modern evidence. I know of one writer who lifted a complete editorial right out of *Uncle Tom's Cabin*. Publication dates meant nothing to the Moscow-trained propagandists.
>
> Here they ran into easily controvertible facts. Negroes worked in Military Government on exactly the same basis as white members. General Clay had a Negro honor guard—handsome men, all over six feet. They were excellently trained, smartly uniformed, and, when they appeared on parade, Russian propaganda about the sorry lot of the American Negro looked pretty silly, just as silly as the new line that the Russians were ready to feed the Germans, while we bolted with the loot.[156]

Howley's rhetorical invocation of the all-black honor guard in his memoirs functioned as its own form of historical propaganda that obscured the truth and extent of African American exclusion in Germany. Blacks did not work in military government on exactly the same basis as white members; in fact, during the course of the occupation, African Americans had been banned from working in infantry units, in the constabulary, as supervisors of white civilian laborers, and even the postal service.[157] It took considerable agitation by actors outside the military, including Truman Gibson and Marcus Ray, who both served as advisers of racial affairs to the Secretary of War, to make the army reevaluate the hypocrisy of its policies abroad.[158]

While some change was gained through these means, the reduction of black troops from American military ranks in Germany ultimately ended due to the manpower requirements of the Berlin Airlift, the massive relief effort undertaken to overcome the Soviet blockade of the city. According to historians Maria Höhn and Martin Klimke, the U.S. military "curbed all further efforts to keep blacks from participating in the occupation in Germany as it generated an urgent demand for troops in transportation supply units," an action that foreshadowed the pragmatic implementation of President Harry S. Truman's Executive Order 9981 ending segregation in the armed forces during the Korean War.[159] "Operation Vittles" (as it was known to the

Americans) flew some 278,228 sorties and delivered 2,326,406 tons of supplies to western sectors of Berlin in a fifteen-month period, necessitating a mass coordination of U.S. transportation companies rivaled only by the game-changing efforts of the Red Ball Express convoy system operating during World War II.[160] Organized two months after D-Day, the Red Ball Express was needed to swiftly bring Allied materiel to the front in France as the railroad system had been bombed out of commission and German forces held most of the French ports. Given that the only way to transport supplies was by truck, Red Ball drivers—75 percent of whom were black—drove day and night for eighty-one days, hauling an estimated 413,193 tons of supplies to the U.S. Army advancing from Normandy to the German border.[161]

The disproportionate assignment of black soldiers to quartermaster and trucking units—which, as I have shown throughout my study, was a normative condition of African American military service from the early to the mid-twentieth century—ironically gave them increased ability to circulate beyond the barbed-wire fences of their military base camps during and after World War II. In France, those Red Ball drivers who chose to do so became important agents in the underground economies that flourished during the war, regularly availing themselves of the sex and "scrip" they encountered during their travels. As one former driver said, "Sometimes girls would come up close to your truck and ask you certain things, you know, if you wanted to take care of business. I had what they wanted and they had what I wanted."[162] Some soldiers participated wholeheartedly in the black market, exchanging everything from cigarettes and gasoline to entire trucks in the administrative fog of war.[163] Their unregulated circulation within the economies of sex and scrip led to the institution of compulsory prophylaxis for the mobile members of the Red Ball Express. Charles Stevenson, a lieutenant with the 3858th Quartermaster Gas Supply Company, noted that all personnel returning from leave were required to take sulfa pills or a shot of penicillin after five men in his unit came down with gonorrhea. "Whenever they logged back in from a pass, we made them take five or six sulfa pills or a shot," he said. "They'd swear up and down they hadn't done anything. But they had orders to take the pills."[164] In occupied Germany, higher rates of venereal disease among black soldiers were also attributed to their disproportionate concentration in segregated quartermaster regiments. While this increased their opportunities for sexual contact with the local population, racial hostility at Red Cross canteens made it more difficult for black truckers to access prophylaxis and receive effective treatment, leading to an increase in venereal infections.[165]

The "superior mobility" of African American truck drivers and supply workers drew scorn and envy from their white American colleagues, feelings that had been held over from their similar use during World War II.[166] Thomas A. Bailey, an academic commissioned by the National War College to undertake an inspection tour of Europe during the summer of 1947, found that white officers' low regard for black troops stemmed from sexual competition. "Many of the blacks had been assigned to commissary work," putting them "in a position to steal food with which to buy the favors of German girls."[167] Likewise, Leon C. Standifer, a white veteran of World War II and the occupation of Germany, offered proof of the ritual inculcation of racial animosity in his memoir, *Binding up the Wounds.* Dedicated "especially [to] the men of the *Schwartze Kater*," a nightclub for African American soldiers in Munich to which he had been given privileged entry, his memoir viewed the American occupation as a contest between interracial masculine supremacy and homosocial reconciliation. Standifer often hitched rides with black truck drivers on his trips throughout Germany. While riding along with Sam'Le Emory, a former Red Ball driver who had introduced him to the "exciting Army subculture" of the Black Tomcat's vaudeville burlesque shows, he recalled a derisive song about quartermaster troops he had learned to sing in England called "Blue-Star Commando": "Take down that gold star, mother, / Your son's not going to die. / He's a blue star commando in the service of supply."[168]

White American resentment at African American mobility in occupied Germany was part and parcel of the impetus behind the black exodus from Berlin. In order to establish its own Jim Crow metropole in Europe, the U.S. Army enforced the surveillance and control of black soldiers, displaced persons, and German women to the best of its ability. But just as Charles Houston had predicted, the exigencies of imperial warfare required the labor of black military workers to function. After the success of the Berlin Airlift, the United States could no longer "carry a dominant role in a militarized world without integrating the Negro into the armed forces to a degree far beyond all present declarations of policy."[169] The resulting increase in the presence of black soldiers in occupied Germany produced tensions that mirrored the hard feelings felt by white Southerners after the end of the Civil War eighty years prior. As Schivelbusch perceptively observed, the U.S. role as occupying power strongly mirrored the relationship between the victorious Union and the defeated South:

> What took place in Germany in the years after 1945 had taken place once before in postbellum America, from the idea of unconditional

surrender to the military occupation, the installation of a military government, and the attempt through reeducation morally to improve the subject population. Instead of slavery and racism, the ideas now to be rooted out were militarism and nationalism. The methods in both campaigns were alike insofar as the population to be reeducated was not believed capable of the strength required for self-purification. Salvation had to be forced on it.[170]

Leon Standifer, who hailed from Clinton, Mississippi, had a similar realization upon encountering a Nazi propaganda poster in the weeks immediately following Germany's surrender. "There were posters on the walls with the silhouette of a spy, and 'Psst' written under it," he said. "Back home we had signs that said, 'Psst, the enemy is listening,' but here the enemy was us."[171] Viewing himself through the eyes of the conquered Germans prompted Standifer to imagine himself as a soldier in the Union occupation army. As he watched a fellow soldier harass a young German woman for her identity card, he was troubled by the discomfiting similarities between his actions and those committed by the "damnyankees" eighty years prior:

> I knew—from stories anyway—what it felt like to be a defeated people. I knew that, during Reconstruction days, decent women shouldn't associate with the enemy. I knew that General Butler, the Beast of New Orleans, had ordered that any woman refusing to speak to a Yankee soldier be arrested as a prostitute.
>
> There was a sign painted on the wall: Ein Volk, Ein Reich, Ein Führer. That had been Hitler's slogan; it meant that all Germanic people were one nation and should be under one leader. It reminded me of the Pledge of Allegiance: "one nation, indivisible, with liberty and justice for all." Our nation was indivisible because the War for Southern Independence had established that states weren't allowed to secede. Hitler had made the country indivisible, but not with liberty and justice for all. I didn't like being an occupation soldier.[172]

Transposing the "lost cause" of southern independence with fall of the Third Reich, Standifer discovered his disdain for occupation service. He abhorred its social upheavals and reversals of power, its violation of white womanhood and its corruption of white masculinity. And yet his intimate friendships with African American soldiers ultimately led him to question and rebut the Jim Crow logics of American rule that had bound black troops to the bottom of the military hierarchy. Though disconcerting for Standifer, the ambiguities of occupation spawned in both periods provided unprecedented opportunities for African American mobility. Viewed in successive historical moments as contagious and immune, black troops came in contact with a world globalized through technological advances in communication, medicine, travel, and warfare, and this shaped their own ideas about race, sexuality, and citizenship. The successes of the Red Ball Express and the Berlin Airlift—much like the employment of black men and women in America's earlier twentieth-century wars—validated the use of black military workers in Germany, and challenged the generational regimes of segregation and subjection that inhibited their ability to move. African American soldiers were undoubtedly cognizant of this midcentury shift in the boundaries of black mobility. As we shall see in a final reflection upon the work of William Gardner Smith, they recurred to a divergent archive of meanings to make sense of their emplacement as occupiers in postwar Berlin.

Much like the Reconstruction period in U.S Southern history, the occupation of Germany replaced one regime of control with another, destabilizing the fixity of the color line, and shifting the meanings of race, nation, and sexuality through military fiat. The social and sexual control of both German womanhood and African American masculinity by southern white military elites in the American zone of Germany can thus be read as a repeated attempt to repair, reconcile, and redeem the white American male body in the postwar moment; reprising a performance of white reunion that, as Amy Kaplan has shown, began by "bringing together blue and gray on distant shores" during the Spanish-Cuban-American War, continued unabated through the regulation of African American soldiers in France, and found a new generation of men and women fit for regulation in the overlapping theaters of World War II.[173]

Epilogue
The Long Arc of Black Military Opportunity

From the beginning of the twentieth century to the end of World War II, black men and women mobilized across oceans and hemispheres to extend America's military dominion beyond its own borders, projecting national debates about race, rights, and sexuality onto the world stage and into the overlapping theaters of global war. In these successive contests of masculine supremacy, the U.S. military resisted the use of African Americans as warriors while welcoming their service as workers, and the abiding debate over their proper employment continued into the postwar period. In April 1946 the War Department released Circular No. 124, "Utilization of Negro Manpower in the Postwar Army Policy," which offered a midcentury evaluation of black military labor in World War II and its prospective uses in the future. While still advocating for segregation in the practice of American militarism, the Gillem Board Report, as it would come to be known, gave an overall positive assessment of African American soldiers in World War II. In fact, before the exigencies of the Berlin Airlift forced it to end its restriction of black troops from overseas assignments, the army had already concluded that the use of "Negro manpower" had been a success, and much more of it would be necessary to have on hand in the event of any future national emergency. Out of nearly 2.5 million African Americans who registered for service in World War II, approximately 909,000 were selected for army use.[1] "The natural and artificial resources of any nation are dependent upon and reflect the vigor of her manpower," the board wrote. "An intelligent patriotism is imperative, if the nation is to vindicate the past, maintain the present, and rise to its future destiny." Cognizant of the "progress made by the Negro citizen between World War I and World War II, particularly in the last five years," the Gillem Report presented the black soldier as "ready and eager to accept his full responsibility as a citizen."[2] Forecasting the army's needs for black manpower in the future, the board made the following recommendations: "That the Negro, desiring to accept his legal and moral responsibility as charged by the Constitution, should be given every opportunity and aid to prepare himself for effective military service in company with every other citizen who is called. That those charged with the utilization of manpower in the military establishment have an equal legal and moral obligation under the Constitution to take all steps necessary to prepare the qualified manpower of the nation so that it will function efficiently and effectively under the stress of modern battle conditions."[3]

The Gillem Report took special note of the roles education and mobility had played in enhancing the war potentials of the modern African American service force, a fact which bode well for the military and American society overall. "The imprints of travel of bettered living and health conditions, plus the increased financial resources, have left a mental stamp which will persist and continue to become more articulate." Moreover, as "a more complete acceptance of the Negro in all the diversified fields of endeavor" continued apace in the United States, creating a "ready market in the intricacies of a modern military machine," the board perceived military service as having effected a transformation of black laborers into *craftsmen*. "Many Negroes who, before the war, were laborers, are now craftsmen, capable in the many instances of competing with the white man on an equal basis. This change in the industrial status has, further, allowed the Negro to give his children more and better education. In many colleges and universities of the North and West, the Negro student is accepted solely on the basis of his individual merit and ability. This rise in the technical and cultural level of the Negro has, in turn, given him a more articulate voice in government."[4]

According to the board, the militarization of the African American population during World War II produced technically proficient men and women of color whose new proximity to ideals of heteronormative citizenship made them choice candidates for military service. As the Gillem Report suggested, the long arc of military opportunity had promoted a possibility seen as anathema by black leftists and white supremacists alike: namely, that beyond their employment during times of war, African Americans might look to military service as a career field. And yet even with this positive endorsement of the present and future use of black manpower, the Gillem Report still recommended segregating black military personnel into racially composite groups, and limiting their enlisted number to a "1 to 10 ratio of the Negro civilian population to the total population of the nation."[5]

While some black newspapers welcomed the Gillem Report as evidence of progress, others, like the *Pittsburgh Courier*, remained fiercely critical of the Jim Crow logics of segregation that continued to encumber African American military service. Soon after the report was released, the Philadelphia paper reprinted an editorial written by Roy Wilkins, then editor of *The Crisis*, that castigated the board for its unwillingness to renounce the segregationist frameworks impeding the effective use of black personnel. "Since the policy of segregation was the basic cause of unrest and low morale and instances of poor performance among Negro troops," Wilkins wrote, "it was reasonable to expect the Gillem Report would attack the basic cause. . . . But it does not do so except to allow for the placement of a few specialists and technicians here and there in the framework of the overhead units at Army installations where Negro personnel with special skills can be utilized to advantage as individuals."[6]

The *Courier* newsroom had a vested interest in the fair treatment of black soldiers in this new imperial moment, as one of their own budding young journalists had been drafted for occupation service in Germany that previous December.[7] The African American novelist and writer William Gardner Smith, who would gain great acclaim for his novel about black occupation service in Germany, *Last of the Conquerors* (1948), began his professional writing career as a beat reporter for the paper at only sixteen years of age. Born and raised in Philadelphia, Smith started working for the *Courier* as a high school senior, taking the pen name "Bill Smith" in newsprint. He received his draft notice one month shy of his nineteenth birthday, and reported to Fort Meade, Maryland, for basic training on January 8, 1946. After qualifying as a marksman, Smith was given orders to Europe, and on June 13 he arrived in the city of Berlin.

Smith was assigned to 661st T. C. Truck Company as a clerk-typist, a position which allowed him to make the most out of his newspaper background and gave him direct access to the former tools of his trade. In fact, alongside his military duties, he continued to write for the *Courier* as a "special correspondent," giving his Philadelphia readership an embedded perspective on black soldiering abroad. He wrote a slew of articles that detailed the injustices faced by black soldiers in Germany, the covert attempt to purge them from overseas service, and their reluctance to return to the United States. With titles like "Army 'Big Shots' Speed 'Purge' of Race Troops from Germany," "Segregation Dogs Soldiers in Europe," and "Innocent Soldier Goes on Rampage; Kills 1, Wounds 3," one wonders how Smith managed to publish explicit antiracist critiques of army policy from overseas without being discovered or reprimanded.[8] Had the army's World War I "Negro subversion" unit still been operative, perhaps his actions would have drawn their attention; but his official military records make no note of any insubordinate behavior on his part. As noted by his biographer, Leroy S. Hodges Jr., Smith's superiors found that he "Kept the records in good condition. Made out Morning Reports. Also was in charge of Motor Pool employing 76 Germans."[9]

Smith worked in the same trucking companies whose superior mobility, as I have previously discussed (chapter 5), created such consternation within the white American military hierarchy in occupied Berlin. As a clerk-typist he was specifically involved in copying and distributing the edicts of military rule in Germany, and was witness to, and a likely participant in, the purge of African Americans from the European theater. In an article written on November 9, 1946, Smith exposed the "secret orders" he had received that detailed the plan to facilitate "a coming mass discharge of colored soldiers" in the "European Black Belt" of Germany. Using as their cover the recently enacted policy of the "blue discharge," which "deprives soldiers who have served over long periods of time of all benefits under the GI Bill of Rights," military commanders were given carte-blanche authority in fast-tracking discharges, and had "turned their scythes on the hitherto untouched Regular Army men."[10] The administrative effect of the blue discharge policy was immediate, as commanders inundated their clerical subordinates with requests to write termination letters. "The response was overwhelming," Smith wrote. "Company clerks and typists were kept working overtime." As evidence of the "highly phrased but basically trivial letters" he and other clerks were commanded to type up, Smith cited the case of a black regular in Mannheim who faced dismissal because of his alleged unkempt appearance. "Despite the prodding of his Sergeant, the First Sergeant, and myself, he has persisted in coming on duty and going on pass with soiled apparel. His tie is especially filthy. I feel the appearance of this man in the presence of our allies and enemies is prejudicial to the good reputation of the United States Army which has maintained a high standard of cleanliness through its long and inspiring history. For this reason I recommend that _____ be discharged under the provisions of Section VIII (The Blue Discharge)."[11]

The figure of the dirty black soldier, so present in the historical discourse of African American military service, had reemerged once more in the European Black Belt as a subject of regulation, control, exclusion, and now disfranchisement. "So this soldier," Smith wrote, "who after serving two and a half years re-enlisted for three years more, now faces the possibility of a Blue Discharge depriving him of his mustering out pay, right to go to college under the GI Bill, and many other advantages—because his necktie was dirty."[12] As a clerk-typist, Smith's role in this necropolitical furlough embodied the kinds of complicities and resistances that previous generations of black military workers had experienced in their entanglements with American militarism. While there is no evidence to suggest that Smith ever wanted to reenlist himself, he knew that the future of African American military service in the postwar period was fraught with precariousness, since the vaunted transformation of black laborers into military craftsmen trumpeted in the Gillem Report had done little to transmute the racist attitudes of the craftsmen's managers.

Smith's European service ended on January 21, 1947, and he arrived in New York harbor on the S.S. *Marine Robin* on February 1. During his return voyage he took time to reflect upon the paradoxical feelings of freedom and constriction he experienced as an occupation soldier in Berlin. As the editor of the ship's paper, Smith had a small office and a typewriter to himself, and he transposed his muddled thoughts into words. As he recounted in an interview a year later, "It was blind, inane stuff at first and I kept pecking out: 'You can so write. Now is the time. Now is the time. Now. Right now.' I kept doing that till the real words came and the book got started."[13]

The results of those efforts, the novel *Last of the Conquerors*, was published by Farrar, Straus, and Company in 1948. Smith's thinly veiled portrait of his time in Berlin was widely acclaimed and sold briskly, receiving positive reviews from mainstream papers as well as niche radical journals. For instance, writing under the pseudonym G. F. Eckstein in the *Fourth International*, the journal of the U.S. Socialist Workers Party, C. L. R. James reviewed the debut favorably alongside Norman Mailer's bestseller *The Naked and the Dead*. For James, both works marked an "unmistakable sign of a new wave of radical intellectuals" and he proclaimed Smith "a natural writer."[14]

Still, reviewers were apt to critique Smith's literary proficiency as a novelist. James himself noted in comparing *Conquerors* to *The Naked and the Dead* that "Smith's book is in every way a much slighter work." A critic in the *Dallas Herald* opined that "the author does not have any great style, and humor and geniality are as little evident in the writing as they are in the leading character, but the story does not call for frivolity."[15] The *Chicago Sun-Times* made a balanced assessment of Smith's literary craftsmanship, appreciating his content but quibbling over his form. "The writing for the most part is strong, simple, and lively. One might be tempted to recommend the excision of some parts which are too hortatory or too biased, but it should be realized these artistic defects usually accompany the novel with a bitter message."[16]

The questionable aesthetic merits of *Conquerors* may explain why Smith's most celebrated work has only recently received sustained engagement and reappraisal by practitioners of African American literary and cultural studies. Bernard Bell, in his foundational survey *The Afro-American Novel and Its Tradition* (1987), largely dismisses the novel as "an interracial love story in which black soldiers ironically discover more freedom in Germany than they found in the United States," and assured his readers that of Smith's four published novels, "the best of these is the last."[17] Bell compares Smith unfavorably to the better-known writers of 1940s black naturalist fiction, including Richard Wright, Chester Himes, and Ann Petry. But as literary scholar Stephanie Brown has recently argued, "even within the genre of African American postwar fiction, Smith's novel has been largely ignored."[18] In fact, Brown credits contemporary feminist historians of the German-American postwar military encounter for *Conquerors*' critical recovery, as their work "has done far more to rehabilitate Smith's novel than has African-American literary studies."[19]

As I conclude this study of black military immunity during the first fifty years of twentieth-century U.S. military engagement, I should admit that my purpose in reflecting upon *Conquerors*' critical reception history at this late stage in my argument is not aimed at recovering Smith as an underappreciated writer of the postwar moment. And while I wholeheartedly agree with Hodges's early assertion that the novel "derives its power from a penetrating examination of Black soldiers in a racially segregated American Army and is the first twentieth-century novel by an Afro-American writer to deal with this sensitive matter," I do not intend, in these final lines, to offer a new reading of his text's significance within the canon of African American literature.[20] To be sure, a number of excellent works in literary, historical, and cultural studies have arrived to give *Conquerors* the sensitive reading it has always deserved. I only hope to show that Smith—like millions of other African Americans, then and now—made the most out of his midcentury encounter with American militarism. Smith departed Germany a year before the Berlin Airlift broke the clasp, if not the strap, of the Black Belt in Europe; yet his communiqués and literary reflections of the American occupation still stand today as a singular record of the fervor of that disorienting and discomfiting moment for black soldiers, reifying their experiences into protest and prose, and continuing a tradition of black military cultural critique that had been centuries in the making.

Brown's insightful reading of the conditions of possibility that helped shape Smith's writing career illustrates this point clearly. She observes that "as a journalist whose tenure at the *Pittsburgh Courier* in the final years of the war had sharpened his appraisal of its impact on African Americans, Smith entered the occupation army in a unique position to observe the social and political ferment that characterized the years between the end of the war and the integration of the military that began with Truman's executive order in 1948."[21] Smith's witness, as subject and scribe of the overseas military apparatus, offered a counter history to America's official military record of occupation, and laid the mythic foundation for what would become the twice-told tale of black soldiering in Germany: that military service in the fallen nation was like a "breath of freedom" for African American men and women.[22] This contagious narrative of black military freedom, popularized by the black press and later reified in the nostalgic memoir of former U.S. Secretary of State Colin Powell, linked black aspiration to a military career occupation, and influenced ensuing generations of African Americans to enlist in the service. Yet rather than anointing Smith's novel as an urtext of the modern African American encounter with American militarism, I would submit finally that we place the whole of his work in the genealogy of black military immunity I have traced in these pages, making him heir to, rather than progenitor of, the long discourse of resistance and complicity, freedom and control that has marked black soldiering in the postwar era, and continues to haunt the contradictory meanings ascribed to African American military service in our contemporary moment.

Notes

Introduction

1. Vagts, "Ivory Towers into Watchtowers," 162.
2. Vagts, "Ivory Towers into Watchtowers," 163.
3. Vagts, "Ivory Towers into Watchtowers," 164–65.
4. Vagts, "Ivory Towers into Watchtowers," 164.
5. Vagts, "Ivory Towers into Watchtowers," 162.
6. Vagts, *History of Militarism*, 11.
7. Vagts, *History of Militarism*, 11.
8. Epstein, Catherine, *Past Renewed*, 316–18; Fair-Schulz and Kessler, *German Scholars in Exile*, 220.
9. Vagts, "Ivory Towers into Watchtowers," 175.
10. Vagts, "Ivory Towers into Watchtowers," 171–72.
11. Vagts, "Ivory Towers into Watchtowers," 173–74.
12. Vagts, "Ivory Towers into Watchtowers," 166–67.
13. Kim Parker, Anthony Cillufo, and Renee Stepler, "Six Facts about the Military and Its Changing Demographics," Pew Research Center, April 13, 2007, https://www.pewresearch.org/fact-tank/2017/04/13/6-facts-about-the-u-s-military-and-its-changing-demographics/; John Gramlich, "The Gap between the Number of Blacks and Whites in Prison Is Shrinking," Pew Research Center, April 30, 2019, https://www.pewresearch.org/fact-tank/2019/04/30/shrinking-gap-between-number-of-blacks-and-whites-in-prison/.
14. Hussain, "Sound of Terror"; "AFRICOM Mission Statement," United States Africa Command, http://www.africom.mil/what-we-do, accessed October 26, 2019.
15. Huntington, *Soldier and the State*, 11, 13.
16. Vagts, *History of Militarism*, 12–13.
17. As of 2015, there were close to 800 installations operating in over seventy countries and territories overseas. See Johnson, *Sorrows of Empire*, 1; Donovan, *Militarism, U.S.A.*; David Vine, "Where in the World Is the U.S. Military?," *Politico*, July–August 2015, https://www.politico.com/magazine/story/2015/06/us-military-bases-around-the-world-119321; and Vine's book-length treatment, *Base Nation*.

Chapter One

1. Elena Schor and Connor O'Brien, "McCain Calls for War Powers Debate after Niger Attack," *Politico*, October 23, 2017, https://www.politico.com/story/2017/10/23/mccain-war-powers-niger-attack-244085; Phillip Carter and Andrew Swick, "Why Were US Soldiers even in Niger? America's Shadow Wars in Africa, Explained," *Vox*,

October 26, 2017, https://www.vox.com/world/2017/10/26/16547528/us-soldiers-niger-johnson-widow-africa-trump.

2. Richard Sisk, "Lawmaker: Family Learned of Soldier's Remains from News Reports," *Military.com*, November 22, 2017, https://www.military.com/daily-news/2017/11/22/lawmaker-family-learned-of-soldiers-remains-from-news-reports.html.

3. Dj Deak, "[New Details/Extended Version] The Niger Ambush," May 24, 2018, YouTube video, 22:55, https://youtu.be/cFmN-1N0SWg.

4. Trouillot, *Silencing the Past*, 26.

5. I thank Frank Kelleter for this generous insight.

6. Monica Mark, "Inside the Botched Raid that Left Four U.S. Soldiers Dead in Niger," *Buzzfeed News*, December 9, 2017, https://www.buzzfeed.com/monicamark/niger-secret-wars-in-africa?utm_term=.txNqXMm13#.np5y8ZK4D.

7. Steve Owen, "Miami Stunt Rider Known as the 'Wheelie King,'" WPLG-TV10 ABC Local 10 News, September 13, 2013, https://www.local10.com/news/florida/miami-stunt-rider-known-as-the-wheelie-king_20151127195827943; Molly Hurford, "U.S. Soldier Killed in Niger Was a Skilled BMX Rider Known as the 'Wheelie King,'" *Bicycling*, October 25, 2017, https://www.bicycling.com/news/a20030630/us-soldier-killed-in-niger-known-as-wheelie-king/.

8. Dj Deak, "[New Details/Extended Version] The Niger Ambush."

9. Joe Tacopino, "Trump to Slain Soldier's Widow: 'He Knew What He Signed up for,'" *New York Post*, October 17, 2017, https://nypost.com/2017/10/17/trump-to-slain-soldiers-widow-he-knew-what-he-signed-up-for/.

10. ABC News, "Transcript: Widow of Fallen Soldier La David Johnson Speaks out," *Good Morning America*, October 23, 2017, https://abcnews.go.com/US/transcript-widow-fallen-soldier-la-david-johnson-speaks/story?id=50655055.

11. Elmer T. Williams, "Was La David Johnson Another Bowe Bergdahl?" *E.T. Williams, The Doctor of Commonsense*, October 23, 2017; George Iliffe, discussion forum, "How They Fell: Army Team 'Fought to the End' in Niger Ambush," *Military.com*, July 21, 2018, https://www.military.com/daily-news/2018/05/11/how-they-fell-army-team-fought-end-niger-ambush.html.

12. Verdery, *Political Lives of Dead Bodies*.

13. Snorton and Haritaworn, "Trans Necropolitics"; Haritaworn, Kuntsman, and Posocco, *Queer Necropolitics*; Ferrániz and Robben, *Necropolitics*, 1.

14. Mbembe, "Necropolitics," 12.

15. Mbembe, "Necropolitics," 34.

16. Mbembe, "Necropolitics," 34–5.

17. Mbembe, "Necropolitics," 34.

18. Associated Press, "More than 1,000 Mourn Sgt. La David Johnson and 3 Fellow Soldiers Killed in Niger," *USA Today*, October 21, 2017, https://eu.usatoday.com/story/news/nation/2017/10/21/more-than-1-000-mourn-sgt-la-david-johnson-and-3-fellow-soldiers-killed-niger/787979001/.

19. 5000 Role Models of Excellence Project, https://www.5000rolemodels.com/, accessed on October 26, 2019.

20. Mbembe, "Necropolitics," 40.

21. Michel Foucault, *Society Must Be Defended*, 256.

22. Foucault, *Society Must Be Defended*, 257.
23. Foucault, *Society Must Be Defended*, 257.
24. Mbembe, "Necropolitics," 24.
25. Mbembe, "Necropolitics," 21.
26. Mbembe, "Necropolitics," 40.
27. For a capsule history of this debate, see Watts, "Yellow Fever Immunities," and Kiple, "Response to Sheldon Watts."
28. McNeill, *Mosquito Empires*, 46, emphasis mine.
29. Watts, "Yellow Fever Immunities," 961.
30. Espinosa, "Question of Racial Immunity," 440–44.
31. Espinosa, "Question of Racial Immunity," 448.
32. Rush, *Account of the bilious remitting fever*, 96.
33. Rush, *Account of the bilious remitting fever*, 97.
34. Jones and Allen, *Narrative of the proceedings of the black people*, 15.
35. Miller, "Wages of Blackness,"183.
36. Jones and Allen, *Narrative of the proceedings of the black people*, 20.
37. Cottrol and Diamond, "Second Amendment," 331; *Constitution Society* website, http://www.constitution.org/mil/mil_act_1792.htm, accessed October 26, 2019.
38. Humphries, *Intensely Human*, 29.
39. Patterson, *Slavery and Social Death*, 96.
40. Aptheker, "Negro Casualties in the Civil War," 21, 75, 76.
41. Aptheker, "Negro Casualties in the Civil War," 22.
42. Aptheker, "Negro Casualties in the Civil War," 25.
43. Aptheker, "Negro Casualties in the Civil War," 12–13.
44. Gatewood, *Smoked Yankees*, 11.
45. Blight, "Meaning or the Fight," 151.
46. Washington, *Booker T. Washington Papers*, 4:389.
47. Washington, *Booker T. Washington Papers*, 4:389.
48. Washington, *Booker T. Washington Papers*, 4:389.
49. Harlan, *Booker T. Washington*, viii.
50. "Let Afro-Americans Prove Their Loyalty," *Cleveland Gazette*, March 26, 1898, 1.
51. "Let Afro-Americans Prove Their Loyalty."
52. "The Negro in the Impending Crisis," *Colored American*, March 19, 1898.
53. "Negro in the Impending Crisis," emphasis mine.
54. "General Order No. 55, May 26, 1898," *U.S. War Department General Orders* (Washington, DC: War Department, Adjutant General's Office, 1898), 140.
55. "Strangest Regiment in World," *Duluth News-Tribune*, July 31, 1898, 6; "One Regiment May Save Santiago," *Philadelphia Inquirer*, July 31, 1898, 2.
56. "Strangest Regiment in World," *Duluth News-Tribune*, July 31, 1898, 6; "One Regiment May Save Santiago," *Philadelphia Inquirer*, July 31, 1898, 2.
57. "Immune Humbuggery," *Augusta Chronicle*, May 30, 1898, 4.
58. "In Favor of the Negro," *Semi-Weekly Times-Democrat*, May 13, 1898, 2.
59. Fletcher, "Black Volunteers in the Spanish-American War," 48–49.
60. Fletcher, "Black Volunteers in the Spanish-American War," 48.
61. "Press Opinions: An Immune Defined," *Augusta Chronicle*, June 23, 1898, 4.

62. "Negro Soldiers," *Parsons Weekly Blade*, April 16, 1898, 2.

63. *Colored American*, June 11, 1898, 4.

64. Huber and Kremer, "Nathaniel C. Bruce," 39.

65. Born three years after the end of slavery on a farm near Danville, Virginia, Bruce knew only too well the well-oiled insult of comparing blacks to animals; but following his mentor, he also believed the labor of both was necessary for the vocational independence of his people. He would later found the first agriculture school for blacks in Missouri, which remained open until shut down by the 1954 *Brown v. Board of Education* Supreme Court decision that outlawed segregated in education. Letter from Nathaniel C. Bruce from the *News and Observer* (Raleigh, NC), May 22, 1898, reprinted in Gatewood, *Smoked Yankees*, 107–8.

66. Gatewood, *Smoked Yankees*, 197.

67. Gatewood, *Smoked Yankees*, 197.

68. Gatewood, *Smoked Yankees*, 198.

69. Gatewood, *Smoked Yankees*, 226.

70. Gatewood, *Smoked Yankees*, 202–3.

71. Gatewood, *Smoked Yankees*, 204.

72. Baudrillard, "The Precession of Simulacra," in *Simulacra and Simulation*, 1–42; McCook, *Martial Graves of our Fallen Heroes*, 19.

73. Jeremy Silvester's study of German settler colonialism in Namibia makes a similar claim about the use of martial graveyards on colonized land; Silvester, "Sleep with a Southwester."

74. Fanebust, *Major General Alexander M. McCook*, 25.

75. Fanebust, *Major General Alexander M. McCook*, 25; Herrera, *For Liberty and the Republic*, 155.

76. McCook, *Martial Graves of our Fallen Heroes*, 200–01.

77. Zelinsky, *Enigma of Ethnicity*, 76; McCook, *Martial Graves of our Fallen Heroes*, 9.

78. McCook, *Martial Graves of our Fallen Heroes*, 18.

79. McCook, *Martial Graves of our Fallen Heroes*, 200.

80. McCook, *Martial Graves of our Fallen Heroes*, 201.

81. McCook, *Martial Graves of our Fallen Heroes*, 201.

82. McCook, *Martial Graves of our Fallen Heroes*, 203.

83. Cirillo, *Bullets and Bacilli*, 92.

84. Kaplan, "Black and Blue on San Juan Hill," 232.

85. McCook, *Martial Graves of our Fallen Heroes*, 393; Bonsal, *Fight for Santiago*, 433.

86. McCook, *Martial Graves of our Fallen Heroes*, 394.

87. Cashin, et al, *Under Fire with the Tenth Cavalry*, 131; Cirilo, 92.

88. Bonsal, *Fight for Santiago*, 434.

89. McCook, *Martial Graves of our Fallen Heroes*, 284.

90. McCook, *Martial Graves of our Fallen Heroes*, 256.

91. McCook, *Martial Graves of our Fallen Heroes*, 256.

92. Washington, *Future of the American Negro*, 130–31.

93. Washington, *Future of the American Negro*, 130. John Bethell writes, "On the American side, some 5,509 regulars and volunteers died of infectious diseases, 202 died of wounds, and 496 were killed in action"; Bethell, "Splendid Little War."

94. Washington, *Booker T. Washington Papers*, 4:492.
95. Washington, *Booker T. Washington Papers*, 4:492.
96. Washington, *Booker T. Washington Papers*, 4:492, footnote 1.
97. "The Gospel of Washington," *Colored American*, October, 10, 1898, 1.
98. "Gospel of Washington."
99. R. C. Ransom, "When the World Heard." *Indianapolis Freeman*, November 12, 1898, 2.
100. Ransom, "When the World Heard."
101. Booker T. Washington, "Booker T. Washington's Chicago Speech as It Was," *Birmingham Age Herald*, November 13, 1898, 15.
102. Washington, "Booker T. Washington's Chicago Speech as It Was."
103. Washington, "Booker T. Washington's Chicago Speech as It Was."
104. Washington, "Booker T. Washington's Chicago Speech as It Was."
105. Washington, *Booker T. Washington Papers*, 4:493, footnotes 2 and 3.
106. Booker T. Washington, *Working with the Hands*, 106. Washington would repeat the claim six years later in an article about Tuskegee's training schools for nurses; see Washington, "Training Colored Nurses at Tuskegee," 168.

Chapter Two

1. "Mrs. Curtis's Mission to New Orleans," *Daily Picayune*, July 21, 1898, 8.
2. "Mrs. A. M. Curtis Goes South," *Colored American*, July 16, 1898, 8.
3. "Mrs. Curtis in Louisiana: Her Mission to Secure Immune Trained Nurses for Service in Cuba—a Page of History," *Colored American*, July 30, 1898, 6.
4. "Gossip Gathered in Hotel Lobbies," *Daily Picayune*, July 17, 1898, 12.
5. "Mrs. Curtis's Mission to New Orleans."
6. "A Council of Women: The National Association of Colored Women Holds a Session in This City," *Colored American*, July 30, 1898.
7. I thank Christa Buschendorf, Emeritus Professor of American Studies at Frankfurt University, for bringing Wells's family history of yellow fever to my attention at the JFK Institute, Freie Universität, Berlin, May 31, 2017.
8. "Mrs. A. M. Curtis Goes South." For more on the Citizens' Committee, see DeCuir, "Attacking Jim Crow." 38-9.
9. See Hine, *Black Women in White*, 3-25; Carnegie, "Black Nurses at the Front," 1252; Washington, "Training Colored Nurses at Tuskegee," 168.
10. "News of Women Workers," *Los Angeles Herald*, August 28, 1898, 22. Curtis is misidentified as "M. A. Curtis."
11. "Quartered Below Mules: Alleged Indignity Offered Immune Nurses on Board the Transport Michigan at Port Tampa," *Boston Daily Globe*, August 1, 1898.
12. United States Department of War, *Correspondence relating to the War with Spain and conditions growing out of the same, including the insurrection in the Philippine Islands and the China Relief expedition, between the Adjutant General of the Army and Military Commanders in the United States, Cuba, Porto Rico, China, and the Philippine Islands, from April 15, 1898 to July 30th, 1902*, Washington, DC: Government Printing Office, 1902, 341.
13. Bolton, *History of the Second Regiment Illinois Volunteer Infantry*, 66-67.

14. Dannett, *Profiles of Negro Womanhood*, 103.

15. "THE COLOR LINE: Drawn by the Proprietor of a Chicago Apartment House," *Los Angeles Times*, September 29, 1894, 1; "Woman of Mystery to Return to Coast," *San Francisco Call*, August 27, 1906.

16. Daniel Murray Papers.

17. "The Fifteen Amendment: Grand Turnout by the Colored Population," *Weekly Alta California*, April 9, 1870. Curtis's father, Hamilton Wilson Sockum (listed as "Wm. Sockum"), was a likely member of the procession of 1500 people marching in honor of the ratification of the Fifteenth Amendment.

18. "Women's Work and Ways," *Plain Dealer* (Detroit, MI), January 6, 1893, 8; "World's Fair Doings: Protection is Guaranteed, Interests of the Colored Exhibitors Will Be Carefully Guarded," *Daily Inter Ocean* (Chicago), January 1, 1893, 5. Jackson, sometimes listed in the archival record as Walla, passed away in 1881.

19. Murphree, *Native America*, 486. Joseph A. Romeo's "The Moors of Delaware" website has been especially useful in tracing the branches of the Sockum family tree. Joseph A. Romeo, "The Moors of Delaware: Genealogical Records of the Descendants of a Colonial Delaware Isolate Community," http://www.moors-delaware.com/gendat/moors.aspx.

20. Murphree, *Native America*, 486.

21. In the 1850 census Sockum and his eleven-member family were all listed as "mulatto," which suggests that the law against selling powder to mixed-race folk was selectively enforced. The prosecuting attorney admitted as such, stating later that "the case originated in the private spite of envious Caucasian neighbors." "1850 United States Federal Census," *Ancestry.com*, Year: 1850; Census Place: Indian River Hundred, Sussex, Delaware; Roll: M432_55; Page: 178A; Image: 357, accessed June 20, 2016. See also Porter, "Anthropologists at Work," 2.

22. Porter, "Anthropologists at Work," 1–2; Weslager, *Delaware's Forgotten Folk*, 31–37.

23. "Somewhat Mixed: The Descendants of Indians and other Races in Delaware," *New Haven Evening Register*, March 13, 1890; Murray Papers.

24. "Boom-De-Ra," *Cleveland Gazette*, March 18, 1893.

25. Barnett and Wells, *Reason Why the Colored American Is Not in the World's Columbian Exposition*, http://digital.library.upenn.edu/women/wells/exposition/exposition.html.

26. "Negro Blood Flows in Her Veins: Reasons for Ejectment Proceedings against Pretty Mrs. Curtis," *Chicago Tribune*, September 28, 1894, 12.

27. "The Color Line, Mrs. A. M. Curtis, Well Known in this City," *San Francisco Chronicle*, September 29, 1894, 14.

28. "Mrs. A. M. Curtis Wins Her Suit: Justice Everett Decides She May Not Be Ejected from Her Home," *Chicago Tribune*, September 30, 1894, 4.

29. Mrs. A. M. Curtis, "Appeal to Colored Voters," *Cox-McPherson Family Papers, 1892–1922*, mss#38-11, Special Collections Department, University of Virginia Library, http://www2.vcdh.virginia.edu/afam/politics/appeal.html, accessed October 27, 2019.

30. Cobb, "Medical History," 296.

31. Cobb, "Medical History," 294, 297. Willard Gatewood is a notable exception in his careful treatment of Curtis. See Gatewood, *Aristocrats of Color*.

32. "Report of Mrs. A. M. Curtis of the Work That Is Being Done in San Francisco by the American National Red Cross and Its Branches, to Hon. William H. Taft, President of the American National Red Cross," American National Red Cross, Bulletin no. 4, issued by the Central Committee (October 1906), 32–37.

33. *Indianapolis Freeman*, August 24, 1912.

34. "Spanish-American War Nurses, Report of Fourth Annual Meeting: President's Address," *American Journal of Nursing* 4, no. 1 (October 1903), 131. Anita Newcomb McGee's address was given in absentia.

35. As Mariola Espinosa maintains in her important article debunking the entrenched belief in black immunity among historians, "The argument that long histories with malaria increased the prevalence of genes that offer some protection to that disease in populations from which Caribbean slaves were drawn—therefore long exposure to yellow fever likely had a similar effect—is simply wrong." See Espinosa, "Question of Racial Immunity," 447. Turnbull's age (forty-two) and race (mulatto) taken from 1880 Census records, *Ancestry.com*, 1880; Census Place: Baton Rouge, East Baton Rouge, Louisiana; Roll: 452; Family History Film: 1254452; Page: 356A; Enumeration District: 103; Image: 0575.

36. "Died," *Daily Picayune*, September 28, 1898, 4.

37. "Transport Brings Many Dead from Cuba," *New York Times*, February 20, 1901.

38. "Fifth Annual Session: National Convention of Army Nurses Meet Here," *Evening Star*, May 1, 1905, 7; *Nurses Journal of the Pacific Coast*, June 1905, 205. Turnbull's date of death and burial notice suggests that she died stateside rather than in Cuba.

39. U.S. Congress, Senate, *Report of Commission Appointed by the President to Investigate the Conduct of the War with Spain*. Washington, DC: Government Printing Office, 1900, 3052.

40. U.S. Congress, Senate, *Conduct of the War with Spain*, 3170; also see Yoshiya Makita, who cites this characterization of the nurses as probable evidence of McGee's antiblack racism; Makita, "Professional Angels of War," 67–86.

41. Hine, *Black Women in White*, 3–4; Sabin, "Sweating, Purging, and a Passion for Care," 12–16.

42. Ward, *Voodoo Queen*, 39–42; Miller, "Wages of Blackness," 183–84.

43. *Mobile Register*, August 24, 1868, 2.

44. *The Annual Statistician and the Economist* (San Francisco: L. P. McCarty and Sons, 1890), 550.

45. Ochsner, "Complex Life of Rudolph Matas," 387–92.

46. Matas, *Surgical Peculiarities of the American Negro*, 28.

47. Matas, *Surgical Peculiarities of the American Negro*, 125.

48. Matas, *Surgical Peculiarities of the American Negro*, 29.

49. Matas, *Surgical Peculiarities of the American Negro*, 125.

50. Matas, "Nursing in Yellow Fever," 200.

51. Matas, "Nursing in Yellow Fever," 201.

52. See Sokolitz, "Picturing the Plantation."

53. "White middle-class Americans did not consider hospitalization a viable alternative to home care. Most often they were treated in their homes by an attending physician and female family members." Hine, *Black Women in White*, 5.

54. Fannie B. Ward, "Custom in House Keeping in Cuba," *The State* (Columbia, SC), September 20, 1898.
55. Fahs, *Out on Assignment*, 241–51.
56. Hunter, *To 'Joy My Freedom*, 60–61.
57. Ward, "Custom in House Keeping in Cuba."
58. Ward, "Custom in House Keeping in Cuba.
59. Ward, "Custom in House Keeping in Cuba."
60. "Colored Nurses Return from the Campaign of Mercy at Santiago," *Daily Picayune*, September 21, 1898, 6.
61. "Colored Nurses Return from the Campaign of Mercy at Santiago."
62. "Colored Nurses from Cuba," *New York Tribune*, September 16, 1898.
63. "Nurses Start South," *New York Tribune*, September 15, 1898.
64. "Colored Nurses from Cuba."
65. "Colored Nurses from Cuba."
66. "Colored Nurses from Cuba."
67. "Colored Nurses from Cuba."
68. "Testimony of Cleveland Moffett." in U.S. Congress, Senate, *Investigation of Conduct of War with Spain*, 2298.
69. "Gruesome Hospital Tales Told by the Army's Most Famous Nurse," *Springfield Daily Republican* (Springfield, MA), October 24, 1898, 10.
70. Spillers, "Mama's Baby, Papa's Maybe," 65.
71. According to the testimony of a white nurse who served at Santiago and Montauk, "Mammy Cobbs, colored" was a good worker who continued nursing at Camp Wikoff after leaving Cuba, "and the officials are unwilling that she should go home. "An Interesting Letter from Miss Florence Applegate, Nurse at Santiago de Cuba," *Daily Picayune*, November 11, 1898, 3.
72. Spillers, "Mama's Baby, Papa's Maybe," 65.
73. "Gruesome Hospital Tales."
74. "Gruesome Hospital Tales."
75. "Gruesome Hospital Tales."
76. "Testimony of Cleveland Moffett," 2298–301; Gillett, *Army Medical Department*, 193–95.
77. "Colored Nurses Return from the Campaign of Mercy at Santiago."
78. "Colored Nurses Return from the Campaign of Mercy at Santiago."
79. Holder, "What's Sex Got to Do with It?," 156; Thomas, "'Plessy vs. Ferguson' and the Literary Imagination."
80. U.S. Constitution, amend. 14, sec. 1, emphasis added.
81. Alexander, "Upgrading of the Negro's Status."
82. Thomas, "'Plessy vs. Ferguson' and the Literary Imagination," 46.
83. Despite Mrs. Curtis's protests to Washington, women nurses were paid only half as much—thirty dollars per month—as their male peers. "Gossip Gathered in Hotel Lobbies," 12.
84. "Colored Nurses Return from the Campaign of Mercy at Santiago."
85. For analysis of the "spectacles of aggressive American manhood" that defined coverage of the conflict, see Kaplan, "Black and Blue on San Juan Hill," 223–25.

86. McCook, *Martial Graves of our Fallen Heroes*, 399.
87. White men (and presumably black men) were excluded as well. For the history of black women's attempts to join the ANC, see Threat, *Nursing Civil Rights*.
88. Trouillot, *Silencing the Past*, 23; Moorer, "Negro Heroines," in *Prejudice Unveiled*, 75.

Chapter Three

1. Marshall, "Atlanta Peace Jubilee"; Hilfrich, "Creating and Instrumentalizing Nationalism."
2. *Christian Recorder*, November 3, 1898; "Those Premature Jubilees," *Plain Dealer* (Cleveland, OH), November 22, 1898, 4; "Not Time for Peace: President Asks that Atlanta Change Name of Its Jubilee," *Tacoma Daily News* (Tacoma, WA), November 11, 1898, 1.
3. "Peter Purity: He writes about the Atlanta Peace Jubilee." *Broad Ax* (Salt Lake City, UT), January 7, 1899, 4. "Peter Purity" may have been the pen name of *The Appeal*'s editor, Charles H. J. Taylor. Woods, "C. H. J. Taylor and the Movement for Black Political Independence," 131.
4. "The Peace Jubilee," *Washington Bee*, April 15, 1899, 4.
5. "What Does it Mean? The Peace Jubilee—The Negro Not Wanted—A Manly Letter," *Washington Bee*, May 27, 1899, 5.
6. *American Citizen* (Kansas City, KS), April 28, 1899; in Marks, *Black Press Views American Imperialism*, 124.
7. "Civilization Should Begin at Home," *Indianapolis Recorder*, April 1, 1899; in Marks, *Black Press Views American Imperialism*, 120.
8. Marks, *Black Press Views American Imperialism*, 124.
9. *Indianapolis Freeman*, October 7, 1899; in Marks, *Black Press Views American Imperialism*, 150.
10. *Indianapolis Freeman*, July 1, 1899; in Marks, *Black Press Views American Imperialism*, 131.
11. *Cleveland Gazette*, July 8, 1899; in Marks, *Black Press Views American Imperialism*, 133.
12. *Voice of Missions* (Atlanta, GA), 7, May 1, 1899.
13. *Helena Reporter* (AL), February 1, 1900; in Marks, *Black Press Views American Imperialism*, 167.
14. Quoted in the *American Citizen*, July 14, 1899; in Marks, *Black Press Views American Imperialism*, 134.
15. Huntington, *Soldier and the State*, 11, 13.
16. Two biographies that offer exemplary treatments of Young's extant corpus are Kilroy, *For Race and Country*, and Shellum, *Black Officer in a Buffalo Soldier Regiment*.
17. *The Crisis*, February 1922, 155.
18. Brooks, *Bodies in Dissent*, 5.
19. *The Crisis*, February 1922, 155.
20. Brooks, *Bodies in Dissent*, 3.
21. Taylor, "Afterword," 1888.

22. Taylor, "Afterword," 1893.
23. Taylor, *Archive and the Repertoire*, 20.
24. McCaskill and Gebhard, *Post-Bellum, Pre-Harlem*, 2.
25. Trouillot, *Silencing the Past*, 73.
26. Trouillot, *Silencing the Past*, 96; Glick, *Black Radical Tragic*, 1.
27. Glick, *Black Radical Tragic*, 3.
28. Hartman, "Venus in Two Acts," 11.
29. *The Crisis*, February 1922, 155.
30. Kilroy, *For Race and Country*, 25–26; Shellum, *Black Officer in a Buffalo Soldier Regiment*, 6–7.
31. Kilroy, *For Race and Country*, 33–34; Shellum, *Black Officer in a Buffalo Soldier Regiment*, 62–63.
32. Shellum, *Black Officer in a Buffalo Soldier Regiment*, 77.
33. Gatewood, *Smoked Yankees*, 115–16.
34. Gatewood, *Smoked Yankees*, 119.
35. Gatewood, *Smoked Yankees*, 119–20.
36. Kilroy, *For Race and Country*, 45
37. Kilroy, *For Race and Country*, x, 34.
38. Gatewood, *Smoked Yankees*, 211.
39. Gatewood, *Smoked Yankees*, 256.
40. Richard Johnson, *My Life in the U.S. Army, 1899–1922*, quoted in Ngozi-Brown, "African-American Soldiers and Filipinos," 48.
41. All quotations from Stephan Bonsal, "The Negro Soldier in War and Peace," 325.
42. Marks, *Black Press Views American Imperialism*, 155; Balce, *Body Parts of Empire*, 91–125.
43. Gatewood, *Smoked Yankees*, 268.
44. Gatewood, *Smoked Yankees*, 258–59.
45. Wells-Barnett, *Lynch Law in Georgia*, 7–8.
46. Cited in Wells-Barnett, *Lynch Law in Georgia*, 8.
47. Gatewood, *Smoked Yankees*, 259.
48. Robinson and Schubert, "David Fagen," 69; Funston, *Memories of Two Wars*, 376.
49. Baker, *Modernism and the Harlem Renaissance*, 114, 77.
50. Brown, "White Backlash and the Aftermath of Fagen's Rebellion," 170.
51. Shellum, *Black Officer in a Buffalo Soldier Regiment*, 118–23.
52. Brown, "White Backlash and the Aftermath of Fagen's Rebellion."
53. Robinson and Schubert, "David Fagen," 75n30, 80–83.
54. Cooper, *Voice from the South*, 30.
55. Kilroy, *For Race and Country*, 52.
56. Vagts, *Military Attaché*, x.
57. "Charles Young Portfolio Sketches," National Afro-American Museum and Cultural Center digital archive, https://www.ohiomemory.org/digital/collection/p15005coll34/id/227, accessed October 29, 2019; Vagts, *Military Attaché*, 13.
58. "Colored Officer Chosen: Capt. Charles Young to Be Military Attache in Haiti and Santo Domingo," *New York Times*, May 1, 1904; cited in Kilroy, 65.
59. Shellum, *Black Officer in a Buffalo Soldier Regiment*, 167.

60. Kilroy, *For Race and Country*, 68.
61. Shellum, *Black Officer in a Buffalo Soldier Regiment*, 113.
62. Kilroy, *For Race and Country*, 66; Heinl and Heinl, *Written in Blood*, 337.
63. Heinl, "Col. Charles Young," 174.
64. Heinl and Heinl, *Written in Blood*, 337.
65. Shellum, *Black Officer in a Buffalo Soldier Regiment*, 171.
66. Shellum, *Black Officer in a Buffalo Soldier Regiment*, 176.
67. Comhaire-Sylvain, *Le Créole Haïten*; Schieffelin and Doucet, "The 'Real' Haitian Creole," 178.
68. Taylor, *Archive and the Repertoire*, 20.
69. Young, *Little Hand-Book of French Creole*, 1–3.
70. Kilroy, *For Race and Country*, 68.
71. Kilroy, *For Race and Country*, 150n29.
72. Kilroy, *For Race and Country*, 69.
73. Young, *Military Morales of Nations and Races*, 80.
74. Young, "Toussaint L'Ouverture," 17.
75. Young, "Toussant L'Ouverture," 27.
76. Young, *Little Hand-Book of French Creole*, 6.
77. Young, "Toussaint L'Ouverture," 29.
78. Young, "Toussaint L'Ouverture," 30.
79. Young, "Toussaint L'Ouverture," 32.
80. Young, "Toussaint L'Ouverture," 37.
81. Young, "Toussaint L'Ouverture," 42.
82. Young, "Toussaint L'Ouverture," 45.
83. Young, "Toussaint L'Ouverture," 75.
84. Young, "Toussaint L'Ouverture," 62–63.
85. Young, "Toussaint L'Ouverture," 68.
86. Young, "Toussaint L'Ouverture," 71.
87. Young, "Toussaint L'Ouverture," 75.
88. "Race Relations Education for the U.S. Army," Washington, DC: Headquarters, Department of the Army, December 1973.
89. Young, "Toussaint L'Ouverture," 75–76.
90. The attempt by Rigaud's partisans to assassinate Louverture is discussed by Bell, *Toussaint Louverture*, 177; Young, "Toussaint L'Ouverture," 77.
91. Young, "Toussaint L'Ouverture," 77.
92. Young, "Toussaint L'Ouverture," 77.
93. Young, "Toussaint L'Ouverture," 81.
94. Young, "Toussaint L'Ouverture," 85.
95. Young, "Toussaint L'Ouverture," 86.
96. Young, "Toussaint L'Ouverture," 87.
97. Young, "Toussaint L'Ouverture," 87.
98. Dormon, "Shaping the Popular Image," 450–71.
99. Young, "Toussaint L'Ouverture," 113.
100. Young, "Toussaint L'Ouverture," 108.
101. James, *Black Jacobins*, 81.

102. Young, "Toussaint L'Ouverture," 32.
103. Young, "Toussaint L'Ouverture," 114.
104. Young, "Toussaint L'Ouverture," 115.
105. Young, "Toussaint L'Ouverture," 116.
106. Young, "Toussaint L'Ouverture," 117.
107. Moses, *Classical Black Nationalism*, 2.
108. Young, "Toussaint L'Ouverture," 127.
109. Young, "Toussaint L'Ouverture," 135.
110. Young, "Toussaint L'Ouverture," 138.
111. Beard, *Toussaint L'Ouverture*, 232
112. Young, "Toussaint L'Ouverture," 140.
113. Young, "Toussaint L'Ouverture," 140. "They have only felled the trunk of the tree (of the freedom of the blacks); branches will sprout, for the roots are numerous and deep"; Beard, *Toussaint L'Ouverture*, 233.
114. Young, "Toussaint L'Ouverture," 140.
115. Young, "Toussaint L'Ouverture," 140.
116. Kilroy, *For Race and Country*, 63.
117. Shellum, *Black Officer in a Buffalo Soldier Regiment*, 175.
118. Kilroy, *For Race and Country*, 63.
119. Young, *Little Hand-Book of French Creole*, 29–42.
120. Kilroy, *For Race and Country*, 68.
121. Kilroy, *For Race and Country*, 67.
122. "Military Attache Robbed," *New York Times*, April 9, 1907.
123. Kilroy, *For Race and Country*, 77; Shellum 180.
124. Washington, *Booker T. Washington Papers*, 11:363–64, 370, 377, 379.
125. Kilroy, *For Race and Country*, 82–96.
126. *Washington Bee*, October 23, 1915; also noted in Kilroy, *For Race and Country*, 101–2.
127. Shellum, *Black Officer in a Buffalo Soldier Regiment*, 226.
128. Shellum, *Black Officer in a Buffalo Soldier Regiment*, 239–44.
129. Young, *Toussaint L'Ouverture*, 104.
130. Kilroy, *For Race and Country*, 121–23.
131. Kilroy, *For Race and Country*, 122.
132. Huntington, *Soldier and the State*, 3.
133. Huntington, *Soldier and the State*, 11, 13, 17–18.
134. Kilroy, *For Race and Country*, 130–31; "Itinerary for Col. Charles Young's Trip from Wilberforce, OH to Washington, DC," Smithsonian Digital Volunteers: Transcription Center, https://transcription.si.edu/project/9638, accessed October 29, 2019.
135. Kilroy, *For Race and Country*, 127; Young, *Toussaint L'Ouverture*, 7.
136. Kilroy, *For Race and Country*, 141.
137. "Negro Officers," *The Crisis*, June 1919, 96.
138. "Negro Officers," *The Crisis*, June 1919, 96.
139. "Negro Officers," *The Crisis*, June 1919, 96.
140. Gilroy, *Black Atlantic*, 20.
141. "Negro Officers," *The Crisis*, June 1919, 96.

142. "Correspondence of the Military Intelligence Division Relating to 'Negro Subversion,' 1917–1941," National Archives and Records Administration, 1987, Washington, DC, 2–3.

143. Case number 10218-364, "IO-NYC to MID. Re: Maj. H.A. Strauss Forwards Copy of Report Gathered by One of Military Intelligence Allies Regarding the 'Negro Agitation,'" August 25, 1919, "Correspondence of the Military Intelligence Division Relating to 'Negro Subversion,' 1917–1941," National Archives at College Park, College Park, MD. Electronic record retrieved from http://www.fold3.com, accessed August 12, 2019.

144. Charles Young, 1864–1922, Telegram from Charles Young to W. E. B. Du Bois, October 31, 1919, W. E. B. Du Bois Papers (MS 312), Special Collections and University Archives, University of Massachusetts Amherst Libraries.

145. W. E. B. (William Edward Burghardt) Du Bois, 1868–1963, Letter from W. E. B. Du Bois to United States Department of State [fragment], November 12, 1919, W. E. B. Du Bois Papers (MS 312), Special Collections and University Archives, University of Massachusetts Amherst Libraries.

146. Kilroy, *For Race and Country*, 147.

147. John R. Hurst, "Haiti," *The Crisis*, May 1920, 29.

148. Charles Young, 1864–1922, Letter from Charles Young to W. E. B. Du Bois, July 20, 1920, W. E. B. Du Bois Papers (MS 312), Special Collections and University Archives, University of Massachusetts Amherst Libraries.

149. Kilroy, *For Race and Country*, 150.

150. Robinson, *Forgeries of Memory and Meaning*, 233.

151. "Letter from Charles Young to Clarence I. Smith Jr.," January 15, 1919, Charles Young Collection, National Afro-American Museum and Cultural Center, Ohio Historical Society, The African-American Experience in Ohio, 1850–1920, http://dbs.ohiohistory.org/africanam/html/detao2f.html?ID=5472, accessed October 29, 2019.

152. Young, "Toussaint L'Ouverture," 142, 143.

153. Young, "Toussaint L'Ouverture," 144.

154. Young, "Toussaint L'Ouverture," 144.

155. Young, "Toussaint L'Ouverture," 144, 149.

156. Young, "Toussaint L'Ouverture," 150.

157. Young, "Toussaint L'Ouverture," 143.

158. Young, "Toussaint L'Ouverture," 151.

159. Young, "Toussaint L'Ouverture," 152.

160. Du Bois, *The Crisis* (February 1922), 155.

161. "Letter from Charles Young to Clarence I. Smith Jr."

162. "Letter from Charles Young to Clarence I. Smith Jr."

163. Kilroy, *For Race and Country*, 50.

164. Kilroy, *For Race and Country*, 152.

165. Kilroy, *For Race and Country*, 152.

166. Shellum, *Black Officer in a Buffalo Soldier Regiment*, 277.

167. Shellum, *Black Officer in a Buffalo Soldier Regiment*, 277.

168. Kilroy, *For Race and Country*, 152.

169. *The Crisis*, February 1922, 155.

170. *The Crisis*, July 23, 1923, 106.
171. Puar and Rai, "Monster, Terrorist, Fag," 130–40.
172. *The Crisis*, July 23, 1923, 106.
173. Du Bois, *Souls of Black Folk*, 3.
174. Clarke, "Pan-Africanism," 54–55.
175. Young, "Toussaint L'Ouverture," 156.
176. Young, "Toussaint L'Ouverture," 156.
177. Young, "Toussaint L'Ouverture," 156; Martineau, *Hour and the Man*, 449.
178. Young, "Toussaint L'Ouverture," 157–58.
179. Young, "Toussaint L'Ouverture," 158.
180. Young, "Toussaint L'Ouverture," 158.
181. Young, "Toussaint L'Ouverture," 160.
182. Young, "Toussaint L'Ouverture," 161.
183. Young, "Toussaint L'Ouverture," 161.
184. Portrait of Toussaint L'ouverture, frontispiece, Joseph Saint-Rémy (Saint-Rémy, of Hayti), *Vie de Toussaint-L'ouverture*. Paris, 1850, British Library, https://www.bl.uk/collection-items/portrait-of-toussaint-louverture, accessed October 29, 2019.
185. Geggus, "Changing Faces of Toussaint Louverture."

Chapter Four

1. Case number 10218-337, "Maj. Loving memo for Capt. Cutler. Re: League for Democracy," June 11, 1919, "Correspondence of the Military Intelligence Division Relating to 'Negro Subversion,' 1917–1941," National Archives at College Park, College Park, MD. Electronic record retrieved from http://www.fold3.com, accessed August 12, 2019.
2. *Washington Bee*, April 6, 1907.
3. *Washington Bee*, October 22, 1904; *Indiana Freeman*, August 15, 1908.
4. American National Red Cross, Bulletin no. 4 (October 1906), 31–2.
5. *Indianapolis Freeman*, August 6, 1904; *Washington Bee*, March 16, 1907.
6. *Washington Bee*, April 6, 1907.
7. *Washington Bee*, March 17, 1906; Randolph, "Remembering Dunbar."
8. *Washington Bee*, June 14, 1913.
9. *The Freeman*, November 7, 1914.
10. *Washington Bee*, May 5, 1917; Guy-Sheftall, *Words of Fire*, 9.
11. *Washington Bee*, June 8, 1918.
12. Case number 10218-279, "Special Bulletin: The Negro Problem in the Army," October 21, 1918, "Correspondence of the Military Intelligence Division Relating to 'Negro Subversion,' 1917–1941," National Archives at College Park, College Park, MD. Electronic record retrieved from http://www.fold3.com/, 1, accessed August 12, 2019.
13. "Special Bulletin: The Negro Problem in the Army," 1.
14. "Special Bulletin: The Negro Problem in the Army," 1.
15. "Special Bulletin: The Negro Problem in the Army," 3; emphasis in the original.
16. Case number 10218-244, "Frank W. Thomas, Staten Island, NY to D, MI. Re: Colored troops at Debarkation Hospital," October 25, 1918, "Correspondence of the Military Intelligence Division Relating to 'Negro Subversion,' 1917–1941," National

Archives at College Park, College Park, MD. Electronic record retrieved from http://www.fold3.com, accessed August 12, 2019.

17. Case number 10218-279, "Summary of Replies to Questionnaire from Intelligence Officers at the Large Training Camps," May 17, 1919, "Correspondence of the Military Intelligence Division Relating to 'Negro Subversion,' 1917–1941," National Archives at College Park, College Park, MD. Electronic record retrieved from http://www.fold3.com, accessed August 12, 2019.

18. Case number 10218-280, "Maj. W. H. Loving to MMS. Re: Investigation of Military Camps," November 24, 1918, "Correspondence of the Military Intelligence Division Relating to 'Negro Subversion,' 1917–1941," National Archives at College Park, College Park, MD. Electronic record retrieved from http://www.fold3.com, accessed August 12, 2019.

19. Crane, *Medical Department of the United States Army in the World War*, 208.

20. Case number 10218-280, "Maj. W. H. Loving to MMS. Re: Investigation of military camps." November 2, 1918, "Correspondence of the Military Intelligence Division Relating to 'Negro Subversion,' 1917–1941," National Archives at College Park, College Park, MD. Electronic record retrieved from http://www.fold3.com, accessed August 12, 2019.

21. Case number 10218-280, "Maj. W. H. Loving to MMS. Re: Investigation of Military Camps," September 14, 1918, "Correspondence of the Military Intelligence Division Relating to 'Negro Subversion,' 1917–1941," National Archives at College Park, College Park, MD. Electronic record retrieved from http://www.fold3.com, accessed August 12, 2019.

22. Case number 10218-280, "Maj. W. H. Loving to MMS. Re: Investigation of Military Camps," September 27, 1918, "Correspondence of the Military Intelligence Division Relating to 'Negro Subversion,' 1917–1941," National Archives at College Park, College Park, MD. Electronic record retrieved from http://www.fold3.com, accessed August 12, 2019.

23. Case number 10218-280, "Maj. W. H. Loving to MMS. Re: Investigation of Military Camps," September 23, 1918, "Correspondence of the Military Intelligence Division Relating to 'Negro Subversion,' 1917–1941," National Archives at College Park, College Park, MD. Electronic record retrieved from http://www.fold3.com, accessed August 12, 2019.

24. Quoted in Barbeau and Henri, *Unknown Soldiers*, 53.

25. Mitchell, *Righteous Propagation*, 101, 293.

26. National Medical Association, "About Us," https://www.nmanet.org/page/About_Us, accessed October 27, 2019.

27. Williams, "Venereal Diseases," 183, emphasis in the original.

28. A. Wilberforce Williams, "Dr. A. Wilberforce Williams Talks on Preventive Measures, First Aid Remedies, Hygenics and Sanitation," *Chicago Defender*, August 30, 1919, 20.

29. Roman, "American Negro and Social Hygiene," 43–44.

30. Scott, *Scott's Official History*, 92–93.

31. "Medical Men in Campaign against Venereal Diseases," *Baltimore Afro-American*, September 27, 1918, 4.

32. Roman, "Syllabus of Lecture to Colored Soldiers," 104.
33. Roman, "Syllabus of Lecture to Colored Soldiers," 105.
34. Roman, "Syllabus of Lecture to Colored Soldiers," 106.
35. Roman, "Syllabus of Lecture to Colored Soldiers," 106. On Roman's brand of sexual Victorianism, see Simmons, "African Americans and Sexual Victorianism in the Social Hygiene Movement," 9, 11, 14–15. A. Wilberforce Williams would also lend his voice to the VD campaign, lecturing in France with the Y.M.C.A. in the summer of 1919. Upon returning to the United States, he would speak of the "splendid work of Mrs. Hunton and Mrs. Curtis, who did much in keeping upon the morale of the boys during this period." "Dr. Wilberforce Williams in Town," *Chicago Defender*, May 10, 1919, 4; "Dr. Wilberforce Williams Lands in New York," *Chicago Defender*, August 30, 1919, 1.
36. Roman, "Syllabus of Lecture to Colored Soldiers," 108.
37. Young, *Surgeon's Autobiography*, 265; "Colonel's Plea Gets Medical Recruits: 174 Young Doctors at Yale Club Enlist after Roosevelt's Stirring Appeal," *New York Times*, May 29, 1917; Goodwin, *Notes for Army Medical Officers*.
38. In his autobiography, Young writes "Father was engaged in nearly all the great battles of the Army of Tennessee in Kentucky, Mississippi, Alabama, and Georgia . . . in several of these battles Father was severely wounded, but he always returned to his regiment, and at the age of twenty-six he was commissioned brigadier general, the youngest, I am told, in the Confederate Army." Likewise, in a biography of George Walker's brother, Miles (who was also a doctor), it was written that "The Walkers were of Revolutionary stock. Six of Dr. Miles J. Walker's father's brothers were in the Confederate army during the war between the states." Young, *Surgeon's Autobiography*, 12; Snowden, *History of South Carolina*, 5:96.
39. Ware, "Brief History of Urology at Baylor Medical Center," 431; also see Bera, Maji, and Bera, "Tribute to Hugh Hampton Young," 169–70; Engel, "Hugh Hampton Young," 458–64.
40. Harbord, *American Army in France*, 73.
41. Young, *Surgeon's Autobiography*, 270.
42. Vandiver, *Black Jack*, 773–75.
43. "It was apparent that the danger of regulated prostitution was not entirely from the disease of the women themselves, but also from the fact that by receiving one individual after another without any douching or even arising from their beds, these women came to possess 'septic tanks' filled with almost every type of venereal infection." Young, *Surgeon's Autobiography*, 309.
44. Gillette, *Army Medical Department*, 254.
45. Walker, *Venereal Disease in the American Expeditionary Forces* [AEF], 41.
46. Brandt, *No Magic Bullet*, 120.
47. Walker, *Traffic in Babies*, iii.
48. Walker, *Venereal Disease in the AEF*, 40.
49. Young, *Surgeon's Autobiography*, 304–6.
50. Young, *Surgeon's Autobiography*, 362.
51. Young, *Surgeon's Autobiography*, 320.
52. Walker, *Venereal Disease in the AEF*, 123–24.

53. Weed, *Medical Department of the United States in the World War*, 6:953.

54. Stevedores were also issued only four-hour "liberty" passes to the leave the camp, which was based on the idea that prophylaxis was only effective if practiced within three hours of sexual exposure.

55. Walker, *Venereal Disease in the AEF*, 122–23.

56. Young, *Surgeon's Autobiography*, 320–21.

57. Kehoe, McCall, and Mix, *Legacy of Hugh Hampton Young*, 13.

58. While we might be cautioned to soberly assess Young's frank admission of having orchestrated the systemic torture of black soldiers as a relic from another age, we should also take note that at least one historian recounted his anecdote as evidence of one "amusing side effect" of chemical prophylaxis. Writing in *Prologue*, the magazine of the U.S. National Archives and Records Administration, the historian recast the black orderly and the African American servicemen he represents as simply "labor troops," thereby obscuring the extent to which the punchline participated in, and drew its force from, intersecting midcentury discourses of race, sexuality, and power. Occurring within the quarterly digest of America's official repository of archival memory, this instance of racial erasure is particularly egregious insofar as the phenomenology of Young's joke points us toward the very real concerns he had about African American soldiers sleeping with white French women—anxieties that he would continue to harbor over twenty years later during the writing of his autobiography—and indicates the technological methods through which he was enabled to register his disapproval. See Smythe, "Venereal Disease," 67.

59. "Review: Venereal Disease in the American Expeditionary Forces," *British Medical Journal* 2, no. 3264 (July 21, 1923), 108.

60. For contemporary critiques of Sims and his medical legacy, see Owens, *Medical Bondage*; Roberts, *Killing the Black Body*; Snorton, *Black on Both Sides*; and Washington, *Medical Apartheid*.

61. Walker conducted a study of 2,817 men who had contracted gonorrhea, chancroid, or syphilis. Among this group, 1,801 men claimed to have contracted a venereal disease *after* using prophylaxis. Breaking them into their respective categories, Walker found that 907 (50.3 percent) contracted gonorrhea, 689 (38.3 percent) contracted chancroid, and 205 (11.4 percent) contracted syphilis. He then compared those numbers to 969 men who had contracted venereal disease *without* taking chemical prophylaxis and received the following results: 523 (54.0 percent) contracted gonorrhea; 315 (32.5 percent) contracted chancroid, and 131 (13.5 percent) contracted syphilis. Walker, *Venereal Disease in the AEF*, 30.

62. Weed, *Medical Department of the United States in the World War*, 6:955.

63. Frank W. Harris, Captain of Engineers, U.S. Army to the Editor, *The Crisis*, June 26, 1919, Du Bois Papers, Reel 8, as cited in Lentz-Smith, *Freedom Struggles*, 124.

64. Barbeau and Henri, *Unknown Soldiers*, 55.

65. Day, "Urologic and Venereal Idiosyncrasies," 166.

66. Arthur B. Spingarn, "The Health and Morals of Colored Troops," *The Crisis*, August 1918, 166. Spingarn's comments in *The Crisis* closely echo his remarks made a month earlier in the *Journal for Social Hygiene* (Spingarn, "War and Venereal Disease").

67. Arthur E. Williams, "From France," *Chicago Defender*, May 17, 1919, 8.

68. Williams, "From France."

69. W. E. B. Du Bois, "Opinion," *The Crisis*, May 1919, 11. Critic Mark Whalan also remarks that "the notion of political advance through national service and sacrifice dominated the tone of the war stories, poems, and drama that featured in the *Crisis* in the war years and for some time afterwards." Whalen, *Great War and the Culture of the New Negro*, 18.

70. "Men of the Month," *The Crisis*, November 1918, 28.

71. Florence Lewis, "A Negro Woman to Her Adopted Soldier Boy," *The Crisis*, December 1918, 66.

72. Lewis, "Negro Woman to Her Adopted Soldier Boy," 67.

73. Hunton and Johnson, *Two Colored Women*, 136. There were about 3,480 YMCA women stationed overseas total. *Summary of the World War Work of the American YMCA* (International Committee of the Young Men's Christian Association, 1920), 112.

74. Hunton and Johnson, *Two Colored Women*, 137.

75. Williams, "Mobilized Diaspora," 248.

76. Hunton and Johnson, *Two Colored Women*, 15.

77. Hunton and Johnson, *Two Colored Women*, 38.

78. Hunton and Johnson, *Two Colored Women*, 151.

79. Hunton and Johnson, *Two Colored Women*, 155–56.

80. Hunton and Johnson, *Two Colored Women*, 157.

81. Lentz-Smith, *Freedom Struggles*, 8.

82. Hunton and Johnson, *Two Colored Women*, 137.

83. Walker, *Venereal Disease in the AEF*, 154, 190.

84. Walker, *Venereal Disease in the AEF*, 154.

85. Walker, *Venereal Disease in the AEF*, 223.

86. Walker, *Venereal Disease in the AEF*, 224.

87. Walker, *Venereal Disease in the AEF*, 224.

88. "*Perversion* of the sexual instinct, as will be seen farther on, is not to be cofounded with *perversity* in the sexual act; since the latter may be induced by conditions other than psychopathological. The concrete perverse act, monstrous as it may be, is clinically not decisive. In order to differentiate between disease (*perversion*) and vice (*perversity*), one must investigate the whole personality of the individual and the original motive leading to the perverse act. Therein will be found the key to the diagnosis." Krafft-Ebing, *Psychopathia Sexualis*, 79–80.

89. Walker, *Venereal Disease in the AEF*, 226.

90. Walker, *Venereal Disease in the AEF*, 225.

91. Walker, *Venereal Disease in the AEF*, 227.

92. Walker, *Venereal Disease in the AEF*, 227.

93. Walker, *Venereal Disease in the AEF*, 228.

94. Walker, *Venereal Disease in the AEF*, 229.

95. Maurer, "Language and the Sex Revolution," 7.

96. Hitchens, Christopher. "As American as Apple Pie," *Vanity Fair*, October 10, 2006, https://www.vanityfair.com/news/2006/07/hitchens200607.

97. Green, *Ely*, 390.

98. Green, *Ely*, 396.

99. Gilman, "Black Bodies, White Bodies."
100. Green, *Ely*, 433.
101. Green, *Ely*, 370.
102. Green, *Ely*, 371.
103. Martha Greuning, "Houston," *The Crisis*, November 1917; Scott, *Scott's Official History*, 94–5.
104. Green, *Ely*, 371.
105. Green, *Ely*, 457.
106. Green, *Ely*, 428.
107. Green, *Ely*, 429.
108. Delany, *Times Square Red*; Kelley, *Race Rebels*, 46–49.
109. Segregation and congregation theorized by Earl Lewis, as quoted by Kelley, *Race Rebels*, 45; black bodies as instruments of pleasure rather than labor theorized by Paul Gilroy, as quoted by Kelley, *Race Rebels*, 48.
110. Bluesman "Mississippi" Fred McDowell, who was born in 1904, said it was the first song he ever learned how to play. Lentz-Smith, *Freedom Struggles*, 106; Baraka, *Blues People*, 92; Fred McDowell, "Big Fat Mama, Meat Shakin on Her Bones," track 1 on *Come and Found You Gone: The Bill Ferris Recordings*, Devil Down Records, CD001, 2010.
111. Handy, *Father of the Blues*, 78.
112. Baraka, *Blues People*, 146.
113. Baraka, *Blues People*, 110.
114. Baraka, *Blues People*, 90.
115. Baraka, *Blues People*, 110–11.
116. Baraka, *Blues People*, 90.
117. Baraka, *Blues People*, 90.
118. Badger, *Life in Ragtime*, 26–27.
119. Badger, *Life in Ragtime*, 51.
120. Sissle, "Memoirs of 'Jim' Europe," 36.
121. Sissle, "Memoirs of 'Jim' Europe," 45.
122. Badger, *Life in Ragtime*, 145–46.
123. Gilroy, *Black Atlantic*, 12, 17.
124. Sissle, "Memoirs of 'Jim' Europe," 95.
125. Sissle, "Memoirs of 'Jim' Europe," 95–96.
126. Baraka, *Blues People*, 143.
127. Sissle, "Memoirs of 'Jim' Europe," 106–7.
128. Pratt's theory of contact zones is explicitly linked to forms of contact occurring within the frameworks of colonialism. However, following the lead of Heide Fehrenbach, who has adapted the use of "contact zones" to describe the politics of race and sexuality accompanying U.S. military occupation in Germany after 1945, I have also employed Pratt's term to consider the effects wrought by American militarism on French ports during World War I. See Pratt, *Imperial Eyes*, 6; and Fehrenbach, "Contact Zones: American Military Occupation and the Politics of Race," in *Race after Hitler*, 17–45.
129. Montrose J. Roses, "Shakespeare in the Trenches," *The Independent* 94 (April–June 1918), 360.

130. Winthrop Ames, "Letter to Noble Sissle," reprinted in Sissle, "Memoirs of 'Jim' Europe," 126.

131. Badger, *Life in Ragtime*, 166.

132. Little, *From Harlem to the Rhine*, 130.

133. The Hellfighter's stellar record provided opportunities for humor when Noble Sissle, the band's drum major, became sick with the mumps and was quarantined for eighteen days. "The men of the band, especially the Porto Ricans [sic], were continually kidding me over the fact that I was the first one to land in the hospital and inasmuch as I was going to the hospital it seems as if I could have picked out some other ailment rather than what is looked upon as a childhood sickness." Little, *From Harlem to the Rhine*, 100–01; Sissle, "Memoirs of 'Jim' Europe," 112.

134. Von Eschen, *Satchmo Blows Up the World*, 20.

135. Von Eschen, *Satchmo Blows Up the World*, 24–25.

136. Reid Badger points out that Sissle incorrectly remembered that the concert was in Tours instead of Nantes. Badger, *Life in Ragtime*, 300.

137. "Ragtime by U.S. Army Band Gets Everyone 'Over There,'" *St. Louis Post-Dispatch*, June 10, 1918, reprinted in the liner notes for *James Reese Europe with his 369th U.S. Infantry "Hellfighters" Band: The Complete Recordings*, Memphis Archives, MA7020, 1996, as well as Sissle's memoirs.

138. Handy, *Father of the Blues*; Robertson, *W. C. Handy*, 160–61; "Tennessee: Memphis Blues," *Time Magazine*, June 10, 1940; *The Tennessee Encyclopedia of History and Culture*, s.v. "Edward Hull 'Boss' Crump," by David Tucker, http://tennesseeencyclopedia.net/entry.php?rec=334, accessed October 29, 2019.

139. Merriam and Garner, "Jazz," 20–21; Maurer, "Language and the Sex Revolution," 6.

140. Badger, *Life in Ragtime*, 50.

141. Dixon-Gottschild, *Waltzing in the Dark*, 98.

142. Badger, *Life in Ragtime*, 51.

143. Browning, *Infectious Rhythm*, 7.

144. Bergmeier and Lotz, "James Arthur Biggs," 113.

145. Watkins, *Proof through the Night*, 321; Tim Gracyk, liner notes for *James Reese Europe with his 369th U.S. Infantry "Hellfighters" Band: The Complete Recordings*, Memphis Archives, MA7020, 1996; Williams, *Torchbearers for Democracy*, 327–28.

146. "How 'Ya Gonna Keep 'Em Down on the Farm (After They've Seen Paree)?," Joe Young and Sam M. Lewis (lyricists), Walter Donaldson (composer), 1918.

147. Brandt, *No Magic Bullet*, 118–20.

148. *When You Go Home: Take This Book with You*, U.S. Army pamphlet published for distribution by the War Department, Commission on Training Camp Activities, Otis Historical Archives, National Museum of Health and Medicine, Armed Forces Institute of Pathology, 1918, 3.

149. Hunton and Johnson, *Two Colored Women*, 39.

150. "Camp Pontanezen, Brest, France," *The Military Surgeon: Journal of the Association of Military Surgeons of the United States* 46 (1920), 301.

151. Hunton and Johnson, *Two Colored Women*, 6.

152. Crowell and Wilson, *Demobilization*, 19–20.

153. "Camp Pontanezen," 305.
154. "Camp Pontanezen," 304–5.
155. "Camp Pontanezen," 305.
156. "Camp Pontanezen," 312.
157. Hunton and Johnson, *Two Colored Women*, 39.
158. Nichols, "Social Hygiene and the Negro."

Chapter Five

1. Rosenberg, *How Far the Promised Land?*, 44–5.
2. W. E. B. Du Bois, "Close Ranks," *The Crisis*, July 1918, 111. For extended commentary on the impact of the "Close Ranks" editorial on Du Bois's legacy and the controversy behind its publication, see Ellis, "'Closing Ranks' and 'Seeking Honors'"; Jordan, "Damnable Dilemma"; Ellis, "W. E. B. Du Bois and the Formation of Black Opinion."
3. Ellis, "'Closing Ranks' and 'Seeking Honors,'" 122.
4. Byron Gunner to Du Bois, July 25, 1918, in Du Bois, *Correspondence*, 1:228.
5. A. Philip Randolph, "Pro-Germanism among Negroes," *The Messenger*, July 1918, quoted in Kornweibel, *Seeing Red*, 78, and in full in Stanford, *If We Must Die*, 120–21.
6. Quoted in Ellis, "W. E. B. Du Bois and the Formation of Black Opinion," 1585.
7. Ellis, "W. E. B. Du Bois and the Formation of Black Opinion," 1585n3. Ellis extends his analysis and treatment of Wilson's case in his monograph *Race, War, and Surveillance*, 89–91.
8. Nalty and MacGregor, *Blacks in the Military*, 93.
9. Padmore, *Life and Struggles of Negro Toilers*, 5.
10. Padmore, *Life and Struggles of Negro Toilers*, 124–25.
11. Padmore, *Life and Struggles of Negro Toilers*, 112.
12. Padmore, *Life and Struggles of Negro Toilers*, 112–13.
13. Civilian military training is defined by one former enlistee as "the process of taking civilians from private life and giving them military training in the army for a certain predetermined period and then returning them to their private life. The object of this training is to form a nucleus of men in private industry with military training who may, if the emergency occurs, form the basis of an enlarged standing army. This training is not to make soldiers of all of our male citizens but to make citizens of all of our males, these citizens are thus prepared to defend our country and its ideals if the occasion should warrant"; Custer, *Citizens' Military Training Camp*, foreword.
14. Padmore, *Life and Struggles of Negro Toilers*, 113.
15. Trinidadian by birth, Padmore traveled to the United States in his early twenties, and spent time at Fisk University, New York University, and Howard University. Padmore, *Life and Struggles of Negro Toilers*, 113.
16. Padmore, *Life and Struggles of Negro Toilers*, 112, 114–15.
17. Hastie, "Negro Officers in Two Wars," 317.
18. Hastie, "Negro Officers in Two Wars," 318–19.
19. Morden, *Women's Army Corps*, 17. For one of the few memoirs chronicling the experiences of African American women during World War II, see Early, *One Woman's War*.
20. Gibson, *Knocking Down Barriers*, 77.

21. White, "Race Relations in the Armed Services," 350.

22. White, "Race Relations in the Armed Services," 351.

23. Cripps and Culbert, "*The Negro Soldier*," 622; Vaughn, "Ronald Reagan and the Struggle for Black Dignity," 2–3.

24. White, "Race Relations in the Armed Services," 350.

25. Army Air Force Special Film Project 151, *Wings for This Man*, A production of the First Motion Picture Unit, Army Air Forces, 1945. Another short film produced by the U.S. Office of War Information, *Negro Colleges in Wartime* (1943), heaps similar praise upon Tuskegee, while also mentioning Prairie View in Texas, Howard University in D.C., and Hampton University in Virginia.

26. Nalty and MacGregor, *Blacks in the Military*, 96–99.

27. Hirschfeld, *Sexual History of the World War*, 298.

28. Hanson, "Protection of Soldiers, Sailors, and Workers," 181.

29. Draper, "Protecting Industry from Venereal Disease," 98, 99.

30. Draper, "Protecting Industry from Venereal Disease," 100.

31. Hegarty, *Victory Girls, Khaki-Wackies, and Patriotutes*, 61–84.

32. U.S. Census 2000, *Statistical Abstract of the United States: 583. Armed Services Personnel—Summary of Major Conflicts*, https://www.allcountries.org/uscensus/583_armed_forces_personnel_summary_of_major.html, accessed October 29, 2019. Covers service between December 1, 1941, and December 31, 1946.

33. Love and Davenport, "Comparison of White and Colored Troops."

34. Sternberg, et al., "Venereal Diseases," 186.

35. Kolmer, "Problem of Falsely Doubtful and Positive Reactions," 510–25.

36. 26,093 had untreated infections, and 10,937 were previously under treatment; Sternberg, et al., "Venereal Diseases," 188.

37. Love and Davenport, "Comparison of White and Colored Troops," 58–59.

38. Sternberg, et al., "Venereal Diseases," 189–90.

39. Lee, *Employment of Negro Troops*, viii. Lee also co-edited the anthology *The Negro Caravan* with Sterling A. Brown and Arthur P. Davis in 1941.

40. Lee, *Employment of Negro Troops*, 277.

41. Lord, *Condom Nation*, 79–80.

42. Prophylactic stations were facilities set up in or near red-light districts for the purpose of "sexual disinfection" after sexual encounters. "Pro-kits" were also produced during the war for the soldier on the go. Each packet contained: "1. 1 Tube containing 5 Grams of Ointment (30% Calomel + 15% Sulfathiazole), 2. Direction Sheet, 3. Soap Impregnated Cloth, 4. Cleansing Tissue"; WW2 US Medical Research Centre, https://www.med-dept.com/articles/venereal-disease-and-treatment-during-ww2/, accessed October 29, 2019.

43. Cripps, *Making Movies Black*, 118.

44. The "Pro-kit" became "the most important venereal disease preventive measure developed during the war" and was advertised as such in the Army media. Sternberg, et al., "Venereal Diseases," 201.

45. Sternberg, et al., "Venereal Diseases," 191.

46. Sternberg, et al., "Venereal Diseases," 194.

47. Lee, *Employment of Negro Troops*, 286.

48. "The difference between the races in incidence of venereal diseases is probably due partly to a difference in social pressure, partly to a difference in ability to control the sex instinct"; Love and Davenport, "Comparison of White and Colored Troops," 59.

49. From early as January 1941 throughout the end of the war, the Federal Bureau of Investigation has placed Robeson under surveillance due to his support of the Soviet Union. Army intelligence agents kept files on him as well. See Duberman, *Paul Robeson*, 253, 285.

50. Cripps, *Making Movies Black*, 118.
51. Sternberg, et al., "Venereal Diseases," 196.
52. White, "Race Relations in the Armed Services," 351.
53. United States Army Service Forces (USASF), *Pocket Guide to West Africa*, 12.
54. USASF, *Pocket Guide to West Africa*, 1.
55. White, "Race Relations in the Armed Services," 352.
56. White, "Race Relations in the Armed Services," 351.
57. USASF, *Pocket Guide to West Africa*, 7.
58. USASF, *Pocket Guide to West Africa*, 6.
59. USASF, *Pocket Guide to West Africa*, 6–7.
60. USASF, *Pocket Guide to West Africa*, 11.
61. Houston, "Critical Summary," 365.
62. Metcalf, *Black Profiles*, 117.
63. Houston, "Critical Summary," 365.
64. Houston, "Critical Summary," 366.
65. Houston, "Critical Summary," 366.
66. Houston, "Critical Summary," 366.
67. W. E. B. Du Bois, "As the Crow Flies," *New York Amsterdam Star-News*, February 14, 1942; also reprinted as "Closing Ranks Again," in Lewis, *Du Bois Reader*, 739.
68. Du Bois, "Closing Ranks Again," 739.
69. Du Bois, "Closing Ranks Again," 739.
70. Du Bois, "Closing Ranks Again," 740.
71. W. E. B. Du Bois, "Africa," *Amsterdam News*, July 12, 1941, reprinted in Lewis, *Du Bois Reader*, 738.
72. Du Bois, "Closing Ranks Again," 741.
73. White, *Rising Wind*, 144.
74. Lee, *Employment of Negro Troops*, 591–92.
75. Lee, *Employment of Negro Troops*, 428.
76. Lee, *Employment of Negro Troops*, 429. St. Lucia was opposed to Puerto Rican troops as well.
77. Lee, *Employment of Negro Troops*, 432; Brawley and Dixon, "Jim Crow Downunder?," 610.
78. Lee, *Employment of Negro Troops*, 434.
79. Lee, *Employment of Negro Troops*, 435.
80. Lee, *Employment of Negro Troops*, 436.
81. Lee, *Employment of Negro Troops*, 436.
82. Lee, *Employment of Negro Troops*, 438.
83. Dumett, "Africa's Strategic Minerals," 392.

84. Horn, "Belgian Congo in the War," 12.
85. Oyebade, "Feeding America's War Machine," 119–31.
86. McGuire, *Taps for a Jim Crow Army*, xvi.
87. McGuire, *Taps for a Jim Crow Army*, 239.
88. Shayne E. Wallesch and Wendy J. Hochnadel, "1944 Troop Ship Crossings," World War II Troop Ships, 2007, http://ww2troopships.com/crossings/1944b.htm.
89. David W. Hogan, "India-Burma: The U.S. Army Campaigns of World War II," U.S. Army Center of Military History, http://www.history.army.mil/brochures/indiaburma/indiaburma.htm, accessed October 29, 2019.
90. "EAB in China-Burma-India," National Museum of the United States Air Force, May 4, 2015, https://www.nationalmuseum.af.mil/Visit/Museum-Exhibits/Fact-Sheets/Display/Article/196660/eab-in-china-burma-india/.
91. "Life-Line to China Re-opened," Universal Newsreel Vol. 18-372, February 12, 1945, https://en.wikipedia.org/wiki/File:Life-Line_To_China_Re-Opened_1945212.ogg, accessed October 29, 2019.
92. Dr. Geraldine Seay, "African Americans and the Ledo Road," Ledo/Stilwell Road, https://www.ledostilwellroad.com/, accessed October 29, 2019.
93. Rudi Williams, "Black WWII Vet Recalls Terrible Time Building 'Ledo Road,'" American Forces Press Service, July 7, 2004, http://archive.defense.gov/news/newsarticle.aspx?id=25745.
94. Williams, "Ledo Road."
95. Williams, "Ledo Road."
96. Stevens, "Black Correspondents of World War II," 400.
97. Williams, "Ledo Road"; Seay, "African Americans and the Ledo Road."
98. Stevens, "Black Correspondents of World War II," 404.
99. Lesch, *First Miracle Drugs*, 25.
100. Young, *Surgeon's Autobiography*, 262–63.
101. Lesch, *First Miracle Drugs*, 3–4.
102. Lesch, *First Miracle Drugs*, 5.
103. Loveless and Denton, "Oral Use of Sulfathiazole," 827–28.
104. Chancroid, also known as soft chancre, is a sexually transmitted bacterial infection that is considered common in tropical countries today, but rare in other parts of the world. Sternberg, et al., "Venereal Diseases," 202–3; "Chancre (Soft Chancre)," New York State Department of Health, last modified November 2006, https://www.health.ny.gov/diseases/communicable/chancroid/fact_sheet.htm.
105. Sternberg, et al., "Venereal Diseases," 234.
106. Sternberg and Turner, "Treatment of Sulfonamide Resistant Gonorrhea"; Lesch, *First Miracle Drugs*, 230.
107. Paul Padget, in Sternberg, et al., "Venereal Diseases," 266.
108. Leonard A. Dewey, in Sternberg, et al., "Venereal Diseases," 216.
109. Dewey, in Sternberg, et al., "Venereal Diseases," 220.
110. Dewey, in Sternberg, et al., "Venereal Diseases," 200.
111. Sternberg, et al., "Venereal Diseases," 269.
112. Sternberg, et al., "Venereal Diseases," 269–70.
113. Hull, *Memoirs*, 2:1186.

114. Sternberg, et al., "Venereal Diseases," 271.
115. Sternberg, et al., "Venereal Diseases," 271–72.
116. Abraham, *Belles of Shangri-La*, 87–99.
117. Sternberg, et al., "Venereal Diseases," 273. Abraham, *Belles of Shangri-La*.
118. Leder, *Thanks for the Memories*, 122.
119. In Briggs, "Communicability, Racial Discourse, and Disease," 274.
120. Sternberg, et al., "Venereal Diseases," 273.
121. Sternberg, et al., "Venereal Diseases," 275.
122. Sternberg, et al., "Venereal Diseases," 274.
123. Sternberg, et al., "Venereal Diseases," 275.
124. Moon, *Sex among Allies*; Lee, *Employment of Negro Troops*, 619. An archive documenting this neocolonial encounter has only recently been discovered and cataloged, and it is hoped that further study will recover the agency of the women who worked in Paradise, Shangri-La, and Idylewilde. See the guide to the George and Katy Abraham Papers, 1915–2005, Collection Number 6777, Division of Rare and Manuscript Collections, Cornell University Library, http://rmc.library.cornell.edu/ead/htmldocs/RMM06777.html, accessed October 29, 2019.
125. Lee, *Employment of Negro Troops*, 616; Sternberg, et al., "Venereal Diseases," 276; Stevens, "Black Correspondents of World War II," 395–96.
126. Sternberg, *Preventive Medicine in World War II*, 276.
127. USASF, *Pocket Guide to Iran*, 10.
128. Sternberg, et al., "Venereal Diseases," 281.
129. Sternberg, et al., "Venereal Diseases," 281.
130. Sternberg, et al., "Venereal Diseases," 282.
131. Sternberg, et al., "Venereal Diseases," 281.
132. Sternberg, et al., "Venereal Diseases," 282.
133. The special issue "The National Postwar Program in Action," *Journal of Social Hygiene* 31, no. 8 (November 1945) is devoted entirely to this question.
134. Schivelbusch, *In a Cold Crater*, 8–9.
135. Timm, "Think It Over!," 50. The one-to-three rape ratio is confirmed by Atina Grossman in *Jews, Germans and Allies*, 49.
136. See Joseph R. Starr, "Fraternization with the Germans in World War II," Declassified report, Occupation Forces in Europe Series, 1945–46 (Frankfurt-am-Main: Office of the Chief Historian, European Command, 1947); Fehrenbach, *Race after Hitler*; Grossman, *Jews, Germans and Allies*; Pfau, *Miss Yourlovin*; and Willoughby, *Remaking the Conquering Heroes*, 31–34.
137. Radio spots numbers 2 and 65, Supreme Headquarters Allied Expeditionary Force office memorandum, 16 March 1945, courtesy of the Allied Museum in Berlin, June 17, 2008. See also the catalog from the Allied Museum's 2001 exhibition *The Link with Home—and the Germans Listened in: The Radio Stations of the Western Powers from 1945 to 1994* (Berlin: Ruksaldruck, 2001).
138. Starr, "Fraternization with the Germans in World War II," 88–9.
139. Höhn and Klimke, *Breath of Freedom*, 54–60; Fehrenbach, *Race after Hitler*, 31–9.
140. Fehrenbach, *Race after Hitler*, 44.
141. Campt, *Other Germans*, 25–29.

142. Campt, *Other Germans*, 59.
143. Ruffner, "Black Market in Postwar Berlin."
144. Quoted in Schroer, *Recasting Race after World War II*, 66.
145. Schroer, *Recasting Race after World War II*, 66.
146. Luther A. Townsley, "Protests of Meader Report Grow," *Atlanta Daily World*, December 14, 1946; "The Meader Report . . . Another Black Eye," *Chicago Defender*, December 14, 1946; "Meader's DP Report Criticized As Unfair," *New York Times*, January 2, 1947; "Medic Flays Slur of Meader Report on GIs," *Chicago Defender*, January 11, 1947; "Meader Report on Venereal Disease Blasted," *Atlanta Daily World*, January 19, 1947.
147. Ruffner, "Black Market in Postwar Berlin."
148. See Wyman, *DPs*.
149. George Schuyler, "Views and Reviews," *Pittsburgh Courier*, February 1, 1947.
150. Ruffner, "Black Market in Postwar Berlin"; Schroer, *Recasting Race after World War II*, 70.
151. Willoughby, *Remaking the Conquering Heroes*, 67.
152. Willoughby, *Remaking the Conquering Heroes*, 71.
153. Höhn and Klimke, *Breath of Freedom*, 40; Fehrenbach, *Race after Hitler*, 25.
154. Willoughby, *Remaking the Conquering Heroes*, 53–72.
155. As quoted in Schroer, *Recasting Race after World War II*, 63; Grathwol, Moorhus, and Steen, *Berlin and the American Military*, 22.
156. Howley, *Berlin Command*, 190.
157. Willoughby, *Remaking the Conquering Heroes*, 70.
158. Höhn and Klimke, *Breath of Freedom*, 72–76.
159. Höhn and Klimke, *Breath of Freedom*, 41.
160. Tine, "Berlin Airlift."
161. Colley, *Road to Victory*, xiv–xv; Weil, "Negro in the Armed Forces," 97; Lee, *Employment of Negro Troops*, 632–33.
162. Colley, *Road to Victory*, 152.
163. Colley, *Road to Victory*, 154–61.
164. Colley, *Road to Victory*, 153.
165. Willoughby posits two additional reasons for increased rates. Since those persons having sexual relations with black troops were more likely to be persecuted by white American and German authorities, they were more likely to resist forced treatment. In addition, more African Americans entered the military with STIs due to extant health care disparities in the segregated South. See Willoughby, "Sexual Behavior of American GIs," 166n31.
166. Willoughby, *Remaking the Conquering Heroes*, 67.
167. Bailey, *Marshall Plan Summer*, 57.
168. Standifer, *Binding up the Wounds*, 155.
169. Houston, "Critical Summary," 366.
170. Schivelbusch, *In a Cold Crater*, 32.
171. Standifer, *Binding up the Wounds*, 10.
172. Standifer, *Binding up the Wounds*, 11.
173. Kaplan, "Black and Blue on San Juan Hill," 232.

Epilogue

1. War Department, Circular No. 124, "Utilization of Negro Manpower in the Postwar Army Policy," Washington, DC, April 27, 1946. Cited hereafter as the Gillem Board Report, 4.
2. Gillem Board Report, 3.
3. Gillem Board Report, 3.
4. Gillem Board Report, 4.
5. Gillem Board Report, 1; also cited in Lanning, *African American Soldier*, 216.
6. "Still Jim-Crow Army, Roy Wilkins Decides," *Pittsburgh Courier*, April 27, 1946.
7. Hodges, *Portrait of an Expatriate*, 11.
8. Sollors, *Temptation of Despair*, 190, especially footnote 32.
9. Hodges, *Portrait of an Expatriate*, 11.
10. Bill Smith, "Army 'Big Shots' Speed 'Purge' of Race Troops from Germany," *Pittsburgh Courier*, November 9, 1946.
11. Smith, "Army 'Big Shots' Speed 'Purge.'"
12. Smith, "Army 'Big Shots' Speed 'Purge.'"
13. Walmy Bald, "Young Man Tackles Great Irony," *New York Post*, August 23, 1948, quoted in Hodges, *Portrait of an Expatriate*, 12.
14. C. L. R. James [G. F. Eckstein, pseud.], "Two Young American Writers," *Fourth International* 11 no. 2, March–April 1950, 53–56.
15. Hodges, *Portrait of an Expatriate*, 18.
16. Hodges, *Portrait of an Expatriate*, 17.
17. Bell, *Afro-American Novel and its Tradition*, 183.
18. Brown, *Postwar African American Novel*, 103.
19. Brown, *Postwar African American Novel*, 103.
20. Hodges, *Portrait of an Expatriate*, 17.
21. Brown, *Postwar African American Novel*, 102.
22. Höhn and Klimke, *Breath of Freedom*, 1.

Bibliography

Libraries and Archives Consulted

Allied Museum, Berlin, Germany
Beinecke Rare Book & Manuscript Library, New Haven, CT
California Digital Newspaper Collection, Center for Bibliographic Studies and Research, University of California, Riverside, Riverside, CA
Coleman Collection, Akron, OH
Library of the John F. Kennedy Institute for North American Studies, Berlin, Germany
National Archives and Records Administration, College Park, MD
Ohio History Connection/National Afro-American Museum and Cultural Center, Wilberforce, OH
Schomburg Center for Research in Black Culture, NYPL, New York, NY
U.S. Army Heritage & Education Center at Carlisle Barracks, Carlisle, PA
UMass Amherst Special Collections and University Archives, Amherst, MA
Wisconsin Historical Society, Division of Library, Archives, and Museum Collections, Madison, WI

Newspapers and Periodicals

American Citizen (Kansas City, KS)
Atlanta Appeal
Atlanta Journal Constitution
Augusta Chronicle
Birmingham Age-Herald
Boston Daily Globe
Broad Ax (Salt Lake City, UT)
Chicago Evening Post
Chicago Sun-Times
Chicago Times-Herald
Chicago Tribune
Christian Recorder (Philadelphia, PA)
Cleveland Gazette
Colored American (Washington, D.C.)
The Crisis
Daily Inter Ocean (Chicago)
Daily Picayune (New Orleans, LA)
Dallas Herald
Duluth News-Tribune
Evening Star
Fourth International
Helena Reporter (AL)
Illinois Record
Indianapolis Freeman
Indianapolis Recorder
Los Angeles Herald
Los Angeles Times
The Messenger
Mobile Register
New Haven Evening Register
New York Tribune
Omaha Progress
Parsons Weekly Blade (Parsons, KS)
Philadelphia Inquirer
Pittsburgh Courier
Plain Dealer (Cleveland, OH)

Plain Dealer (Detroit, MI)
Semi-Weekly Times-Democrat
  (New Orleans, LA)
San Francisco Call
San Francisco Chronicle
Springfield Daily Republican
  (Springfield, MA)

The State (Columbia, SC)
St. Louis Post-Dispatch
Tacoma Daily News
Voice of Missions (Atlanta, GA)
Washington Bee
Weekly Alta California

Articles

Alexander, Raymond Pace. "The Upgrading of the Negro's Status by Supreme Court Decisions." *Journal of Negro History* 30, no. 2 (April 1945): 117-49.

Aptheker, Herbert. "Negro Casualties in the Civil War." *Journal of Negro History* 32, no. 1 (January 1947): 10-80.

Bera, Malay K., Tapas K. Maji, and Keya P. Bera. "A Tribute to Hugh Hampton Young: The Father of Modern Urology." *Indian Journal of Surgery* 69, no. 4 (August 2007): 169-70.

Bergmeier, Horst P. J., and Rainer E. Lotz. "James Arthur Biggs." *Black Music Research Journal* 30, no. 1 (Spring 2010): 93-181.

Bethell, John T. "'A Splendid Little War': Harvard and the Commencement of a New World Order." *Harvard Magazine* (November-December 1998). https://harvardmagazine.com/1998/11/war.html.

Blight, David. "The Meaning or the Fight: Frederick Douglass and the Memory of the Fifty Fourth Massachusetts." *Massachusetts Review* 36, no. 1 (Spring 1995): 141-53.

Bonsal, Stephan. "The Negro Soldier in War and Peace." *North American Review* 185, no. 616 (June 7, 1907): 321-27.

Brawley, Sean, and Chris Dixon. "Jim Crow Downunder? African American Encounters with White Australia, 1942-1945." *Pacific Historical Review* 71, no. 4 (November 2002): 607-32.

Briggs, Charles L. "Communicability, Racial Discourse, and Disease." *Annual Review of Anthropology* 34 (2005): 269-91.

Brown, Scot. "White Backlash and the Aftermath of Fagen's Rebellion: The Fates of Three African-American Soldiers in the Philippines, 1901-1902." *Contributions in Black Studies* 13, article 5 (1995). https://scholarworks.umass.edu/cibs/vol13/iss1/5/.

Carnegie, M. Elizabeth. "Black Nurses at the Front." *American Journal of Nursing* 84, no. 10 (October 1984): 1250-52.

Clarke, John Henrik. "Pan-Africanism: A Brief History of an Idea in the African World." *Présence Africaine* 145 (1988): 26-55.

Cobb, W. Montague. "Medical History: Austin Maurice Curtis, 1868-1939." *Journal of the National Medical Association* 46, no. 4 (July 1954): 294-98.

Cottrol, Robert J., and Raymond T. Diamond. "The Second Amendment: Toward an Afro-Americanist Reconsideration." *Georgetown Law Journal* 80, no. 2 (1991-92): 309-61.

Cripps, Thomas, and David Culbert."*The Negro Soldier* (1944): Film Propaganda in Black and White." *American Quarterly* 31, no. 5: "Film and American Studies" (Winter 1979): 616–40.

Day, George H. "Urologic and Venereal Idiosyncrasies Presented by the Negro: A Comparative Study." *Transactions of the Section on Urology of the American Medical Association at the Seventy-First Annual Session, held at New Orleans, La., April 26 to 30, 1920*. Reprinted from the *Journal of the American Medical Association*. Chicago: American Medical Association Press, 1920, 163–72.

Dormon, James H. "Shaping the Popular Image of Post-Reconstruction American Blacks: The 'Coon Song' Phenomenon of the Gilded Age." *American Quarterly* 40, no. 4 (December 1988): 450–71.

Draper, Warren F. "Protecting Industry from Venereal Disease," *Journal of Social Hygiene* 27, no. 3 (March 1941): 98–102.

Dumett, Raymond. "Africa's Strategic Minerals during the Second World War." *Journal of African History* 26, no. 4: "World War II and Africa" (1985): 381–408.

Ellis, Mark. "'Closing Ranks' and 'Seeking Honors': W. E. B. Du Bois in World War I." *Journal of American History* 79, no. 1 (June 1992): 96–124.

———. "W. E. B. Du Bois and the Formation of Black Opinion during World War I: A Commentary on 'The Damnable Dilemma.'" *Journal of American History* 81, no. 4 (March 1995): 1584–90.

Engel, Rainer Maria Ernst. "Hugh Hampton Young: Father of American Urology." *Journal of Urology* 169, no. 2 (February 2003): 458–64.

Espinosa, Mariola. "The Question of Racial Immunity to Yellow Fever in History and Historiography." *Social Science History* 38, nos. 3–4 (January 2014): 437–53.

Fletcher, Marvin. "The Black Volunteers in the Spanish-American War." *Military Affairs* 38, no. 2 (April 1974): 48–53.

Geggus, David. "The Changing Faces of Toussaint Louverture: Literary and Pictorial Depictions." John Carter Brown Library, electronic publication (April 2013). https://www.brown.edu/Facilities/John_Carter_Brown_Library/exhibitions/toussaint/index.html.

Gilman, Sander L. "Black Bodies, White Bodies: Toward an Iconography of Female Sexuality in Late Nineteenth-Century Art, Medicine, and Literature." In *"Race," Writing and Difference*, edited by Henry Louis Gates, 223–61. Chicago: University of Chicago Press, 1985.

Hanson, Millard C. "Protection of Soldiers, Sailors, and Workers from Syphilis and Gonorrhea: I. From the Standpoint of the Public Health Officer." *Journal of Social Hygiene* 27, no. 4 (April 1941): 181–85.

Hartman, Saidiya. "Venus in Two Acts." *Small Axe* 12, no. 2 (June 2008): 1–14.

Hastie, William H. "Negro Officers in Two Wars." *Journal of Negro Education* 12, no. 3: "The American Negro in World War I and World War II" (Summer 1943): 316–23.

Heinl, Nancy G. "Col. Charles Young: Pointman." *The Crisis* 84, no. 5 (May 1977): 173–76.

Hilfrich, Fabian. "Creating and Instrumentalizing Nationalism: The Celebration of National Reunion in the Peace Jubilees of 1898." In *Celebrating Ethnicity and*

Nation: American Festival Culture from the Revolution to the Early 20th Century, edited by Jürgen Heideking, Geneviève Fabre, and Kai Dreisbach, 228–56. New York: Berghahn, 2001.

Holder, Ann S. "What's Sex Got to Do with It? Race, Power, Citizenship, and the 'Intermediate Identities' in the Post-Emancipation United States." *Journal of African American History* 93, no. 2 (Spring 2008): 153–73.

Horn, Max. "The Belgian Congo in the War." In *Belgian Congo at War*, 7–12. New York: Belgian Information Center, 1942.

Houston, Charles H. "Critical Summary: The Negro in the U.S. Armed Forces in World Wars I and II." *Journal of Negro Education* 12, no. 3: "The American Negro in World War I and World War II" (Summer 1943): 364–66.

Huber, Patrick J., and Gary R. Kremer. "Nathaniel C. Bruce, Black Education and the 'Tuskegee of the Midwest.'" *Missouri Historical Review* 86, no. 1 (October 1991): 37–54.

Hussain, Nasser. "The Sound of Terror: Phenomenology of a Drone Strike." *Boston Review*, October 16, 2013.

Jordan, William. "'The Damnable Dilemma': African American Accommodation and Protest during World War I." *Journal of American History* 81, no. 4 (March 1995): 1562–83.

Kaplan, Amy. "Black and Blue on San Juan Hill." In *Cultures of United States Imperialism*, edited by Amy Kaplan and Donald E. Pease, 219–36. Durham, NC: Duke University Press, 1993.

Kiple, Kenneth. "Response to Sheldon Watts: Yellow Fever Immunities in West Africa and the Americas in the Age of Slavery and Beyond: A Reappraisal." *Journal of Social History* 34, no. 4 (Summer 2001): 969–74.

Kolmer, John A. "The Problem of Falsely Doubtful and Positive Reactions in the Serology of Syphilis." *American Journal of Public Health* 34, no. 5 (May 1944): 510–25.

Love, Lieut.-Col. A. G., and Major C. B. Davenport. "A Comparison of White and Colored Troops in Respect to Incidence of Disease." *Proceedings of the National Academy of Sciences of the United States of America* 5, no. 3 (March 15, 1919): 58–67.

Loveless, James A., and William Denton. "The Oral Use of Sulfathiazole as a Prophylaxis for Gonorrhea." *Journal of the American Medical Association* 121, no. 11 (March 13, 1943): 827–28.

Makita, Yoshiya. "Professional Angels of War: The United States Army Nursing Service and Changing Ideals of Nursing at the Turn of the Century." *Japanese Journal of American Studies* 24 (2013): 67–86.

Marshall, Elizabeth. "Atlanta Peace Jubilee." *Georgia Historical Quarterly* 50, no. 3 (September 1966): 276–82.

Matas, Rudolph. "Nursing in Yellow Fever and the Duties of Trained Nurses in Epidemics." *Trained Nurse and Hospital Review* 35, no. 4 (October 1905): 199–207.

Maurer, D. W. "Language and the Sex Revolution: World War I through World War II." *American Speech* 51, nos. 1–2 (Spring–Summer 1976): 5–24.

Mbembe, Achille. "Necropolitics." *Public Culture* 15, no. 1 (Winter 2003): 11–40.

Merriam, Alan P., and Fradley H. Garner. "Jazz—The Word." *Jazz Review* (March–August 1960): 373–96. Reprinted in *The Jazz Cadence of American Culture*, edited by Robert G. O'Meally, 7–31. New York: Columbia University Press, 1998.

Miller, Jacquelyn C. "The Wages of Blackness: African American Workers and the Meanings of Race during Philadelphia's 1793 Yellow Fever Epidemic." *Pennsylvania Magazine of History and Biography* 129, no. 2 (April 2005): 163–94.

Ngozi-Brown, Scot. "African-American Soldiers and Filipinos: Racial Imperialism, Jim Crow and Social Relations." *Journal of Negro History* 82, no. 1 (Winter 1997): 42–53.

Nichols, Franklin O. "Social Hygiene and the Negro." *Journal of Social Hygiene* 15, no. 7 (October 1929): 408–13.

Ochsner, John. "The Complex Life of Rudolph Matas." *Journal of Vascular Surgery* 34, no. 3 (September 2001): 387–92.

Oyebade, Adebayo. "Feeding America's War Machine: The United States and Economic Expansion in West Africa during World War II." *African Economic History* 26 (1998): 119–40.

Porter, Frank W. "Anthropologists at Work: A Case Study of Nanticoke Indian Community." *American Indian Quarterly* 4, no. 1 (February 1978): 1–18.

Puar, Jasbir K., and Amit Rai. "Monster, Terrorist, Fag: The War on Terrorism and the Production of Docile Patriots." *Social Text* 20, no. 3: "911–A Public Emergency" (Fall 2002): 117–48.

Randolph, Matt. "Remembering Dunbar: African-Americans and Amherst College, 1888–1961." In *Amherst in the World*. Amherst, MA: Amherst College Press, 2020.

Robinson, Michael C., and Frank N. Schubert. "David Fagen: An Afro-American Rebel in the Philippines, 1899–1901." *Pacific Historical Review* 44, no. 1 (February 1975): 68–83.

Roman, Charles V. "The American Negro and Social Hygiene." *Journal of Social Hygiene* 7, no. 1 (January 1921): 41–47.

———. "Syllabus of Lecture to Colored Soldiers." *Journal of the National Medical Association* 10, no. 3 (July–September 1918):104–8.

Ruffner, Kevin Conley. "The Black Market in Postwar Berlin: Colonel Miller and an Army Scandal." *Prologue Magazine* 34, no. 3 (Fall 2002). https://www.archives.gov/publications/prologue/2002/fall/berlin-black-market-1.html.

Sabin, Linda. "Sweating, Purging, and a Passion for Care: The Yellow Fever Nurse in the Deep South in the Early Nineteenth Century." In *Nursing Interventions through Time: History as Evidence*, edited by Patricia D'Antonio and Sandra B. Lewenson, 3–16. New York: Springer, 2011.

Schieffelin, Bambi B., and Rachelle Charlier Doucet. "The 'Real' Haitian Creole: Ideology, Metalinguistics, and Orthographic Choice." *American Ethnologist* 21, no. 1 (February 1994): 176–200.

Silvester, Jeremy. "'Sleep with a Southwester': Monuments and Settler Identity in Namibia." In *Settler Colonialism in the Twentieth Century: Projects, Practices, Legacies*, edited by Caroline Elkins and Susan Pederson, 271–86. London: Routledge, 2005.

Simmons, Christina. "African Americans and Sexual Victorianism in the Social Hygiene Movement, 1910-40." *Journal of the History of Sexuality* 4, no. 1 (July 1993): 51-75.

Smythe, Donald. "Venereal Disease: The AEF's Experience." *Prologue* 9 (Summer 1977): 65-74.

Snorton, C. Riley, and Jin Haritaworn. "Trans Necropolitics: A Transnational Reflection Violence, Death, and the Trans of Color Afterlife." In *The Transgender Studies Reader*, edited by Susan Stryker and Aren Z. Aizura, 66-76. New York: Routledge, 2013.

Sokolitz, Rebecca. "Picturing the Plantation." In *Landscape of Slavery: The Plantation in American Art*, edited by Angela D. Mack and Stephen G. Hoffius, 30-57. Columbia: University of South Carolina Press, 2008.

Spillers, Hortense J. "Mama's Baby, Papa's Maybe: An American Grammar Book." *Diacritics* 17, no. 2, "Culture and Countermemory: The 'American' Connection" (Summer 1987): 64-81.

Spingarn, Arthur B. "The War and Venereal Disease among Negroes." *Journal of Social Hygiene* 4, no. 3 (July 1918): 333-46.

Sternberg, Thomas H., Ernest B. Howard, Leonard A. Dewey, and Paul Padget. "Venereal Diseases." In *Communicable Disease Transmitted through Contact or Unknown Means*, edited by Leonard D. Heaton, 139-331. Vol. 5 of *Preventive Medicine in World War II*. Edited by John Boyd Coates Jr., Ebbe Curtis Hoff, and Phere M. Hoff. Washington, DC: Office of the Surgeon General, US Department of the Army, 1960.

Sternberg, Thomas H., and Thomas B. Turner. "The Treatment of Sulfonamide Resistant Gonorrhea with Penicillin Sodium: Results in 1,686 Cases." *Journal of the American Medical Association* 126, no. 3 (September 16, 1944): 157-61.

Stevens, John D. "Black Correspondents of World War II Cover the Supply Routes." *Journal of Negro History* 57, no. 4 (October 1972).

Taylor, Diana. "Afterword: War Play." *PMLA* 124, no. 5: "War" (October 2009): 1886-95.

Thomas, Brook. "'Plessy vs. Ferguson' and the Literary Imagination." *Cardozo Studies in Law and Literature* 9, no. 1 (Spring-Summer 1997): 46-51.

Timm, Annette F. "'Think It Over!': Soldiers, Veronikas and Venereal Disease in Occupied Berlin." In *It Started with a Kiss: German-Allied Relations after 1945*, edited by Florian Weiss, 50-56. Berlin: Jaron Verlag, 2005.

Tine, Gregory C. "Berlin Airlift: Logistics, Humanitarian Aid, and Strategic Success." *Army Logistician: Professional Bulletin of United States Army Logistics* 37, no. 5 (September-October 2005): 39-41. https://alu.army.mil/alog/issues/sepoct05/Berlinairlift.html.

Vagts, Alfred. "Ivory Towers into Watchtowers." *Virginia Quarterly Review* 17, no. 2 (Spring 1941): 161-78.

Vaughn, Stephen. "Ronald Reagan and the Struggle for Black Dignity in Cinema, 1937-1953." *Journal of Negro History* 77, no. 1 (Winter 1992): 1-16.

Ware, Elgin W. "A Brief History of Urology at Baylor Medical Center." *Baylor University Medical Center Proceedings* 16, no. 4 (October 2003): 430-34.

Washington, Booker T. "Training Colored Nurses at Tuskegee." *American Journal of Nursing* 11, no. 3 (December 1910): 167–71.

Watts, Sheldon. "Yellow Fever Immunities in West Africa and the Americas in the Age of Slavery and Beyond: A Reappraisal." *Journal of Social History* 34, no. 4 (Summer 2001): 955–67.

Weil, Frank E. G. "The Negro in the Armed Forces." *Social Forces* 26, no. 1 (October 1947): 95–8.

White, Walter. "Race Relations in the Armed Services of the United States." *Journal of Negro Education* 12, no. 3: "The American Negro in World War I and World War II" (Summer 1943): 350–54.

Williams, A. Wilberforce. "Venereal Diseases." *Journal of the National Medical Association* 10, no. 4 (October–December 1918): 183–84.

Williams, Chad. "A Mobilized Diaspora: The First World War and Black Soldiers as New Negroes." In *Escape from New York: The New Negro Renaissance beyond Harlem*, edited by Davarian L. Baldwin and Minkah Makalani, 247–69. Minneapolis: University of Minnesota Press, 2013.

Willoughby, John. "The Sexual Behavior of American GIs during the Early Years of the Occupation of Germany." *Journal of Military History* 62, no. 1 (January 1998): 155–74.

Woods, Randall B. "C. H. J. Taylor and the Movement for Black Political Independence, 1882–1896." *Journal of Negro History* 67, no. 2 (Summer 1982): 122–35.

Books

Abraham, George. *The Belles of Shangri-La and Other Stories of Sex, Snakes, and Survival from World War II*. New York: Vantage, 2000.

Badger, Reid. *A Life in Ragtime: A Biography of James Reese Europe*. New York: Oxford University Press, 1995.

Bailey, Thomas A. *The Marshall Plan Summer: An Eyewitness Report on Europe and the Russians in 1947*. Stanford, CA: Hoover Institution Press, 1977.

Baker, Houston A. *Modernism and the Harlem Renaissance*. Chicago: University of Chicago Press, 1987.

Balce, Nerissa S. *Body Parts of Empire: Visual Abjection, Filipino Images, and the American Archive*. Ann Arbor: University of Michigan Press, 2016.

Baraka, Amiri [LeRoi Jones]. *Blues People: Negro People in White America*. New York: Morrow Quill, 1963.

Barbeau, Arthur, and Florette Henri. *The Unknown Soldiers: African American Troops in World War I*. New York: Da Capo, 1996.

Barnett, Ferdinand Lee, and Ida B. Wells, eds. *The Reason Why the Colored American Is Not in the World's Columbia Exposition*. Reprint of 1893 edition. Edited by Robert W. Rydell. Urbana and Chicago: University of Illinois Press, 1999.

Baudrillard, Jean. *Simulacra and Simulation*. Translated by Sheila Faria Glaser. Ann Arbor: University of Michigan Press, 1994.

Beard, John Relly. *Toussaint L'Ouverture: A Biography and Autobiography*. Boston, MA: James Redpath, 1863.

Bell, Bernard W. *The Afro-American Novel and Its Tradition*. Amherst: University of Massachusetts Press, 1987.

Bell, Madison Smartt. *Toussaint Louverture: A Biography*. New York: Pantheon, 2007.

Bolton, Horace W. *History of the Second Regiment Illinois Volunteer Infantry from Organization to Muster-out*. Chicago: R. R. Donnelly and Sons, 1899.

Bonsal, Stephen. *The Fight for Santiago: The Story of the Soldier in the Cuban Campaign, from Tampa to the Surrender*. New York: Doubleday and McClure, 1899.

Brandt, Allan. *No Magic Bullet: A Social History of Venereal Disease in the United States since 1880*. New York: Oxford University Press, 1985.

Brooks, Daphne A. *Bodies in Dissent: Spectacular Performances of Race and Freedom, 1850–1910*. Durham, NC: Duke University Press, 2006.

Brown, Stephanie. *The Postwar African American Novel: Protest and Discontent, 1945–1950*. Jackson: University Press of Mississippi, 2011.

Brown, Sterling A., Arthur P. Davis, and Ulysses Lee, eds. *The Negro Caravan: Writings by American Negroes*. New York: Citadel, 1941.

Browning, Barbara. *Infectious Rhythm: Metaphors of Contagion and the Spread of African Culture*. New York: Routledge, 1998.

Campt, Tina. *Other Germans: Black Germans and the Politics of Race, Gender, and Memory in the Third Reich*. Ann Arbor: University of Michigan Press, 2004.

Cashin, Herschel V., Charles Alexander, William T. Anderson, Arthur M. Brown, and Horace W. Bivins. *Under Fire with the Tenth Cavalry*. Chicago: American Publishing House, 1902.

Cirillo, Vincent J. *Bullets and Bacilli: The Spanish-American War and Military Medicine*. New Brunswick, NJ: Rutgers University Press, 2004.

Colley, David P. *The Road to Victory: The Untold Story of World War II's Red Ball Express*. New York: Warner, 2000.

Comhaire-Sylvain, Suzanne. *Le Créole Haïten: Morphologie et Syntaxe*. Port-au-Prince: Caravelle, 1936.

Cooper, Anna Julia. *A Voice from the South*. Xenia, OH: Aldine Printing House, 1892.

Crane, A. G. *The Medical Department of the United States Army in the World War*. Vol. 13, Part One, *Physical Reconstruction and Vocational Education*. Washington, DC: U.S. Government Printing Office, 1927.

Cripps, Thomas. *Making Movies Black: The Hollywood Message Movie from World War II to the Civil Rights Era*. New York: Oxford University Press, 1993.

Crowell, Benedict, and Robert Forrest Wilson. *Demobilization: Our Industrial and Military Demobilization after the Armistice, 1918–1920*. New Haven, CT: Yale University Press, 1921.

Custer, John Douglas. *The Citizens' Military Training Camp at Fortress Monroe, Virginia, July 7 to August 5, 1937*. Unpublished typescript, November 28, 1940.

Dannett, Sylvia G. L. *Profiles of Negro Womanhood*. Vol. 2, *20th Century*. New York: M. W. Lads, 1966.

DeCuir, Sharlene Sinegal. "Attacking Jim Crow: Black Activism in New Orleans, 1925–1941." PhD diss., Louisiana State University and Agricultural and Mechanical College, 2009.

Delany, Samuel R. *Times Square Red, Times Square Blue*. New York: New York University Press, 1999.
Dixon-Gottschild, Brenda. *Waltzing in the Dark: African American Vaudeville and Race Politics in the Swing Era*. New York: St. Martin's, 2000.
Donovan, James A. *Militarism, U.S.A.* New York: Charles Scribner's Sons, 1970.
Duberman, Martin. *Paul Robeson*. New York: Knopf, 1988.
Du Bois, W. E. B. *The Correspondence of W. E. B. Du Bois*. Vol. 1, *Selections, 1877-1934*. Edited by Herbert Aptheker. Amherst: University of Massachusetts Press, 1997.
―――. *The Souls of Black Folk: Essays and Sketches*. Chicago: A. C. McClurg, 1903.
Early, Charity Adams. *One Woman's War: A Black Officer Remembers the WAC*. College Station: Texas A&M University Press, 1989.
Ellis, Mark. *Race, War, and Surveillance: African Americans and the United States Government During World War I*. Bloomington: Indiana University Press, 2001.
Epstein, Catherine. *A Past Renewed: A Catalog of German-Speaking Refugee Historians in the United States after 1933*. Cambridge: Cambridge University Press, 1993.
Fahs, Alice. *Out on Assignment: Newspaper Women and the Making of Modern Public Space*. Chapel Hill: University of North Carolina Press, 2011.
Fair-Schulz, Axel, and Mario Kessler, eds. *German Scholars in Exile*. Lanham, MD: Lexington, 2011.
Fanebust, Wayne. *Major General Alexander M. McCook, USA: A Civil War Biography*. Jefferson, NC: McFarland, 2013.
Fehrenbach, Heide. *Race after Hitler: Black Occupation Children in Postwar Germany and America*. Princeton, NJ: Princeton University Press, 2005.
Ferrániz, Francisco, and Antonius Robben, eds. *Necropolitics: Mass Graves and Exhumations in the Age of Human Rights*. Philadelphia: University of Pennsylvania Press, 2015.
Foucault, Michel. *"Society Must Be Defended": Lectures at the Collège de France, 1975-76*. Edited by Mauro Bertani and Alessandro Fontana. Translated by David Macey. New York: Picador, 1997.
Funston, Frederick. *Memories of Two Wars: Cuban and Philippine Experiences*. New York: Charles Scribner's Sons, 1911.
Gatewood, Willard B., Jr. *Aristocrats of Color: The Black Elite, 1880-1920*. Fayetteville: University of Arkansas, 2000.
―――. *"Smoked Yankees" and the Struggle for Empire: Letters from Negro Soldiers, 1898-1902*. Fayetteville: University of Arkansas Press, 1987.
Gibson, Truman K. *Knocking Down Barriers: My Fight for Black America*. Evanston, IL: Northwestern University Press, 2005.
Gillette, Mary C. *The Army Medical Department, 1917-1941*. Washington, DC: Center for Military History, 2009.
Gilroy, Paul A. *The Black Atlantic: Modernity and Double Consciousness*. Cambridge, MA: Harvard University Press, 1993.
Glick, Jeremy M. *The Black Radical Tragic: Performance, Aesthetics, and the Unfinished Haitian Revolution*. New York: New York University Press, 2016.

Goodwin, T. H. *Notes for Army Medical Officers*. Philadelphia, PA, and New York: Lea and Febiger, 1917.

Grathwol, Robert P., Donita M. Moorhus, and Gareth L. Steen, eds. *Berlin and the American Military: A Cold War Chronicle*. New York: New York University Press, 1999.

Green, Ely. *Ely: Too Black, Too White*. Amherst: University of Massachusetts Press, 1970.

Grossman, Atina. *Jews, Germans and Allies: Close Encounters in Occupied Germany*. Princeton, NJ: Princeton University Press, 2007.

Guy-Sheftall, Beverly. *Words of Fire: An Anthology of African-American Feminist Thought*. New York: New Press, 1995.

Handy, W. C.. *Father of the Blues: An Autobiography*. Edited by Arna Bontemps. New York: Macmillan, 1941.

Harbord, James G. *The American Army in France, 1917-1919*. Boston, MA: Little, Brown, 1936.

Haritaworn, Jin, Adi Kuntsman, and Silvia Posocco, eds. *Queer Necropolitics*. New York: Routledge, 2014.

Harlan, Louis. *Booker T. Washington: The Wizard of Tuskegee*. New York: Oxford University Press, 1983.

Hegarty, Marilyn E. *Victory Girls, Khaki-Wackies, and Patriotutes: The Regulation of Female Sexuality during World War II*. New York: New York University Press, 2008.

Heinl, Robert D., and Nancy G. Heinl. *Written in Blood: The Story of the Haitian People, 1492-1971*. Boston, MA: Houghton Mifflin, 1978.

Herrera, Ricardo A. *For Liberty and the Republic: The American Citizen as Soldier, 1775-1861*. New York: New York University Press, 2015.

Hine, Darlene Clark. *Black Women in White: Racial Conflict and Cooperation in the Nursing Profession, 1890-1950*. Bloomington: Indiana University Press, 1989.

Hirschfeld, Magnus. *The Sexual History of the World War*. New York: Cadillac, 1946.

Hodges, Leroy S., Jr. *Portrait of an Expatriate: William Gardner Smith, Writer*. Westport, CT: Greenwood, 1985.

Höhn, Maria, and Martin Klimke. *A Breath of Freedom: The Civil Rights Struggle, African American GIs, and Germany*. New York: Palgrave Macmillan, 2010.

Howley, Frank. *Berlin Command*. New York: G. P. Putnam's Sons, 1950.

Hull, Cordell. *The Memoirs of Cordell Hull*. 2 vols. New York: Macmillan, 1948.

Humphries, Margaret. *Intensely Human: The Health of the Black Soldier in the American Civil War*. Baltimore, MD: Johns Hopkins University Press, 2006.

Hunter, Tera W. *To 'Joy My Freedom: Southern Black Women's Lives and Labors After the Civil War*. Cambridge: Harvard University Press, 1997.

Huntington, Samuel P. *The Soldier and the State: The Theory and Politics of Civil-Military Relations*. Cambridge, MA: Harvard University Press, 1967.

Hunton, Addie W., and Kathryn M. Johnson, *Two Colored Women with the American Expeditionary Forces*. Brooklyn, NY: Brooklyn Eagle, 1920.

James, C. L. R. *The Black Jacobins: Toussaint L'Ouverture and the San Domingo Revolution*. New York: Vintage, 1963.

Johnson, Chalmers. *The Sorrows of Empire: Militarism, Secrecy, and the End of the Republic*. New York: Metropolitan, 2004.

Jones, Absalom, and Richard Allen. *A Narrative of the Proceedings of the Black People, during the Late Awful Calamity in Philadelphia, in the Year 1793: and a Refutation of Some Censures, Thrown upon Them in Some Late Publications*. Philadelphia, PA: Franklin's Head, 1794.

Kehoe, Marjorie Winslow, Nancy McCall, and Lisa A. Mix. *The Legacy of Hugh Hampton Young, Pioneer in Urology: A Guide to the Papers of Hugh Hampton Young*. Baltimore, MD: Alan Mason Chesney Medical Archives, 1991.

Kelley, Robin D. G. *Race Rebels: Culture, Politics, and the Black Working Class*. New York: Free Press, 1994.

Kilroy, David P. *For Race and Country: The Life and Career of Colonel Charles Young*. Westport, CT: Praeger, 2003.

Kornweibel, Theodore. *Seeing Red*. Bloomington: Indiana University Press, 1998.

Krafft-Ebing, Richard. *Psychopathia Sexualis*. New York: Rebman, 1906.

Lanning, Michael L. *The African American Soldier: From Crispus Attucks to Colin Powell*. New York: Citadel, 2004.

Leder, Jane Mersky. *Thanks for the Memories: Love, Sex, and World War II*. Westport, CT: Praeger, 2006.

Lee, Ulysses. *The Employment of Negro Troops*. Washington, DC: Center for Military History, 1994.

Lentz-Smith, Adriane. *Freedom Struggles: African Americans and World War I*. Cambridge, MA: Harvard University Press, 2009.

Lesch, John E. *The First Miracle Drugs: How the Sulfa Drugs Transformed Medicine*. New York: Oxford University Press, 2007.

Lewis, David Levering, ed. *W. E. B. Du Bois: A Reader*. New York: Henry Holt, 1995.

Little, Arthur W. *From Harlem to the Rhine: The Story of New York's Colored Volunteers*. New York: Covici and Friede, 1936.

Lord, Alexandra M. *Condom Nation: The U.S. Government's Sex Education Campaign from World War I to the Internet*. Baltimore, MD: Johns Hopkins University Press, 2010.

Marks, George P. *The Black Press Views American Imperialism, 1898-1900*. New York: Arno, 1971.

Martineau, Harriet. *The Hour and the Man: A Historical Romance*. London: E. Moxon, 1841.

Matas, Rudolph. *The Surgical Peculiarities of the American Negro: A Statistical Inquiry Based upon the Records of the Charity Hospital of New Orleans, L.A., Decennium 1884-94*. Reprinted from the Transactions of the American Surgical Association, Vol. 14, 1896.

McCaskill, Barbara, and Caroline Gebhard, eds. *Post-Bellum, Pre-Harlem: African American Literature and Culture, 1877-1919*. New York: New York University Press, 2006.

McCook, Henry Christopher. *The Martial Graves of Our Fallen Heroes in Santiago de Cuba*. Philadelphia, PA: G. W. Jacobs, 1899.

McGuire, Phillip. *Taps for a Jim Crow Army: Letters from Black Soldiers in World War II*. Lexington: University of Kentucky Press, 1983.

McNeill, J. R. *Mosquito Empires: Ecology and War in the Greater Caribbean, 1620-1914*. New York: Cambridge University Press, 2010.

Metcalf, George R. *Black Profiles*. New York: McGraw Hill, 1970.
Mitchell, Michele. *Righteous Propagation: African Americans and the Politics of Racial Destiny after Reconstruction*. Chapel Hill: University of North Carolina Press, 2004.
Moon, Katherine H. S. *Sex among Allies: Military Prostitution in U.S.-Korea Relations*. New York: Columbia University Press, 1997.
Moorer, Lizelia Augusta Jenkins. *Prejudice Unveiled: And Other Poems*. Boston, MA: Roxburgh, 1907.
Morden, Betty J. *The Women's Army Corps, 1945-1978*. Washington, DC: Center for Military History, 2000.
Moses, Wilson Jeremiah, ed. *Classical Black Nationalism: From the American Revolution to Marcus Garvey*. New York: New York University Press, 1996.
Murphree, Daniel S. *Native America: A State-by-State Historical Encyclopedia*. Vol. 1, *Alabama–Louisiana*. Santa Barbara, CA: Greenwood, 2012.
Murray, Daniel Alexander Payne. *The Daniel Murray Papers*. Series: *Murray's Historical and Biographical Encyclopedia of The Colored Race Throughout The World*, reel 3. The State Historical Society of Wisconsin, http://digital.library.wisc.edu/1711 .dl/wiarchives.uw-whs-micro577, accessed December 6, 2019.
Nalty, Bernard C., and Morris J. MacGregor, eds. *Blacks in the Military: Essential Documents*. Wilmington, DE: Scholarly Resources, 1981.
Owens, Deidre Cooper. *Medical Bondage: Race, Gender, and the Origins of American Gynecology*. Athens: University of Georgia Press, 2017.
Padmore, George. *The Life and Struggles of Negro Toilers*. London: Red International of Labor Unions Magazine for the International Trade Union Committee of Negro Workers, 1931.
Patterson, Orlando. *Slavery and Social Death: A Comparative Study*. Cambridge, MA: Harvard University Press, 1982.
Pfau, Ann Elizabeth. *Miss Yourlovin: GIs, Gender and Domesticity during World War II*. New York: Columbia University Press, 2008.
Pratt, Mary Louise. *Imperial Eyes: Travel Writing and Transculturation*. London: Routledge, 1992.
Roberts, Dorothy. *Killing the Black Body: Race, Reproduction, and the Meaning of Liberty*. New York: Vintage, 1997.
Robertson, David. *W. C. Handy: The Life and Times of the Man Who Made the Blues*. New York: Knopf, 2009.
Robinson, Cedric J. *Forgeries of Memory and Meaning: Blacks and the Regimes of Race in American Theater and Film before World War 2*. Chapel Hill: University of North Carolina Press, 2007.
Rosenberg, Jonathan. *How Far the Promised Land? World Affairs and the America Civil Rights Movement from the First World War to Vietnam*. Princeton, NJ: Princeton University Press, 2006.
Rush, Benjamin. *An account of the bilious remitting fever, as it appeared in the city of Philadelphia in the year 1793*. Philadelphia, PA: Thomas Dobson, 1794.
Schivelbusch, Wolfgang. *In a Cold Crater: Cultural and Intellectual Life in Berlin, 1945-1948*. Translated by Kelly Barry. Berkeley: University of California Press, 1998.

Schroer, Timothy L. *Recasting Race after World War II: Germans and African Americans in American-Occupied Germany*. Boulder: University Press of Colorado, 2007.

Scott, Emmett J. *Scott's Official History of the American Negro in the World War*. Chicago: Homewood, 1919.

Shellum, Brian. *Black Officer in a Buffalo Soldier Regiment: The Military Career of Charles Young*. Lincoln: University of Nebraska Press, 2010.

Sissle, Noble. "Memoirs of Lieutenant "Jim" Europe." Unpublished manuscript, 1942. Library of Congress Music Division, Washington, DC.

Snorton, C. Riley. *Black on Both Sides: A Racial History of Trans Identity*. Minneapolis: University of Minnesota Press, 2017.

Snowden, Yates, ed. *History of South Carolina*. Vol. 5. Chicago: Lewis, 1920.

Sollors, Werner. *The Temptation of Despair: Tales of the 1940s*. Cambridge, MA: Harvard University Press, 2014.

Standifer, Leon C. *Binding up the Wounds: An American Soldier in Occupied Germany, 1945–1946*. Baton Rouge: Louisiana University Press, 1997.

Stanford, Karin L. *If We Must Die: African American Voices on War and Peace*. Lanham, MD: Rowman and Littlefield, 2008.

Taylor, Diana. *The Archive and the Repertoire: Performing Cultural Memory in the Americas*. Durham, NC: Duke University Press, 2007.

Threat, Charissa J. *Nursing Civil Rights: Gender and Race in the Army Nurse Corps*. Urbana: University of Illinois Press, 2015.

Trouillot, Michel-Rolph. *Silencing the Past: Power and the Production of History*. Boston, MA: Beacon, 1995.

United States Army Service Forces, Special Service Division. *A Pocket Guide to Iran*. Washington, DC: War and Navy Departments, 1943.

———. *A Pocket Guide to West Africa*. Washington, DC: War and Navy Departments, 1943.

Vagts, Alfred. *A History of Militarism: Romance and Realities of a Profession*. New York: W. W. Norton, 1937.

———. *The Military Attaché*. Princeton, NJ: Princeton University Press, 1967.

Vandiver, Frank E. *Black Jack: The Life and Times of John J. Pershing*. 2 vols. College Station: Texas A&M University Press, 1977.

Verdery, Katherine. *The Political Lives of Dead Bodies: Reburial and Postsocialist Change*. New York: Columbia University Press, 1999.

Vine, David. *Base Nation: How U.S. Military Bases Abroad Harm America and the World*. New York: Metropolitan, 2015.

Von Eschen, Penny. *Satchmo Blows up the World: Jazz Ambassadors Play the Cold War*. Cambridge, MA: Harvard University Press, 2004.

Walker, George. *The Traffic in Babies: An Analysis of the Conditions Discovered during an Investigation Conducted in the Year 1914*. Baltimore, MD: Norman, Remington, 1918.

———. *Venereal Disease in the American Expeditionary Forces*. Baltimore, MD: Medical Standard Book Company, 1922.

Ward, Martha. *Voodoo Queen: The Spirited Lives of Marie Laveau*. Jackson: University Press of Mississippi, 2004.

Washington, Booker T. *Booker T. Washington Papers*. Vol. 4, *1895-98*. Edited by Louis R. Harlan. Urbana: University of Illinois Press, 1975.

———. *Booker T. Washington Papers*. Vol. 11, *1911-12*. Edited by Louis R. Harlan and Raymond W. Smock. Urbana: University of Illinois Press, 1981.

———. *The Future of the American Negro*. Boston, MA: Small, Maynard and Company, 1899.

———. *Working with the Hands: Being a Sequel to "Up from Slavery" Covering the Author's Experiences in Industrial Training at Tuskegee*. New York: Doubleday, 1904.

Washington, Harriet A. *Medical Apartheid: The Dark History of Medical Experimentation on African Americans from Colonial Times to the Present*. New York: Harlem Moon, 2006.

Watkins, Glenn. *Proof Through the Night: Music and the Great War*. Berkeley: University of California Press, 2003.

Weed, Frank W. *The Medical Department of the United States in the World War*. Vol. 6, *Sanitation in the AEF*. Washington, DC: Government Printing Office, 1926.

Wells-Barnett, Ida B. *Lynch Law in Georgia*. Chicago: Chicago Colored Citizens, 1899.

Weslager, C. A. *Delaware's Forgotten Folk: The Story of the Moors and Nanticokes*. Philadelphia: University of Pennsylvania Press, 2012.

Whalan, Mark *The Great War and the Culture of the New Negro*. Gainesville: University Press of Florida, 2008.

White, Walter. *A Rising Wind*. Garden City, NY: Doubleday, Doran, 1945.

Williams, Chad. *Torchbearers for Democracy: African American Soldiers in the World War I Era*. Chapel Hill: University of North Carolina Press, 2010.

Willoughby, John. *Remaking the Conquering Heroes: The Social and Geopolitical Impact of the Post-War American Occupation of Germany*. New York: Palgrave, 2001.

Wyman, Mark. *DPs: Europe's Displaced Persons, 1945-1951*. Ithaca, NY: Cornell University Press, 1998.

Young, Charles. *Little Hand-Book of French Creole, as Spoken in Hayti*. Typewritten manuscript, 1905. Washington, DC: U.S. Army Military Research Collection.

———. *Military Morales of Nations and Races*. Kansas City, MO: Franklin Hudson, 1912.

———. "Toussaint L'Ouverture: A Negro History Drama in Five Acts." Unpublished manuscript, 1910. Courtesy of the National Afro-American Museum and Culture Center, Wilberforce, Ohio.

Young, Hugh Hampton. *A Surgeon's Autobiography*. New York: Harcourt, Brace and Company, 1940.

Zelinsky, Wilbur. *The Enigma of Ethnicity*. Iowa City: University of Iowa Press, 2001.

Index

Note: Illustrations are indicated by page numbers in *italics*.

AEF. *See* American Expeditionary Force (AEF)
Africa: in World War II, 183–84, 187, 189, 196. *See also* West Africa; *specific countries*
African Americans: black extinction theory and, 62–63; in Civil War, 25–27; as naturally immune, 23–25, 49–50, 61, 63–64, 227n35; patriotism of, 186; in Social Darwinism, 61–62; in Spanish-Cuban-American War, 20, 27–34, 38–39, 50–52, 77–78, 80–81, 86–88; in World War I, 134, 136–37, 141–45, 155–57; in World War II, 183–84, 186–203. *See also* entries at black
AFRICOM, 9, 13–14
Afro-American Novel and Its Tradition, The (Bell), 217–18
Afro-Cuban: emancipation, 31; self-determination, 31; women, African American women vs., 67–68
Alaska, 189
Allen, Richard, 24
Alvah, Donna, 106
American Expeditionary Force (AEF), 108, 133–35, 138, 145, 150. *See also* World War I
American Indian Wars, 26
Ames, Winthrop, 157
ANC. *See* Army Nurses Corps (ANC)
Anti-Slavery Society, 55
Aptheker, Herbert, 26
Arlington National Cemetery, 41, 43, 59–60
Armour, Philip D., 56

Armstrong, Louis, 158
Army Nurses Corps (ANC), 76, 229n87
Ascension Island, 189

Baartman, Sarah "Saartjie," 149
Bailey, Thomas A., 210
Bain, Elizabeth, 145–46
Baker, Houston A., 90
band, military, 154–61, 240n133
Baraka, Amiri, 153–54, 156
Barton, Clara, 66
Beard, George, 33–34, 88
Belgian Congo, 189–91, 196
Bell, Bernard, 217–18
Berlin Airlift, 208–10, 212–13, 218
Bermuda, 188
Bethune, Mary McLeod, 58
Binding Up the Wounds (Standifer), 210
"black codes," 56, 73
black extinction theory, 62–63
black international, 8
black masculinity, 83, 128, 161, 172–82
blackness: and burial practices at war, 9, 21; immunity and, 21–26; slavery and, 20; in Toussaint, 102
blues music, 152–54, 156–57
Blues People: Negro Music in White America (Baraka), 153–54
Bonsal, Stephan, 89
Bradford, Isabelle R., 59–60
Braithwaite, William Stanley, 141
Briggs, Charles L., 198
Brooks, Daphne A., 84, 158
Brown, Stephanie, 218–19
Brown v. Board of Education, 224n65
Bruce, Nathaniel, 31–32, 224n65

263

Brymn, Tim, 161
"Buffalo Soldiers," 26, 92, 116
burial practices, at war, 21, 35–42, 36–37, 39–41, 75–76

Camp Grant, 116, 128
Campt, Tina, 204
Camp Wikoff, 39, 69–70, 72, 228n71
Camp Zachary Taylor, 129
Canada, 189
Center of Military History (CMH), 176
Central African Republic, 189
Chad, 189
chancroid, 135, 138, 163, 196, 244n104. *See also* venereal disease
chemical prophylaxis, 134–35, 138–39, 179, 199, 237nn58, 61
Chile, 189
China, 182–83, 185, 187, 190, 192–94
cigarettes, 126, 209
citizenship: and African American inferiority discourse, 17; militarism and, 73, 84; military service and, 20–21, 26, 29, 35; necropolitical, 50, 76; and pathology of difference, 28; "separate but equal" doctrine and, 74
Citizens Military Training Camps, 169–70
civilian control, of military power, 2
Civil War, 20–22, 25–28, 46–49, 65–67, 69–71, 133, 210
Clarke, John Henrik, 119
Clay, Lucius, 205, 207
Clef Club, 154
CMH. *See* Center of Military History (CMH)
colonialism, 20, 83–85, 94, 119, 122, 169, 188, 191, 201, 224n73, 239n128, 245n124
colorism, 53
Congo, 189–91, 196
Connolly, Donald H., 201
conscription, 4–7, 76, 90, 127, 148–49, 169–71, 200

contact zones, 8, 152, 157, 160, 164, 170, 239n128
contagion: militarism and, 187; prostitution and, 197, 200; theorization of, 5–12
Cooper, Anna Julia, 125
Cordin, C. W., 88–89
Cousins, Benjamin, 37
Creole language, 94–95, 97
Crowell, Benedict, 163
Crump, Edward H. "Boss," 159
Cuba, 6, 27, 34–35. *See also* Afro-Cuban; Spanish-Cuban-American War
Curtis, Austin, 56
Curtis, Namahyoka Gertrude, 48–60, 54, 59, 79–80, 124–26

DAR. *See* Daughters of the American Revolution (DAR)
Daughters of the American Revolution (DAR), 60–61
Davie, Mose J., 193–94
Day, George H., 139
defections, 90–91
Delany, Martin R., 92, 110
Delany, Samuel R., 152
Delaware, 56
"Delaware Moors," 55
Denton, William, 195
desertions, 90–91
De Vleeschauwer, Albert, 190–91
Dewey, Taliaferro Miles, 87
Diagne, Blaise, 170
displaced persons (DPs), after World War II, 205–7, 210
Dominican Republic, 93–94, 107
Douglass, Frederick, 27, 93
Draper, Warren F., 174–75
Du Bois, W. E. B., 84, 86, 108, 112, 117–19, 141–42, 166, 169, 186–87
Dubose, Edmund, 91
Dunbar, Paul Laurence, 58, 94, 97

Easy to Get (film), 173–74, 177–82
Eisenhower, Dwight D., 2, 188

Ellington, Duke, 158
Ellis, Mark, 168
embarkation camps, 162–64
Employment of Negro Troops, The (Lee), 176
Enloe, Cynthia, 152
Espinosa, Mariola, 22–23, 227n35
Espionage Act, 167
Europe, James Reese, 154–55
Executive Order 9981, 208, 218

Fagen, David, 90–92, 111, 168
Fehrenbach, Heide, 204
fellatio, 145–48
Fifty-Fourth Massachusetts Infantry, 26
films, 171–82
Finlay, Carlos, 62
5000 Role Models, 19
Florida A&M University, 193–94
Foucault, Michel, 18–20
Fourteenth Amendment, 5, 50, 73–74
France, 6–7, 94, 99, 103–4, 135, 140–49, 157–62, 170
Free African Society, 24
French Equatorial Africa, 189, 196
French Revolution, 103

Gabon, 189
Gambia, 189
gender: fellatio and, 147; inclusion, 8; racial immunity and, 60–65; slavery and, 65. *See also* women
General Order No. 55, 29
General Order No. 77, 134
Germany, after World War II, 202–12, 215
germ theory of disease, 61–62, 133
Ghana, 189
Gibson, Truman K., 171, 208
Gillem Board Report, 213–15, 217
Gillespie, Dizzy, 158
Gilroy, Paul, 155
gonorrhea, 138, 162–63, 177, 237n61. *See also* venereal disease

Goodwin, T. H., 133
graves, mass, 18. *See also* burial practices, at war
Gray, William, 24
Green, Elisha "Ely," 148–51
Greenland, 189
Gunner, Byron, 166

Haiti, 10, 83, 93–95
Haitian Revolution, 79, 84, 96–97, 103, 119. *See also* Louverture, Toussaint; *Toussaint L'Ouverture: A Negro History Drama in Five Acts* (Young)
Handy, W. C., 153, 159
Hanson, Millard, 174
Harbord, James G., 134
Harding, James V., 190–91
Hartman, Saidiya, 92
Hastie, William H., 170
Hawaii, 189
Hayward, William, 155
Hellfighters, 157–65, 240n133
heroism, 35, 38, 74, 76–77, 80, 141–42
Herrera, Ricardo, 34
Hitchens, Christopher, 147
Hobson, Winslow, 87
Hodges, Leroy S., Jr., 215
Höhn, Maria, 208
Houston, Charles H., 184–85, 210
Howard University, 169–70, 185
Howe, Tom, 37
Howley, Frank, 207–8
"How 'Ya Gonna Keep 'Em Down on the Farm (After They've Seen Paree')?," 161–62
Hull, Cordell, 197
Humphries, Margaret, 25
Huntington, Samuel P., 106, 109
Hunton, Addie Waites, 142–44, 162–63

Iceland, 189
immune nurses, 23–26, 48–52, 59–61, 63–73
"Immune Regiments," 5, 27

Index 265

immunity: biological, 21–26, 60–65, 227n35; black investment in, 27–34; gender and, 60–65; political, 29, 34–47; relative, 63–64; senses of term, 5–6; slavery and, 6, 9, 21–26, 227n35; supposed, of African Americans, 23–25, 49–50, 61, 63–64, 227n35; theorization of, 5–12
imperialism, 44, 50, 80, 169, 183–84, 187
India, 192–94
International Conference of Negro Workers, 169
interracial sexuality, 129, 131–32, 136, 179, 217–18
interwar period, 166–71, 195
Iran, 196, 200–201
Islamic State, 14, 18
Italy, 196–97

Jackson, Arrena, 56
Jackson, Walter, 55
James, C. L. R., 79, 103
Jamison, Roscoe C., 141
jazz music, 153–54, 158–60, 165
Jim Crow, 53, 136, 214. *See also* Plessy v. Ferguson; segregation
Johnson, Kathryn Magnolia, 142–44, 162–63
Johnson, La David, 13–17, 19, 21
Johnson, Myeshia, 17
Johnson, Richard, 88–89
Jones, Absalom, 24
Jones, LeRoi. *See* Baraka, Amiri
Jones, William Richard, 40–42, 42–43

Kaplan, Amy, 38
Kelley, Robin D. G., 152
Kenya, 189
Keyes, Geoffrey, 207
Kilroy, David, 106–7, 109–10
Klimke, Martin, 208
Know for Sure (film), 177
Korean War, 200, 208
Krafft-Ebing, Richard, 146

Lane, Charles, 124
language, 88–89, 94–95, 97
Last of the Conquerors (Smith), 215, 217–18
"last stand," 15–16
Laveau, Marie, 61
Laveaux, Étienne, 100
League of Democracy, 124, 126
Ledo Road, 193–94
Lee, Ulysses, 176, 181, 188
Leftwich, Aaron, 37
Lentz-Smith, Adriane, 139
Lesch, John E., 195
Lewis, Earl, 239n109
Lewis, Florence, 142
Lewis, James, 51
Lewis, Kenneth, 142
Lhérisson, Justin, 94
Liberia, 112, 197–200
Life and Struggles of Negro Toilers, The (Padmore), 168–69
Little, Arthur, 157
Little Handbook of French Creole, as Spoken in Hayti (Young), 94
Long, John Davis, 27–28
Louis, Joe, 180
Louverture, Toussaint, 78, 85–86, 95, 168. *See also Toussaint L'Ouverture: A Negro History Drama in Five Acts* (Young)
Loving, W. H., 124, 128–31
lynching, 90, 124

MacArthur, Douglas, 188–89
malaria, 194, 227n35
marronage, 90–91, 140, 152–53
masculinity: black, 83, 128, 161, 172–82; oral sex and, 146; sexual freedom and, 148
Mason, Lydia Ann, 55
mass graves, 18. *See also* burial practices, at war
Matas, Rudolph, 62–65
Maurer, D. W., 147
Mbembe, Achille, 17–18, 20

266   Index

McCook, Henry Christopher, 34–41, 75–76
McCorkle, Harry, 35–36
McDaniel, Etta, 177
McDowell, Fred, 239n110
McGee, Anita Newcomb, 60–61
McGuire, Phillip, 192
McKaine, Osceola, 124
McKinley, William, 34, 45, 48, 51, 53, 57, 77, 80
McNeill, J. R., 21–22
Meader, George, 205–6
media, 176–77. *See also* films
mercurochrome, 195, 199
Metcalf, Ralph, 180
Mexican-American War, 25
Mexico, 108
MID. *See* Military Intelligence Division (MID)
Middle East, 189, 200–201
Middle Passage, 156
militarism, 1–2; contagion and, 187; in interwar period, 167–68; and "last stand" trope, 15–16; Pan-African, 119; race and, 20–21
military band, 154–61, 240n133
military-industrial complex, 2
Military Intelligence Division (MID), 93–94, 107, 111–12, 126
military power: civilian control of, 2
military studies, 1
military worker: as term, 4
Militia Act of 1862, 25
Miller, Francis P., 205–6
Miller, Jacquelyn, 24
Mills, Ada, 93
Mitchell, U.S.S., 193
Moffett, Cleveland, 70
Moorer, Lizelia Augusta Jenkins, 76
Morton, Ferdinand Joseph "Jelly Roll," 153
Mott, Lucretia, 55
Murray, Daniel, 53, 55
music: blues, 152–54, 156–57; jazz, 153–54, 158–60, 165; and military bands, 155–58, 240n133; ragtime, 153–55, 158–61; sexuality and, 159–60

NACW. *See* National Association of Colored Women (NACW)
Namibia, 224n73
Nanticoke people, 55
Narrative of the Proceedings of the Black People, during the Late Awful Calamity in Philadelphia (Jones and Allen), 24
National Association for the Advancement of Colored People (NAACP), 108, 166–67
National Association of Colored Women (NACW), 51
necropolitics, 17–21
"Necropolitics" (Mbembe), 17–18
Negro Colleges in Wartime (film), 242n25
"Negro Soldiers, The" (Jamison), 141
Newfoundland, 189
New Orleans, Louisiana, 48–49
New Zealand, 134, 182, 189
Niagara Movement, 166
Nicholas, H. W., 93
Niger, 13–17
Nigeria, 189
Nord-Alexis, Pierre, 94
nurses: immune, 23–26, 48–52, 59–61, 63–72; plantation, 9, 50, 65, 70

Office for Military Government in Germany (OMGUS), 205
Ogé, Elvire, 102–3
OMGUS. *See* Office for Military Government in Germany (OMGUS)
oral sex, 145–48
Orientalism, 201
Owens, Chandler, 166–67
Owens, Jesse, 180

Padmore, George, 168–70, 185, 241n15. *See also* venereal disease
Panama, 189
Parran, Thomas, Jr., 198
patriotism, 28–30, 65, 74, 180, 186, 213

Index 267

Payne, French, 37
Pearl Harbor attack, 186
Pershing, John, 133–34, 140–41
Phelps, John, 37
Philadelphia, yellow fever epidemic in, 23–24
Philippines, 6, 27, 80–83, 88–91
"picturization," 171
plantation nurse, 9, 50, 65, 70
Plessy, Homer Adolf, 51
Plessy v. Ferguson, 52, 73–74
Pope, Benjamin, 60
Pratt, Mary Louise, 239n128
pro-kits, 242n42, 44
Prontosil, 195
prophylaxis, chemical, for venereal disease, 134–35, 138–39, 179, 199, 237nn58, 61
prostitution, 134–36, 145, 151–53, 197, 199–201
Puerto Rico, 27, 50, 80, 155, 194, 243n76
Pullman Porters Union, 169
"Punitive Expedition," 108

quarantine, 50, 64, 69, 129, 131, 149, 198–99, 240n133
Quarles, Benjamin, 192
"Questionnaire Concerning Colored Troops," 127–28

race: militarism and, 20–21; necropolitics and, 18–21; venereal disease and, 131–32, 175. *See also* African Americans; *entries at* black; *entries at* white
race riots, 149–50
racism: in Foucault, 19–20; institutionalized, 83; in Young, 86
ragtime music, 153–55, 158–61
Randolph, Asa Philip, 166–67, 171
Ransom, R. C., 45–46
Ray, Marcus, 208
Reagan, Ronald, 172–73
Red Ball Express, 209, 212
Red Cross, 60, 66, 125, 143, 209
Republican Party, 57, 125

"Rhineland Bastard," 204
Rigaud, André, 100–102
riots, race, 149–50
Robeson, Paul, 180–81, 181n49
Robinson, Michael, 89
Rolph-Trouillot, Michel, 15
Roman, Charles Victor, 132–33
Roosevelt, Theodore, 93
Ross, Harry, 32–33
Rush, Benjamin, 23
Russell, Lewis, 91

Saint-Rémy, Joseph, 123
Schivelbusch, Wolfgang, 202, 210
Schmeling, Max, 180
Schuyler, George, 206
Scott, Emmett, J., 161
Second Confiscation Act, 25
"Second Great Migration," 175
segregation, 52–53, 57, 73–74, 152, 189, 192, 208, 213–15. *See also* Jim Crow; *Plessy v. Ferguson*; "separate but equal" doctrine
Senegal, 170
"separate but equal" doctrine, 73–74. *See also Plessy v. Ferguson*; segregation
sexual freedom, 148
sexuality, 6, 194–202; of black men, 128, 130, 133, 181; "contact zones" and, 239n128; interracial, 129, 131–32, 136, 179, 217–18; in media, 140–42; music and, 159–60; patriotism and, 132–33; in postwar Germany, 204. *See also* prostitution
sexually transmitted infections. *See* venereal disease
Shellum, Brian, 106
sickroom, 64–65
Sierra Leone, 189
Silvester, Jeremy, 224n73
Sims, J. Marion, 138, 149
Sissle, Noble, 155–56, 158, 160, 240n133
slavery: blackness and, 20; Creole language and, 94; in Cuba, 31; gender and, 65; Haitian Revolution and, 95;

268 *Index*

immune nurses and, 61, 63–65; immunity and, 6, 9, 21–26, 227n35; marronage and, 90; Middle Passage and, 156; and plantation nurse myth, 50
Smith, William Gardner, 215–19
SOCAFRICA. *See* Special Operations Command Africa (SOCAFRICA)
SOCFWD-NWA. *See* Special Operations Command Forward, North and West Africa (SOCFWD-NWA)
Social Darwinism, 61–62
social hygiene movement, 132–33, 140–41, 162, 173–74, 201
Sockum, Hamilton, 56, 226n21
Sockum, Levin, 55–56
Sothern, E. H., 157
Sousa, John Philip, 159–60
South Africa, 189–90
Spanish-Cuban-American War, 20, 27–34, 38–39, 50–52, 77–78, 80–81, 86–88
Spanish language, 88–89
Special Operations Command Africa (SOCAFRICA), 13
Special Operations Command Forward, North and West Africa (SOCFWD-NWA), 13
Spingarn, Arthur B., 140
Standifer, Leon C., 210–12
St. Lucia, 188, 243n76
Star of Ethiopia, The (Du Bois), 108
Steele, John, 37
Stephanopoulos, George, 17
Sternberg, George M., 51, 58, 65
Stevens, John D., 194
Stevenson, Charles, 209
Strother, Albert, 37
sulfanilamide, 195. *See also* chemical prophylaxis; venereal disease
sulfathiazole, 195–96, 199. *See also* chemical prophylaxis; venereal disease
Surgical Peculiarities of the American Negro, The (Matas), 62

Sylvain, Georges, 94
syphilis, 128–29, 175–76, 179–80. *See also* venereal disease

Taylor, Diana, 84, 86
Terrell, Mary Church, 58, 125–26
theater: in conceptualization of war, 84–85
Thirteenth Amendment, 73–74
Toussaint L'Ouverture: A Negro History Drama in Five Acts (Young), 85, 95–108, 113–15, 119–23
Treaty of Paris, 77
Trinidad, 188
Trotter, William Monroe, 166
Truman, Harry, 208
Trump, Donald, 16–17
tuberculosis, 175–76
Turnbull, Minerva, 59
Tuskegee Soldiers, 171
Two Colored Women with the American Expeditionary Forces, 142–43

Uniform Militia Act, 25
U.S. African Command, 9, 13–14

Vagts, Alfred, 1–3, 12, 93
venereal: as term, 127–28
venereal disease: chemical prophylaxis for, 134–35, 138–39, 179, 199, 237nn58, 61; in films, 171–82; incidence of, 130; in media, 140–42; race and, 131–32, 175; treatments, 195–96; women and, 174–75
Venezuela, 189
Vie de Toussaint-L'Ouverture (Saint-Rémy), 123
Von Eschen, Penny, 158
voodoo, 61, 95–98, 114

WAAC. *See* Women's Army Auxiliary Corps (WAAC)
Walker, George, 133, 135, 138–39, 145–47, 149, 237n61
Walker, Maggie L., 58

war: as black, 27–34; burial practices in, 21, 35–42, 36–37, 39–41, 75–76; theater models and metaphors in conceptualization of, 84–85; as white, 18–21. *See also specific wars*
Ward, Fannie Brigham, 66, 68
War of 1812, 25
Washington, Booker T., 5, 27–28, 32, 42–47, 58, 108, 172
Washington, George, 24
Washington, Margaret Murray, 58
Wells-Barnett, Ida B., 51
West Africa, 183–84, 197. *See also specific countries*
Whalan, Mark, 238n69
White, Walter, 171, 182, 187, 206
whiteness: military enlistment and, 48; as normative standard, 22; in Toussaint, 102; war and, 18–21
white privilege, 53
white supremacy: in black media, 29; black military service and, 25, 30, 46–47, 76, 81, 149; and burial practices at war, 35; public health and, 23; World War I and, 168; World War II and, 184, 192; in Young, 85–86, 119
Wilkes, Sam, 90
Wilkins, Roy, 214–15
Williams, Arthur E., 140–41
Williams, A. Wilberforce, 131
Williams, Chad, 143
Williams, Fannie Barrier, 58
Willoughby, John, 207, 246n165
Wilson, Frederica, 19
Wilson, Robert, 163
Wilson, Woodrow, 166, 168
Wings for This Man (film), 172–83

Woman Wage-Earner's Association, 125–26
women: Afro-Cuban *vs.* African American, 67–68; and burial practices at war, 76; French, in World War I, 145–47; as matriarchs in World War I, 142–43; plantation nurse myth and, 50; in postwar Germany, 204–5; prostitution and, 136; sexuality and, 194–202; in Spanish-Cuban-American War, 47; venereal disease and, 174–75. *See also* gender; nurses
Women Army Corps, 188
Women's Army Auxiliary Corps (WAAC), 171
Women's Republican Association, 57
Working with the Hands (Washington), 47
World War I, 2, 6–7, 109–10, 124–26, 129, 134, 136–37, 141–45, 155–57, 166, 186. *See also* American Expeditionary Force (AEF)
World War II, 2, 183–84, 186–203. *See also* Germany

yellow fever, 23–25, 27, 48–49, 61–62, 64, 70, 75, 105, 194. *See also* immune nurses; Spanish-Cuban-American War
Yellow Fever Commission, 62, 65
Young, Ada, 92–93, 106–7
Young, Charles, 77–123, 78, 186; black masculinity and, 83; death of, 117–18; Fagen and, 91–92; in Liberia, 112–13; NAACP recognition of, 108; retirement of, 83–84; at Wilberforce University, 86–87
Young, Hugh Hampton, 133–38, 149, 194–95, 236nn38, 43, 237n58

www.ingramcontent.com/pod-product-compliance
Lightning Source LLC
Chambersburg PA
CBHW031801220426
43662CB00007B/488